14 95
X

COMING
TO
TERMS

COMING TO TERMS

Feminism, Theory, Politics

EDITED BY ELIZABETH WEED

ROUTLEDGE
New York   London

Published in 1989 by

Routledge
An imprint of Routledge, Chapman and Hall, Inc.
29 West 35 Street
New York, NY 10001

Published in Great Britain by

Routledge
11 New Fetter Lane
London EC4P 4EE

Library of Congress Cataloging in Publication Data

Coming to terms : feminism, theory, politics / edited by Elizabeth
   Weed.
      p. cm.
     Bibliography: p.
     Includes index.
     ISBN 0-415-90067-0; ISBN 0-415-90068-9 (pbk.)
     1. Feminism—Philosophy.   2. Feminist criticism.   3. Identify.
 I. Weed, Elizabeth. 1940–
HQ1154.0644   1989
305.4′2′01—dc19   89-6021
                                               CIP

British Library Cataloguing in Publication Data

Coming to terms: feminism, theory, politics
   1. Society. Role of women. Role of women
 in society. Feminist theories
 I. Weed, Elizabeth   II. Pembroke Center
for Teaching and Research on Women
305.4′2′01

ISBN 0-415-90067-0
ISBN 0-415-90068-9   Pbk

Contents

Acknowledgments

The essays in this volume address some of the most insistent questions raised by the Pembroke Center's ongoing research project on "Cultural Constructions of Gender." What successes the Center has had in focussing collaborative attention on such questions are due in great measure to Joan Wallach Scott's leadership as the Pembroke Center's founding director (1981–85). Joan Scott's brilliant contributions to the field of history are matched by her innovative institutional achievements, and Brown University, the Pembroke Center for Teaching and Research on Women, and feminist inquiry in general are the beneficiaries of her work. It has been my personal good fortune to benefit, as a friend and colleague, from Joan's powerful intelligence and extraordinary generosity, for which I thank her.

Many helped with this collection. Special thanks go to Karen Newman, present director of the Pembroke Center, for her support; to Barbara Anton for her unfailing help; and to Elizabeth Barboza who, as coordinating secretary, makes everything possible. A warm thanks to Miven Booth, Michele Burke, Nicole Cunningham, Colette Matzzie, Melissa Murphy, and Phyllis Oscar, who helped at various stages of the project, and to Erika Rundle and Carol Irving for their proofreading. I am most grateful to Christina Crosby for her advice throughout, and to Barbara Babcock, Karen Newman, Joan Scott, Naomi Schor, and Ellen Rooney for their helpful comments on the introduction. My sincere gratitude, finally, to the contributors to this volume for their patience, generosity, and good humor.

The Pembroke Center is endebted, for its research projects, to the Ford Foundation, the National Endowment for the Humanities, and Brown University, none of which is responsible for the wide range of opinions expressed in this volume, but all of which are to be credited for their strong support of collaborative feminist scholarship.

I wish to acknowledge permission to reprint essays from the following sources: "Changing the Subject," in *Feminist Studies, Cultural Studies,* ed. Teresa de Lauretis

(Bloomington: Indiana University Press, 1986), and in Nancy K. Miller, *Subject to Change* (New York: Columbia University Press, 1988); "Julia Kristeva: Take Two" in Jacqueline Rose, *Sexuality in the Field of Vision* (London: Verso, 1986); "Dreaming Dissymmetry: Barthes, Foucault, and Sexual Difference," in *Men In Feminism*, eds. Alice A. Jardine and Paul Smith (New York: Methuen, 1987); "Gender: A Useful Category of Historical Analysis," in *American Historical Review*, vol. 91, no. 5 (December 1986), and in Joan Wallach Scott, *Gender and the Politics of History* (New York: Columbia University Press, 1988); and "A Manifesto for Cyborgs: Science, Technology, and Socialist Feminism in the 1980s," *Socialist Review*, no. 80 (March-April 1985).

Introduction: Terms of Reference

There is no academic field in which debates around theory, politics, and the production of knowledge are more animated than in feminist studies. The enormous development of feminist scholarship across the disciplines in the last two decades has had its institutional effects, not the least of which have been widely publicized debates on the role of the humanities and Western civilization in the university. Feminism figures prominently in current questions about theory and the constitution of knowledge, and indeed many of the issues raised are related in some way to the inescapable impact on the academy of feminism's transformation of knowledge. Moreover, the political interests of feminism are wide ranging, joining the academic and political in ways that extend from the study of structures of domination in representations of gender, to the examination of problems of reproductive technologies, to the study of the position of third world women in international development and multinational expansion.

When the Pembroke Center for Teaching and Research on Women held a conference on "Feminism/Theory/Politics" in 1985, it aimed to look at issues of theory and politics within feminist scholarly practice itself. The conference was designed to examine the complex intersections among these terms, with feminism, however multiple, as the starting point; with theory, namely post-structuralist theory, central to the inquiry; and with the whole inscribed within the context of the political, the political remaining, as it were, the last word. Of the contributors to the volume a number participated in that conference: Joan Scott, then director of the Pembroke Center, presided over it; Nancy Miller, Jacqueline Rose, Margaret Ferguson, Naomi Schor, Mary Ann Doane, Carroll Smith-Rosenberg, Evelyn Brooks-Higginbotham, Leila Ahmed, Barbara Harlow, and Gayatri Chakravorty Spivak presented papers. With the conference as a point of departure, this volume was assembled as an expanded examination of the same problematic triad. All of the contributors have been in one way or another affiliated with the Pembroke Center. A number have participated in the Pembroke Seminar: Naomi Schor, Heather Findlay, Mary Ann Doane, Denise Riley, Rey Chow, Christina Crosby, and Ellen Rooney. And in 1986, Donna Haraway visited the Pembroke Center and participated in a colloquium on her "Cyborgs" paper at which Crosby, Scott, and Doane offered the commentaries included here. As a collection, the essays were selected for their focused examination—individually and collectively—of the questions of feminism/theory/politics. Inevitably, the very focus limits the range of feminisms, theories, and politics represented by the volume, and while the contributors have a broad range of interests, they work primarily out of the disciplines of literature and semiotics, history, philosophy, and the history of science. That is not to say that there is a critical consensus among the contributors, nor that they would necessarily underwrite the terms of the debate as they are inscribed by the thematic framing of the collection. What can be seen as common are the terms of reference of the inquiry—a set of theoretical and political issues involved in the feminist production of knowledge.

In many ways U.S. academic feminism has never ceased to play out the contradictions and tensions of its position in the late 1960s at the intersection of "identity politics" (women's liberation movement, Civil Rights, gay liberation, and so forth), on the one hand, and the massive theoretical critique of liberal humanism and its philosophical foundations, on the other. These tensions have been inflected over the years in such different and discontinuous oppositions as French feminism versus U.S. feminism, anti-essentialism versus essentialism, theory versus politics; and they are still evidenced in current debates about the politics of theory and the strategies of situational politics.

The contradictions produced at the crossroads are, indeed, striking. The current feminist movement emerged in the context of the Civil Rights movement and brought with it its own historical foundation in an enlightenment discourse of individual rights. It was at that time, too, that the continental critique of that very enlightenment discourse and its Western metaphysical roots began to make itself felt in the U.S. academy. At the moment, then, that Western feminism was emphatically reasserting women's identity and rights, a strong critical movement was dismantling the very concept of a free-choosing individual and putting into question such notions as identity, agency, reason, and intentionality.

It is increasingly evident that the convergence of U.S. "identity" movements and the post-structuralist critique of "identity" is neither coincidental nor a "simple" historical contradiction. Certainly, the continental structuralist and post-structuralist critical movement has its own history in the French, European, and third world politics of the 1950s and 1960s, exposed most visibly in the events of 1968, and that history has little resemblance to the U.S. context into which continental theory was transplanted in the 1960s. However, there is something distinctive about the meeting of U.S. feminism and post-structuralist theory, and that seems to be the intense challenge both pose to the very grounds of liberalism, that is, to the nature and status of the individual. Indeed, what makes that meeting so interesting is that while post-structuralism is squarely "against" the liberal individual, feminism is in no simple way for such an abstraction. Feminism's interrogation of the history of Western Man as the economy of the One and the same, forges a connection between feminism and post-structuralism that further twists the knot of contradictions. At the same time, while the liberal rights discourse and the post-structuralist critique of it are imbricated within feminism in complex ways, it is not a question of somehow reconciling the two. On the contrary, it is that imbrication which produces the ideological contradictions that make feminism such a productive site for cultural criticism.

One of the difficulties of discussing the meeting of liberalism and post-structuralism in feminism is that none of the terms can simply stand for itself. The U.S. liberal rights system is a rich and complex one. One of its great sources of strength is its ability to contain challenges to it; it is flexible, sometimes unpredictable, and not easily reducible to formulaic critiques of it. It is, moreover, the channel through which most social change is currently realized. At the same time, the system is at present being strained from at least two directions. First, the appeal to rights has become a generalized political tool crossing other political agendas in diverse ways: from the many rights movements nationally, to international "human rights" strategies, to such other interventions as "animal rights" and "species rights." It is in response to the proliferation of "minority" rights movements, of course, that pluralism has emerged in the U.S. in recent years as a dominant model for negotiating the demands on the system. Secondly, the discrepancy between the principles of rights and actual social formations are becoming more and more glaring. The "feminization of poverty" is a factual reality, as is the social and economic deterioration of the position of blacks in the U.S. since the 1960s. These strains on the system represent problems both for liberal purists (who must acknowledge the growth of serious poverty in this country despite apparent gains in "rights") and for radical purists (who cannot simply point to poverty as a way of dismissing, as ideological containment, the gains of rights movements under advanced capitalism).

If liberalism is a complex affair, so is post-structuralist theory. The assemblage of critical theories which carry the (somewhat unfortunate and sometimes misleading) name of "post-structuralist" incorporates work that is very different and often conflicting. In the U.S. critical environment those theories derive a coherence from their generalized resistance to Western metaphysical grounds of knowledge and the systems of domination they enable. However, the U.S. appropriation of continental theory has tended to emphasize post-structuralism's discursive production as "academic" theory (philosophical, linguistic, etc.) at the expense of its political resonance. The reception of post-structuralist theory in this country has indeed been a complex affair partly because of the differences between the U.S. and French-European contexts, and partly because of the U.S. academy's own complicated theoretical-political formations.

In order to speak of feminism's engagement with liberalism and post-structuralism one must speak first of feminism's own involved history of theory and politics. The traditional taxonomies of feminism are well known, and recent classifications are ever more nuanced. Yet, for all the varieties within the movement, it seems safe to say that the "second wave" of feminism in the U.S. was principally inscribed within the liberal system of individual rights and that the various strains of feminism have had to engage in one way or another with the terms of that inscription. It is in this sense that "liberal feminism" is the mainstream feminism, all the while intersecting in multiple ways with "other" feminisms—socialist, marxist, post-structuralist, black, lesbian, chicana, and so forth—which themselves overlap.

If feminism tends to intersect with post-structuralism, that is because there are constitutive tensions even within mainstream feminism, because feminism can never be completely at home within the structure of individual rights. A demand for rights typically employs the category of the rights-bearing individual and forms a challenge to the principles of inclusion and exclusion which constitute it: property ownership, national origin, gender, race, and so forth. The addition of any new group to the category of rights-bearing individual can then never be simply incremental but always invokes in some way the (Derridean) logic of the supplement which points to the deficiencies or incompleteness of the supplemented whole. Although supplemental negotiations have long been a part of the history of Western liberalism, rights struggles around gender (and race in different ways) have always met with a particular kind of intractability. Indeed, that intractability displays something that feminists have come to know well: the liberal individual's— Man's—resistance to intimations of deficiency, especially when those intimations are themselves expressed through gender.

Stephen Heath sketches out what is at stake in *The Sexual Fix:* "With the development of industrialism and urbanization [his focus is on nineteenth-century Britain, but also generally on the West in the modern period] what are then seen as traditional forms of community definition and cohesion give way to a social organization, that of capitalism, in which, precisely, society and the individual become the terms of reference, in which the social relations of the individual— the 'individual and society'—become the problem as such."[1] Making the connections among the social, the individual, and the family, Heath sees the family as the breeding ground of the individual, one of the primary sites where the "problem" of the individual is addressed through the organization, the shoring up, the securing of (masculine) identity. Moreover, this very shoring up is both a social and a psychical process and requires the Woman as the negative term to ground male positivity. Identity and subjecthood are then constructed as male, and Woman, powerfully (re)constructed in the modern discourse of sexuality, is the means for this and the guarantee.

Even today, as Joan Scott reminds us in her analysis of the "Sears case" (in her *Gender and the Politics of History*), there is a certain unabated social anxiety produced around questions of equity for women. The case—a class action suit first brought against the Sears-Roebuck Company in 1978 for systematic discrimination against women—recently gained national notoriety in its use of feminist scholars from opposing political positions as expert witnesses. What seemed to get lost in the debates, as Scott points out, is the problematic nature of the principal structuring argument of the case as that of "equality versus difference": "When equality and difference are paired dichotomously, they structure an impossible choice. If one opts for equality, one is forced to accept the notion that difference is antithetical to it. If one opts for difference, one admits that equality is unattainable."[2] One might well ask by what legal and logical artifice the notion of "equality," which is precisely a concept of equivalences within and among *differences* (or, as Scott puts it, a "deliberate indifference to specified differences," p. 173), is permitted to elide into the sense of "equal" as "same." There is, in fact, a certain undecidability here, and this undecidability at the heart of one of democracy's fundamental concepts has been the terrain of a long history of struggles. And yet, the struggles about gender seem to produce a repetitive resistance permissable only through a dogged biologism. Indeed, at this time, when the denial of legal rights on explicitly essentialist grounds (race, ethnicity) is scrupulously prohibited—or rather, at a time when the essential category "human" is supposed to include everyone—there seems to be a considerable slippage in the prohibition when it comes to gender. Because sexual difference, of all the differences, appears to be the one most grounded in biology—and perhaps because the (white) woman is the most domesticated of the Others—the invocation of the commensurability of women's social and biological functions seems permissible and "natural." Moreover, the effects of this slippage are not limited to consolidations of gender differences. The very fact that an appeal to biology (however mediated through culture) is quite permissible in debates on women's rights—while such an appeal is currently not acceptable in areas of race, class, religion, and ethnicity—indicates, perhaps, the role women and feminism play in "managing" the residue of the profoundly essentialist beliefs of our very recent past. One need only look at the ongoing pathologizing of poor black women and other poor women of color (a process even more pervasive now than at the time of the Moynihan report) to see a virtually unmasked essentialism-as-racism at work, a racism that is enabled by the biologically laden category of gender.

It is not surprising that essentialism continues to nag at feminism, that the "sex/gender" distinction continues to figure as a dominant ground for much feminist work. At the very core of feminism is a struggle against the historical constitution of individual (masculine) identity with its collapse of the female into the biological or into the "naturally" ordained realm of the functional; and as Heath has suggested, that struggle takes on a particular focus in nineteenth-century constellations of the individual and the social. In her study of these formations (in "Does Sex Have a History? 'Women' and Feminism"), Denise Riley argues that the "social" emerged in mid-nineteenth-century Britain as a concern with the intimate conditions of working-class domestic life, and that the social-familial connection became progressively feminized—partly through the efforts of socialist feminists and women's philanthropic organizations. One result of the constitution of the social-familial was that the political was dislocated, the political taking on "an air of privacy and invulnerability, of 'high politics' associated with judicial and governmental power in a restricted sense."[3] Women (increasingly collapsed into "the sex" in the emerging discourses of sexuality) were aligned with this sense of the social, essentially secured, as it were, in their place. Men were aligned as distinct from the social and this distinction gave rise to the opposition "man versus society" with "the couplet man/society, and the ensuing riddle of their relationship, becoming the lifestuff of anthropology, sociology, social psychology—the problem of how the individual is in the world." Riley goes on: "if the social which partly encapsulates women, is then set against 'man' or the individual in this way, then the alignments of the sexes in 'society' are *conceptualized* as askew. It is not so much that 'women' are omitted as that they are too thoroughly included" (p. 43).

When U.S. feminism emerged in the late 1960s with its famous slogan "the personal is the political," it put into play a whole system of interlocking elements not unrelated to Riley's description of nineteenth-century Britain, although some of the terms, of course, had shifted. The personal/political certainly evoked the public/private, which was by now a fully naturalized concept overlaid onto the social, with both hierarchies, while not identical, complexly articulated and at work in the drama of the individual versus society of the late 1960s. There was a way, indeed, in which the anti-war and countercultural movements of the period were that drama. Moreover, there was a way in which they were a family affair, that is, the focus of intense concern on the part of the sons and families of the white middle class who were outraged by the state's intrusion into the personal-private lives of young men for the purpose of an unjust, unpopular war (blacks being involved in anti-war efforts through the different route of anti-racist struggles, and the working class dismissed by the anti-war movement as "hard hats"). With the anti-war sentiment came, through the "youth culture," a thoroughgoing rebellion of the young against the established values and conventional mores of their elders, with the result that the whole economy of the public/private realm, so excessively regulated in the 1950s, was unsettled and redistributed.

Feminism's intervention into this context took the form of a demand for the inclusion of women in the category of "individual." (White) men traditionally have access to all categories of personal/political, public/private in that they are constituted as individuals distinct from these categories; for them the 1960s were precisely a time of renegotiation of the terms of access. For women, however, the feminine was still seen as fully personal and private. For feminism the issue was differentiation and that differentiation was effected by a reclamation of the political. Indeed, "the personal is political" reclaims the "political" while deconstructing the political/personal and the public/private. The "political," having been dislocated by the liberal discourse, as Riley says, into a realm of high politics which had rendered it less visible and in many ways more private than the so-called "private," was now forced into the open. It is true that in the late 1960s everything became "political." But for feminism, everything became political through a transformation of the categories of the political and the *personal,* the gendered personal being, as Joan Scott argues in this volume, that which is always excluded from high politics but which—through the opposition male/female—operates forcefully in the structuring of power. The reversal of the political/personal hierarchy by feminism means that the political is already marked by, constituted by the personal, and most important, it means that both terms are displaced.[4]

What causes the tensions and contradictions even for mainstream feminism is that the demand for individuation for women on the one hand, is not in some unproblematic way compatible with the ideological insights produced by the displacement of the personal and political on the other. The widespread practice of consciousness-raising groups in the 1960s and early 1970s did much to generate one of feminism's most important recognitions: that one's desire may not be one's own, that what one calls one's self may be constructed elsewhere. The whole practice of consciousness-raising was, of course, highly organized and effective. Largely an affair, again, of the white middle class—both in its participants and in the issues it raised—it nonetheless touched many people. *Ms* magazine even had a special "click" section where readers shared personal moments of ideological unveiling, of the recognition that the "subjective" is constructed within systems of power. The problem was, and is, what implications feminists might draw from such recognitions: what stance feminism can take toward identity and the individual, what negotiations are possible given the structures of power and domination so forcefully revealed.

The history of U.S. feminism has, in fact, been a history of ambiguity toward the contradictions it exposes. For some feminisms, the consciousness-raising model served as a passage from false consciousness to truth and to a building of the proper category of women through the received terms of liberal individualism. For others, like black, marxist, psychoanalytic, and post-structuralist feminisms, analyses of the ideological constructions of gender led, in different and sometimes overlapping ways, to more radical critical practices. Within scholarly feminism, those tending in the latter direction—that is, those which have multiplied contradictions and resisted containment—have made the intersections between feminism and post-structuralism increasingly evident.

Even as one makes such distinctions, however, one must qualify them. Feminism is not a simple terrain divided into the liberal-humanist versus the theoretical-radical. In feminism the categories of humanist, liberal, post-structuralist, marxist, formalist, and so forth, cross one another and overlap in multiple and sometimes unpredictable ways. Moreover, the necessity for all the "other" feminisms to engage with the terms of liberal feminism has meant that the problems of the liberal discourse have in one way or another absorbed U.S. feminist scholarship for many years. That is not to say that individual scholars have all been preoccupied with such questions as individuation, identity, agency, experience, sexuality, and so forth. Rather it is that in ways that have been difficult to ignore, these questions have been continually produced and debated in many and different circles, partly because they are highly naturalized terms in U.S. political debates, and partly because the particular organization of knowledge in the U.S. academy favors such issues. But also—and here again is where even liberal feminism cannot contain itself easily within its own terms—these questions have been produced partly because they are constitutive problems within contemporary feminism. Any examination of women's problems must in some way confront the very notion of gender differentiation, of what constitutes the category of "women"; and for problems in the modern era and in the West, that question leads to sexuality. As Mary Ann Doane says, "[w]hatever the social, historical, economic effects of sexism, they are linked, in however mediated a fashion, to a definition of women as the *sex,* with respect to the zero degree of masculinity." Doane's comment is an historically specific one. It locates feminism as both constituted by and resistant to the mode of intense individualism characteristic of recent Western history: with the individual as the basic unit of economic, social, and affective organization, and individual identity powerfully formed through, and consolidated by, sexual differentiation. The terms of feminism are, then, given to it by the social formations in which it is produced, and feminist practice becomes an ongoing theoretical and political process of reinscribing or dismantling those terms.

A common criticism directed against mainstream feminism is that it has been too absorbed by the categories of the individual, too self-absorbed. Certainly there has been significant movement in recent years away from a universalized concept of female identity and experience to a more plural understanding of "women" and to a notion of "situational identities" determined by the exigencies of the social field. These shifts are surely welcome, and signal, perhaps, the exhaustion of some of feminism's more insistent categories. At the same time, one must be wary of seeing "differences" as the cure for feminism. It is all too easy to slip into a simple pluralism which, while replacing assimilation as an ideal, nonetheless keeps power relations intact and simply inflects the many within the paradigm of the one. Moreover, it is all too easy to allow the pluralistic ideal to cover over a full endorsement and reinscription of the categories of identity, epistemology, and experience, and for the thematics of "multiple identities" to conflate subject, social subject, and individual. In "What Is To Be Done," Ellen Rooney cites Jenny Bourne's argument that the privileging of identity has, in fact, undermined feminist politics: "Identity Politics is all the rage. Exploitation is out (it is intrinsically determinist). Oppression is in (it is intrinsically personal). What is to be done has been replaced by who I am."

The problem for feminism is—still—one of resistance and displacement. And yet, in the process of resisting there is no simple formula for expunging the terms of a dominant discourse. "Resistance," as Wlad Godzich reminds us, is a "leaning against" in the very process of "opposing."[5] Or, as Doane says in her reading of Donna Haraway's essay, "there is no clean break" with constitutive historical structures. The "old" dualisms of self/other, inside/outside, personal/political linger on, even when they are not (as they frequently are) actively redeployed. The essays in this volume all address in some way these problems of resistance and displacement. As the authors' notes indicate, some of the earlier essays trace the terms of earlier debates, but it is precisely those traces which mark our current discourse.

Identity, as feminism's compulsion, speaks compulsively of the problem of difference. Since Simone de Beauvoir, we have understood that in the Western production of male/female, the male is both the positive and the neutral and the female is constructed as the negative term. Subsequent feminist theory has read in Western conceptual systems a deep aversion to heterogeneity and an anxious containment of it through the operations of logic and power. Feminist readings have also pointed to certain cultural obsessions of recent Western history: the fetishization of women as/against lack, and the necessity continually to shore up structures of masculinity.

One of the difficulties of working with such embedded ideological formations is that those formations both enable and limit critical responses to them. Readings of female "negativity" have indeed called forth work on female positivity, often figured by a simple reversal through the very thematics which embellish the opposition: the thematics of choice, voice, agency, and knowledge. With work of a "positive" nature the question is always the extent to which problematic terms are reconsolidated. There is a way in which positive work is necessary: feminism as an historicized project cannot but be an activity of retrieval; as a political enterprise it cannot do without a category of "women." However, to what end women and gender are retrieved and how the political category of "women" is formed are open to much debate. Recent work on feminist epistemology, for example, like earlier work on female moral development, allows for an easy slippage into essentialism (as Scott says in her "Gender" article), and it reinscribes universalist categories (as women of color and others have been quick to point out). Yet there is work that is far removed theoretically from a nostalgia for self-presence, which has its own "dream of dissymmetry," as Naomi Schor calls it in this volume. As Schor says in *Reading in Detail:* "Whether or not the 'feminine' is a male construct, a product of a phallocentric culture destined to disappear, in the present order of things we cannot afford not to press its claims even as we dismantle the conceptual systems which support it." Schor's insistence on the need for a feminine specificity is political. It represents a recognition on xviii / Introduction: Terms of Reference

the part of some feminists—a growing recognition since the writing of "Dreaming Dissymmetry" in 1985—that much of post-structuralist theory which is not explicitly feminist is simply blind to sexual difference or, in its desire to get beyond the opposition male/female, underestimates the full political weight of the categories. Moreover, Schor goes on in *Reading in Detail* to make a connection between the need for feminine specificity and the struggle against male violence. Although Schor's argument is particular to her history of the detail from its sublimation in Hegel to its "desublimation" in Barthes, it has a general resonance. Asserting that there is no evidence that women's art is more "particularistic" than men's, she writes: "Indeed, further investigation of this question may lead us to formulate a surprising hypothesis, namely that feminine specificity lies in the direction of a specifically feminine form of idealism, one that seeks to transcend not the sticky feminine world of prosaic details, but rather the deadly asperities of male violence and destruction." Schor's feminine specificity here does not precede the circumstances of the field in which it is produced. It is not a "positive" specificity, but it is a fully necessary one.[6]

There is another branch of feminism which also grounds specificity in political necessity and which resists the generalized category of "women." Since the beginnings of the current feminist movement, and with particular insistence since the late 1970s, women finding themselves outside the frame of dominant feminism—black women, other women of color, ethnic women, working-class women, third world women—have contested the terms of its discourse. They have pointed not only to the inadequacies of the prevailing concept of "women" but to white feminism's own historical consolidation of Western, white, and middle-class interests. In "White Women Listen! Black Feminism and the Boundaries of Sisterhood," an essay appearing in *The Empire Strikes Back,* Hazel Carby says that "in arguing that most contemporary feminist theory does not begin to adequately account for the experience of black women we also have to acknowledge that it is not a simple question of their absence, consequently the task is not one of rendering their visibility. On the contrary we will have to argue that the process of accounting for their historical and contemporary position does, in itself, challenge the use of some of the central categories and assumptions of recent mainstream feminist thought."[7] Three of those fundamental categories which Carby goes on to discuss are "the family," "patriarchy," and "reproduction." Moreover, not only can one not simply add black women to feminist categories, one cannot in any formulaic way articulate the two discourses of race and of gender. One can, as Carby says, point out similarities between constructions of race and gender: both are naturalized through reference to biology; as social constructs neither has much internal coherence; and social legislation cannot solve the problems of either. However, Carby argues, after Michèle Barrett, the parallels are of little use because "as soon as historical analysis is made, it becomes obvious that the institutions which have to be analyzed are different, as are the forms of analysis needed" (p. 212–13).

In "Does Sex Have a History?," Denise Riley argues that while the biological female has had a more or less continuous history, the history of "women" is discontinuous, indeed, a good deal more so than that of "Woman," the powerful signifier of the Western symbolic order. For Riley, " 'women' is historically and discursively constructed, always in relation to other categories which themselves change. 'Women' is a volatile collectivity in which female persons can be very differently positioned so that the apparent continuity of the subject of 'women' isn't to be relied on. . . ."[8] In a later context Riley goes on: "There are indeed no moments at which gender is utterly unvoiced. But the ways in which 'women' have always been there, spoken in advance of some more formally collectivized and prominent 'emergence,' will be different, so that we can only decipher some newer articulation of 'women' by establishing what layers it is being spoken upon and against . . ." (p. 40).

For Carby and Riley, then, 'women' is a meaningful and useful term when carefully historicized in relation to other relevant categories. Although the term is in itself unstable and unreliable, there is little danger of lapsing into "sexual indifference," or indifference to gender, because 'women' are indeed continually produced by social formations. The whole problem of establishing a positive identity for women is thus displaced since such a project makes sense only if the term 'women' can be somehow isolated or essentialized. And the lack of a reliable positive identity does not mean an endless proliferation of differences. It means, rather, that the very categories of difference are displaced and denaturalized through the articulation of those categories with the structures of domination in which they were historically produced.

A deconstructionist argument would assert that there is a way to resist replicating those structures of domination, a way to resist essentializing and hypostatizing the processes which produce categories of race, class, and gender. These categories, constructed relationally and oppositionally in history, cannot settle into self-identity if that differentially produced identity is shown always to be different from itself. Such a critical practice does not entail sublation, but neither does it preclude meaning as those skeptical of deconstruction's value for politics assert. The deconstructive practice is inscribed in, and only possible within, a signifying system which, as Spivak points out, necessarily produces its meaning, its referentiality, through a movement of transcendence.[9] Deconstruction does not deny meaning; it resists meaning. And resisting meaning in politics can signal attentiveness to one's own coercive operations. The most concrete of feminism's problems—such as domestic violence or rape—while produced by the circumstances of the social field, are produced as problems to be addressed only through active and often contested processes of representation. Those processes need not reconsolidate dominant interests if we as critical-political subjects acknowledge, as Spivak says (in *In Other Worlds*), that the production of political explanations entails exclusion, and that "although the prohibition of marginality that is crucial in the production of any explanation is politics as such, what inhabits the prohibited

margin of a particular explanation specifies its particular politics."[10] The deconstructive practice need not end once an explanation is produced, and explanation
need not replicate domination if political positions are attentive to their own
relations to margin and center.

The difficulty with theoretical-political arguments against identity and for the
instability of "women," of course, is that they do not simply "solve" the problem.
For feminism, identity, like essentialism, is an issue that won't go away, that itself
stubbornly resists displacement. Constituted through Woman and women, identity
claims them too as its own. It can be argued that white feminism's slowness in
recognizing its own universalizing moves was not simply due to self-interest and
racism (although there is a lot of truth in Donna Haraway's sardonic remark that
"[w]hite women . . . were forced kicking and screaming to notice . . . the non-
innocence of the category 'woman'." White feminism's blindness was caused partly
by the extraordinary explanatory power of its own critical reading of Western
Man and his Other and of the semantic richness of the figure of the feminine.
For white middle-class women this entailed a reading of one's identity from the
other side as it were, and in that sense was compelling as negative identification,
as identification with the negative. Indeed, Jacqueline Rose points out (in *Feminine
Sexuality*) that in Jacques Lacan's later theories of sexuality and language "woman
is constructed as an absolute category (excluded and elevated at one and the same
time), a category which serves to guarantee the unity on the side of the man.[11]
Although "Woman" does not exist, of course, other than as man's support, the
very unified nature of the concept has had its own seductive history and effects.

Recent feminist concerns have moved somewhat away from the closed economy
of radical alterity. Woman has given way to women, difference to differences,
identity to multiple identities. The romantic sentiments of individual loss and
alienation which permeated high modernism (and still linger over some post-
structuralist thematics of the displaced subject) seem not to be feminism's sentiments. One finds rather a feminist celebration of heterogeneity and proliferating
identities. The shift seems to be away from psychic identity as an ever slipping
fiction of coherence through language and representation to an emphasis, particularly on the part of chicana, black, and other theorists and critics, on ideological
processes of subject positioning. The operations associated with "identity" are
now seen as more fully implicated in social formations. To cite Haraway: "Identities
seem contradictory, partial, and strategic. . . . Gender, race, or class consciousness
is an achievement forced on us by the terrible historical experience of the contradictory social realities of patriarchy, colonialism, and capitalism."

Feminism is focusing increasingly on the identity-effects produced by those
contradictory social realities and "identity" has emerged—as the semantically
surfeited term it is—to occupy large areas within feminist work: multiple identities,
strategic identities, identity politics. Like other feminist thematics, the term has
at least a double life and can be used to both radical and recuperative ends.

Haraway's evocations of cyborg identities dazzingly appropriate in order to disrupt. And Haraway finds affinities with the work of women of color, such as that of Cherríe Moraga which "explores themes of identity when one never possessed the original language, never told the original story, never resided in the harmony of legitimate heterosexuality in the garden of culture, and so cannot base identity on a myth or a fall from innocence and right to natural names, mother's or father's." Such work does, indeed, fracture identity, interrupt coherence, and displace origins.

Problems arise in the appropriation of "identity," however, when the emphasis shifts from attention to subject positions and the fracturing of coercive coherence to questions of authorship and consciousness. These questions—particularly the retrieval of authorship—strike deeply at the heart of many feminisms. Nancy Miller addresses the problem directly in "Changing the Subject" when she brings together feminism's project and Roland Barthes's "Death of the Author," arguing that because the female "has juridically been excluded from the polis, hence decentered, 'disoriginated,' deinstitutionalized, etc., her relation to integrity and textuality, desire and authority, displays structurally important differences from that universalist position." In displaying feminism's anxiety about agency, Miller points to a key tension in the debates between feminism and post-structuralism. From one side of the debate, the stubborn problem for feminism is that agency has been denied to women in the past and seems essential to political change in the future. From the other side, the problem with agency construed this way is that it seems to require authorship, and that entails an inviolable site of intentionality.

In short, the problem for those concerned with social change is that such a view of authorship can secure the individual and the rational subject in their place with all of the political fragmentation and isolation that implies. Yet, there are ways out of the impasse, ways to resist this recontainment and to argue that agency does not require authorship in the sense of a transcendent subject present to itself, proprietor of action and master of causality. There is another kind of intervention which attempts to displace questions of coherence and origin and to interrogate the effects of its own constitution, again not to deny what is necessary for political action but to resist what is dangerously seductive because familiar. It is the politics which ask "what is to be done?" rather than "who am I?" which attempt to avoid the identificatory structures available everywhere, those structures which enable us to see women of color but not race, blacks but not whites.

Some of the recent work on feminist epistemology in such fields as philosophy, cognition, and moral development, point to a continued, perhaps renewed interest in theories of female agency. While the emphasis may be shifting to a concept of knowledge as relationally produced rather than revealed, the structure of epistemology remains nonetheless rooted in a cogito, representation, and a metaphysics of presence. Moreover, a reliance on epistemology tends precisely to underwrite the notion of a one-to-one correspondence between power and knowledge in its focus on agency and intentionality. One finds a related set of questions in feminism's version of what has become a veritable cultural fixation: the narrative or story. From cultural criticism's reading of the master narratives of the West, to developmental psychology's theorizing of life stories, to newsweekly and t.v. journalism's construction of seductive scenarios of politics and history, our collective fascination with the narrative seems to have intensified into a shared hermeneutical thematics. Some evocations of the narrative are fully informed theoretically, others are simply formulaic, but the interest is a shared one. It is the interest of our times, related to what Stephen Heath calls "the powerful work of *social* representation of 'the individual,' the socially cohesive realization of the latter, people given that sense: stories of life, of lives, patterns of recognition, the ceaseless account of the social as meaning for the individual, experience always in these individual terms."[12] Whether through the work of the nineteenth-century novel or of twentieth-century television, the narrative is part of the identity-sexuality fix.

The current deployment of this preeminent mode of realism has to do not only with a certain cultural "crisis" of the referent, but with a destabilization of the narrative form itself in its capacity as what de Lauretis calls a "strategy of coherence."[13] If the narrative has become a major commodity fetish in its simulation of the "real thing," there are implications for feminism's use of the form. It is indeed used everywhere as the metaphor and means for women to break the silence, to tell their own stories, to forge their own critical and theoretical narratives. Perhaps the greatest risk involved with such a thematics—a risk related to the question of epistemology—is that its very appeal to the factitious nature of the narrative, which is salutary in its loosening of the power of the referent, also focuses attention anew onto the question of women's agency. However it is figured, this simple view of agency can be seen as just another lure. As de Lauretis says in a discussion of film in *Technologies of Gender,* if feminist (film) work embraces the narrative mode, "it should be narrative and oedipal with a vengeance," working "to represent the duplicity of the oedipal scenario itself and the specific contradiction of the female subject in it."[14]

For feminism, the most common ground for knowledge and agency has historically been experience. Though common, experience is nonetheless an embattled term: "women's experience" has for one area of feminism served to reveal authenticity and to ground theory and politics; for another, " 'I' carries with it," as Paula Treichler has written, "the baggage of a bourgeois and humanistic tradition which privileges the individual and grounds discussion in an ideology which makes certain kinds of analysis impossible."[15] The received notion of experience certainly has blocked ways of disrupting the subject/society opposition. It continually reinforces the terms of the opposition, cleaving anew, as it were, the personal and the political. Experience becomes the authentic and the authoritative and with it comes—paradoxically for feminism—the whole apparatus of subject/object and the demarcating of the proprietor. One is blocked from thinking other ways of valuing human life, other modalities of freedom. Moreover, the very separation of the personal and the political allows one term to stand for the other; one risks reducing the political to the merely personal and lapsing into what Ellen Rooney has called "the politics of feeling good."

One of the reasons experience has been such a stubborn category for feminism is that it seems to be a natural access to sexuality, that complex process so crucial to feminism and to the individual and which seems so intimately one's own. There certainly have been critical-theoretical efforts to denaturalize sexuality. The work of Michel Foucault, Stephen Heath, or Denis Riley has given sexuality a history, and, as Doane says, "[a]s soon as sexuality has a history, it becomes a representation, a discourse. In this important work, the history of sexuality becomes its indictment. . . ." From another direction, psychoanalysis has shown that the edifice of the individual subject is built with great difficulty, that the working up of identity through sexuality is an elaborate and precarious process. Perhaps the most powerful intervention has come, finally, from work which has located sexuality in its Western specificity as part of the deployment of gender, race, and class in the construction of a psychic-economic-political Other.

On the one hand, then, there is good reason to argue that rather than experience revealing sexuality, sexuality, in the context of Western individualism, constructs experience. On the other hand, there are feminisms which argue that there is truth located within an experienced sexuality. And yet, even within those positions, one finds a certain refusal of that "truth," or at least an ambivalence to it, and one of the places that ambivalence can be found is in mainstream feminism's apparent difficulty with heterosexuality. If one looks at the principal feminist debates around sexuality in recent years, one sees that they have focused on lesbianism, pornography, and motherhood, which, while important topics in them-selves, can also be seen, in the absence of discussions of heterosexuality in its specificity, as displacements from that topic. On a theoretical psychoanalytic level, of course, all discussions of sexuality are discussions of heterosexuality and of women's negotiation of lack through such strategies as mimesis, mimicry, and masquerade. And yet, there is a level on which sexuality is not identical to heterosexuality, and it is in that space of difference that the specificity of het-erosexuality has been neglected, or avoided. Lesbianism in its most radical form— that is, when it is not posited as an authentic sexuality—certainly represents the most extreme displacement, as in the work of Monique Wittig where female homosexuality is outside the economy of heterosexuality and lesbians simply are not "women." The focus on motherhood has done the critical work of retrieving maternity from the male imaginary. And in the debates on pornography, the anti-pornography critics have analogically folded heterosexuality into violence against women, while the anti-anti-pornography people have either been dominated by a lesbian discourse of sexual liberation or have moved deftly to analyses of the juridical, the broadly social, or the political-economic, leaving the specificities of heterosexuality behind.

Feminist work on male subjectivity, such as Kaja Silverman's, is very important in this regard, although, again, the approach is indirect. Indeed, the very indirectness of much of feminist treatment of heterosexuality may be precisely the point. If feminist critical work shows an apparent reluctance to deal straightforwardly, as it were, with heterosexuality, if the kind of positivity that has been constituted both experientially and theoretically for lesbianism and maternity has not been constituted for heterosexuality, the explanation might have something to do with the constitutive contradictions within feminism itself and with the inadequacies of the notion of experience. Feminism has long argued that Woman as Other to white, Western Man is an uninhabitable category negatively constituted as it is through sexuality in relation to male identity. And yet, as de Lauretis has said and as we know, "women continue to become woman."[16] There is no escaping that pull within Western culture, although when one is lesbian, or black, or a mother one seems to have some purchase against the category. Since heterosexuality collapses always into sexuality, there is little purchase there to be had, as feminist psychoanalytic theory has often told us. Feminism's general unease, then, with heterosexual specificity points to a certain acknowledgement that the place of "women" in the West is in no simple way more inhabitable (or more accessible through experience) than that of Woman, in that "women" too is always historically marked by sexuality. In itself "women" cannot offer a categorical place of recognition, an identity.

If sexual difference becomes ever more destabilized, living as a female will become an easier project, but that will result from the continued displacement of "women," not from its consolidation. Mainstream feminism's complicated relationship to heterosexuality does not mean, of course, that there is any unified position in feminism with regard to heterosexuality as a way of organizing subjectivity or as a sexual practice (although most feminists are critical of heterosexuality's historical role in the formation of these practices and in political-economic structures of domination). It certainly does not mean that relations between actual women and men have been rendered more difficult by feminism, as some critics of the movement have maintained. What it does mean is that feminism's—especially white, middle-class feminism's—relationship to "women's experience" is a good deal more problematic than one would sometimes believe.

For those outside mainstream feminism, "women's experience" has never ceased to be problematic. The common ground of sisterhood, long held as white feminism's ideal, was always a more utopian than representative slogan. Worse, it was coercive in its unacknowledged universalism, its unrecognized exclusions. In Haraway's discussion of mainstream feminism's deep investment in and deployment of the "comfortable categories" of Western metaphysics, she cites Katie King's work, which observes that as different segments within the women's movement constitute their political agendas, incorporating and marginalizing other feminisms, they do so by building explicit ontologies and epistemologies which "police deviation from official women's experience." And yet, there is another side to "experience," an experience which allows the black critic to assert, as Hazel Carby does, that "most contemporary feminist theory does not begin to account for the experience of black women." It is this kind of "experience" which enabled feminism to displace the personal and the political, which allows Moraga to trace a different relationship to the oedipal subjection of white culture. When experience is used in this way, not to pin down the truth of the individual subject but as a critical effort to open up ideological contradictions, it resembles, as Mae Henderson has argued, the Afro-American ritual of "testifying." Testifying combines "both the concept of story and the notion of critical self-consciousness. It is the testimony of the individual confirming and confirmed by the community, shaping and shaped by history that finally authorizes and authenticates the account." Understood in this way, testifying is not the story of an individual truth produced and policed by a group, but a critical commentary on ideological formations. For Henderson, an appeal to experience is an appeal to situate scholarship—both scholar and the object of study—historically, socially, and politically: "In doing so, we will avoid the occulting potential of ideology and the reductive risks of assuming sameness, even as we enjoy our freedom (recognize our necessity) to acknowledge difference."[17]

Efforts within feminism to loosen family ties and to resist the lures of identification, are nowhere more important than in work on the "third world." Western feminism's own roots place it squarely on the terrain of colonialism, and as Barbara Harlow says, it "has at times assumed for itself the prerogative of the exemplary 'civilizing mission' of its own colonial past." Leila Ahmed argues forcefully that the notion that "egalitarianism" or "humaneness" belongs fully to feminism and the Western rights discourse is simply ethnocentric. Moreover, such ethnocentrism reinforces what Ahmed sees as a long history of orthodox Islam's hegemonic erasure of resistance and dissent, precisely that history which she locates in Sufism's non-oppressive organization of gender.

However, a feminism which is not proprietary, which tries to be attentive to the problems of ethnocentrism, can still confront difficulties in its interrogation of the third world. In asking "Can the Subaltern Speak?" in *Marxism and the Interpretation of Culture*), Spivak's answer is no, not in any unproblematic sense. The "third world woman" is produced by historical, political-economic, and epistemological formations: "Between patriarchy and imperialism, subject-constitution and object-formation, the figure of the woman disappears, not into a pristine nothingness, but into a violent shuttling which is the displaced figuration of the 'Third World woman' caught between tradition and modernization." In the context of a complexly layered discussion of *suttee*, Spivak addresses Foucault's distinction in the *History of Sexuality* between repression (which "functions well as a sentence to disappear, but also as an injunction to silence, affirmation of non-existence; and consequently that of all this there is nothing to say, to see, to know") and "the prohibitions maintained by the simple penal law." For Spivak, the reading of the history of sexuality in the West cannot hold for the third world woman in question: "The case of *suttee* as exemplum of the woman-in-imperialism would challenge and deconstruct this opposition between subject (law) and object-of-knowledge (repression) and mark the place of 'disappearance' with something other than silence and nonexistence, a violent aporia between subject and object status.[18] The problem of an "identificatory" critical practice is not limited, then, to an uninterrogated liberal feminism which looks for "women" everywhere, seeking them, producing them, and in the process imposing its own specular economy of interest; the very reading of Western "subjection" in sexuality can be, indeed, something that one learns to read against.

Along an intersecting but different route from Spivak's, Rey Chow argues that in its constitution of the third world as an object of study, Western post-structuralist theory can tend, in its very attentiveness to " 'the capacity for contradiction' in the dominating stance," to be blind to overdetermined instances of domination within the specific culture at hand. Certainly post-structuralist theory and criticism (like all theory and criticism) must resist the pleasure of always finding itself in its very reading. Indeed, given the complexity of Western hegemony in today's global social formations, the study of the West's operations is at once increasingly necessary and increasingly difficult because of the seductiveness of its totalizing force. It is not, as Chow says, that there is some innocent solution in the "earnest excavations of the forgotten." What Chow calls for is a way in which the contradictions of the other can themselves come forth, in their specificity.

There is a way in which Chow's call is, after all, feminism's project: to enable the contradictions of the other to come forth in their specificity. The strength of the feminist enterprise lies in the close connections most areas of scholarly feminism have maintained with the problems and sufferings people face in their capacity as women. This ongoing involvement with concrete politics has meant repeated demands from one or another quarter for specificity. When those demands have not been a simple nostalgic appeal for female identification, they have been feminism's greatest strength and have helped the feminist discourse resist even its own movements of domination. To cite Denise Riley once again, " 'women' is a simultaneous foundation of and irritant to feminism, and this is constitutionally so."[19] It is that irritant which has made feminism such a productive discourse.

In her commentary in this volume, Margaret Ferguson refers to the "uneasy relations among a set of heterogeneous terms"—politics/psychoanalysis/feminism—the same uneasy relations, perhaps, that one finds among the terms feminism/theory/politics. Might that uneasiness be part of a general mode of self-reflection characteristic of many areas of feminist inquiry today? Has feminism labored, does it labor still to take on the "master narratives" as well as the master theoretical discourses only to find that it has replicated the moves of dominance in the constitution of its own discourse? If the specificity of Western feminism is sexuality, what happens to the force of this analysis if concern for the social subject leaves the psychical subject behind? And how does one deploy the psychoanalytic discourse in the reading of non-Western subjects and social formations?

Yet unease does not tell the whole story, for feminism is in no sense in retreat. The very strength of the essays collected here points to the productive future of un-ease, as it were, the future of a discourse that can't stay in its place. The volume marks a time of critical ferment in a significant segment of the field of feminist studies, and that ferment is quite apparent in the animated exchange among the essays, the commentaries, and the texts they engage. The exchanges among the essays take place over different periods of time and in different contexts; moreover, five of the essays are reprinted from other publications (those of Miller, Rose, Schor, Scott, and Haraway) and carry with them the traces of still different debates. There has been little effort given to smoothing out the time lags among the essays, and allusions to the 1985 Pembroke Center conference and to Haraway's colloquium have been retained. My hope is that those traces of production and the resulting layering and imbrication of the texts will, in fact, invoke something of the density and movement of the debates.

Certainly the essays are hard to pin down and the five sections of the book function more like intersections than divisions. The best illustration of this is the relations among the first three sections: "Feminist Politics of Interpretation," "Sexual Difference and Indifference," and "Writing History." Essentially the same categories as those of the original Pembroke Center conference, they served then as now to designate three of academic feminism's major concerns. It is not surprising (although it is instructive) to find questions of interpretation and representation addressed in some way more directly by the historians than by the literary critics. In Joan Scott's strong reading of the intersections of feminist history and theory, she looks for ways to account for gender in history without always telling the same old story. With theories of patriarchy or psychoanalytic theory, "[h]istory becomes, in a sense, epiphenomenal, providing endless variations on the unchanging theme of a fixed gender inequality"; with marxist theory the story is always elsewhere and sexuality is largely written out. In proposing a reading of the histories of power through the binary opposition of man/woman, Scott reminds us that history resides under the virtually intact dominion of representation and that one (perhaps *the*) powerful guarantor of that dominion is gender. The next essay, Carroll Smith-Rosenberg's "The Body Politic," leads us in Riley's words, straight to the key question of what sense we can give to the idea of a "female language" or the slightly different " 'female voice,' as an echo or resource to be caught in history." By looking at the language of several generations of politically resistant women in the U.S. between the Civil War and the 1920s, Smith-Rosenberg raises the ever difficult issue of what is at stake in the deployment of the very terms that one might be trying to displace. And for Evelyn Brooks-Higginbotham (to whom I will return shortly) the reading of black women's history is a complex process entailing the triple representation of American History, Afro-American history, and women's history.

Like the historians, Nancy Miller and Jacqueline Rose take on questions of representation but they do so by focusing on problems of the subject. In a nuanced reading of Julia Kristeva's work, Rose explores the vexed question of the political and the psychoanalytic and rejects the reading of the two as mutually exclusive: "To say that the unconscious cannot be politicized does not necessarily entail setting up psychoanalysis as an alternative to all politics. To argue that questions of sexuality are not—in a one to one relation—managed or exhausted by traditional political discourse or transformation does not mean that we have to discard these questions from political understanding and debate." Ferguson, citing Louis Althusser, asks if there can't be an *indirect* politicization of the unconscious, and Mary Ann Doane, evoking Rose's work in her consideration of Schor and Findlay, argues for a shifting of terms, pointing to psychoanalysis' utopian tendencies and its "misrecognition (as authoritative science)." Nancy Miller's subject is the female reading/writing subject, particularly as against Roland Barthes's "Death of the Author." But Miller's subject is also "subject to change"; it is mobile, touching many of the questions addressed elsewhere in the volume. The essay is indeed a kind of hetero-text, multiplying questions, splitting typeface, agreeing to close but refusing to settle.

It is fitting that the essays in the second section, the section on sexuality, engage several master (male) theorists, declining finally to accept them fully on their own terms. In her essay, Naomi Schor argues with (the ever-seductive and ubiquitous) Roland Barthes's embodiment of a sexual discourse of indifference, and with Michel Foucault's blindness to women's specificity if not to their alterity. She wonders finally if "the discourse of sexual indifference/pure difference is not the last or (less triumphantly) the latest ruse of phallocentrism." For Heather Findlay, heterosexuality figures prominently in the containment of Jacques Derrida's deconstructive reading of the Woman. For her, Derrida's premature foreclosure of homosexuality in his reading of homosexuality and heterosexuality as "coming to the same thing" means, as well, a certain foreclosure of deconstruction's radicality.

With Evelyn Brooks-Higginbotham's essay—from the inside of history so to speak—the volume takes a turn toward a question present from the outset and now more fully addressed: the limits of feminism. For Brooks-Higginbotham, the categories constituting her field of history—"women," "black," "American,"—are not inflections within an economy of pluralism; they form a "triple paradox" which permits neither of totalization nor of easy articulation: black and female, black and American, American and female. For Riley, the limits of feminism are its very history, which forces one to admit "the historical as well as the semantic vacillations of 'women.'" Leila Ahmed is concerned both with the historical relationships of Western feminism to orthodox Islam and with the connections between that relationship and the Sufi movement's historical resistance to Islamic orthodoxy. Through her discussion of the eighth-century mystic Rabi'a, she asserts that one can look to Islamic history, prior to and independent of the Western discourse of rights, for a non-oppressive social organization. Rey Chow also finds a suppressed similarity between the West and the "non-West," but in this case it is a resemblance of complicity between the Chinese modernist intellectual and strains of current Western theory. In Chow's reading, not only does Western theory risk replicating Hegel, but in ignoring its own process of Othering it remains blind, like the writer Lu Xun, to crises it cannot incorporate.

With Chow's essay, the focus turns sharply to the politics of "theory." Like Chow, Barbara Harlow forcefully criticizes "homogenization within dominant theoretical constructions which disallows the complications raised by unsanctioned historical contradiction." Harlow's indictment of dominant modes of theory and feminism, which she sees as constituting yet another intellectual "international division of labor," is accompanied by evocations of feminist political practice related to the conditions of specific political struggles.

Donna Haraway's "A Manifesto for Cyborgs: Science, Technology, and Socialist Feminism in the 1980s" focuses on feminism's relationship to the social relations of science and technology under late capitalism. For Haraway, "post-modern" is a critical-theoretical designation of current social formations and, invoking a similar argument by Fredric Jameson, she asserts that "'post-modern' is not an option, a style among others, but a certain cultural dominant requiring radical reinvention of left politics from within." Her concern is that socialist and marxist feminisms' too easy adoption of the "comfortable old hierarchical dominations"—family/market/factory; public/private; nature/culture; white capitalist patriarchy—renders them ineffective when confronted with the international subdivision of labor, the mobility of capital, and the complex systems produced by communications technologies and biotechnologies. In their engagement with Haraway's essay, Joan Scott, Christina Crosby, and Mary Ann Doane all raise questions which both parallel and challenge Haraway's own. One of Scott's concerns is to locate the boundaries between the cyborg as rhetorical strategy and as messenger of technological determinism. Crosby, too, appreciates the double life of the cyborg ("incalculably dangerous in the form of a cruise missile," but offering "opportunities that haven't yet been calculated for forming new alliances") and underlines the irony of the revelation that "the informatics of domination which cover the globe are both a grid through which power is exercised and the pathways along which resistance runs." But Crosby, like Scott, looks for something that the "Cyborg" essay itself posits; a specificity of political response. Doane observes that although the "informatics of domination" evoked by Haraway (through which power becomes dispersed, invisible, difficult to resist) seems to make the "old dualisms" anachronistic in their simple location of domination, the efficacy of the cyborg is, in fact, dependent on those dualisms: "The specificity of the cyborg's resistance, its pleasure and potency, lies in its territorial transgression of the boundaries between nature and culture, body and mind, the organic and the technological." While Doane, like Haraway, recognizes that transgression is inadequate to the complexity of technologically maintained powers, she sees the cyborg's value precisely as myth, with all the slippage of the real and the imaginary that that term implies.

Although Gayatri Spivak's essay also addresses the problem of "women in the integrated circuit," or third world women in international capitalism, it is of a radically different nature. Where Haraway uses a rich thematics of alliances, creative circuitry and networks, Spivak, as Ellen Rooney so rightly observes, multiplies differences ("[d]istance, discontinuity, divisions, fractures; these are the pervasive topoi of Spivak's text"): differences among women in the first world, between women in the first and third worlds, between the colonial and the neo-colonial, between empiricists and theorists, between herself and her audience, and among academic disciplines. One of the many effects of Spivak's proliferation of discontinuities is that the difficulty of any kind of political-academic practice is put into relief. Her focus on the interrogating subject as well as on the third world female subject underlines the problematic nature of working within the Western academic framework once the alibi of an access to individualism is fully removed. Rooney, in her rigorous reading of Spivak, proposes that Spivak's "modest disciplinary suggestions" for future academic work offered at the end of the essay might well cede to an analysis which Rooney reads at the heart of Spivak's discussion but which is never made explicit: the need for a politics which indeed "is more or other than an alibi of sisterhood," and which confronts directly the problems of global political economy.

No End in Sight

If this introduction and the volume have a rhetorical term of their own, it is citation. Indeed, feminism itself forms a particularly rich citational discourse with much circulating of work, much commenting and repeating of texts. Morevoer, citation is linked to what Naomi Schor points to as feminism's insistence on doubling—from mimeticism, mimicry, and masquerade, to double identification and female fetishism. It is an appropriate term for something as serious as politics, with an edge, perhaps, on irony which, as Nancy Miller remarks (in an earlier version of "Changing the Subject"), can misfire. Citation carries less content of its own. There is a sense, of course, in which it authorizes, but the citation I pose is not the kind which substantiates, it is not for attribution. On the contrary, it cites, like all feminist doubling, to open up a space of difference.

What, then, of feminism as a critical practice in the citational mode? Such a practice remembers, as Derrida argues, that all terms are citational; that is, it is the very repeatability of a term that demonstrates its inscription in a (differential) system of meaning. Moreover, any repetition, no matter how identical, is always also a difference and it is that space of difference which allows for a feminist reading of the ideological workings of social formations.[20] At the same time (and this is the second part of the double endeavor), a citational mode helps the feminist project to resist its own ideological moves, to read its own blind spots. A citational practice resists forgetting. It reads and speaks double, like "word play," keeping more than one meaning working at a time. With it, nothing can stay unmarked for long.[21]

The problem with Man is that it remained for so long an unmarked term; the problem with whiteness, as Hazel Carby has said, is that it still refuses to become a racialized category.[22] One challenge for feminism now is to keep "women" in a citational mode, to resist the seductive lures of identity and the politics of the "personal." Moreover, some of the most productive feminist criticism in the end has "nothing to do" with women as subjects but rather with the cultural operations of the figures of femininity and masculinity. The critical advantage of the feminist project has been that when one area of feminism has settled on a truth, another has emerged to disrupt that truth, to keep at bay truths too easily produced by cultural and political formations. If feminism's special strength is the specificity of its politics, we must attend to structures of knowledge which will allow that specificity to be produced. As long as feminism remains a process of coming to terms but never arriving, always interrogating the very terms it constitutes and never mastering them, it will continue to be a challenging mode of inquiry.

Feminist Politics of Interpretation

1

Changing the Subject

Nancy K. Miller

In the spring of 1985 I wrote "Changing the Subject" for two conferences that provided me with an occasion after "Arachnologies" to elaborate my thinking about the women writer and her feminist reader in relation both to questions of feminist theory and to the various post-structuralist discussions of writing and sexual difference. The first of these events was held at the Pembroke Center, Brown University in March 1985; its agenda was flagged in the punctuation of its title, "Feminism/Theory/Politics"; the second, held at the Center for Twentieth-Century Studies of the University of Wisconsin-Milwaukee in April 1985, was entitled "Feminist Studies: Reconstituting Knowledge."

The session at which I spoke at the Pembroke conference was called "The Feminist Politics of Interpretation," and the panelists were asked to reflect upon a crux of issues very similar to the general charge of the Milwaukee conference as Teresa de Lauretis described it in her opening remarks (now the introduction to Feminist Studies/Critical Studies). *Both call for an interrogation of the current state of feminist projects: "What is specifically feminist about the varieties of feminist critical practice? Are feminist strategies of reading written and visual texts transferable to the study of such things as social and political institutions?" (Pembroke conference, emphasis added). In de Lauretis's letter to participants: "there are a general uncertainty, and among feminists, serious differences as to what the specific concerns, values and methods of feminist critical work are, or ought to be. . . . Speakers will seek to identify the specificity of feminism as a critical theory" (Milwaukee conference, emphasis added).*

These are not easy questions, and in this essay I have not attempted to describe the specificity of feminist theory and practice directly. Instead I have chosen to rehearse a certain number of positions against, from, and through which feminist critical theory might define itself as it emerges within the discourse of literary studies. This rehearsal identifies two chronologies, post-structuralist and feminist; two rhetorics, dilatory and hortatory; and, to return to the figure of the "exquisite dance of textual priorities" named by Hortense Spillers and evoked by de Lauretis at the opening of the conference (13), two moves, or rather a hesitation between, say, the calls of a square dance and the ritual of a minuet, as the dance searches for the right steps and rhythm, perhaps the waltz satirized by Dorothy Parker, or as one of the participants suggested after the conference, the fox-trot (which has interesting possibilities).[1]

Though I may indeed be looking for a third tropology (in the feminist spirit of always mapping the territory of future perspectives), I want just as strongly to leave the hesitation in place, and refuse the temptation of a synthesis, because the question forming before us is none other than the question of female subjectivity, the formation of female critical subjects. And this, in face of the current trend toward the massive deconstitution of subjectivity, is finally the figure I'm looking for.

Authorship, Writing, and the Reader

The question of authorship has been on the agenda of intellectuals and literary critics in France since at least 1968, a date that also marks a certain theoretical repositioning in political and social chronologies. In 1968, for example, Roland Barthes contended in "The Death of the Author" that the author, as we have known him, has lost what was thought to be a "natural" authority over his work. The author gives way to *writing*, a theory and practice of textuality which, Barthes argued then, "substitutes language itself for the person who until then had been supposed to be its owner" (143). From such a perspective, the emergence of this disembodied and ownerless *écriture* in fact requires the author's suppression.[2] In the structuralist and post-structuralist debates about subjectivity, authority, and the status of the text that continue to occupy and preoccupy the critical marketplace, the story of the Author's disappearance has remained standard currency.

Now, to the extent that the Author, in this discourse, stands as a kind of shorthand for a whole series of beliefs about the function of the work of art as (paternally authorized) monument in our culture, feminist criticism in its own negotiations with mainstream hegemonies might have found its positions joined by the language of those claims. It is, after all, the Author anthologized and institutionalized who by his (canonical) presence excludes the less-known works of women and minority writers and who by his authority justifies the exclusion. By the same token, feminist criticism's insistence on the importance of the reader— on positing the hypothesis of her existence—might have found affinities with a position that understands the Birth of the Reader as the necessary counterpoint to the Death of the Author. (Barthes actually puts it a good deal more apocalyptically: "the birth of the reader must be at the cost of the death of the Author" [148].)

The political potential of such an alliance, however, has yet to be realized. The removal of the Author has not so much made room for a revision of the concept of authorship as it has, through a variety of rhetorical moves, repressed and inhibited discussion of any writing identity in favor of the (new) monolith of anonymous textuality or, in Foucault's phrase, "transcendental anonymity" (120). If "writing," then, as Barthes describes it, "is that neutral, composite, oblique space where our subject slips away, the negative where all identity is lost, starting with the very identity of the body writing" (142), it matters not *who* writes. In the same way, the shift that moves the critical emphasis from author to reader, from the text's origin to its destination, far from producing a multiplicity of addressees, seems to have reduced the possibility of differentiating among readers altogether: "the reader," Barthes declares, "is without history, biography, psychology" (148). What matters who reads? The reader is a space and a process. The reader is only *"someone"* written *on*. (I also think that the failure of an effective critical alliance is more generally due to the fact that the relationship between mainstream feminism and the practices and positions that have come to be grouped together under the label of deconstruction or post-structuralism in U.S. academic scenes has not been one of a *working* complicity: of fighting the same institutional battles. But this deserves a discussion of its own.)

I want nonetheless to make a distinction between the asymmetrical demands generated by different writing identities—male and female, or more perhaps more usefully, hegemonic and marginal. It is inarguable that the destabilization of the paternal—patriarchal, really— authority of authorship (Milton's for example) brought about through deconstruction has been an enabling move for feminist critics. But it does not address the problem of his "bogey" at the level of subjectivity formation. The effect *of his identity and authority on a female writing identity remains another matter and calls for other critical strategies. The psychological stress of that negotiation in literature for the nineteenth-century woman writer has been formulated dramatically by Gilbert and Gubar in* Madwoman in the Attic. *Here I am trying to resituate that question at the level of theory itself, or rather theory's discourse about its own project.*

So why remember Barthes, if this model of reading and writing by definition excludes the question of an identity crucial to feminist critical theory? Well, for one thing because Barthes's interest in the semiotics of literary and cultural activity—its pleasures, dangers, zones, and codes of reference—intersects thematically with a feminist emphasis on the need to situate, socially and symbolically, the practices of reading and writing. Like the feminist critic, Barthes maneuvers in the spaces of the tricky relations that bridge the personal and the political, the personal and the critical, the interpersonal and the institutional (his seminar, for example). Barthes translates seductively from within French thought the more arduous writings of Derrida, Lacan, Kristeva, for or into literature; and in the same gesture represents metonymically outside the Parisian scene (or in North American literature departments) most of the concepts that animate feminist (and other) literary critics not hostile to Theory's stories: currently, the post-structuralist epistemologies of the subject and the text, the linguistic construction of sexual identity.

In the preface to *Sade, Fourier, Loyola* (1971) Barthes returns to the problem of authorship: "For if," he writes, "through a twisted dialectic, the Text, destroyer of all subject, contains a subject to love—un sujet à aimer—that subject is dispersed, somewhat like the ashes we strew into the wind after death" (8). And he continues poignantly in the same sentence, "were I a writer, and dead [*si j'étais écrivain, et mort*] how I would love it if my life, through the pains of some friendly and detached biographer, were to reduce itself to a few details, a few preferences, a few inflections, let us say: to 'biographemes' " (9). What interests me here, more than yet another nomination, another code, is Barthes's acknowledgment of the persistence of the subject as the presence in the text of perhaps not some*one* to love in person, but the mark of the need to be loved, the persistence of a peculiarly human(ist?) desire for connection. It is as though thinking of a writer's life—a "life" of Sade, a "life" of Fourier appended to a reading of their writing— generated a thinking of self: for Barthes then imagines himself "a writer."[3] But we have just seen the writer is already dead, his ashes scattered to the winds; and the self fatally dispersed. Thus no sooner is the subject restored metaphorically to a body through love, than he is dispersed figuratively through death. If one is to find the subject, he will not be in one place, but modernly multiple and atopic.

Will *she?*

The postmodernist decision that the Author is Dead and the subject along with him does not, I will argue, necessarily hold for women, and prematurely forecloses the question of agency for them. Because women have not had the same historical relation of identity to origin, institution, production that men have had, they have not, I think, (collectively) felt burdened by *too much* Self, Ego, Cogito, etc. Because the female subject has juridically been excluded from the polis, hence decentered, "disoriginated," deinstitutionalized, etc., her relation to integrity and textuality, desire and authority, displays structurally important differences from that universal position. .

In Breaking the Chain, *Naomi Schor takes up Barthes's analysis in* S/Z *of the cultural discourse on "femininity," which he locates for the sake of argument in a passage from Balzac's* Sarrasine. *Curiously, this is also the passage that serves as the opening citation of "The Death of the Author": "This was woman herself. . . . (etc.) Following Schor's lead, it is interesting to puzzle the connections that for Barthes join* ;écriture *and "woman" in a definition of textuality that refuses a coherent subjectivity.*

In "Mapping the Postmodern" Andreas Huyssen asks: "Isn't the 'death of the subject/ author' position tied by mere reversal to the very ideology that invariably glorifies the artist as genius, whether for marketing purposes or out of conviction and habit? . . . [D]oesn't poststructuralism, where it simply denies the subject altogether, jettison the chance of challenging the ideology *of the subject (as male, white, and middle-class) by developing alternative and different notions of subjectivity?" (44).*

In "Women Who Write Are Women," Elaine Showalter, arguing against Cynthia Ozick's belief (subsequently rearticulated by Gail Godwin in the same publication) that "writing transcends sexual identity, that it takes place outside of the social order," pointedly observes that in the gender asymmetry of dominant culture "the female witness, sensitive or not, is still not accepted as first-person universal" (33).

It seems to me, therefore, that when the so-called crisis of the subject is staged, as it generally is, within a textual model, that performance must then be recomplicated by the historical, political, and figurative body of the woman writer. (That is, of course, if we accept as a working metaphor the location of women's subjectivity in female authorship.) Because the discourse of the universal historically has failed to include the testimony of its others, it seems imperative to question the new doxa of subjectivity at this juncture of its formation.

Feminist critics in the United States have on the whole resisted the fable of the author's demise on the grounds that stories of textuality which trade in universals—the Author or the Reader—in fact articulate marked and differentiated structures of what Gayatri Spivak has called masculine "regulative psychobiography." Feminist critics, I argue in "The Text's Heroine," have looked to the material of the female authorial project as the scene of perhaps a different staging of the drama of the writing subject. But what does it mean to read (for) the woman writer when the Author is Dead? Or, how can "reading as a woman"—a deconstructionist phrasing of a reconstructionist feminist project—help us rethink the act of reading as a politics? I'd like to see a more self-conscious and deliberate move away from what I think remains in dominant critical modes, a *metaphysics* of reading. As Foucault asks in "What Is an Author": "In granting a primordial status to writing (*écriture*), do we not, in effect, simply reinscribe in transcendental terms the theological affirmation of its sacred origin?" (120).

In her presentations at both the Pembroke and the Milwaukee conferences, Spivak contrasted the psychobiography of a male subjectivity based on naturalized access to dominant forms of power with that of the "postmodern female subject" created under late capitalism (emblematized by the hegemony of the computer chip): women of color whom imperialism constructs as a permanent casual labor force doing high-tech work for the multinationals. Her relation to networks of power is best understood through the concept of "women in the intergrated circuit," which Donna Haraway describes as "the situation of women in a world . . . intimately restructured through the social relations of science and technology" (84–85). It is not self-evident what form testimony would take in such an economy.

Speaking from within a certain "new French feminism," Hélène Cixous makes a homologous argument for the need to recognize a deuniversalized *subjectivity: "until now, far more extensively and repressively than is ever suspected or admitted, writing has been run by a libidinal and cultural—hence political, typically masculine—economy" (879). This definition of a sexually "*marked writing*" that expresses and valorizes masculine access to power emerges from the critique of phallogocentrism, but because of its place in the network of Derridean operations, it remains at odds with the reconstructive impulses of much feminist literary* criticism in the United States: the analysis of canon formation and reformation through the study and valorization of women's writing.

Thus, in his concluding remarks to the section of On Deconstruction devoted to feminist criticism, Jonathan Culler builds on Peggy Kamuf's troping of signature and identity in "Writing as a Woman": "For a woman to read as a woman is not to repeat an identity or an experience that is given but to play a role she constructs with reference to her identity as a woman, which is also a construct, so that the series can continue: a woman reading as a woman reading as a woman" (64). The question for feminist critical theory is how to imagine a relation between this logic of deferral and the immediate complexities of what Adrienne Rich calls "a politics of location" (Blood, Bread, and Poetry, 215).

I want to offer one kind of political reading with a passage from a famous account of a female "psychobiography." I take it as an example of what has been characterized as the "first moment" or first stage of feminist criticism, a criticism Jonathan Culler describes as "based on the presumption of continuity between the reader's experience and a woman's experience" (46). The account is Adrienne Rich's "When We Dead Awaken: Writing as Re-Vision," which, she explains in a retrospective frame, was originally given as a talk on "The Woman Writer in the Twentieth Century" in a forum sponsored by the Commission on the Status of Women in the Profession at the MLA in 1971. I cite Rich's return to the context of her talk by way of suggesting that we review these issues both in "women's time" and in men's, the Eastern Standard Time of mainstream events. (I'm referring here to Elaine Showalter's personal take on the history of feminist criticism.)[4]

Rich notes:

> A lot is being said today about the influence that the myths and images of women have on all of us who are products of culture. I think it has been a peculiar confusion to the girl or woman who tries to write because she is peculiarly susceptible to language. She goes to poetry or fiction looking for her way of being in the world, since she is looking eagerly for guides, maps, possibilities; and over and over . . . she comes up against something that negates everything she is about; she meets the image of Woman in books written by men. She finds a terror and a dream, she finds a beautiful pale face, she finds La Belle Dame Sans Merci, she finds Juliet or Tess or Salomé, but precisely what she does not find is that absorbed, drudging, puzzled, sometimes inspired creature, herself, who sits at a desk trying to put words together. (39)

Rich's woman "susceptible to language," like Roland Barthes, goes to literature as a writing subject: she does not, however, find there "un sujet à aimer." She finds instead, a terror and a dream. To find "somebody to love," as the song goes, Rich, like Barthes, would have to find someone somehow like her in her desire for a place in the discourse of art and identity from which to imagine and image a writing self—"absorbed, drudging, puzzled"—at a desk. For the girl "susceptible to language" the words have established a split she cannot overcome: Woman whose image, whose "beautiful pale face" has installed in her place a regime of the specular and excluded her from production.[5] Woman leaves the woman poet in exile.

In her 1983 essay, "Blood, Bread, and Poetry: The Location of the Poet" (where she outlines the borders of scenes of writing in North America and in Central America), Rich returns to the biography of her reading, or the history of its subject, to develop in more explicitly political terms the implications of the split between the girl and the poet, "the girl who wrote poems, who defined herself in writing poems, and the girl who was to define herself by her relationships with men" (40). To close "the gap between poet and woman," Rich argues here, the fragmentation within the writing subject requires the context of a "political community" (536). For Rich, on *this* side of identity, the condition of dispersal and fragmentation Barthes valorizes (and fetishizes) is not to be achieved, but overcome:

> I write for the still-fragmented parts in me, trying to bring them together. Whoever can read and use any of this, I write for them as well. I write in full knowledge that the majority of the world's illiterates are women, that I live in a technologically advanced country where forty per cent of the people can barely read and twenty per cent are functionally illiterate. I believe that these facts are directly connected to the fragmentations I suffer in myself, that we are all in this together. (540)

In "Blood, Bread, and Poetry," Rich maps the geopolitics of a poetics of gender. This vision of a global context for women's writings emerges from a program of text production as a collective project. In the sixties, under the logic of "the personal is the political," the communication with the community involved writing "directly and overtly as a woman, out of a woman's experience," taking "women's existence seriously as theme and source for art" (535). In "When We Dead Awaken," Rich had contrasted this euphoric turn to feminocentric production— a more prosaic, or rather less lyrical account of the agenda valorized by Cixous (in "The Laugh of the Medusa")—with the anxieties of the fifties where, she writes, "I began to feel that my fragments and scraps had a common consciousness and a common theme, one which I would have been very unwilling to put on paper at an earlier time because I had been taught that poetry should be 'universal,' which meant, of course, nonfemale" (44). Now, in the eighties, the formula "the personal is the political" requires a redefinition of the personal to include most immediately an interrogation of ethnocentrism; a poetics of identity that engages with the "other woman."[6] If for Rich in 1971 the act of women's reading as a critique of the dominant literature was seen not merely as "a chapter in cultural history" (135) but as "an act of survival," in 1983 the act of women's writing becomes inseparable from an expanded definition of, and expanded attention to, the social field in which the practices of reading and writing are located and grounded. Now the question arises, if the ethics of feminist writing involve writing for the woman who doesn't read—to push this model to its limits—then what would be required of a responsive, responsible feminist reading?

The question will remain open and generate other questions. Does the specificity of feminist theory entail reading for the other woman? Would this mean reading *as* the other woman? In her place? Wouldn't this assumption reinstate a universal or an interchangeability of women under the name of woman and thereby "collapse," as Denise Riley put it to me at the Pembroke conference, "the different temporalities of 'women' " which she glosses as "the uneven histories of the different formations of different categories of 'women' from the side of politics"? In more strictly literary terms, I would now say that we must think carefully about the reading effects that derive from a poetics of transparence—writing directly from one's own experience, especially when doubled by an ethics of wholeness—joining the fragments.

Rich speaks in this essay of her discovery of the work of contemporary Cuban women poets in a book edited by Margaret Randall called Breaking the Silences. *And it is in part because of reading this book (her* tolle e lege) *that she decides to go to Nicaragua (a decision which provides the occasion for "Blood, Bread, and Poetry"). To what extent does this active/activist model of reading establish the grounds for a prescriptive esthetics—a "politically correct" program of representation—of the sort that shaped the arguments of Barbara Smith and Sondra O'Neale at the Milwaukee conference?[7]*

Against the necessarily utopian rhetoric of an unalienated art that Rich reads in Cuban women poets ("the affirmation of an organic relation between poetry and social transformation" [537]) I want now to juxtapose the discourse with which I began this discussion of critical strategies. On the back jacket to *Sade, Fourier, Loyola* Barthes states the "theoretical intention" of his project. It is a kind of self-referential challenge: to discover "how far one can go with a text speaking only of its writing [*écriture*]; how to suspend its signified in order to liberate its materialist deployment." "Isn't the social intervention achieved by a text," he asks rhetorically, located in the "transport" of its writing, rather than in the "message of its content"? In the pages of the preface, Barthes addresses the problem of the "social responsibility of the text," maintaining that since there is "today no language site outside bourgeois ideology," "the only possible rejoinder" to, say, the establishment, is "neither confrontation, nor destruction, but only theft: fragment the old text of culture, science, literature, and change its features according to formulae of disguise, as one disguises [*maquille*] stolen goods" (10).

We see here the double move we saw earlier in "Death of the Author": on the one hand disperse the subject, on the other, fragment the text, and repackage it for another mode of circulation and reception.

Dispersion and fragmentation, the theft of language and the subversion of the stereotype attract Barthes as critical styles of desire and deconstruction, rupture and protest. Certain women writers in France like Hélène Cixous, Luce Irigaray, and I would argue, paradoxically, Monique Wittig, have also been attracted to this model of relation: placing oneself at a deliberately oblique (or textual) angle to intervention. Troped as a subversion—a political intertextuality—this positionality remains in the end, I think, a form of negotiation within the dominant social text, and ultimately, a local operation.

Because it is also my sense that the reappropriation of culture from within its own arenas of dissemination is still a political urgency, I will recast my earlier question about the female subject in feminist theory to ask more narrowly now: what does it mean to read and write as a woman *within* the institutions that authorize and regulate most reading and writing in the university?

"Oubliez les Professeurs"

In Charlotte Brontë's *Villette* acute attention is paid to the construction of female subjectivity, and in particular to the way in which female desire as quest aligns itself uneasily with the question of mastery (including, importantly, mastery of the French language), mastery and knowledge within an academy necessarily, in 1853, a female one. In the scene I will review here, the heroine, Lucy Snowe, is dragged off to be examined by two professors, "Messieurs Boissec and Rochemorte" (the etymology is of course motivated). This examination perceived by Lucy as a "show-trial" set up to prove that she indeed was the author of a remarkable essay the men suspected their colleague M. Emmanuel, Lucy's professor/friend, of having written for her (forging her signature in order to document his pedagogical agency) provides us with a vivid account of the institutional power arrangements that historically have constructed female experience. These two specimens of deadwood interrogate Lucy:

> They began with classics. A dead blank. They went on to French history. I hardly knew Mérovée from Pharamond. They tried me in various 'ologies, and still only got a shake of the head, and an unchanging "Je n'en sais rien." (493)

Unwilling or unable to reply, Lucy asks permission to leave the room.

> They would not let me go: I must sit down and write before them. As I dipped my

> pen in the ink with a shaking hand, and surveyed the white paper with eyes half-blinded and overflowing, one of my judges began mincingly to apologize for the pain he caused. (494)

They name their theme: "Human Justice."

> Human Justice! What was I to make of it? Blank, cold abstraction, unsuggestive to me of one inspiring idea. . . . (495)

Lucy remains blocked until she remembers that the two examiners were in fact known to her; "the very heroes" who had "half frightened [her] to death" (495) on the night of her arrival in Villette. And suddenly, thinking how little these men deserved their current status as judges and enforcers of the law, Lucy falls, as she puts it, "to work."

> "Human Justice" rushed before me in novel guise, a red, random beldame with arms akimbo. I saw her in her house, the den of confusion: servants called to her for orders or help which she did not give; beggars stood at her door waiting and starving unnoticed; a swarm of children, sick and quarrelsome, crawled round her feet and yelled in her ears appeals for notice, sympathy, cure, redress. The honest woman cared for none of these things. She had a warm seat of her own by the fire, she had her own solace in a short black pipe, and a bottle of Mrs. Sweeny's soothing syrup; she smoked and she sipped and she enjoyed her paradise, and whenever a cry of the suffering souls about her pierced her ears too keenly—my jolly dame seized the poker or the hearth-brush. . . . (495–96)

Writing "as a woman," Lucy Snowe domesticates the public allegories of Human Justice. Her justice is not blind (hence serenely fair) but deaf to the pathetic cries that invade her private space: arbitrary and visibly self-interested, marked not by the sword and scales of neoclassical iconography, Lucy's "red, random beldame," smokes her pipe and sips her syrup.

However perversely, I am tempted to take this scene in which a woman is brought forcibly to writing as a parable of—which is not to say a recommendation for—the conditions of production for female authorship (or for the practice of feminist criticism). Because she reappropriates the allegory of timeless indifference particularized through the identification of the men and fictionalized through the imagined body of an aging woman, Lucy both overcomes the terror of the blank page and undermines the regime of a universal self-reference.

I should perhaps have mentioned that the chapter in which this writing out takes place opens with a line rich in implications for the conclusion of my argument: "Oubliez les professeurs." Now in context, this imperative is a warning issued by Mme. Beck that Lucy not think of M. Paul for herself. But clearly in this collegial psychodrama the relation to *him* is not only a question of female rivalry and the love plot. As I have just suggested, the scene asks more generally the question of women's relation to the arbitrariness of male authority, to the grounds of their power and their laws.

Lucy, we know, can't forget her particular professor, for she is moved more than she will say by his offer of friendship. But in her apprenticeship to the world of work, she has learned to make distinctions. To accept M. Paul does not mean that she accepts the system of institutional authorization in which their relation is inscribed. Nor is the point of her essay, its style, lost on M. Paul who, having read the exam paper, calls her "une petite moqueuse et sans coeur" (496). Lucy's mockery, which is the flip side of her pathos, could also be figured as irony, which is, I think, a trope that by its status as the marker of a certain distance to the truth, suits the rhetorical strategies of the feminist critic.[8]

The chapter in which the scene of writing is staged is called "Fraternity," for it is here that M. Paul asks Lucy to be the "sister of a very poor, fettered, burdened, encumbered man." His offer of "true friendship" (501), of a "fraternal alliance" (503), while not exempt from its own ironies, nonetheless announces a less depressing mode of relations between women and institutional authorities than that of the "daughter's seduction" diagnosed by Jane Gallop, for it figures a working ground of parity.[9] At the end of Brontë's novel, through the enabling terms of the alliance, Lucy Snowe has not only her own seat by the fire but her own house and school for girls. Within that space, she makes Paul a "little library"; he whose mind, she had said earlier, was her library, through which she "entered bliss" (472). And of course, in his absence, and in his place, she writes the narrative of *Villette*.

This being said, one might, in the final analysis, do better to restore to the fraternal its historical dimensions. Women writers' idealization of fraternity belongs to a long and vexed tradition of feminist discourse about equality and difference that in 1949 provided Simone de Beauvoir with the last words of *The Second Sex:* "To gain the supreme victory, it is necessary . . . that by and through their natural differentiation men and women unequivocally affirm their brotherhood [*fraternité*]" (814).

Subject to Change

In 1973, in an essay called "Toward a Woman-Centered University," Adrienne Rich described her vision of a future for feminist studies. In it we read: "The university I have been trying to imagine does not seem to me utopian, though the problems and contradictions to be faced in its actual transformations are of course real and severe" (153). Yet looking back over the past ten to fifteen years of Women's Studies, can we say that "masculine resistance to women's claims for full humanity" (as Rich defines the project) has been overcome in any serious way? Nothing could be less sure.

In fact, I think that though we may have our Women's Studies programs, our centers, journals, and conferences, feminist scholars have not succeeded in instituting the transformative claims we articulated in the heady days of the mid-seventies. Supported by the likes of William Bennett, Rochemorte and Boissec are going strong: they continue to resist, and to attack, feminism's fundamental understanding that the deployment of the universal is inherently, if paradoxically, partial and political. And the M. Pauls, who like Terry Eagleton et al. offer friendship and the promise of "fraternal alliance," seem to be saying at the same time: "feminism is theoretically thin, or separatist. Girls, shape up!" (Spivak, "The Politics of Interpretations," 277). More serious, perhaps, because it is supported by the prestige of philosophy, the ultimate purveyor of universals, is the general failure on the part of most male theorists, even those most interested in "feminine identity," to articulate sufficiently in the terms of their own enunciation what Rosi Braidotti calls "the radical consciousness of one's own complicity with the very power one is trying to deconstruct" (*Ms.*). Like the humanists, they have not begun to question the grounds on which they stand, their own relation to the "sexual differential" that inhabits "*every* voice" (Spivak, 277); their own difference from the universal, from the institution which houses them, and from which they speak.

But we have of course participated in our own failure to challenge the " 'ologies" and their authorities in a significant way. Our greatest strength in the seventies, I would argue, was our experience, through consciousness raising, of the possibility of a collective identity resistant to but intimately bound up with Woman—in fact our account, analysis, and valorization of experience itself (de Lauretis makes the point forcefully at the end of *Alice Doesn't*). For reasons I cannot fully articulate here, but which have to do on the one hand with the difficulty of constructing theoretically the discourse of women's experience, a difficulty derived in part from the feminist bugaboo about essentialism—which can only be understood in relation to a massively theorized "antiessentialism" (Russo, 228); and on the other, particularly for those of us working in things French, with the prestige of a regime of accounts of post-gendered subjectivities, we seem to have have gotten stuck between two varieties of self-censorship.

In the face of a prevailing institutional indifference to the question of women, conjoined with a prevailing critical ideology of the subject which celebrates or longs for a mode beyond difference, where and how to move? On what grounds can we remodel the relations of female subjects to the social text? In the issue of *Tulsa Studies* devoted to the current state of feminist criticism (republished in *Feminist Issues in Literary Scholarship*) there is at least one pressing call to forget the professors, theorists masculine and feminine, to "reject male formalist models for criticism" in the belief, Jane Marcus writes, that "the practice of formalism professionalizes the feminist critic and makes her safe for academe" ("Still Practice," 90). We must, I think, see this as too simple. Not only because, as Nina Auerbach argues in the same issue, "whether we like it or not, we live in one world, one country . . . one university department with men" (155), but because we don't. If Women's Studies is to effect institutional change through critical interventions, we cannot afford to proceed by a wholesale dismissal of "male" models. Rather, like Lucy in the school play (in another forced performance), who refuses to play a man's part dressed in men's clothes and instead assumes *"in addition"* to her "woman's garb" the signifiers of masculinity (209; emphasis added), the effectiveness of future feminist intervention calls for an ironic manipulation of the semiotics of performance.[10]

Earlier in *Villette,* Ginevra pressed Lucy to explain herself, to reveal some deeper truth that seems to elude her grasp: "Who *are* you, Miss Snowe?" And Lucy, "amused at her mystification," replies, "Who am I indeed? Perhaps a personage in disguise. Pity I don't look the character" (392–93). But Ginevra is not satisfied with this flip account: "But *are* you anybody?" This time Lucy is slightly more forthcoming, supplying information, at least, about her social insertion: "Yes . . . I am a rising character: once an old lady's companion, then a nursery-governess, now a school-teacher" (394). Ginevra persists in thinking there is more to Lucy than Lucy will say, but Lucy will offer nothing more. If we take Lucy Snowe's account of herself at face value, not persisting like Ginevra in a hermeneutics of revelation that is structured, Barthes has taught us, on oedipal narratologies, we begin to take the measure of Brontë's radical achievement in this novel: creating a heroine whose identity is modulated through the cadences of work; through the effects of institutions. This is not to suggest that Lucy's subjectivity is re-contained by a work history, circumscribed by its hierarchies of class. On the contrary, we have seen Ginevra's conviction that despite the institutional inscription, Lucy somehow continues to escape her, not only because Ginevra is looking for a social language she can understand—"a name, a pedigree"—but because in some palpable and troubling way, Lucy, like the Lacanian subject she anticipates, also resides elsewhere in the "field of language" which constitutes her otherness to herself (Mitchell, 241).

I want to float the suggestion, then, and by way of a gesture toward closure, that any definition of the female writing subject not universalized as Woman that we try to theorize now must include Lucy Snowe's ambiguities: in work, in language. This is a process that recognizes what Elizabeth Weed describes as the "impossible . . . relation of women to Woman" (74) and acknowledges our ongoing contradictions, the gap and (and perhaps permanent) internal split that makes a collective identity always a horizon, but a necessary one.[11] It is a fragmentation we can, however, as feminist readers work with and through. This is the move of resistance and production that allows Lucy to find language "as a woman" despite the power of the " 'ologies," despite the allegory of *human* justice.

At the end of "Femininity, Narrative, and Psychoanalysis" (1982), an essay in which she takes as her example Emily Brontë's Wuthering Heights, Juliet Mitchell outlines a question by way of providing herself with a solution of closure to her discussion of the female (writing) subject and a critique of Kristeva's valorization of the semiotic, the heterogeneous space of the subject-in-process. To her own question of what identity and text might mean construed along the lines of such a theoretical model—"in the process of becoming what?"—Mitchell responds: "I do not think that we can live as human subjects without in some sense taking on a history; for us, it is mainly the history of being men or women under bourgeois capitalism. In deconstructing that history, we can only construct other histories. What are we in the process of becoming?" (294).

Mitchell shrewdly leaves the question open, but since this is my essay and not hers, I have felt it important to risk a reply. At the Pembroke conference, I ended by saying: I hope we are becoming women. Because such a reply proved too ironic to occupy the privileged place of the last word, I will now say: I hope we are becoming feminists. In both phrases, however, the hope I express for a female future is a desire for all that we don't know about what it might mean to be women beyond the always already provided identity of Women with which we can only struggle; the hope for a negotiation that would produce through feminism a new "social subject," as de Lauretis puts it in Alice Doesn't (186), and that I have figured here as the work of female critical subjects.

2

Julia Kristeva: Take Two

Jacqueline Rose

It seems appropriate in this context to talk about Julia Kristeva who has, I think, for many of us represented something of an emblem as a woman theorist writing within the brief of this conference's title—Feminism/Theory/Politics—or at least as a woman whose work has had repercussions which touch on the crucial and complex relationships among the three. Also because Kristeva's work has recently seemed to shift in difficult ways which oblige us to reflect on a whole moment of theorization in France which could be said to have been determinant in constituting the very field in which a conference such as this is possible. There are a number of women—some of whom are here—who have translated, worked on, and written about Kristeva from a multiplicity of positions (Kristeva, 1980; Jardine, 1981; Spivak, 1981; Jones, 1984)* which seemed to have polarized recently into the case for or against. In all of.this I have felt that something has started to slip through the net or is in danger of being lost from our discussion which, for want of a better expression, I will call psychic life, although I am very aware that the question of how to articulate that domain with the political becomes harder and harder to pose. I think this is Kristeva's problem and I certainly see it as mine. Rather than judge Kristeva positively or negatively, I have tried to write from within it.

In an article published in 1975, Julia Kristeva wrote: "The symbolic order is assured as soon as there are images which secure unfailing belief, for belief is in itself the image: both arise out of the same procedures and through the same terms: *memory, sight and love.* ..."[1] The article appeared in a special issue of *Communications* on *Psychoanalysis and the Cinema* which marked a type of turning

---

*The texts Jacqueline Rose is referring to are Julia Kristeva, *Pouvoirs de l'horreur, Essai sur l'abjection* (Paris: Seuil, 1980); Alice Jardine, "Pre-Texts for the Transatlantic Feminist," *Yale French Studies,* 62 (1981); Gayatri Chakravorty Spivak, "French Feminism in an International Frame," *Yale French Studies,* 62 (1981); Ann Rosalind Jones, "Julia Kristeva on Femininity: The Limits of a Semiotic Politics," *Feminist Review,* 15 (Winter, 1984). (ed. note).

point within semiotics when psychoanalysis was brought to bear on the cultural analysis of the sign. Cinema was central to that shift because it so clearly rested on the twin axes of identification and fantasy—mechanisms built into the very structure of the apparatus and then merely given their most appropriate and predictable content, bodied forth as it were, in Hollywood's endless sagas of love. Writing on identification, Freud had put love and hypnosis together because of the idealization, subjection, compliance, and sapping of initiative which they are capable of inducing in the subject.[2] In view of which, Julia Kristeva's latest book— *Histoires d'amour* (1983) (Histories of Love or Love Stories)—which takes a cinematic image, that of *ET*, as the truth of a culture suffering a dearth of love and idealization, appears as something of an ironic twist.[3] What has happened? How can we best understand this move? Where has Julia Kristeva been and gone?

The question can only be posed, I believe, historically and psychoanalytically, which means tracing out a conceptual movement and context which, for Kristeva at least, has constantly been informed by psychoanalysis—a movement which then turns back on itself in so far as psychoanalysis provides many of the terms through which it can itself be understood. Kristeva is also a self-diagnostician, and the psychic drive or investment of much of her writing can often be lifted straight out of her texts. "I desire the Law," she writes in a key chapter of this latest book[4] voicing a panic which—psychoanalysis itself might have anticipated— was bound to be the ultimate effect of that earlier onslaught on the securing identity of the image, which Kristeva and the *Tel Quel* group had castigated throughout the 1970s as little more than bourgeois deceit.

Julia Kristeva's work belongs to that semiotic tradition most closely identified with the work of Roland Barthes, in which the analysis of the structure of language rapidly became a critique of the stabilizing illusion of the sign, and of those forms of writing, in particular the nineteenth-century novel, which were seen to embody and guarantee that illusion for a bourgeois society binding its subjects into the spurious unity of a culture inaccessible to change. The unity of the culture and the psychic unity of subjects went together, with the second as pre-condition of the first, complementary facades which bound over the psychic and social divisions beneath. Kristeva now argues that this dual emphasis set her apart from the pitfalls of structuralism and of what became for many the predominant strand of "post-structuralism" alike: "For some the important task was to 'deconstruct' phenomenology and structuralism as a minor form of metaphysics unaware of being so. For others, amongst whom I count myself, it was indispensable to give the structure its 'dynamic' by taking into consideration, on the one hand the speaking subject and his or her unconscious experience, and, on the other, the pressures of other social structures."[5]

The point was made by Kristeva in 1974: "Crude grammatology abdicates the subject . . . uninterested in symbolic and social structures, it has nothing to say in the face of their destruction or renewal."[6]

It is worth noting already therefore that the appeal to the unconscious was part of a move to bring back history and social structures into that form of "structuralism and after" which, in direct proportion to its repudiation of metaphysics, was seen by Kristeva as increasingly locked within its terms.

From that original diagnosis, Julia Kristeva then set herself a wager—which she herself has defined as exorbitant[7]—to confront language at the point where it undoes itself, pushing against that illusion of safety through which alone it can function, uncovering the psychic forces which sustain that illusion but which equally put it at risk. From among the *Tel Quel* group with whom she was associated from the late 1960s, Kristeva could be seen as the only writer who took to its limits the engagement between psychoanalysis and semiotics (already in 1969 she was calling her work a "sémanalyse"),[8] an engagement which had in many ways seemed to stall at the concepts of "identification," "interpellation," and "the subject's position in language" which had been brought in, via Lacanian psychoanalysis, to buttress Louis Althusser's theory of ideology and the state.

In a move whose force and difficulty can perhaps only be fully understood now, Kristeva chose to drive that engagement with language and the sign into the most violent depths of their own process, where the dangers for psychic coherence, and indeed for the social (Kristeva's previous book, *Pouvoirs de l'horreur,* could be seen as her book about fascism)[9] made that earlier concept of subjectivity and its illusions look as comforting and facile as the literary forms which had been the object of its critique.

"Site of maximum abjection," the only place where the "savagery" of the speaking being can be heard,[10] psychoanalysis became for Kristeva the means of taking that shift to subjectivity and the unconscious at its word (body and letter) through a clinical engagement with the acquisition, dissolution, and pathology of language, all of which had lain beneath the earlier analysis of literary form and style. The more explicit psychoanalytic project followed directly therefore from the investigation of avant-garde writing. It reflected the need to confront speech in the throes of a pathology otherwise in danger of being restricted to its aesthetic mode. There is also an important historical link between psychoanalysis and the literary avant-garde in France through the surrealists. Against a medical institution largely unsympathetic to psychoanalysis which addressed madness "from the place of reason" with a prophylactic aim, the surrealists had tried in the 1920s and 1930s to speak of madness "from the place of madness itself."[11]

I *"Only the superego must see the light of day"*[12]

That such a wager (such a speech) should finally be impossible is in fact given in advance by Kristeva's early writing. Kristeva's work has become best known for the concept of the "semiotic" which she defines as the traces of the subject's difficult passage into the proper order of language (the symbolic or "thetic" instance). It inherits Freud's concept of the primary processes as well as that of the drive—aspects of subjectivity which are only ever partially bound into the norms of psychic and sexual life. It then inflects these concepts through Lacan's account of subjectivity which gives language, or representation, central importance as the means through which these norms are vehiculed into place. Disorders of psychic identity and linguistic disorders are tied into each other, a link which is permitted by the psychoanalytic emphasis on the centrality—and fragility—of speech. But if Kristeva concentrates on the signs of that fragility (troubles of phonological, syntactic, and enunciating laws), she can only do so in terms of the order of language against which they break. The "semiotic" can never wholly displace the "symbolic" since it relies on that very order to give to it its, albeit resistant, shape.

In Kristeva's analysis of Mallarmé's poetry, for example, she describes the sound patterns of the language in terms of the basic mechanisms of the drive (explosion, implosion), drawing on Roman Jakobson's famous article "Why Mama and Papa?" which traced the consonant opposition to the primary vocal gestures and needs of the infant.[13] But even if these oppositions can evoke once again these earliest affective processes, they can only do so now by underscoring the phonological patterns which form the ground rules of ordinary speech. They are also immediately caught up in—and cannot operate without—the semantic content which is made explicit by the text, as well as being held in check by a syntax, disrupted but still recognizable, which Mallarmé himself referred to as his "sole guarantee."[14] Kristeva talks of Mallarmé's use of syntax as at once a "supercompetence" and a "risk" for the subject.[15] In the section of La révolution du langage poétique on "The semiotic apparatus of the text," she concentrates on the shifters (the movement of the first person pronoun across the text), allusions to other texts (the place of the text in a history of writing), and syntax (transformations and their rules) as much as on the phonological patterns of the language which are all too easily assimilated to the idea of a body at play. On this Kristeva is explicit: the body can only ever be *signified*, it is never *produced*. *Après-coup*, rather than regression, this is neither a pure body in process nor a total disintegration of speech.

Furthermore, the extent to which the "semiotic" is confined to the expression and celebration of its heterogeneity and disruptive charge alone is the index not only of its psychic, but also of its *political* limitations. This is a point which has been overlooked in most commentaries on Kristeva's writing.[16] In La révolution du langage poétique, Lautréamont and Mallarmé are chosen by Kristeva because of the sexual and linguistic scandal which they represented for bourgeois moral and literary forms—an excess confined to marginal expression by a repressive culture and state (we can recognize in this analysis the project of the later Russian Formalists—"A Slap in the Face of Public Taste"—to which Kristeva adds a psycho-sexual emphasis).[17] But in so far as these writers fail to move back in the opposite direction and to take up the recognizable social institutions and meanings from which they have been banned, so they fall prey to aestheticism, mysticism, and anarchy. In a later article on dissidence Kristeva will talk of the "verve anarchiste" of the Paris Commune against "power, institutions and beliefs,"[18] but there has never been a promotion of anarchy as such. For Kristeva, to abdicate symbolic norms—to enact that abdication—opens the way to psychosis: "The way to psychosis—foreclusion of the thetic instance—remains open . . . and this situation translates the ideological limitations of the avant-garde."[19]

For Kristeva, as far back as 1974 therefore, the "logical, thetic, binding, instance" (also called meaning or "sens") was the "*sine qua non* of practice."[20] Mallarmé's refusal of politics, Lautréamont's silence on sexual and familial ideologies, were the direct consequence of a failure to re-engage that instance, even though it is the crisis to which they so relentlessly subject it which constitutes the value of their work. The question therefore becomes not how to disrupt language by leaving its recognizable forms completely *behind,* but how to articulate the psychic processes which language normally glosses over *on this side of* meaning or sense. The avant-garde text, like the speech of the psychotic and the neurotic symptom, speaks a truth in a form which is too easily banished.

Despite the apparent dualism of that semiotic/symbolic division, there is therefore no strict demarcation between them. There cannot be if the semiotic is to find articulation and if the symbolic is to feel its effects. The symbolic is not, as has been argued, a rigid, monolithic structure,[21] but unstable and shifting. Kristeva's recognition of this is simply the other side of her acknowledgment that the semiotic has to work through the very order of language it defies. Their relationship is one of a "dynamic." "Complete repression (were such a thing possible) would entail consequences preventing the symbolic function."[22] It is in fact a tenet of Freudian psychoanalysis that repression can never be absolute. If it were, the very concept of repression could not be thought.

It is worth stressing these points simply because they show how closely Kristeva's concept of social transformation, as early as 1974, already approximated to the idea of the analytic *cure.* Kristeva has often been criticized for inadequately posing her appeal to semiotic heterogeneity in terms of social practice, although this was in fact her own criticism of the avant-garde text. But that criticism, advanced by Kristeva herself, relied in turn on the notion that resistance must finally be articulated in a voice which can be heard, and this necessarily involves, as it does in the analytic setting, a partial reintegration of speech. Paradoxically, the very aspect of the theory which stopped Kristeva's writing from spinning off into the gratuitous celebration of noise is the aspect now criticized for its psychically normative implications; as if "being an analyst" (the opening words of Kristeva's own statement on the back of this latest book), and working towards an at least partial symbolization of the repressed meant, by definition, abdicating any commitment to social change. In the 1970s, Kristeva herself criticized psychoanalysis on exactly these grounds,[23] but a closer look shows that some form of "integration" was always seen by her as the pre-condition of any effectivity in the social; it is the concept of what that effectivity should aim for which has altered. This fact suggests to me at least that Kristeva's discarding of Marxism can hardly be laid at the door of her increasing involvement with psychoanalysis. From the very beginning, the psychoanalytic insight and the concept of practice *together* acted as a check on the original critique of the subject as a purely ideological ideal. Psychosis—we can be thankful—was never offered as a revolutionary ideal.

The problems raised by Kristeva's challenge to language and identity can perhaps be recognized as another version of a more familiar political question: how to effect a political transformation when the terms of that transformation are given by the very order which a revolutionary practice seeks to change. The presence of "revolution" in the title of that early book was never, it should be stressed, part of a suggestion that psychic or aesthetic disruption could substitute for other forms of politics. But it did aim at this larger issue of the conditions, and limits, of revolutionary change. In 1974, Kristeva located this logical "impasse," or bind, in the Marxist theory of a class whose abolition, along with that of class itself, will emerge out of the same historical conditions which produced it. The proletariat has a privileged consciousness of a social totality tending towards its own elim- ination, which also means eliminating the very class and consciousness which had grasped its totality as such.[24] It is a concept of self-negation which, in a less quoted but central chapter of *La révolution du langage poétique,* Kristeva then carries over into her discussion of the subject's relation to language and psychic life. In his paper on "Negation," Freud had made the negative instance the pre-condition of logical thought—the subject expels part of itself in order that it may come to be.[25] This description of loss as the founding moment of subjectivity then forms the basis, via Lacan, of Kristeva's concept of psychic life. But equally important, it already bears the weight of that other question—whose difficulty has become more and more pressing—of a transformation which will finally mean relinquishing the very forms of self-recognition through which it was first desired. The classic opposition between revolution and reform takes on another meaning when what is involved is the subject's very ability to hold itself together in speech.

The problem was perhaps bound to emerge as soon as the question of identity (psychic and sexual) was introduced into the analysis of how a specific social order is upheld. The turn to subjectivity and sexuality had originally been part of a rejection of those forms of economism or traditional Marxist analysis which excluded these questions from politics or else seemed to relegate them to second place. This was central to *Tel Quel's* commitment to Maoist China and the concept of a cultural revolution in the seventies. But in so far as the conception of sexuality was a psychoanalytic one, so it rapidly touched on aspects of subjectivity which cannot be "managed" even by more progressive institutional and familial forms. Although *Tel Quel* prefaced their Summer 1974 issue (No 58) with a quotation from Wilhelm Reich on the socially liberating power of sexuality, it was clear from the outset that, unlike Reich, their idea of sexuality was not that of a quantity to be released but of processes which unsettle the most fundamental self-definition of the subject. No priority, therefore, to "psychic liberation,"[26] first because the psychic was always the *non-sufficient* condition of genuine social transformation, second because it was precisely not "liberation" that was at stake. For that very reason, the psychoanalytic movement immediately found itself hedged in on both sides: by an appeal back and away from questions of sexuality to the politics of a purely class opposition which it had been the crucial intention to shift,[27] or else by a call from off the very edge of language. It could be argued— and was argued by Kristeva—that by ignoring language, or not seeing language as an issue, the first of these positions firmly entrenches itself within its laws. Kristeva herself has said over and again that her own aim is to avoid both of these alternatives: no absolutism of the "thetic" which then gets erected as a theological law, but no denial of the "thetic" which brings with it the fantasy of "an irrationalism in pieces."[28]

In assessing the changes in Kristeva's work, we need therefore to distinguish a number of different levels.

Firstly, what appears to me as an increasing recognition on Kristeva's part that there can be no direct politicization of the unconscious since this is to confuse political and psychic resistance or, more simply, struggle and symptomatic distress.

Secondly, a discarding on Kristeva's part of revolutionary politics (Marxist and then Maoist), and, since 1977, of any political discourse which totalizes the social, in favor of a highly individualistic conception of dissidence and worth.[29] Kristeva has set the latter against all politics—including feminism—but this does not necessarily follow; the critique of totalities, for example, could be related to recent feminist criticism of the monolithic language and organization of the Left.[30] To this extent, Kristeva's image of feminism as a political movement in these moments is drawn from only one half of the description which she herself gives of it in "Women's Time."[31]

Thirdly, a continuing focus on questions of psycho-sexual identity whose basic insight has not changed: that identity is necessary but only ever partial and therefore carries with it a dual risk—the wreck of all identity, a self-blinding allegiance to psychic norms. To hold onto both sides of this dynamic is, Kristeva argues, almost impossible, although one is in fact always implicated in both. Certainly Kristeva sees psychoanalysis as one of the few places in our culture where this dynamic is fully allowed to speak, at the same time as her work also veers from one side to the other of the divide.

Clearly these are related, but we collapse the levels into each other at a price. To say that the unconscious cannot be politicized does not necessarily entail setting up psychoanalysis as an alternative to all politics. To argue that questions of sexuality are not—in a one-to-one relation—managed or exhausted by traditional political discourse or transformation does not mean that we have to discard these questions from political understanding and debate. The fact that Kristeva now seems to withdraw the analytic insight from the directly political arena does not mean that it was always and necessarily asocial from the start. Nor can psychoanalysis be seen, in a simple way, as the sole cause and determining factor in the political shift. Kristeva's abandonment of that earlier concept of revolution can also be related to changes—some of which have been welcomed by feminism— in the field of politics itself. It would be possible to argue, for example, that some form of political pluralism, case for local initiatives, and multiple political strategies, follows more logically from the rejection of revolutionary Marxism which, for *Tel Quel* and their subsequent journal *Infini,* has been accompanied by an unmistakable shift to the right. It was, after all, feminism which first argued that subjectivity (the "personal") was a political stake. Kristeva's move can in fact be turned back on itself, since she herself has never discarded the attempt to understand the different and changing forms of social articulation through which identities are moved in—and out of—place.

II   *"A freudful mistake"*[32]

I do not think we should be surprised, therefore, nor too comfortably critical or dismissive, when Kristeva proceeds to fall, at various points throughout her work, into one or other side of the psychic dynamic which she herself describes. The latest book, with its appeal to the "father of individual pre-history," can certainly be seen, as I have already suggested, as a race back into the arms of the law. But Kristeva's own work, and responses to Kristeva, have equally been marked by the opposite impulse, notably around the concept of the semiotic which has acquired something of an existence of its own, outside the realm of meaning without which, strictly, it does not make sense. The attraction of the theory was always that it pointed to aspects of language which escaped the straitjacket of symbolic norms. But this has also made the theory vulnerable to some very archaic notions of the content of the repressed. Variously, and at times conjointly, Kristeva has attributed to the semiotic: femininity, color, music, body, and affect—concepts whose oppressive lyricism has at times been welcomed by feminism but which feminism has also been the quickest to reject. It is also through these concepts that Kristeva takes her leave of Jacques Lacan. The concept of "affect," for example, comes through André Green, a member of the *Association Psychanalytique de France,* founded when its members split with Lacan in 1964 (Kristeva trained as an analyst with this school). Published in 1973, one year before *La révolution du langage poétique,* Green's book *Le discours vivant* developed the concept of affect in Freud as part of a critique of Lacan's central premise that psychic life is ruled by the exigencies of representation and the linguistic sign.[33] In an article published in the journal of the *Association* in 1979, Kristeva reiterated Green's critique of Lacan—that Lacan's concept of language assimilates into itself and absorbs "what the dualism of Freudian thought holds to be strangely irreducible: drive, affect," although she immediately qualifies: "Is there any need to recall that the position which takes the semiotic as heterogeneous does not arise from a concern to integrate some alleged concreteness, brute corporality, or energy-in-itself into a language suspected of being too abstract ... This semiotic is without primacy and has no place as origin."[34]

There is no doubt, however, that the push here is against language itself, even though Kristeva herself is again the best analyst of the dangers this might imply. In an interview in 1977 on the United States, Kristeva praised the "non-verbal" aspects of modern American culture which draw more "radically and profoundly than in Europe" on the realms of "gesture, colour and sound," but then she asked whether that same non-verbalization might not also be the sign of a resistance, the almost psychotic hyper-activity of a violent and overproductive culture incessantly on the go.[35] Even if we do not accept the representation of American culture, Kristeva's own check on the celebration of a place beyond language is worthy of note.

It is, however, almost impossible not to assign the status of origin to the semiotic once it is defined as beyond language in this way. Elsewhere Kristeva defines heterogeneity as the "archaisms of the semiotic body," "logically and chronologically prior to the institution of the symbolic," "genetically detected in the first echolalias of infants." And it is this concept of priority which lies behind Kristeva's psychoanalytic interest in the acquisition of language and in object relations theory which concentrates on the interaction between the mother and child. But the emphasis on this relationship immediately produces a split between the order of the mother and of the father, giving to the first the privilege of the semiotic and separating it out from the culture in which it is inscribed. Juliet Mitchell has discussed how in the 1920s and 1930s attention was focused on this relationship because it was felt to hold the key to the pre-oedipal sexuality of the female child. She also argues that the effect of this was to close off the question of sexual difference—of the symbolically produced and only ever partial division between men and women, masculinity and femininity, a division which this theory takes for granted and thus helps to reproduce.[36] Lacan's emphasis on the symbolic was first of all developed against this tendency. It represented an attempt to return to the larger questions of cultural determination figured in Freud's myth of the beginnings of culture in *Totem and Taboo*.[37] In Kristeva's case, the attention to the mother does not ignore these wider issues but becomes part of a more general question about the place of the mother-child relation in the constitution of cultural taboos (see below). But as soon as Kristeva gives to this relation the status of origin—psychic or cultural, or both—it is handed over to the realm of the senses, outside of all history and form. Kristeva uses this quotation from Freud to support the identification of the semiotic with an essentially maternal domain: "It [an advance in intellectuality] consists, for instance, in deciding that paternity is more important than maternity, although it cannot, like the latter, be established by the evidence of the senses."[38]

For Kristeva, this relinquishing of the maternal is loss, as much as advance, and it is never complete, but this does not alter the fully ideological division between maternal and paternal, senses and ideation which it serves to reinforce.

But the problematic nature of this tendency in Kristeva's thought is perhaps best illustrated by the very term of the semiotic itself, which Kristeva calls "chora" or receptacle after Plato's cosmology (The Timaeus), where it stands for the mediating instance in which the copies of the eternal model receive their shape. Plato himself describes the "chora" as maternal, and from the beginning Kristeva based the link to Freud on this: "this rhythmic space without thesis or position, the process where signifiance comes to be, Plato indicates as much when he designates this receptacle nursing, maternal."[39] But if Plato did so, it was because the mother was seen as playing no part in the act of procreation, a receptacle or empty vessel merely for the gestation of the unborn child.[40]

III   "I hate Maria and when I see her portrait I go down on my knees"[41]

It seems to me now that the concept of the semiotic, especially in those formulations which identify it with the mother and place it beyond language, is the least useful aspect of Kristeva's work, even though it is the concept for which she is best known. For what happens to this maternally connoted and primitive semiotic is first that it is defined as the hidden underside of culture (we can recognize the proximity of this to the classical demonic image of femininity) and then idealized as something whose value and exuberance the culture cannot manage and has therefore had to repress (a simple reverse of that first image which makes femininity the ideal excluded instance of all culture).

Kristeva herself charts these dramatic reversals from idealization of the woman to degradation and back again throughout her discussion of the writings of Mallarmé and Céline. But she does so by analyzing them as fantasies whose violent oscillations, especially in the case of Céline, bring greater and greater violence in their train. Furthermore, as Kristeva has constantly insisted, idealization of the semiotic in itself involves a denial or cover up of the psychic pain and violence which in fact characterizes the early interaction between the mother and child. This is why Kristeva is able at one and the same time to lay out the horrors of the fantasmatic structure which underpins the writings of an author like Céline, while at the same time praising that writing for exposing a psychic drama which—with massive social repercussions—is constantly denied, projected onto the other, and then played out by the culture at large.[42] Céline's writing is a *symptom*. It reveals *horror* as a matter of *power*—the power of fascination when we are confronted with the traces of our own psychic violence, the horror when that same violence calls on social institutions for legitimation, and receives it.

In *Pouvoirs de l'horreur,* Kristeva takes up the question with which she ended *La revolution du langage poetique:* "How can negativity, or the reject be articulated in the social?,"[43] returning to a mostly forgotten emphasis of that earlier book— the negativity or reject, horror or abjection as she now calls it, which characterizes the semiotic realm. She then charts the way that different religious cultures have drawn up the boundaries (soiling, abomination, sin) of what they can—bodily— contain. It is another version of the problem which has run right through her writing—of what can be articulated on this side of culture without breaking its limits, only the account of what needs to be spoken has got considerably worse.

Kristeva could also be seen here as feeding back the issue of pre-oedipal sexuality into the theorization of cultural origins which Freud—following his changed account of femininity—had himself failed to do. She makes the point that discussions of the incest taboo have concentrated on the place of the father together with the forms of disorder (obsessional neurosis and paranoia) associated with his prohibitory role, leaving the mother precisely as the idealized relic of what comes to be forbidden, a kind of lost territory which says nothing of the psychic ambivalence of that early relation, nor of the disorders (psychosis and phobia) with which it can be clinically linked. Kristeva's increasing interest in those analysts who concentrate on the most difficult aspects of that early relation (Rosenfeld, Bion) stems from this critique. If this is object-relations theory, therefore, it is with a difference, since there is no concept of "adequacy" at stake. Rather it seems that, in response to an idealization latent in her own formulations, Kristeva was replying that the semiotic is no "fun."

For what does it mean, we can ask, to place the mother at the source and fading point of all subjectivity and language, a point which, as Kristeva herself has argued, threatens the subject with collapse? Surely this is already the effect of an idealization which barely conceals the reproach, felt threat, and feared loss of identity, fermenting underneath?

As soon as Kristeva asks this question, then the whole of her work seems to turn on itself, implicating her own concepts in the fantasies, ambivalence, and projections which she describes. Kristeva had criticized Mallarmé for the way that he targets, or fixates onto the woman the disruptions of language played out in his writing, making the woman the bearer of their eternal secret, mystifying them and thus depriving them of what might otherwise be their more unsettling social effects.[44] And in *Pouvoirs de l'horreur,* she describes the way in which Céline fantasizes his own mortality as feminine and projects it onto the woman who then appears as a persecutor, for the life she not only gives, but denies. Much of this book is about the way in which the limits of language and its dissolution are constantly thought in terms of sexual difference, the way that cultures define and secure their parameters by relegating the woman to their outer edge.

Yet, in a twist which gives back to these same fantasies the weight of a primordial truth, Kristeva asks whether they may not find their basis in a femininity whose overpowerful and physical reality effectively places cultures at risk. Is the repudiation of this power of the mother ("maleficent in its power to give mortal life") indeed the pre-condition of symbolic identity on which all cultures rest? Is this same power "*historic* or *fantasmatic*," "*attributed*" to the woman, or is the early relation to the mother its "*unconscious base*"?[45] Kristeva says that her question is not about primacy or cause and effect, although at one point she does describe the taboo on the mother as the "primary mytheme" of all culture,[46] which seems to give the psychic a primacy and brings her uncomfortably close to the form of argument advanced against Bronislaw Malinowski in the 1920s and 1930s by Ernest Jones. In fact Kristeva oscillates, but in the process she has turned a much older debate about the relationship between psychic and social determination in the production of social forms into a query about the origins and persistence (not least of all in her own writing) of some of the most disturbing images of femininity in our culture.

Kristeva's work splits on a paradox, or rather a dilemma: the hideous moment when a theory arms itself with a concept of femininity as different, as something other to the culture as it is known, only to find itself face to face with, or even entrenched within, the most grotesque and fully cultural stereotypes of femininity itself. Unlike some of her most virulent detractors,[47] however, Kristeva at least knows that these images are not so easily dispatched. It is not by settling the question of their origins that we can necessarily dismantle their force.

IV   Feminism and Its Fantasies

Kristeva's relationship to these highly charged and ambivalent images, and the way that she works at the limits of psychic identity explain, I think, the strength but also the tension of her writing for feminism. Kristeva has never fully identified with feminism and it has never been the place from which she has chosen to speak, although she does describe her place as a woman as central to her overall project: "It was necessary perhaps to be a woman to attempt to take up that exorbitant wager of carrying the rational project to the outer borders of the signifying ventures of men."[48]

Kristeva has, however, been attractive to feminism because of the way that she exposes the complacent identities of psycho-sexual life. But as soon as we try to draw out of that exposure an image of femininity which escapes the straitjacket of symbolic forms, we fall straight into that essentialism and primacy of the semiotic which is one of the most problematic aspects of her work. And as soon as we try to make of it the basis for a political identity, we turn the concept inside out, since it was as a critique of identity itself that it was originally advanced. No politics without identity, but no identity which takes itself at its word. The tension is captured in the title of one of Kristeva's best known articles— "D'une identité l'autre"—which has been translated as "From One Identity to Another," but which is also aimed at the opposite: "identity and its other"— that is, the other of identity itself.[49] This is why Kristeva has increasingly distanced herself from a feminism which she has described as "too existentialist"[50] (this relates specifically to psychoanalysis and echoes Juliet Mitchell's 1974 critique of feminist rejection of Freud,[51]) and which she sees—wrongly as far as I am concerned—as a monolithic entity which, in its claim for identity and power (identity as power), repeats and reinforces the rigidity of the culture which produced it.[52]

At its most simple, therefore, the question becomes: what could it mean to construct a political identity out of processes heralded as the flight of identity itself (see Nancy K. Miller in this collection). Especially given that recognition of the aberrant nature of those processes was, in a sense, the price we paid for moving out of a psychic functionalism which had underlain the earlier accounts of the subject's ideological place.

At the same time, Kristeva gives to women the privilege of the central dilemma caught by her writing: how to challenge the very form of available self-definition without losing the possibility of speech. Against the offered and familiar alternatives of bureaucracy and madness, it is women for Kristeva who know the necessity of, and demand, a place on the historical stage, while also calling the bluff of a psychic and sexual order of things which they pass through and across: the central word *"traverser,"* a word central to Kristeva's writing, implies that you go *through* certainly, but also *out.*[53]

Of these two directions—towards identity and its other side—Kristeva calls the second "negativity," which recalls the negativity of the semiotic and underlines the psychic difficulty at stake. It can be summarized as a refusal: "Ce n'est jamais ca"—"No, it's not that" or "That won't do," which, taken together with the translation "Woman Can Never Be Defined," make the woman the subject as well as the object of the statement.[54] The other side of this negativity, Kristeva calls the "ethics" of femininity, or women's commitment to an ethics which saves them, as she puts it, from a "Nietzschean rage."[55] Criticized recently for linking this to women's experience of motherhood,[56] Kristeva is nonetheless echoing a long-standing feminist demand that this aspect of femininity should be allowed a voice in constructing the priorities of the political domain. And while this may seem to come close to a history of oppressive discourses which have given to women as mothers the privilege of the ethical (and not a great deal else), for Kristeva *ethics* has nothing whatsoever to do with *duty* or the idea that women should people the race. No ethics *without* maternity, but not mothering as ethical *duty* or *role:* "The ethical which aims for a negativity is opposed to ethics understood as the observation of laws."[57] Ethics plus (as) negativity describes a subjective position which avoids conformity (the first without the second) and esotericism or marginality (the second without the first), capturing alternatives which have historically presented themselves to feminism: between an equality which risks absorption into the law, and an absolute difference which can only defy it.

But perhaps even more difficult in relation to feminism, and less commented on, is this issue of the negative aspects that Kristeva identifies in the semiotic which feminism has at times been tempted to claim as its own special realm. Difficult precisely because Kristeva has not stopped at the positive aspects of this process but has gone over to the other side, dredging up archaic images of the mother which, for all their status as fantasy (because of their status as fantasy) are not without their effects. If we stop at the critique of identity—the celebration of a heterogeneity which it is too easy politically to rebuff—we avoid this more troubling area which consists of the psychic ambivalence of the drives. But if we follow this through, then we find ourselves having to relinquish an idealized vision of the lost maternal continent which we have often and so fiercely wished to protect: "Death explodes inside the peace we thought to have absorbed (nirvana, intoxication, silence)."[58] But once that has been said, it becomes impossible to avoid talking about fantasy, not just by men of women, but also amongst women, and even within feminism itself: "to extol a centripetal, becalmed and softened feminine sexuality, only to exhume most recently, under the cover of idylls amongst women, the sado-masochistic ravages beneath."[59]

A question, or image, of feminine paranoia? In what appears to me as one of the most powerful moments of self-diagnosis in her text, Kristeva certainly says so[60] (the structure of paranoia was already there in the article I started with on the hallucinatory power of film). But since Freud at least we have ceased to use diagnosis as a cause for dismissal, still less as a category of abuse. Rather it is the moment when Kristeva recasts *for* women the problem of identity to which she has constantly returned. For what could be a simple love between women, since identity is always in opposition *to?* And yet what could be a place without identity, other than a falling into the realm of the unnameable, body without language, a realm to which women have often and so oppressively been confined? Even between women (that mother-daughter relationship of which politically we have asked so much), the act of differentiation-recognition of the other leads—if not to violence—then at least, and of necessity, to psychic pain.

V   *"The King is with the body"*[61]

This latest book *(Histoires d'amour)* is therefore no idyll since "hatred . . . underpins, carries, determines" the identity it now pleads for and the love whose history it describes.[62] "Narcissus in troubled waters"—one of the chapter headings of the previous book—is there to caution us against a return to identity, narcissism, and idealization which, at first glance, bears all the signs of a retreat. Kristeva now outlines the pre-condition for a psychic identity which neither the abjection of the mother nor the punishing imago of the oedipal father can ground, repair, or sustain. She finds this pre-condition in a primary identification with a non-oedipal "father of individual pre-history": "pre-history" because, it seems, Kristeva is still searching for an ideal and prior psychic instance now lost on the side of the mother (too abject for words), "non-oedipal" because she still wants to save this idealization from the tyranny of the symbolic in which ideals are shaped.

Yet again we can ask what separation (or splitting) this is. For although Freud does refer to the child's early identification with such a pre-oedipal father, there is ambivalence (abjection?) in this identification *from the very first,* and in a key passage from *Group Psychology and the Analysis of the Ego* to which Kristeva refers, he describes this identification as a derivitive of the oral drive which assimilates and annihilates its object.[63] Kristeva calls this identification the advent of the psychic and a deferring of the oral drive, but she has been asked whether this imaginary father and the phallic mother might not be one and the same thing.[64] In fact Kristeva's concept seems at times to come close to Maud Mannoni's attempt to ground psychic identity in the paternal genealogy of the child.[65] It is worth noting, however, that it is only those moments in Kristeva's own writing where she too rigidly demarcates identity and drive, symbolic and semiotic, conscious and unconscious, and distributes them between the realms of the father and the mother, that allows for this paternal return.

It is nonetheless a striking move from Kristeva's early assertion that paternal power will symbolically flourish wherever the question of sexuality is not specifically and critically posed.[66] An assertion which echoed the belief within feminism that the key to women's subordination lay in the symbolic enshrinement and perpetuation of patriarchal law. For even if we now recognize that the passage from symbolic system to the concrete instances of women's subordination cannot be made so easily or so fast,[67] the analysis holds surely still as a castigation of the values in which a culture embodies its own worth. At the same time it must be said, however, that once the precise connections between symbol and concrete power have been questioned or opened up for debate, then we cannot say what political effects will follow from a recognition of the father and his place in the psychic life of the child.

Nor is it a simple idealization which is being promoted here, the idea of a paternally grounded identity which simply receives and comforts the subject. Kristeva criticizes interpretations of Judaic writing which uncover the latent violence of its rhetoric and celebrate part object without identity, or letter without the law, but she nonetheless knows that the risk awaiting those who obey the law of the father is the paranoia of the chosen.[68]

As I understand it, what is most clearly at stake is a psychic necessity: at its most simple, the confrontation of the therapist with the pain of a fragmentation without identity or place. For even the one who plays with language through writing has of course come through to the other side: "The writer: a phobic who succeeds at metaphor so as not to die of fear but to resuscitate through signs."[69]

I do not think that Kristeva should be criticized therefore for her commitment to the concept of psychic identity, nor for her increasingly analytically informed aim to understand the processes through which it is produced—a commitment which does not have to imply a collusion with the way that identity is paraded in the culture at large. Since, far from this involving a denial of the other psychic forces which have been at the center of her writing, it could be seen as the only place from which they can be known. This recognition was there from the outset and, as I have tried to argue, it was this, paradoxically, which saved Kristeva's writing from the anarchy of its own terms. Nor do I think that Kristeva should be dismissed for her analysis of love as a strategy which allows individual subjects to negotiate the troubled psychic waters which she herself so graphically describes. To which we could add that this love does not have to be incompatible with politics. Did not Kristeva herself say that without love of women there was no point in going to China in 1974?[70]

In this latest book, Kristeva pleads for love in response to what she sees as a dearth of idealization in our culture (shades of Christopher Lasch?), a dearth which is precipitating an abolition of psychic space which gives nothing but abjection the reign. "I plead for the Imaginary as antidote to the crisis."[71] But then, as is so often the case, Kristeva provides the self-diagnosis: "doubtless a Cartesian deformation to dream of such a pre-Cartesian subject in love"; the critique: "only for mirrors infatuated with stable images do crises exist"; and the caution: "we lack today an amatory code, but it would be an imposture to propose new ones."[72]

Finally, one can also point to the overall consistency of Kristeva's project in which this latest book has its place. In 1983 Kristeva argued, against an easy misreading of the title of Tel Quel's new journal Infini, that for her at least it does not represent the return of a "religious psychology or ideology" but rather the "never abandoned effort to take transcendence seriously and to track down its premise into the most hidden recesses of language. My prejudice is that of believing that God is analysable. Infinitely."[73]

For me Kristeva's work remains important because of the way it is poised on that interface of politics/psychoanalysis/feminism. In response to the demand for an attention to sexuality, some forms of Marxism will argue for a return to the politics of class. In response to the questions of psychic identity raised by sexuality, feminism seems at moments to come close to dropping the psychoanalytic understanding of sexuality itself, or at least Julia Kristeva who, it should also be said, has too long served as an ideal. But sexuality—the crucial ways it determines and structures our lives—cannot be understood without acknowledging the importance of fantasy, and fantasy in turn reveals aspects of subjectivity which crush the splendor of our (conscious) dreams.

Kristeva's reversals from celebration of the semiotic to abjection and back to a (now paternal) ideal reveal the instability of fantasy itself. They also underscore the problem which arises when political discourse turned on the category of identity and its illusions and accused it of upholding or of being the pre-condition of all other social norms—recognizing in that moment that if sexuality was so intractable, it is because it strikes at the heart of identity itself. And having once gained that insight, we cannot just drop the question of identity and its impasses from the debate.

Kristeva was not the first to bring these issues onto the political stage. They are there already in the confrontation with violence, in the debates about the limits of censorship, about sado-masochism, pornography, and the law. Kristeva writes across *("traverser")* these problems and has pushed them to (her own) breaking point. Her work gives us the measure of the difficulties when politics tries to open itself up to the ravages of the unconscious mind.

3

Commentary: Postponing Politics

Margaret W. Ferguson

This commentary is necessarily marked by its original occasion, a 1985 conference session on "the feminist politics of interpretation" in which an audience heard, for the first time, two difficult and fascinating papers and then listened to my oral response to texts that I had read several times. The situation placed me in a position of potentially abusive power vis-à-vis both the audience and the authors of the papers, who had read each others' work but not my commentary, and who had to sit quietly and listen to me after finishing their presentations. They did however then have a chance to interrogate and dispute my commentary and, eventually, to revise their essays in response to it, and in the light of the discussion in which members of the audience also participated. The written text that follows was itself revised in response to some revisions that Nancy Miller made in her text; but my commentary remains very much an occasional essay— which is to say that certain strands of its critique now seem "fallen" to me, faded, dated. They will nonetheless, I hope, hold some archeological (or, to borrow a word from Nancy Miller, arachnological) interest for feminist readers. In any event, the untimely strands of my critique cannot be easily disentangled from those which seem to me, and to the editor of this volume, still timely enough to transport to a new discursive field.

My chief aim in this response will be to highlight a few of the points of significant connection—and also of major disagreement—between Nancy Miller's and Jacqueline Rose's papers as they directly and indirectly address the topic of our session, "the feminist politics of interpretation." I shall then pose a few specific questions to each author and also to myself about the ways in which our disciplinary formation (or deformation) as literary critics may be shaping, and perhaps limiting, our understandings—and practices—of feminist politics. Though Nancy Miller and Jacqueline Rose address the topic of this session from different theoretical perspectives that imply rather different understandings of what the terms "feminist" and "politics" might mean, both papers offer a performative definition of the third term in our session's title, "interpretation," as *commentary* on some kind of pre-existing text. The implications of this remain to be teased out; we might begin to do so by reflecting on the fact that both of our speakers—one British, the other North American—-approach the topic of this session via a line of inquiry mapped chiefly, and relatively recently—beginning in the late sixties—in France. Both papers suggest, albeit with quite different affective and conceptual emphases, that the question of a "feminist politics of interpretation" cannot be seriously formulated, much less answered, without some confrontation with texts written in the language which Charlotte Brontë's Lucy Snowe, as Nancy Miller pointedly reminds us, mastered sufficiently to confound her professors by repeating, in response to queries about French history and various "ologies," "je n'en sais rien." Though one might want to examine the socio-economic and ideological causes, and effects, of the prestige accorded to French theory by many American and British intellectuals during the post-War era, and particularly during the post-Vietnam War era, I shall not pursue that line of inquiry here; instead, I'll accept provisionally the premise that informs the discursive practice of both Miller and Rose, namely that French discussions of the subject of "the subject"—or alternatively, of what both Miller and Rose call "identity"—are of central importance to those who call themselves, in English, "feminists." Some of you, especially if you are trained in disciplines other than literary studies, may be asking why this should be so, and correlatively, why both speakers chose to devote a significant amount of energy to interpreting arguments about identity formulated by two French intellectuals—Roland Barthes and Julia Kristeva—neither of whom chose to identify him- or herself as a "féministe." Leaving aside now the issue of the seductive attraction that Kristeva may acquire by her very refusal to ally herself in any straightforward way with feminism as a collective national and international movement, let me just review for you the major reason why Kristeva and Barthes do seem important for American feminist theory at this time.

In a sentence that interestingly poses the problem of identity as a problem of *social identification,* specifically, as that mode of identification which confers originating or possessive power on a man whose proper name is associated with a certain discursive tradition, Rose writes that "Julia Kristeva's work belongs to that semiotic tradition most closely identified with the work of Roland Barthes, in which the analysis of the structure of language rapidly became a critique of the stabilizing illusion of the sign, and of those forms of writing . . . which were seen to embody and guarantee that illusion for a bourgeois society binding its subjects into the spurious unity of a culture inaccessible to change." Rose goes on, however, to suggest, without saying so directly, that Kristeva should not be simply perceived as part of a Barthesian tradition but rather as a figure "set apart" from the pitfalls of both structuralism and poststructuralism by virtue of her dual emphasis on the psychic and social divisions that operate, dynamically, beneath the facades of cultural and psychic unity. Kristeva, as Rose powerfully but also ambivalently and sometimes protectively presents her, objects to the same tendency

in structuralism and poststructuralism that leads Nancy Miller to question Barthes—
the tendency, in Kristeva's phrase, to "abdicate the subject." As Rose presents
her, therefore, Kristeva can be seen as an ally, albeit a difficult one, of the American
feminist critic who, according to Nancy Miller, may find in Barthes's theory of
the "death of the author" a premature foreclosure of the question of the *female*
subject and her subjectivity. "It seems to me . . . that when the so-called crises
of the subject is staged, as it generally is, within a textual model," Miller writes,
"that performance must then be recomplicated by the historical, political, and
figurative body of the woman writer."

Stated crudely, then, the major point of connection between Miller's and Rose's
papers is that both argue for a certain *retrieval* of the question of the subject,
specifically, of the female subject. But they differ quite strikingly in their understandings of how this work of retrieving the (female) subject is to be accomplished
and for what ends it is to be pursued.

The differences between Miller's and Rose's conceptions of the question of
identity and its stakes appear as much in their practices of argumentation as in
their explicit statements about the subject. Miller adopts the rhetorical strategy
of opposing the authoritative and, as she says, in certain ways "seductive" voice
of Barthes to the voice of an American woman writer, Adrienne Rich. Miller uses
Rich to articulate a critique of Barthes, who is taken—perhaps too easily—as
representing or speaking for a postmodernist theory of anonymous textuality that
rearticulates an old story of masculine dominance through its reliance on ostensibly
universal concepts such as that of "the Author" and "the Reader."

Miller's critical point, exfoliated with quotations from Naomi Schor, Andreas
Huyssen, Elaine Showalter, and Gayatri Spivak, seems very well taken, and still
(in 1988 as much as if not more than in 1985) controversial in the context of
the North American scene of higher education and publication thereon (e.g.,
such recent books as Allan Bloom's *The Closing of the American Mind* and
E. D. Hirsch's *Cultural Literacy*). Nonetheless, it seems important to question Miller's strategic choice of Barthes to represent the French theoretical attack on the
humanist ideal of the subject. She partly explains her choice when she writes that
Barthes "translates (seductively) from within French thought the more arduous
writings of Derrida, Lacan, Kristeva, for (or into) literature." But this formulation
points, it seems to me, to a problem that's both signaled and evaded by the
parenthetical phrases, a problem pertaining to the evaluation and conceptualization of "literature" as a realm separate from, and somehow more desirable (because
easier?) than "French thought." If we examine the (ideological) values informing
Miller's sentence and her use of Barthes in general, we may surmise that her
institutional training and position, not to mention her own talents as a stylist, are
strongly influencing her argument. That's not of course surprising, but it's nonetheless worth thinking about what intellectual moves are precluded by an argument that implicitly values a quality of seductiveness that is evidently a feature

of Barthes's rhetorical *style*. His style, moreover, is associated not only with a certain conception of literariness but also with a perceived *likeness* between his critical practice and that of literary feminists: his "interest in the semiotics of literary and cultural activity—its pleasures, dangers, zones, and codes of refer- ence—intersects thematically with a feminist emphasis on the need to situate, socially and symbolically, the practices of reading and writing." I would suggest that it is precisely this gesture of finding an *ally* in Barthes that needs more critical scrutiny if North American feminist critics are to move forward in the project of "situating" their own as well as others' practices of reading and writing in a social field. For Barthes's "Death of an Author" (originally published as Miller notes in 1967)—in contrast, say, to Michel Foucault's "What is an Author" (first published in 1969)—does very little to contextualize historically an authorial death the news of which—as Mark Twain said of his own—has (perhaps) been greatly exagger- ated. Moreover, by focusing on Barthes rather than Foucault (his essay is cited in the revised version of the essay, but briefly) Miller arguably makes a Barthesian move for (and "into") a realm conceived as literary. I belabor this point, perhaps, but I want to dramatize the *existence* of an alternative critical path which might, in a shorthand way, be associated with Foucault insofar as his work characteris- tically moves away from literature—or, more precisely, athwart the very cate- gories of literature and "literariness"—by taking as its object of inquiry social, discursive, and institutional formations. In "What is an Author?" Foucault clearly stresses more than Barthes does the social and institutional matrix in which the concept of the author is historically implicated; also in contrast to Barthes, Fou- cault insists that his attack on the notion of the subject is not the record of an "event" but rather a heuristic strategy designed to expand the object of inter- pretation from paper texts to other kinds of phenomena. His aim as he cunningly describes it in an interview of 1977 is "to get rid of the subject itself, that is to say, to arrive at an analysis which can account for the constitution of the subject within a historical framework."[1]

Miller's decision to put Barthes rather than Foucault into dialogue with Adrienne Rich is, as I've suggested, an overdetermined one. It is from the position of a university teacher in the U.S. who teaches French literature and feminist theory, and who has been actively engaged in significant curricular battles, that Miller contrasts Rich with Barthes and then uses her indirectly (and in a series of tricky moves, I think) to articulate an important but nonetheless distinctly limited political argument: that the immediate task of the feminist reader is to work for change within the North American educational institution. This argument seems prob- lematically narrow both in its scope and in its purchase on the concept of "politics"—and it seems narrow partly because it emerges from a discussion in which Miller has used Rich—against Barthes—to open up some very interesting questions about feminist "geopolitics" in the 1980s. The questions Miller's essay raises have to do with Rich's own revisionary argument that the feminist slogan of the sixties, "the personal is the political," now (in Miller's words) "requires a redefinition of the personal to include most immediately an interrogation of ethnocentrism; a poetics of identity that engages with the 'other woman.'" Discussing Rich's discovery of contemporary Cuban women's poetry in a book edited by Margaret Randall called *Breaking the Silences,* and meditating on the challenge that the situation of Latin American women poses for the North American feminist, Miller asks, "if the ethics of feminist writing involve writing for the woman who doesn't read ... then what would be required of a responsive, responsible feminist reading?" I would suggest that this line of questioning could be extended, in the direction of a more pragmatic political query, if we were to ask, What do the practices of reading and writing taught and tested in North American schools have to do with illiteracy, and the poverty that accompanies it, in Central America? An answer to that question would involve many mediatory steps, but they seem important for academic feminists to consider in the light of arguments made by Brian Street, John Guillory, and others who have recently called critical attention to the ways in which competing *ideologies* of literacy are central to the vexed socio-economic relations between First and Third World countries in general, and between the U.S. and Latin American in particular.[2]

Another important question that Miller raises in her discussion of Rich is how analytically useful the category of gender is, at least in and of itself, once one begins the difficult task of coordinating a feminist critique with a critique of ethnocentrism. The implications of this question aren't however, it seems to me, fully explored. It's as if Miller is addressing a problem through a provocative but gingerly technique that entails, first, quoting voices critical of liberal feminist assumptions (she cites Denise Riley, for instance, on the need for feminist critics to take account of "the different temporalities of 'women' ... the uneven histories of the different formations of different categories of 'women' from the side of politics") and second, juxtaposing contradictory voices such as Rich's—arguing for the existence of an "unalienated art" of women's poetry in Cuba—and Barthes's, maintaining that there's "no language site outside bourgeois ideology." Miller does not, however, dwell on the problems implied by her quotations. Instead, she effectively closes off the questions about "cross-cultural feminism" which she has raised in order to move back to the site of the Anglo-American educational institution, back to a canonical text and to the 19th-century white women's struggle with identity. This discursive move, I would suggest, forecloses prematurely Miller's very interesting critique of Barthes and of the position of privileged interest he represents.

As a composite of large and small choices, none of them wholly free but none— as I think Miller herself is intent on arguing—wholly beyond the reach of the subject-as-agent—Miller's critical practice itself poses, for me, a question similar to the one that Jacqueline Rose formulates with regard to Kristeva: how does one participate in an effort to effect a political transformation when the terms of that transformation are given by the very order that a revolutionary practice seeks to change? How, to put it another way, does the modern western intellectual persist in anything that might be called a belief in "radical" change in the light of those sophisticated analyses of the individual subject's (logical as well as political) subordination to discursive and cultural *systems* which have been offered by so many important French theorists (not to mention the members of the Frankfurt School) in the last twenty-five years?

The relevance of this very large general question for Miller's specific argument is, I think, that by declining to explore—or, more feasibly, perhaps, at least to make explicit the problematic existence of—any *relation* between the final section of her essay, "Subject to Change," and the issues about the "geopolitics of a poetics of gender" raised in the earlier section on Rich's encounter with Latin American women writers, Miller implicitly perpetuates a version of the ideological dualism which, in other discursive forms, clearly serves the interests of those currently devising U.S. policy in Latin America. This is the division between what happens "inside" this country (domestic news) and what happens "outside" its (official) geographical borders. Traces of such an ideological division appear, I think, at the crucial moment in Miller's essay when she turns "back" from the narrative of Rich in Latin America to France, the U.S., Barthes, and Lucy Snowe. At that point, Miller seems—if I read her rightly—to ally herself with those French feminists whose "subversive" and highly tropological politics consist of an act of self-positioning that remains a "form of negotiation within the dominant social text, and ultimately, a local operation." But the implied distinction between a politics that occurs "within" a "dominant social text" and one that occurs "without"—a distinction reiterated when Miller writes in the next paragraph of the feminist political imperative to reappropriate culture "from within its own arenas of dissemination"—offers an oversimplified metaphorical map of the current geopolitical world. As Ariel Dorfman and others have forcefully argued, and in a way that casts a bleak light on Adrienne Rich's notion of an "unalienated" Cuban women's art, the culture of the U.S. and Western Europe no longer has any merely "local" arena of dissemination.[3] One consequence of this argument is that Nicaraguan literacy campaigns as well as those partly funded by the U.S. in various Third World countries are arguably well "*within* the institutions that authorize and regulate most reading and writing in the [U.S.] university" (Miller's emphasis).

What I want to suggest, tentatively, is that a certain oppositional effect—evident in Miller's tactic of contrasting Rich and Barthes and evident also in the citation from Brontë that pits Lucy Snowe against her deadwood (male) French professors—works here to deflect Miller's intellectual energies from lines of inquiry that would follow logically from a feminist position she herself adumbrates in the section of her essay that broods on Rich's "vision of a global context for women's writing." What I find myself wishing, then—and of course it's always easier to

imagine new shapes for others' arguments than to formulate one's own—is that
Miller had pursued further the line of inquiry which she marks, among other
ways, by quoting approvingly one of the voices most critical of the ethnocentrism
of much liberal American feminist criticism. Gayatri Spivak, as Miller quotes her,
sees the " 'sexual differential' " as inhabiting "*every* voice," albeit differently.

Spivak's comment, which comes from her response to a set of papers, including
one by Julia Kristeva, originally presented at a *Critical Inquiry* conference on "The
Politics of Interpretation," can serve as a key to what I take to be the major
point of difference between Miller and Rose, namely that Rose, following Kristeva,
tracking her as it were with great rigor and sympathy, is more consistently and
deeply reluctant than Miller is to accept the idea that there *are* phenomena we
can name generally as "women" or as "female subjectivity" or even as the irreducible historical "fact" of the "female body." "The belief that 'one is a woman'
is almost as absurd and obscurantist as the belief that 'one is a man,' " Kristeva
said in an interview in 1974.[4] Rose's paper, especially if it is read in conjunction
with her subtly nuanced introduction to the volume entitled *Feminine Sexuality:
Jacques Lacan and the "école freudienne,"* which she co-edited with Juliet Mitchell,
provides an important context for understanding what Kristeva could possibly
mean by such a statement (one that is guaranteed to raise most American women's
hackles when it's quoted out of context).

It is not my aim here to discuss Kristeva's theories or Lacan's; to do that would
take a labor of interpretation as patient and long as Rose's paper itself. What I
do want to query, as I did with Miller's paper, are aspects of the form and
structure of Rose's argumentation, in particular her choice—and again, it is not
a wholly free one—to cast her essay as an interpretation of one French woman
writer's historical oscillations of critical position and to present her work as
important because it is "poised on that interface of politics/psychoanalysis/fem-
inism." Let me consider that latter formulation first; it raises questions about how
we construe the uneasy *relations* among a set of heterogeneous terms.

The brilliance of Rose's explication of Kristeva is that it continually invites us
to rethink the relation between politics, psychoanalysis, and feminism. But finally,
it seems to me, Rose's style of writing privileges the middle of these terms,
psychoanalysis, not in a simple sense of making it a synthesizing or dialectically
sublating term, but rather in the sense of suggesting that psychoanalysis, as a
mode of rigorous interpretation, exerts an ethically and epistemologically valuable
checking power over the tendency toward illusion in feminist and marxist collective
movements. The oblique privileging of psychoanalytic insight and method appears,
I would suggest, as an effect of Rose's discourse, which repeatedly portrays
Kristeva—the woman who is willing to use of herself the phrase "being a
psychoanalyst" but not the phrase "being a woman" or "being a feminist" or
"being a marxist"—as a figure seeking a difficult balance between two inadequate
alternatives. The psychoanalytic movement, Rose writes, "found itself hedged in

on both sides: by an appeal back and away from questions of sexuality to the politics of a purely class opposition . . . or else by a call from off the very edge of language. . . . Kristeva herself has said over and over again that her own aim is to avoid both of these alternatives: no absolution of the 'thetic' which then gets erected as a theological law, but no denial of the 'thetic' which brings with it the fantasy of 'an irrationalism in pieces.' " Or consider a later formulation from Rose's paper: "For Kristeva *ethics* has nothing whatsoever to do with *duty* or the idea that women should people the race. No ethics *without* maternity, but not mothering as ethical *duty* or *role*. . . . Ethics plus (as) negativity describes a subjective position which avoids conformity (the first without the second) and esotericism or marginality (the second without the first), capturing alternatives which have historically presented themselves to feminism: between an equality which risks absorption into the law, and an absolute difference which can only defy it."

These are examples of a style that implicitly but with great rhetorical authority presents psychoanalysis as a negative knowledge which resists illusion. And even though Rose seeks, in this paper, to make the bar between feminism and psychoanalysis more permeable—in part via a critique of those moments in Kristeva's work where she crosses a conceptual line and falls into problematic dualisms (goes "over to the other side, dredging up archaic images of the mother"), I wonder if Rose herself, constrained by a certain disciplinary investment in psychoanalysis, doesn't offer, in this paper, a premature check on our understanding of what the third term in her triad—politics—might mean for participants in this audience (or readers of this book), most of whom are students or teachers in academic institutions, or for Rose herself, as a teacher and as an interpreter of psychoanalysis. When she says that "there can be no direct politicization of the unconscious since this is to confuse political and psychic resistance," I would ask her to go a step further and discuss whether or not there can be, and if so by what means and for what ends, an *indirect* politicization of the unconscious? This would seem a crucial question for feminists today and indeed for anyone concerned with recent theoretical efforts, by Louis Althusser, Annette Kuhn, AnnMarie Wolpe and others, to define ideology as entailing not the "false consciousness" of classic marxist doctrine but instead something more like the system of the "imaginary" as Lacan describes it.[5] Ideology is surely a notion that permeates the bar which Rose implicitly erects, following Kristeva, when with a pessimistic eloquence worthy of Freud Rose concludes by writing that Kristeva's "work gives us the measure of the difficulties when politics tries to open itself up to the ravages of the unconscious mind." Is there, however, nothing to be done but measure and come to a fuller appreciation of such difficulties, important as it is to acknowledge them? It seems significant that Rose herself has chosen to present, at this conference, a paper which challenges North American feminists (who have been criticized by Juliet Mitchell for their tendency to assume a too easy malleability of the human mind) to confront a figure who is difficult not only because of her theories of human identity but also because of her reluctance to call herself a feminist—to perform an act of self-identification which would mark her as a member of some sort of collective enterprise. Kristeva herself acknowledges the importance of strategic naming, but she does so in a way that separates, too easily, I think, the realm of political action from the "deeper" one of theoretical interpretation. Let me quote once more from the 1974 interview cited earlier, but this time I shall go farther in the text:

> The belief that "one is a woman" is almost as absurd and obscurantist as the belief that "one is a man." I say "almost" because there are still many goals which women can achieve: freedom of abortion and contraception, day-care centers for children, equality on the job, etc. Therefore, we must use "we are women" as an advertisement or slogan for our demands. On a deeper level, however, a woman cannot "be"; it is something which does not even belong in the order of being. (p. 137)

Rose doesn't cite this passage (she is, to be fair, concerned with a later stage in Kristeva's career); and I don't think she would construe the break between political action and intellectual work quite the way Kristeva does in this interview. Nonetheless, I wonder if Rose's argument, by its implicit advocacy of psychoanalysis as a mode of knowledge and an ethics, doesn't simply bypass the question Kristeva's remark might usefully prompt, that is, what is the relation between collective political action of any kind and the model of work provided by psychoanalysis—especially if one thinks of it not just as a body of texts but as an institutional practice? As a practice, it entails two persons struggling alone in a room with and against each other (and with and against their own and the other's unconscious) toward that transformation which Kristeva calls the cure. Rose's paper itself is a rather striking textual analogue for the psychoanalyst's labor: she struggles in this paper with and against Kristeva's writing in an interpretive scenario that raises all sorts of fascinating questions about the (female) interpreter's identification with her (female) subject.

What I would suggest in conclusion is that both Nancy Miller and Jacqueline Rose illustrate modes of interpretation that are brilliant and provocative but also problematically marked by their respective institutional positions and psychic investments therein—by what we might therefore term *professional ideologies*. Symptomatic of that ideological marking, I would contend, is the fact that both of these papers point approvingly toward a theoretical move that they don't quite make in their discursive practice. This is the move Miller describes as a necessary one for male theorists who have not, she argues, sufficiently questioned "the grounds on which they stand . . . their own difference from the universal, from the institution which houses them, and from which they speak." I agree with this point and I agree also with the argument she powerfully pursues through her analysis of Brontë's *Villette*: the grounds upon which (white) educated men have historically stood are very different and as a rule much less shaky than those upon which (white) educated women have stood. I would nonetheless argue that we who occupy female subject positions in the U.S. today, and who also call ourselves feminists, need to question *our* grounds, and our (relatively) protected economic positions within certain institutions, no less rigorously than our male (like us mostly white and middle class) colleagues need to do. And I would apply this injunction as much to my own performance here as to my colleagues' essays.

To what extent have I skewed and cut short my own lines of inquiry because of institutional pressures and investments I cannot wholly grasp, including the pressures of decorum exerted by the conference situation itself (and by the status of a "commentator" positioned as such in a published volume)? Have I not shrugged off the main challenge of this session by deciding to focus my remarks and analytic energies, such as they are, on the texts of my fellow interpreters rather than on one (or more) of the questions raised by the conference organizers, a question that is very hard for a literary critic to answer performatively—in practice— though she may well say yes to it in theory? The question is, "Are feminist strategies of reading written and visual texts transferable to the study of such things as social and political institutions [among them, I would add, our own universities]?"* Each of us in this session has gestured toward this question without, I think, doing very much to answer it. Perhaps it cannot usefully be answered as a general question anyway, but needs to be rephrased with reference to concrete instances, both historical and putative, of such a transfer. In the process of "transferring" interpretive methods from one object of study to another, of course, the object will inevitably be transformed too. It is clear, for instance, that the movement known as the "new historicism," which originated among Renaissance scholars trained primarily in literature, attempts to transfer interpretive methods from texts of high culture such as Spenser's *Faerie Queene* to various phenomena, among them the institution of the Tudor monarchy, conceived as "social texts." But even that phrase suggests that disciplinary ideologies may be skewing the interpretation of social institutions: what aspects of the Tudor monarchy or State might elude the (metaphorical) category of "text" altogether!

I am arguing here, in the hortatory and cautionary mode characteristic of persons recommending to others something they have not done properly themselves, an interpretive practice that would be constantly on the lookout for the biases and indeed the lacunae generated by what I have called "professional ideologies." In advocating a stance of self- and as one might call it, "caste"-critical vigilance, I am joining Nancy Miller and Jacqueline Rose in arguing for a "retrieval" of the theoretical category of the subject in academic feminist critical practice; I

---

*One of the questions posed to the "interpretation" panel at the 1985 conference. (ed. note).

am also arguing that the retrieval needs to include, in theory and in practice, the difficult notion of the subject who is inevitably "interpellated" (Althusser's phrase) by ideologies larger and more powerful than the individual consciousness but who is at the same time capable of a certain political *agency*. This concept of agency, invoked also by Nancy Miller, is not synonymous with traditional liberal notions of individual consciousness or self-determination. Among other differentiating factors is one which the literary critics in this session including myself have repeatedly implied, often by the term "feminism," but have not yet named in a way that would give our title term "politics" as much force as one might wish.

Sexual Difference and Indifference

4

Dreaming Dissymmetry: Barthes, Foucault, and Sexual Difference

Naomi Schor

> ... the risk of essence may have to be taken.
> —Stephen Heath, "Difference"

On the very first page of the important preface to *Powers of Desire: The Politics of Sexuality,* a bulky 1983 anthology bringing together some of the most significant recent texts on feminism and the discourses of sexuality, the three editors pay hom(m)age—or is it femmage—to Michel Foucault, historian of sexuality. Briefly summarizing Foucault's paradoxical reading of so-called sexual liberation as in fact a further turn of the screw of repression or oppression, the editors praise Foucault for his, "subtle rendering of the general argument that sex and capitalism have gone hand-in-hand too long for sex to be interpreted at face value as a radical force."[1] On the very next page, however, Foucault is summarily dismissed as just another purveyor of "the obsessive male sexual discourse that runs through the centuries from St. Augustine to Philip Roth."[2] The editors point out that if for men who have regulated the discourse of sexuality throughout the history of Western civilization, silence is an option, for women whose relationship to sex has traditionally been aphasic, "it is too soon ... for silence."[3] Setting aside for the moment the question of Foucault's phallogocentrism, of the inscription of his discourse on sexuality in the order of male discursive practices, I want to make another point. The mention of Foucault at the very beginning of this lengthy preface is striking in two ways: it is the only mention both of a *French* and a *male* theoretician in this otherwise indigenous, not to say ethnocentric overview of the burgeoning field of feminist discourse on sexuality. One could imagine a homologous anthology which would represent the French point of view and while I will not speculate here on its table of contents, I think it is safe to assume that though most likely equally ethnocentric, it would be less gynocentric, because as historians of French Feminisms have often pointed out, in France recent feminist thought has always functioned in dialogue with the reigning male *maîtres à penser,* notably Lacan and Derrida. One figure is almost never mentioned in this context and that is Roland Barthes. And yet, I will want to argue here that it is perhaps in Barthes, who was in his own words a sort of "echo chamber"[4] of contemporary French thought, that we can most easily grasp the dominant male discourse on sexuality in post-structuralist France, what I will call the *discourse of in-difference* or of *pure difference,* for they are in fact one and the same.

Barthes's major rhetorical strategy is seduction and many feminists—there are some notable exceptions—[5] have succumbed without much resistance to his subtle persuasion. Nor is this seduction totally misguided for there is much in Barthes that speaks to some of the central preoccupations of French neo-feminisms. Most seductive, most resonant has been the later Barthes's valorization of the body and its pleasures, his insistence that one must write the body, that writing must render the very grain of the voice, that most intimate and idiosyncratic corporeal imprint. Then there is also Barthes's valorization of jouissance, the most intense form of sexual pleasure which French women writers and theorists have in the wake of Lacan claimed for the feminine.[6] There is another more subtle reason why so many feminists have felt a special sympathy for Barthes: even at his most doctrinaire, Barthes's voice is never strident; it is a voice whose grain reveals vulnerability and not an obsession with force and penetration. Rejecting the violence of "arrogance," Barthes speaks from the margin, aligning himself with the excluded of the bourgeois social order, with all those who resist ordering. There are, however, a growing number of signs that in the ongoing process of dismantling the master discourses of the past twenty years feminists are beginning to resist the seductions of Barthes's texts and to examine the ways in which these seductive texts participate nonetheless in a masculine discourse on sexuality, which is not to say, of course, that women, indeed feminists do not also practice this discourse, for they do. In what follows I propose to answer the question of the feminist critique of and complicity with what I take to be one of the dominant discourses on sexuality by undertaking to read from a feminist perspective some texts first by Barthes and then by Michel Foucault, with particular emphasis on his more recent work, notably the second and third volumes of his *History of Sexuality.*

In a fragment of *Roland Barthes by Roland Barthes* entitled "*Pluriel, différence, conflit*—Plural, difference, conflict," speaking of himself in the third person, Barthes writes:

He often resorts to a kind of philosophy vaguely labeled *pluralism.*

Who knows if this insistence on the plural is not a way of denying sexual duality? The opposition of the sexes must not be a law of Nature; therefore, the confrontations and paradigms must be dissolved, both the meanings and the sexes must be pluralized. . . . (p. 69)

Denied sexual difference shades into sexual indifference and, following the same slippery path, into a paradoxical reinscription of the very differences the strategy was designed to denaturalize. This sequence of events is traced out in a recent review article on Barthes's *A Lover's Discourse (Fragments d'un discours amoureux)* by Stephen Heath who writes: "The subject of *Fragments,* of its discourse on love, is unisex, an indifference, only a 'lover' (the scenes permutate 'he' and 'she', hetero and homosexual love, marking as little as possible the differences of sexes." Heath is quick to point out the dangers inherent in this sort of erasure of the inflections of gender, what we might call the *effet pervers* or perverse effect of Barthes's sexually unmarked erotics: the return of a "certain myth of the 'feminine'," as when Barthes writes: "the man who waits and suffers from it is miraculously feminized," and, further, "the future will belong to the subjects *in whom there is something feminine.*" Heath comments: "To envisage a future that will belong 'to the subjects in whom there is something feminine' might be heard on the one hand as the projection of a new order, beyond the phallic (. . .), on the other as a derivation from the existing order, a repetition of its image and essentialization and alibi, its perspective of 'Woman.' "[7] Jane Gallop, on the other hand, speculates a propos of Barthes's *The Pleasure of the Text,* that "the wish to escape sexual difference might be but another mode of denying women."[8] To decide whether or not Barthes's discourse of indifferentiation ends up re-essentializing woman and/or denying her specificity altogether I want to study in some detail a recurrent strategy Barthes deploys when confronted with the question of difference, a synecdoche for femininity since in Western conceptual systems the feminine is always defined as a *difference from* a masculine norm. It is the recurrence of this strategy or move that interests me, for on this matter there is no gap between Barthes's pre-structuralist, high structuralist, and post-structuralist discourse. Redundancy, according to Barthes, does not always ensure communication; on the contrary, as he notes in the fragment of *Roland Barthes* entitled "Les idées méconnues—Misunderstood Ideas," the recurrence of an idea from one book to the other virtually guarantees its incomprehension: "it is *precisely* where I dare encourage myself to the point of repeating myself that the reader 'drops' me" (p. 103).

I would like to begin with perhaps the most famous example of Barthes's displacement of sexual difference. It is located in *S/Z,* Barthes's brilliant and highly influential analysis of a bizarre tale by Balzac which tells of the ill-starred love of the sculptor Sarrasine for la Zambinella, a Roman castrato whom Sarrasine willfully persists in mistaking for a woman despite the many early warnings he receives. Barthes's choice of this formerly obscure tale by Balzac seems motivated in part by a desire to dramatize the dangers of essentialism—"Barthes," according to John Sturrock, "began . . . as an enemy of essentialism and he has remained one"[9]— and in late Western culture those dangers can best be dramatized by de-essentializing woman, woman as cultural construct, universal woman as opposed to women as historical subjects, Woman with a capital W. And no text could better serve to dramatize the dangers of essentializing woman than *Sarrasine*, for it is precisely Sarrasine's blind reliance on the conventional signs of femininity that lead to his death; essentialism in the case of Sarrasine is fatal.[10] In order to de-essentialize "woman," Barthes enlists a familiar strategy: what Heath first termed displacement, Barthes's general strategy for shaking up the "habits of intelligibility" of the doxa.[11] Noting that the female characters of the novella are split by a difference internal to femininity, Barthes writes:

> ... sexual classification is not the right one. Another pertinence must be found. It is Mme Lanty who reveals the proper structure: in opposition to her (passive) daughter, Mme de Lanty is totally active: she dominates time (defying the inroads of age); she radiates (radiation is action at a distance, the highest form of power); bestowing praises, making comparisons, instituting the language in relation to which man can recognize himself, she is the primal Authority ... In short, the precursor of Sappho who so terrifies Sarrasine, Mme de Lanty is the castrating woman, endowed with all the hallucinatory attributes of the Father: power, fascination, instituting authority, terror, power to castrate. Thus, the symbolic field is not that of the biological sexes; it is that of castration: of *castrating/castrated, active/passive*. It is in this field, and not in that of the biological sexes, that the characters in the story are pertinently distributed.[12]

At first glance there is much here that is of use to feminist theory. What Barthes does here in exemplary fashion is to de-naturalize difference, stressing what Kaja Silverman has called the "disequivalence between sexual and symbolic differentiation in Balzac's tale,"[13] uncoupling man and activity, woman and passivity. If the characters in *Sarrasine* cannot be usefully classified according to their biological sexes it is because that classification relies on the double equation: masculine = active, feminine = passive which has at least since Aristotle fixed woman in the inferior position in the sexual hierarchy. Feminists have long fought to break down the assignation of fixed sexual roles to biological men and women and claimed for women but also for men the possibility of oscillating between activity and passivity, and to that extent Barthes's substitution of the active/passive for the male/female paradigm can be seen as beneficial. However, if one takes a closer look at what is going on in this passage we note the following: no change has really been effected in the representation of woman, since Mme de Lanty does not cease to be classified as a woman, rather she has been reclassified as that most fearsome of female monsters: the castrating woman, the phallic mother with all her terrifying attributes of super-power. What Barthes calls the women's camp has now become that of "active castration," a questionable reversal: first because it lends credence to a phantasmatic construct of maternal super-power, second because it is *merely* a reversal, which leaves standing what Barthes was to call some years later the "binary prison" (*R. B.*, p. 133) of sexual classification.[14]

In *S/Z* Barthes seeks to de-biologize difference by substituting the paradigm castrating/castrated for the paradigm male/female. This suggests that what is really at stake in *S/Z* is sexual difference, but a symbolic rather than an anatomical one. This presumption is quickly dispelled when one turns to an essay Barthes wrote on the same Balzac tale, entitled "Masculine, Feminine, Neutral." In this early version of what was to become *S/Z*, Barthes suggests that the centrality of sexual difference in *Sarrasine* is in fact illusory, a lure: "Its apparent center is sexuality."[15] Because for Balzac—and, of course, for Barthes—the castrato escapes the binary sexual taxonomy into the neutral, Barthes argues that in *Sarrasine* we are in fact outside the symbolic realm of sexuality altogether:

> In reality, and linguistics attests to this fact, the neutral cannot be directly implicated in a sexual structure; in Indo-European languages, the opposition of the masculine and the feminine is less important than that of the animate and the inanimate; indeed it follows from it:
>
> *Animate (Masculine/Feminine)/Inanimate (Neutral).*

If this is so the question in *Sarrasine* is not the transgression of the bar of castration that separates the masculine from the feminine—since they are located on the same side of the bar which divides the animate from the inanimate—rather what Barthes calls a "transgression of objects." Thus the paradigm of sexual difference is canceled by the opposition of life and death.

So far we could speak merely of displacement: the paradigm man/woman is displaced by two other paradigms, in the first instance castrating/castrated, in the other, animate/inanimate. But as I turn to my third and final example of Barthes's strategy of indifferentiation, I want to introduce another term to characterize Barthes's move. Borrowing, however loosely, from Lucretius via Harold Bloom, I want to call Barthes's movement away from sexual difference, a *clinamen* or swerve.[16] I prefer this term to the more common displacement, because displacement implies taking a concept or a word and transporting it over to another conceptual field, thereby creating a new and startling configuration. Whereas displacement denotes a *shift*, the clinamen as I am using it here denotes a *shift away from*; whereas in displacement the two paradigms co-exist, in the Barthesian clinamen one paradigm is literally effaced by the other. But in order to demonstrate that what is at stake here is not a displacement (either single or double), rather a clinamen (however minimal), and further that the clinamen is a swerve away not merely from sexual difference but specifically away from femininity, let us look at my third and final example, which is drawn from *The Fashion System*.

The Fashion System was originally meant to be Barthes's doctoral thesis. It was begun in 1957, completed in 1963, and first published in France in 1967. Its long voyage into print spans roughly Barthes's years as a high structuralist. The book is intended to be, "the structural analysis of women's clothing as currently described by Fashion magazines."[17] Now although *The Fashion System* is essentially an attempt to carry out Saussure's program for a general science of signs by studying the language of fashion, Barthes subsumes the signifiers of fashion to those of language and is concerned here exclusively with fashion in its textual inscription, that is in the captions that gloss the pictures in the glossy magazines. Because as Barthes notes in one of those parentheses where he tucks away some of his more memorable asides, Fashion is a discourse that "deals only with the Woman, for women" (p. 258), one might expect that Barthes would at some point in the book have to deal with woman or at the very least femininity. And that expectation seems to be borne out when we note that one of Barthes's subheadings is precisely "Femininity." Because *The Fashion System* is possibly Barthes's least pleasurable text to read I skip ahead to the section on femininity. It begins on a fairly conventional note, but then comes the clinamen, the moment at which Barthes's paradigm shift becomes an erasure of the very femininity foregrounded in the section title. Fashion, according to Barthes, "understands the opposition between masculine and feminine quite well; reality itself requires that it do so" (p. 257). What distinguishes women's clothes from men's are often details and despite the clear distinction between men's and women's fashions some degree of cross-dressing is permissible, at least for women, for whereas:

> there is a social prohibition against the feminization of men, there is almost none against the masculinization of women: Fashion notably acknowledges the *boyish look*. *Feminine* and *masculine* each have their own rhetorical version; *feminine* can refer to the idea of an emphatic, quintessential woman (. . .); when noted, the *boyish* look itself has more a temporal than a sexual value: it is the complementary sign of an ideal age, which assumes increasing importance in Fashion literature: the *junior;* structurally, the *junior* is presented as the complex degree of the *feminine/masculine:* it tends toward androgyny; but what is more remarkable in this new term is that it effaces sex to the advantage of age; this is, it seems, a profound process of Fashion: it is age which is important, not sex . . . (pp. 257–258).

Perhaps the best word to describe Barthes's erasure of sex, now to the advantage of the neutral, now to the advantage of age is Foucault's term "desexualization." Foucault's use of the word "desexualization" occurs, perhaps not coincidentally, in his response to an interviewer's question regarding the women's and homosexuals' liberation movements. Foucault says:

> The real strength of the women's liberation movements is not that of having laid

claim to the specificity of their sexuality and the rights pertaining to it, but that they have actually departed from the discourse conducted within the apparatuses of sexuality. These movements do indeed emerge in the nineteenth century as demands for sexual specificity. What has the outcome been? Ultimately, a veritable movement of de-sexualization, a displacement effected in relation to the sexual centering of the problem, formulating the demand for forms of culture, discourse, language, and so on, which are no longer part of that rigid assignation and pinning-down to their sex which they had initially in some sense been politically obliged to accept in order to make themselves heard.[18]

In both Barthes and Foucault the move toward desexualization takes the form of a fascination with limit-cases of difference: to Barthes's *Sarrasine* corresponds Foucault's *Herculine Barbin*. The volume whose English edition bears the mock-libertine title, *Herculine Barbin: Being the Recently Discovered Memoirs of a Nineteenth-Century French Hermaphrodite,* is made up of an introduction by Foucault, the memoirs of Herculine, excerpts from the medico-legal texts on the case, and finally a fictionalized version of the story by the German psychiatrist Oscar Panizza. Herculine Barbin was born in 1838 in Vendée. She was educated in Catholic women's schools, first a convent then a normal school where she obtained her teaching certificate. Herculine's first post as a schoolmistress was with a widow with three daughters. During the three years Herculine spent there she and one of the daughters became lovers. Found out by a doctor who examined her, Herculine decided to request an official change of her civil status. In 1860, when Herculine was 22 years old, she was officially reclassified as being of the male sex, and changed her name to Abel. Alone, miserable, and destitute Abel committed suicide in Paris in February 1868, leaving his memoirs and body to posterity. For Foucault what is of interest in this sad story is the new relationship between desire and the law that was being put into place at the very moment when Herculine's story was unfolding. Whereas in the past hermaphrodites were free to choose their sex, in the eighteenth and nineteenth centuries a new order of discourse decreed that all hermaphrodites were "pseudo-hermaphrodites," that is: beneath the ambiguity of their anatomy lay concealed a single "true" sex, whose discovery it was the task of the medical profession to carry out. Accordingly, Foucault reads the memoirs of Herculine as utopianism masquerading as nostalgia. He contends that the memoirs reveal a longing for the "happy limbo of a non-identity."[19] Indeterminacy is bliss; if only Herculine/Abel had been able to continue indefinitely in her/his sexual in-between state, she/he might have lived happily ever after.[20] In his fragment "Active/passive" Barthes describes the utopia of indeterminacy this way: "once the alternative is rejected (once the paradigm is blurred) utopia begins: meaning and sex become the object of a free play, at the heart of which the (polysemant) forms and (sensual) practices, liberated from the binary prison, will achieve a state of infinite expansion. Thus may be born a Gongorian text and a happy sexuality" (*R. B.,* p. 133).

The memoirs of Herculine Barbin first appeared in 1978 when Foucault was still committed to pursuing the *History of Sexuality* inaugurated in 1976 in its originally announced form. The five volumes Foucault projected writing suggested that the entire project would be ruled by the dream of escaping from what he termed the "austere" binarisms of the sexual order. However, in the course of working on his History, as he explains in the preface to the first volume of what we might call the new *History of Sexuality,* he found himself obliged to revise completely his original plan. He realized that in order to carry out his project it was necessary to study the genealogy of man as subject of and to desire.

> . . . in order to understand how the modern individual could experience himself as a subject of a "sexuality," it was essential first to determine how, for centuries, Western man had been brought to recognize himself as a subject of desire.[21]

To do this he would have to return to the classical foundations of Western civilization, to the ethics of sex elaborated by the philosophers of Ancient Greece and Imperial Rome. The archeological move backward to the origin of Western sexual discourse on sexuality provides a much needed perspective on the discourse of sexuality. Sexuality, it will be remembered, is the term Foucault reserves for the discourse on sex elaborated by the bourgeoisie during the nineteenth century in order to codify the respective and complementary places of men and women in society. Now precisely because sexuality is a discourse with fairly precise spatio-temporal boundaries, the question becomes what came before. In his latest books Foucault sketches out a more comprehensive periodization than that proposed in *The Will to Power,* where Church doctrine had constituted his historical horizon. In the West, man's relationship to his own desire has according to Foucault's Hegelian design passed through three phases: 1) the *aphrodisia,* which is to say the classical discourse on sexual ethics: 2) the "flesh," that is the Christian discourse on sexuality; and, finally, the very recent 3) sexuality in its restricted Foucauldian sense. Foucault's last two books explore in depth only one of these stages, the first, but look ahead to the others. Three diverse but related aspects of Foucault's curiously restrained and limpid final works—so different in tone from the feisty polemics of *The Will to Power*—seem to me of particular interest to feminist analyses of sexuality: first, the scrupulous attention Foucault pays to the gender of the enunciating subject; second, the subtle way in which he decenters the "woman question"; and third and finally, the pride of place he accords a model of heterosexual relations based on reciprocity and mutual respect.

From the outset Foucault makes clear that the *aphrodisia* was a discourse which circulated only among men: "It was an ethics for men: an ethics thought, written, and taught by men, and addressed to men—to free man, obviously" (p. 22). Given this remarkable statement it becomes difficult to maintain as do the authors of *Powers of Desire* that Foucault participates in the obsessive male discourse on sexuality. Or rather, if he does so, he does so in his last works with an intense awareness of the phallocentrism of that discourse; though Foucault can never write from the place of enunciation of a woman—nor does he attempt to—he makes it very clear that he is not complicitous with the "hommosexual" (Lacan and Irigaray) communication circuit he so insistently lays bare. Because of the eminence of Foucault's position on the intellectual scene, his categorical assertion of woman's exclusion from the aphrodisia, as both sender and receiver, encoder and decoder, matters; that Greco-Roman civilization excluded woman, as well as other marginal members of society (slaves, young boys) from access to the symbolic codes will surely come as no surprise to students of classical antiquity, but that it is Michel Foucault who is insisting on this exclusion will surprise feminists. What Foucault does here is to recognize as he never had before in his work the centrality of gender—a question which simply does not arise in *The Will to Power.* Woman as object of discourse and subject of history is, of course, spectacularly in evidence in *The Will to Power,* where Foucault argues that one of the key strategies deployed by the power-knowledge system to ground its tentacular investment of the human body is what he calls the "hysterization" of the female body: a three-step operation involving first a reduction of woman to her sex, second a pathologization of that sex, third a subordination of the female body to the reproductive imperative. But the question of gender cannot be said to inform Foucault's project. In *The Will to Power* we are introduced to a History of Sexuality wherein the notion that the history of sexuality might be different if written by women is never entertained; a single universal history is presumed to cover both sexes, as though the History and, more important, the Historian of sexuality himself had no sex.

Throughout Foucault's presentation of the aphrodisia he continues to insist on their phallocentrism though, significantly, the word is conspicuously absent from the text. Thus he observes that temperance, that discipline of self mastery which ensures the exercise of one's freedom, is a masculine virtue par excellence. This does not mean that women are not enjoined to practice this virtue, but: "where women were concerned, this virtue was always referred in some way to virility" (p. 83). In other words temperance, like Freudian libido, is always masculine. Similarly, Foucault emphasizes the ways in which what he calls the "ejaculatory schema" of the sexual act is in the teachings of a Hippocrates simply transferred from male sexuality onto the female: in this old dream of symmetry—which survives well into the pornographic texts of a Sade or a Cleland—the two are assumed to be isomorphic. "This 'ejaculatory schema,' through which sexual activity as a whole—and in both sexes—was always perceived, shows unmistakably the near-exclusive domination of the virile model." However even within the isomorphism of masculine and feminine sexual activity, a hierarchy is at work: "The female act was not exactly the complement of the male act; it was more in the nature of a duplicate, but in the form of an weakened version" (p. 129). Female sexuality in this schema has no specificity other than its distance from the male norm.

In Freud the valorization of the same does not preclude, indeed requires the centrality of the Other; phallocentrism revolves around the riddle of femininity. What Foucault reveals is that in Greco-Roman moral discourse—mythology tells another story—phallocentrism is not also a gynocentrism; what is problematic and intellectually challenging for classical thinkers is the pederastic relationship to boys, that is the erotic relationship between two free men separated only by an age difference; what is problematic in the conceptual framework of the aphro-disia is not female passivity, which is viewed as so natural as to be non-problematic, but masculine passivity, the feminization of man. The line of demarcation passes here not so much between men and women, or even between homosexuals and heterosexuals, but between active and passive men, with the result that the opposition between men and women and the concomitant obsessive focus on the enigma of femininity is decentered, even as the myth of a happy pederasty is exploded:

> Later, in European culture, girls or married women, with their behavior, their beauty, and their feelings, were to become themes of special concern; a new art of courting them, a literature that was basically romantic in form, an exacting morality that was attentive to the integrity of their bodies and the solidity of their matrimonial commitment—all this would draw curiosity and desires around them. No matter what inferior position may have been reserved for them in the family or in society, there would be an accentuation, a valorization, of the "problem" of women. Their nature, their conduct, the feelings they inspired or experienced, the permitted or forbidden relationship that one might have with them were to become themes of reflection, knowledge, analysis, and prescription. It seems clear, on the other hand, that in classical Greece the problematization was more active in regard to boys, maintaining an intense moral concern around their fragile beauty, their corporal honor, their ethical judgment and the training it required. (pp. 213–214)

But then again, the aphrodisia is not a monolithic discourse; in the course of its passage from Greece to Rome a subtle and gradual shift takes place and eventually the fascination with boys is displaced by a preoccupation with woman. In the section of Le souci de soi, entitled "Woman," woman assumes a new centrality in the context of a reconceptualization of marriage. "The intensification of the concern with the self goes hand in hand here with the valorization of the other."[22] And with this dawning recognition of alterity what I will call conjugal man is born. The model of conjugal relations posited by the Stoics is radically opposed to the model that prevailed in Athens; if under both regimes woman has no existence outside of the marital couple, under this new ethos, the couple becomes a privileged social unit, bound together by mutual respect and obligations. Fidelity is no longer woman's natural destiny, men too are held to the same standard. Reciprocity replaces domination. And heterosexual married love displaces ped-erastic love as the valorized model of eroticism and privileged locus of problem-atization. This does not mean, of course, that homosexual love ceases to be practiced or permitted in Imperial Rome, merely that the love for boys no longer is problematized. Foucault's tone throughout these two books is as already noted remarkably dispassionate; he exposes the interlocking discourses on pederasty and conjugality without ever suggesting the superiority of the one to the other, without ever taking a clear position in regard to them: the texts are, as it were, allowed to speak for themselves, presentation pre-empts representation. And yet despite the impersonality of the voice, or perhaps because of it, a system of values is established, and a model of human sexual relations which is both heterosexual and conjugal is promoted, precisely because it recognizes the alterity of woman.

There are from a feminist perspective at least two problems with Foucault's eerily timely reconstruction of the Stoic ethics of sexuality—an ethics of sexual austerity fueled by a preoccupation with what we might call anachronistically physical fitness: the woman who becomes in Foucault's words, "the other par excellence" is "the wife-woman [la femme-épouse]" (p. 192) and, furthermore, alterity is, of course, not specificity. And therein lies the clearest and most persistent dissymmetry between men and women in feminism today: whereas many theo-reticians, some of them women, have eagerly seized upon and used the tools of deconstruction to dismantle metaphysical woman, no feminist theoretician *who is not also a woman* has ever fully espoused the claims to a feminine specificity, an irreducible difference. Even the most enlightened among the male feminists con-done claims to female specificity *only* as a temporary tactical necessity for pressing political claims; in the promised utopia of sexual indifferentiation and multiple singularities, they assure us, there will no longer be any place or need for sexual difference, it will simply wither away. At the risk of being a wallflower at the carnival of plural sexualities, I would ask: what is to say that the discourse of sexual indifference/pure difference is not the last or (less triumphantly) the latest ruse of phallocentrism? If one lends an ear to what some of the most sophisticated feminist theoreticians are writing these days, the resistance to the hegemony of the discourse of indifference is powerful and growing. That difference does have a future is forcefully argued by Myra Jehlen who, taking note of the emergence of a politics of difference in recent American feminist writings, comments:

> In the evolution of feminist analysis . . . this about-face hardly signifies that women have, typically, changed their minds. On the contrary, it reflects a deeper analysis. In the first place the claim of difference criticizes the content of the male universal norm. But beyond this, it represents a new understanding that if the other is to

live, it will have to live as other, lest the achievement of integration be crowned with the fatal irony of disappearance through absorption.[23]

A chiasmus best figures the cross-purposes of those who currently maintain, respectively, masculine and feminine positions on difference: whereas those who adopt the masculine position press for an end to sexual difference and only grudgingly acknowledge claims for feminine specificity, those who adopt the feminine position concede the strategic efficacy of undoing sexual oppositions and positionalities, all the while pursuing the construction of difference. The most active site of the feminine resistance to the discourse of indifference is a certain insistence on doubling, which may well be the feminine mode of subverting the unitary subject: mimeticism (Irigaray and Kolodny), the double and even double double identification of the female film spectator (Mulvey, Doane, de Lauretis), women's writing as palimpsest (Gilbert and Gubar), female fetishism (Kofman, Berg, Schor), the foregrounding of the "other woman" (Gallop), the elaboration of a "doubled strategy" of deconstruction and construction (Martin) are some of the varied forms this insistence on doubling has taken and is taking.[24] Whether as producers or consumers of cultural artifacts and theories the claim in all these texts is that women occupy in modern Western culture a *specific liminal cultural position* which is through a tangled skein of mediations somehow connected to their anatomical difference, to their femaleness. Women are bilingual, bifocal, bitextual. Now "perhaps," as Simone de Beauvoir writes in The Second Sex, "these differences are superficial, perhaps they are destined to disappear. What is certain is that right now they do most obviously exist."[25] Or as Hélène Cixous writes in *La jeune née,* after having imagined a· utopia of multiple differences not unlike those of her male contemporaries, Barthes and Foucault: "But we are still floundering about—with certain exceptions—in the Old order."[26] Doubling holds open *for now* a space that has only begun to be explored: the pitch black continent of what patriarchal culture has consistently connoted as feminine and hence depreciated. Before tearing down the cultural ghetto where the feminine has been confined and demeaned, we need to map its boundaries and excavate its foundations in order to salvage the usable relics and refuse of patriarchy, for to do so is perhaps the only chance we have to construct a post-deconstructionist society which will not simply reduplicate our own.

5

Is there a Lesbian in this Text?
Derrida, Wittig, and the Politics of the
Three Women

Heather Findlay

Like most modern movements, critical, political, and literary, feminism has been organized by many theorists into stages, "generations," and spaces. In this essay, I wish to address a recent theoretical debate over a particular typology of feminist politics. The discussion will center on philosophical and philosophical-psychoanalytic texts by Jacques Derrida and Elizabeth Berg, with special attention to what I will call the trope of the three women.[1] I will suggest that the three women are differentiated not only by their relation to truth, or their feminist politics, but also by their sexual preferences. By constructing the second woman as a type of lesbian separatist, these texts effectively scapegoat her, and thereby clear the way for the ascension of the third woman. Yet lesbianism is more than just an appendage here—I will also argue that various moments in the rhetoric of deconstruction require heterosexuality as a characteristic of its affirmative heroine, and erase the possibility of a specifically female homosexual practice.

Yet I will not champion the second woman over the third; nor is the aim of my analysis to uncover the real lesbian buried under layers of ideological mystification in Derrida's texts. This all-too-easy personification and consequent admiration is part of the process that raised the third woman to her place of authority in the first place. Instead, I will try to show that the difference played out between the third and second women is analogous to the difference between "the stages that are not stages" of Derrida's theory of deconstruction as outlined in *Positions*. The effect of this analogy between feminine figures, critical operations, and the "stages" of deconstruction is that difference—for my purposes, *lesbian* difference—is yet again contained. In the name of systematizing his previous work, Derrida stresses that heterogeneity, the privileged mode of deconstructive theory, is not to be confused with or inhabited by homogeneity or sameness. The obvious problem occurs when the "hetero-" and the "homo-" of critical practices become the sexualities of the practitioners, and the difference posited by the "homo" finds itself contained and shut out by deconstructive discourse. As is evident, my reading focuses less on the specific claims made by Derrida's and Berg's texts, than on how the processes of theorization and figuration (specifically personification in this case) cause the third and second women, the "have" and the "have not" of feminist deconstruction, to become straight and gay respectively.

Three positional figures of femininity stand at the center of *Spurs*, Jacques Derrida's reading of Nietzsche: the first woman as untruth; the second woman as truth; and the "affirmative," contradictory, dionysiac third woman. Derrida privileges this third woman as the most disruptive of possible "feminine operations"; Elizabeth Berg, one of Derrida's feminist readers, goes a little further and privileges the third woman as the most disruptive *feminist* position. In her essay "The Third Woman," Berg embellishes the distinctions among Derrida's three women, traces their intertextual relationships with writings by Sigmund Freud, Luce Irigaray, and Sarah Kofman, and makes explicit the feminist political ramifications behind each position. In "Choreographies," an interview with Derrida by Christie V. McDonald which also addresses the question of woman as it is presented in *Spurs*, Derrida further elaborates the political potential of the third, affirmative woman.[2] Each of these writings both depict a tripartite typology of femininity and eulogize the third woman over her inferior second. What is at stake here?

The answers lie partly in my own interrogative method. In order to destabilize the hierarchy that Derrida and Berg establish between the third and second women, I must, at first, adopt the critics' techniques: their philosophical and psychoanalytic subjects need political persuasions, their literary figures need bodies, and these bodies need sexualities. In this way, the second woman in particular can gain ascendency—momentarily but with endless ramifications—before some of the more insidious elements of the older sister's power over the younger can be articulated and criticized.

Derrida "politicized" the motif of the third woman in 1976 when, in *Spurs*, he escorted her into a prominent stylistic position in deconstructive writing on the question of "woman."[3] Berg, six years later, dubbed the affirmative woman's movement as "an important step for feminist theory" ("The Third Woman," p. 19). In Derrida's and Berg's view, the third woman's political style is more subversive than the stance of the feminist which to Derrida is "nothing but the operation of a woman who aspires to be like a man" (*Spurs*, pp. 64,65). Her political agenda does not call for a "simple reversal" of phallocentrism as does the second's, and sexual difference is displaced, with no feminists going about "distributing sexual identity cards" ("Choreographies," p. 69). Derrida adds that the third position "presents itself only in the form of the most unforeseeable and most innocent of chances. The most innocent of dances would thwart the *assignation à résidence*, escape those residences under surveillance; the dance changes place and above all changes *places*." Because the third woman does not and cannot choose a single position, Berg argues that she cannot be pinned down, and makes possible

> the penetration of women into the masculine world and the order of the symbolic. If women could be, and are, both active and passive, both masculine and feminine, there is no contradiction between the exigency of participation in masculine activity and the refusal to be assimilated into a masculine mode. ("The Third Woman," p. 13)

This double-gestured praxis is what feminism must learn from the affirmative woman, who resists appropriation and subverts the truth value of castration by living in contradiction. Undecided when it comes to truth, history, castration, and political positions, the third woman also oscillates between a female and male object choice. To Berg, she refuses to resolve the "paradox of bisexuality" (p. 19); and to Derrida, her desire, her style, and her "elytron" "float between the masculine and the feminine."[4]

This bisexuality, however, is limited. A close reading reveals that its undecidability is decidedly "straight"forward. Derrida employs metaphors from various discourses in order to discuss the affirmative woman's relation to truth and nontruth. Her philosophical operations, which Derrida terms her spurs, owe their force to their paradoxical meanings and "bisexual" connotations: at once the spur is the phallus *and* the woman's lack, or the medusa-like threat of castration *and* the fetishistic relief of this threat (see *Spurs*, pp. 36–41). Yet along with the spur's philosophical operations comes a seductive subtext: the spur always seduces in both feminine and masculine poetic garb, with its veils and barbs in constant intercourse. When she is affirmative, such affirmation manifests itself in images of heterosexual flirtation. The spur

> is the oblongi-foliated point (a spur or spar) which derives its apotropaic power from the taut, resistant tissues, webs, sails, and veils which are erected, furled and unfurled around it. (*Spurs*, pp. 40,41)

Is "bisexual writing" heterosexual copulation? Yes and no: it is also female genitalia, Nietzsche's umbrella, his ear, a veiled phallus, a tongue, or a clitoris. Yet it is never lesbian sex, homosexuality, or "feminine operations" between woman and another woman. Moreover, the third woman "affirms herself, in and of herself, in man" ("*Elle ne s'est pas affirmée par l'homme mais s'affirme elle-même, en elle-même et dans le homme*").[5] In other words, when she deconstructs, the third woman does so "in and of herself" but in the end "in man." After the open-ended, opaque introductory (fore)play of meaning, the sentence is sealed with a kiss—between man and woman. Precisely at the moment he *figures* bisexuality as part of a critique of self-presence,[6] Derrida heterosexualizes this figure, and the exclusion of homogeneity carries with it the elision of feminine homosexuality.[7]

When Berg differentiates among her three women by assigning psychoanalytic positions to them, she returns to Freud but omits the sexual orientations that Freud assigns to them. The third woman in Freud's "Female Sexuality" "follows the third, very circuitous path" and arrives at "the final normal feminine attitude, in which she takes her father as her object." Repeating her unconscious love for her father in the rest of her love relations, Freud's third woman is a heterosexual woman. The second woman, on the other hand, has a "masculinity complex" which "can result in a manifestly homosexual object choice."[8] Berg uses psychoanalysis to personify Derrida's feminine operations, and to give them political positions, and this very effort of personification carries with it a re-inscription of Freudian notions of feminine normality: passivity, repression, and heterosexuality. The personification of Berg's second, moreover, suffers under (in Freud's words) "the phantasy of being a man in spite of everything," and has the tendency to become an outright homosexual. Berg's text, in lining up its psychoanalytic typology with Derrida's philosophical one, and then personifying these types, implicitly repeats a normalization that Derrida must perform on *his* affirmative woman, primarily by straightening her out.[9]

As for the second woman, in *Spurs,* in Derrida's philosophical pretexts, and in Berg's article she is "censured, debased and despised" (*Spurs,* pp. 96,97). And as in the figuration of the third woman, part of the second woman's reputation is due to her sexual preference. Unlike the third woman, however, the second woman's reputation is decidedly bad, and her sexuality is arguably deviant. For Berg, "the second woman is also present in the narcissistic woman . . . she is self-sufficient, and her power resides in her very indifference to men, one might say in her utter separation from the masculine world" ("The Third Woman," p. 18). Berg takes the narcissism in her definition from Freud who theorizes that the second avenue for femininity includes the narcissistic retention of clitoral sexuality and—we must remember this although Berg does not—manifest homosexuality.

Politically, then, the second woman resembles the "militant feminist," and in "Choreographies" her effects in the cultural sphere are, to Derrida, "nothing but the operation of a woman who aspires to be like a man" (*Spurs,* p. 65). In the attempt to personify the second woman, Berg and Derrida suggest that she is a lesbian separatist (she is "indifferent to men" and utterly separate from the masculine world) who looks to be, and looks too much like, a man. Worse, she goes about "distributing sexual identity cards" ("Choreographies," p. 69).[10]

The figuration of the second woman as a homosexual continues: Derrida in "Choreographies" aligns what Berg reads as the second woman's political thinking with the dialectic, and points out that the homogeneity of her reactive politics restricts her to repeating phallocentric problematics. "In the same manner," he continues, "phallocentrism and homosexuality can go, so to speak, hand in hand, and I take these terms, whether it is a question of masculine or feminine homosexuality, in a very broad and radical sense" ("Choreographies," p. 72). In this charged passage, deconstruction's critique of a reductive reading of the dialectic (or "homosexual dialectics" as it appears later in the passage) becomes homophobia when the discourse becomes suspicious of this dialectic in the name of "homosexuality . . . in a very broad and radical sense." Note also that phallocentrism and homosexual dialectics go "hand in hand"—a figure which (like the figures in *Spurs*) both personifies these concepts and puts them into a sexual subplot. These are moments when deconstruction takes theoretical operations and turns them into figures; when dialectical negation becomes an invert, and when the figure of the second woman becomes a lesbian caught in "the inversion of negation,"[11] the by-product of such a figuration is, I would argue, homophobia.

Hence, through figuration, a difference within deconstructive operations has become a difference between feminine figures. A similar containment of difference can be found in *Positions,* where Derrida schematizes deconstruction itself. In *Positions,* Derrida divides deconstruction, like femininity in *Spurs,* into "spaces." Like the second and third women, deconstruction's stages are coded as inverted and bi(sexual). Notice the appearance of the invert and the bisexual in this passage dealing with the distinction between deconstructive moments:

> We must also mark the interval between inversion, which brings low what was high, and the irruptive emergence of a new "concept," a concept that can no longer be, and never could be, included in the previous regime. If this interval, this biface or biphase, can be described only in a bifurcated writing.[12]

One stage comes about in the process of "inverted writing," while the addition of the next stage makes deconstruction "bifurcated." Similar to the bisexual third woman in *Spurs,* however, the often sexualized figures that tend to accumulate in deconstructive theory when it theorizes bifurcated writing are heterosexual metaphors. One of the most notorious examples of this is the figure of the hymen. As Gayatri Spivak describes the figure:

> No longer castration (the realization of sexual difference as the model for the difference between signifier and signified) as the origin of signification. Rather *involve* that sexual difference in the "concrete representation" (in the long run these words must be criticized, of course) of the making of meaning: dissemination into the hymen. Into the (n)ever-virgin, (n)ever-violated hymen of interpretation, always supplementing through its fold which is also an opening, is spilled the seed of meaning; a seed that scatters itself abroad rather than inseminates.[13]

The bisexual, bifurcated figures of hymen and dissemination that Spivak and

Derrida "involve" here entail *heterosexual* difference; difference is normalized and contained precisely when the critical operation is both theorized and figured (note Spivak's words "concrete representation"—words she singles out as needing to be critically examined) as a sexual operation. As for the interval of inversion, like the operations of the second woman in deconstructive texts on sexual politics, the systematization of deconstruction reduces it to a stage of secondary importance.

At the moment it homosexualizes and scapegoats "inversion" in deconstruction, the language of *Positions* simultaneously moves deconstruction out of the realm of the "political." Although Derrida argues that deconstruction is not teleological, nor is it a "question of a chronological phase," his figuring of deconstruction as a schema entails such a teleology; moreover, the schematization places the possibility of deconstruction's political effects at the beginning of a teleology, but not at the end. The passage in question reads as follows: Derrida warns that, in the "general strategy of deconstruction," if one ignores inversion (or what is here called "overturning")

> one might proceed too quickly to a *neutralization* that *in practice* would leave the previous field untouched. . . . We know what always have been the practical (particularly *political*) effects of *immediately* jumping beyond oppositions, and of protests in the simple form of *neither* this *nor* that. (*Positions*, p. 41, emphasis Derrida's)

This is the "stage" which Derrida refers to earlier as "inversion." In the above passage, inversion is seen as the operation characteristic of political oppositionism or "protests in the simple form of *neither* this *nor* that," and as necessary politically in order to name, expose, and begin to deconstruct power asymmetry on both the theoretical and "practical (particularly *political*)" levels. However, as Derrida goes on to point out, in order fully to dismantle the field which presents the opposition, "inversion" as such must recede and "bifurcation" must take its place. Significantly, Derrida does *not* present this final operation as having potentially political effects. Unlike inversion, it is not a "practical" necessity. As a result, Derrida effectively neutralizes the political effects of his discourse at the moment his "general strategy of deconstruction" moves beyond inversion.

Crucially, these moves are necessitated by the very theorizing of deconstruction into a "general strategy." *Positions* as a text is very aware of the fact that it is, in Jean-Louis Houdebine's words, "gathering into a 'sheaf' the different directions that your [Derrida's] research had taken . . . the general system of its economy." More than this gathering, summarizing, and thematizing, the moment of *Positions* may require "even announcing, as concerns 'the efficacy of a thematic of *différance*,' the possibility of its *relève*" (*Positions*, p. 39). In other words, the representation of a "thematic of *différance*"—the construction of a deconstructive schema—is also deconstruction's "*relève*" which is both its summary and its relief, or its passage into something else. *Positions,* then, sounds the death knell for that of which it speaks; all of the figures that I've examined arise from the process of deconstruction's *rigor mortis,* or its strict codification into a theory or system. It appears that gays, lesbians, and political radicals are not invited to the funeral, for this *rigor mortis* causes, as I have been arguing, the differences within deconstruction to become differences within a typology of "stages." Together, as a developmental narrative, these "stages" negate homosexuality as a phase, reinscribe heterosexuality as telos, and depoliticize the effects of deconstruction.

Derrida makes it apparent that he sees nothing deconstructive about homosexuality—male or female—in the closing remarks of "Choreographies." He suggests a new "dream" for feminism which aims "beyond the opposition feminine/masculine, beyond bisexuality as well, beyond homosexuality and heterosexuality which come to the same thing." Having collapsed homosexuality into heterosexuality, since they "come to the same thing," he writes,

> Of course, it is not impossible that desire for a sexuality without number can still protect us, like a dream, from an implacable destiny which immures everything for life in the figure 2. And should this merciless closure arrest desire at the wall of opposition, we would struggle in vain: there would never be but two sexes, neither one more nor one less. ("Choreographies," p. 76)

Derrida offers his dream as a theoretical alternative to a heterosexual reality, an "implacable destiny," a "merciless closure" that arrests desire at the wall of the opposition male/female. Yet what if all desire were not arrested in heterosexual opposition? What if female homosexuality were internal to sexuality in general (including heterosexuality) and yet irreducibly different from it? What if lesbian feminists did not "come" to the same thing as heterosexual feminists? The possibility of a lesbian specificity and its implications for the dreams and nightmares of sexuality in general would have to be addressed. Such an address is erased by the text's exclusion of the specificity of lesbianism (homosexuality and heterosexuality come to the same thing) and by the text's vision of sexuality as an implacable struggle between two sexes, woman and man.

In order to demonstrate the construction of the second woman as lesbian, I have had to read her into Derrida's and Berg's texts, and cause her to "act out" in the pages of *Spurs,* "The Third Woman," "Choreographies," and *Positions.* In the process, I intentionally *misread* Derrida in particular; that is, I examine those parts of *Spurs* that the author explicitly warns his readers to ignore. In "Choreographies," Derrida defends his text in these words:

> Some have reacted at times even more perfunctorily, unable to see beyond the end of phallic forms projecting into the text; beginning with style, the spur of the umbrella, they take no account of what I have said about the difference between style and writing or the bisexual complication of those and other forms. ("Choreographies," p. 69)

Derrida asks the reader to look beyond the phallus in *Spurs,* and take comfort in the fact that underlying the projecting, penetrating spur, there exists a fundamental bisexuality. Derrida's prescriptions are interesting in the light of two considerations. First, the readership of "Choreographies" is predominantly feminist. The interviewer Christie V. McDonald is a feminist critic, the subject she chooses to discuss is Derrida's work on "woman" and his ideas on feminism in general, and the text is published in an edition of *Diacritics* dedicated to feminist theory. Hence Derrida's words can be read as exhibiting a certain anxiety over what he imagines might be a feminist critique of *Spurs.*[14] Second, and in the same vein, the author's directives bear a certain similarity to Freud's in "Femininity" (1933) at the moment he attempts to ward off a feminist criticism directed at his lecture:

> For the ladies, whenever some comparison turned out unfavorable to their sex, were able to sputter a suspicion that we, the male analysts, had been unable to overcome certain deeply-rooted prejudices against what was feminine, and that this was being paid for in the partiality of our researches. We, on the other hand, standing on the ground of bisexuality, had no difficulty in avoiding impoliteness. We only had to say, "This doesn't apply to *you.* You're the exception; on this point you're more masculine than feminine."[15]

Derrida, like Freud, falls back on his theory of bisexuality as a type of security against "the ladies" and their imagined feminist reading. Yet if, following Irigaray, we find Freud's theory of bisexuality to be just another tricky play of mirrors in which masculinity reflects itself as its supposed other,[16] where do we find Derrida?

Can homosexuality be deconstructive? The point of my arguments, critical as they might be of deconstruction, is not to say that nothing productive inheres in the intersection of homosexuality and deconstruction,[17] but rather that—sadly enough—recent work in feminism and deconstruction assumes that there is nothing productive about this intersection, to the point of casting homosexuality as deconstruction's other. One writer who comes to this intersection from a new angle, however, is Monique Wittig. In *Le corps lesbien,* for example, we have a text that is supposedly written in "total rupture with masculine culture" (Morrow edition, p. 9); a book of Amazon love poems which sees itself as an utterly separatist document, indifferent to man's desires. While the *guérillères* of Wittig's second novel have "inverted" a phallogocentric state, thrown men off their island, and are living in a separate, lesbian culture, the text of *Le corps lesbien* incorporates strategies which make the lesbian deconstructive—that is, affirmative and supplemental to a simple reversal of a sexual hierarchy.

Wittig inverts the binary opposition of man/woman, but adds another facet to the play of specular opposites: the element of the lesbian. Indeed, Wittig's vision has never been immured in the mirror-like figure 2: in a 1980 article in *Feminist Issues,* Wittig states emphatically that "lesbians are not women," exactly because the signifier "woman" has no meaning except in relation to "man"—hence lesbians are a third sex.[18] I would argue that *Le corps lesbien* is deconstructive and homosexual not only because a lesbian wrote it, or because it is about lesbians, or even because as a text it is deconstructive without foreclosing homosexuality; most significantly, the homosexuality of the text *enables* its deconstructive characteristics. The positing of a third sex, a sex which is not man or woman, is what unsettles even the "inverted" status of the text (Wittig, of course, marks the intrusion of this lesbian subject materially by "marking" the subject pronouns with a bar: "*j/e*" and "*m//écrive*" for example). Perhaps the difference between Derrida's and Berg's "seconds" and Wittig's lesbian is precisely her lesbian *difference* (remember: in "Choreographies" homosexuality and heterosexuality "come to the same thing"). In the world of *The Lesbian Body,* it is not just "woman" that replaces "man" in the overturned hierarchy; it is "lesbian."

This lesbian difference poses a significant dilemma for deconstruction—a dilemma that some discourses within deconstruction have tried to erase. But the discourse of *Le corps lesbien* poses seductive questions for a deconstructive reader: what is the significance, for example, of the subject j/c, who, in the very act of presenting herself pronominally in language, must stutter or break off in that very act? Moreover, what is the significance of a cultural symbolic, like that imagined in the pages of *Le corps lesbien,* organized around the logos of Sappho? Sappho's truth is a truth expressed in writing, not speech; the text offers a poet, a *writer* as its goddess figure, thereby identifying Sappho's reign as instituting an order of writing rather than speech. Moreover, Sappho herself is always seen as a text: either as the constantly shifting collection of fragments that we know as Sappho's corpus, or as the blank page she occupies in Wittig's later work, *Lesbian Peoples: Material for a Dictionary.* Here the entry for "Sappho" is left blank, inviting the inscription of yet another text that will be "Sappho," and underscoring a reading of Sappho that would not produce her as presence.[19] In addition, what are the implications of a theology whose goddess is multiple (Sappho appears under many names), carnal, and subject to deconstruction like J/e, the "protagonist" of the poems? The logos of the discourse of *Le corps lesbien,* raised up through a process of inversion, is fundamentally textual, sexual, and without a singular origin.

One of the prose-poems in *Le corps lesbien* explicitly raises the question of logos and language in the context of Wittig's Amazon culture. In the poem, the women awake to *"la disparition pure et simple des voyelles"* ("the pure and simple disappearance of the vowels") and language, unable to be articulated properly, becomes a joke:

> *L'effet nouveau du mouvement de tes joues et de ta bouche la difficulté des sons à se frayer un passage hors de ta bouche sont si comiques que le rire m//étouffe, j/e tombe à la renverse, les larmes m/e coulent, j/e te regarde immobile muette, le rire m/e gagne de plus en plus, tu te trouves brusquement contaminée, tu éclates, tes joues se colorent, tu tombes à la renverse tandis qu'on entend leurs clameurs au dehors leurs interpellations de longues phrases incompréhensibles prononcées par l'une d'entre elles et reprises par de nombreuses autres répétées sans cesse.* (p. 116)[20]

This poem poses the question of the significance of a language whose end is not so much to transmit meaning as it is to amuse in its very materiality? In the context of *Le corps lesbien,* not only does *j/e* break the silence, but she does so in the form of play or even *jouissance.* Derrida writes of the spur in just these terms: "Our tongue [*langue*] promises us such a pleasure, provided at least that we do not articulate" (*"nous en assure la jouissance pourvu qu'on n'articule pas"*) (*Spurs,* pp. 38–39). The lesbians in Wittig's book have discovered, by pure and simple chance, a deconstructive language, a *langue* that does not articulate.

I wish to look at one more poem in order to ask some questions about Wittig's text's relationship to castration because, in both *Spurs* and "The Third Woman," the Truth of castration is seen as the point around which the distinctions between the affirmative woman and her secondary sister turn.[21] The second woman serves as the philosopher's and the psychoanalyst's proof of castration, particularly because she refuses to believe in it (in Freud's discourse, she persists, in spite of everything, in thinking that she is a man): "she either identifies with truth," writes Derrida, "or else she continues to play with it at a distance as if it were a fetish, manipulating it, even as she refuses to believe in it" (*Spurs,* pp. 96–97). It is the third woman's talent, however, to go beyond believing or not believing, to fetishize without assuming a hidden truth. In Wittig's poem, a lesbian version of the Egyptian myth of Isis and Osiris, most noticeable is the omission of that aspect of the myth which deals with castration; the poem, in a sense, refuses to believe in the she-Osiris's castration. Yet lack and loss are disseminated over the lesbian body of Osiris, and suspended in an irrecuperable state of bodily fragmentation and reconstruction. Unlike the Egyptian myth, there is no missing thirteenth piece, instead there are thirteen pieces which are constantly lost and found. Whereas castration is clearly negated, it is also affirmed *in a new sense*—in Derrida's words, "as previously defined, castration does not take place" ("*au sens que je disais tout à l'heure, la castration n'a pas lieu*") (*Spurs,* pp. 96–97).

Wittig's myth of Isis and Osiris is particularly demonstrative of the signifying processes at work in *Le corps lesbien.* The thirteen pieces of Osiris's fragmented body, for example, reappear in Wittig's text as the average of thirteen poems between each page of boldfaced, listed lesbian body parts. The images of Osiris's split subject reappear in almost every poem as the lovers tear each other apart and exhibit one another in exoscopy. The stability of the lesbian body is seen as fundamentally precarious: every moment of bodily reconstruction is accompanied by destruction. The simultaneous emphasis on the building and destroying of bodily architecture appears in the Isis poem: after Isis completes her search and reassembles her lover, Osiris is done and "undone" at once; "*toi alors m/on Osiris m/a très belle tu m/e souris défaite épuisée*" ("m/y Osiris most beautiful one you smile at m/e undone exhausted") (p. 87).

Wittig fills the text of *Le corps lesbien* with deconstructive moves such as these. In fact, I find myself tempted to believe that Wittig shares a hidden, extended joke with the master of deconstruction in the pages of her work: for example, is the violent disarticulation of Osiris's body a "deconstructing" lesbian? Does one of the poems lesbianize the discovery of the critical operation of "displacement" when the lovers realize offhandedly, as they sport in the island's baths, that the mass of their bodies casts out an equal amount of water? Are Wittig's marked pronouns—the *j/e* maintained and cancelled at once—a play not only on Lacan's $S̷$ but also on Derrida's *sous rature*? Is *j/e* the subject of a "straight" language who is both constituted by, and violently excluded from, that language? If the bar that separates *je* from herself is not simply a stutter, but also a chuckle, as far as I can tell, Wittig keeps it to herself; but if Derrida were to hear it, I think he would find the laughter contagious.

6

Commentary: Post-Utopian Difference

Mary Ann Doane

One suspects that, given the generic constraints of a conference paper, nothing at all can be said about sexuality. Perhaps we all believe at some level that, in reality, sexuality has to do with bodies, touching, closeness, the physical—all of those things which are most susceptible to referentiality. Anti-discursive. Sexuality has to do with the unique—*my* body, not *the* body, *my* pleasure, not the pleasure of any old text. It is the last stronghold of the private, the untheorizable. But we have also been taught to understand that this is the myth. Well-versed in the *discursive* nature of sexuality. The very force of representations of sexuality resides in their claim to incarnate the truth of nature, the natural body, securely authorized by the indisputable binary opposition of sexual difference, untarnished by the vicissitudes of history. This snare of sexuality indicates the significance, for feminism, of the Freud who made the claim, "It is popularly believed that a human being is either a man or a woman," in the hopes of undermining such a belief.[1] This is the Freud who attempted to disengage sexuality from notions of identity and biology, the Freud who, seeing sexuality everywhere, greatly expanded its range and rewrote its definition. Sexuality, in becoming the property of the psychical, retaining a certain autonomy in relation to the biological, seems less fixed in its forms, less tyrannical in its effects.

Situating sexuality at the level of the psychical is one way of subjecting it to a process of denaturalization. Another strategy—exemplified by the work of Michel Foucault in *The History of Sexuality* and Stephen Heath in *The Sexual Fix*— is to historicize it.[2] As soon as sexuality has a history, it becomes a representation, a discourse. In this important work, the history of sexuality becomes its indictment and one senses very strongly that there can be no non-complicit representation of sexuality. In both Foucault's and Heath's critical analyses, sexuality as a concept is produced in order to buttress a bourgeois notion of identity, to encourage a rampant individualism. Contemporary discourses of sexuality—sexology in particular—claim to assure me of my identity—an identity attached to a sexualized and hence purportedly liberated body. In the historical approach, the concept of sexuality pinpoints a precise historical moment—a conjuncture in which the

70

unified and coherent bourgeois subject, threatened increasingly by a fragmentation imposed from without, finds its haven in a sexualized, orgasmic body.

But the discourses of sexuality are many and varied—not only sexology but pornography, advertising, medical discourse, and, at the level of theory and analysis, historical discourse and psychoanalysis—so that it might be more accurate to distinguish between different sexualities, in the plural, as they are produced by the various discourses. Or, perhaps, to eliminate the notion of sexuality altogether. Nevertheless, I think it is critically important that the same term—sexuality—be maintained across these different discourses, that psychoanalysis, for example, somehow be held accountable for articulating a relation between its notions of sexuality and desire and the pornographic construction of sexuality. In psychoanalysis, the term sexuality frequently denotes something quite apart from sexual identity—the rigid binary oppositions of male/female, masculine/feminine. For Jean Laplanche, for example, sexuality is grounded "entirely *in the movement which dissociates it* from the vital function."[3] It is "a perversion of the instinct in the traditional sense—a perversion in which the specific object and the organic purpose both vanish."[4] Sexuality becomes pure drive, dissociated from both its object and any sexually differentiated body. And in the Lacanian schema, desire is a remainder—what is left over when need is subtracted from demand. It is specified in relation to its very insatiability, the absence of an object. In both cases, sexuality is neutered. It is defined entirely outside of the context of a polarization of the sexes, of femininity as a foil to masculinity. Yet, in this way, psychoanalysis collaborates in the discourse of *in*difference outlined by Naomi Schor. And in this sense it must be problematic for feminism. For the specificity of feminism—its difference, in contradistinction to class or racial analysis—is that it locates sexuality as the primary site of oppression. Whatever the social, historical, economic effects of sexism, they are linked, in however mediated a fashion, to a definition of the woman as *the* representation of sexuality, as *the sex,* with respect to the zero degree of masculinity. In this context, the woman's relation to a desiring subjectivity must be negotiated.

In Naomi Schor's argument, the evasion of sexuality as a site of conflict or confrontation for a feminist politics takes the form of a refusal of sexual difference and is exemplified most fully in the work of Roland Barthes. It is in Barthes "that we can most easily grasp the dominant male discourse on sexuality in post-structuralist France, what I will call the *discourse of in-difference* or of *pure difference,* for they are in fact one and the same." The term indifference connotes not only the repudiation of any difference linked to sexuality but also a failure of interest, apathy, a lack of investment. Indifferent to feminism and its political aims, Barthes generates a profusion of *pure* differences whose dissociation from the sexed body is absolute. The body itself is certainly there, for Barthes, in discourse, but it is neutered or androgynous or, perhaps, as with Foucault's fascination with Herculine Barbin, an undecidable body. Difference is elsewhere and multiple. In Barthes,

Schor finds evidence of a veiled utopian thinking or of a desire to simply wish away the problem posed by the polarization of masculine and feminine. The *clinamen*—or swerve away from femininity pinpointed by Schor—is in a way the necessary consequence of the heritage of structural linguistics and of a more contemporary tendency to valorize the dissemination, the multiplication, and dispersal of differences—to make fundamental and inescapable the theory of a language which ultimately has no commerce with the body. Hence, we have the apparent paradox that a theory of pure difference could be equated with one of indifference. The pure difference is a linguistic one. Masculinity and femininity are the impurities which continue to contaminate our thinking.

In the first volume of Foucault's *History of Sexuality* and in most of the work of Barthes, then, it is quite accurate to note a certain refusal to engage with a feminist analysis of sexual difference—for what are ultimately different reasons I believe. Foucault can view feminism only as a form of local resistance within a totalizing network of power relations while Barthes hopes to move beyond the local and to annihilate an oppressive sexual identity by invoking the *jouissance* of pure difference. However, one can just as easily attribute the repudiation or attenuation of sexual difference in Barthes's work to the discourses of Balzac or the fashion industry which he analyzes in texts such as *S/Z* or *Système de la Mode*. Yet, in *The Pleasure of the Text* or *Roland Barthes by Roland Barthes,* the privileging of or even desire for in-difference reveals itself to be a structuring component of Barthes's theory of both signification and political positioning. From this perspective, it is worth extending the crucial quote from "Pluriel, différence, conflit," cited by Schor:

> the meanings and the sexes [must] be pluralized: meaning will tend toward its multiplication, its dispersion (in the theory of the Text), and sex will be taken into no typology (there will be, for example, only *homosexualities,* whose plural will baffle any constituted, centered discourse, to the point where it seems to him virtually pointless to talk about it).
>
> Similarly, *difference,* that much-vaunted and insistent word, prevails because it dispenses with or triumphs over conflict. Conflict is sexual, semantic; difference is plural, sensual, and textual; meaning and sex are principles of construction, of constitution; difference is the very movement of dispersion, of friability, a shimmer; what matters is not the discovery, in a reading of the world and of the self, of certain oppositions but of encroachments, overflows, leaks, skids, shifts, slips . . .
>
> According to Freud (in the book about Moses), one touch of difference leads to racism. But a great deal of difference leads away from it, irremediably.[5]

From the slippage whereby sex and the text become one and the same (rationalized by a collapse of sexual difference onto linguistic difference), we move to a "beyond" of the war between the sexes, and finally to what seems to me to be a much more productive emphasis upon the complicity/collaboration of the solitary difference in the establishment and maintenance of an oppressive identity. The problem with the difference of sexual difference is precisely that it is single rather than multiple—its formulation assents to the lure of binarism, to the mastery of a dominant binary opposition. And as Heather Findlay points out in her essay on Derrida's "third woman," that binary opposition is most easily and readily *thought* in terms of heterosexuality. Yet Barthes, when he speaks of *homosexualities* "whose plural will baffle any constituted, centered discourse," refuses to repeat Derrida's gesture of conflating homosexuality with homogeneity.[6] It is institutionalized heterosexuality, on the contrary, which ultimately promotes an ideology of oneness, unity, sameness by effectively reducing the play of difference.

In response to this fairly strong theoretical framework, Naomi Schor outlines the pitfalls of such a position. Barthes's theory, particularly when it is pushed to the point "where it seems to him virtually pointless to talk about it"—sexual difference that is, heralds the risk of a return to the generic "he." As Schor points out, "Denied sexual difference shades into sexual indifference and, following the same slippery path, into a paradoxical reinscription of the very differences the strategy was designed to denaturalize." Schor's paper, entitled "Dreaming Dissymmetry," evokes the work of Luce Irigaray, particularly her critique of Freud in the section of *Speculum* entitled "The Blind Spot of an Old Dream of Symmetry."[7] For Irigaray, the difference of the long history of Western metaphysics makes no difference since it is a difference in the service of the Same. The term "Blind Spot" indicates precisely an inability to see difference, a deficiency in vision— or, perhaps more accurately, the process of seeing in otherness only a mirror image of the same. Hence, the necessity of dreaming dissymmetry, of pursuing the sometimes convoluted and contradictory project of negotiating a specifically female subjectivity or sexuality in order to counter what Irigaray refers to, in the same vein as Schor, as the "sexual indifference that subtends" representation.[8] From this perspective, then, the only way to "disconcert the staging of representation"[9] is through something like Irigaray's mimeticism—the strategy of fully, even excessively, occupying the position which one has been assigned. Schor's argument for dissymmetry rejoins the work of other feminist theorists attempting to elaborate a feminine specificity in the areas of feminine reading and writing, female spectatorship, subjectivity, or sexuality. The premise of this work is the belief that the only feasible way to counter the effacement of the woman perpetuated by the discourse of indifference is to posit a feminine specificity which is asymmetrical to that of the male.

I find the argument to be an extremely appealing one, but also problematic in that it seems continually to run up against cogent theoretical indictments of the concept of identity. For identity—Barthes's "one touch of difference"—seems also to be the anchor and guarantee of sexual and racial oppression. But I ultimately believe it is necessary to think our way through or beyond the theoretical impasse. In the historical approach of both Foucault and Heath, sexuality is that term which insures the unity, coherency, and political isolation of the subject of late capitalism—that subject's identity, in short. Sexual identity, far from being repressed or effaced, is too much with us, in the discourses and images which surround us every day. What is at stake here is the ideological bind of comfort and security—it is with reference to this bind, I think, that Stephen Heath claims, in *The Sexual Fix,* "No doubt it's comforting at times to be a sex and have a relation with the other."[10] This, usually heterosexual, obsessive coupling is predicated upon the maintenance of the given identities: man/woman, masculine/feminine. The localization and specification of identity as the bad object or, perhaps, the bad concept, is not a strategy which is limited to the historical discourse on sexuality. It has, in fact, a prestigious heritage—from Saussure's privileging of differences over positive terms in language to Barthes's rampant textualization to the psychoanalytic insistence that coherency and identity are fictions of the ego. Identity, with its connotations of rigidity and paralysis, is anathema to any theory which valorizes movement, process, dispersal, and dissemination.

And this denigration and rejection of identity as a viable concept would seem to be corroborated by the long history of identifying the woman—as virgin, whore, the Other, otherness itself, the Truth, the dark continent, *jouissance,* or what have you, a history which reaches the peak of absurdity in Freud's identification of the woman (the woman over thirty, that is) as the very excess of identity. The problem is not that no one knows who she is or what she wants but that she has too much identity, more than the male. I am thinking of the following passage from the essay, "Femininity":

> A man of about thirty strikes us as a youthful, somewhat unformed individual, whom we expect to make powerful use of the possibilities for development opened up to him by analysis. A woman of the same age, however, often frightens us by her psychical rigidity and unchangeability. Her libido has taken up final positions and seems incapable of exchanging them for others. There are no paths open to further development; it is as though the whole process had already run its course and remains thenceforward insusceptible to influence—as though, indeed, the difficult development to femininity had exhausted the possibilities of the person concerned.[11]

Once femininity is finally attained, after a long and difficult development, its very rigidity precludes the possibility of movement or transformation. Inevitably this will be a problem for *any* attempt to theorize femininity—whether from a feminist point of view or not. Its achievement is something of a Pyrrhic victory. The young woman of thirty, set in her psychical ways, may frighten Freud, but she also reassures him of his own flexibility.

Happily, however, this is not the Freud who is so appealing to feminist theory.

Feminist theorists are attracted to psychoanalysis precisely because in its current, particularly Lacanian, formulations, it de-emphasizes or even dissolves such moments in Freud, stressing instead the splittings and slippages of subjectivity and the consequent instability of psychical identity. In opposition to ego psychology, any identity with which psychoanalysis is concerned is an identity which somehow never coagulates. Despite Naomi Schor's isolation and concentration upon the work of Barthes and Foucault, I think it is fair to claim that in contemporary feminist theory, psychoanalysis is *the* discourse of/on sexuality. Its effects have been much more profound than those of the historical discourse on sexuality. Yet, it also generates ambivalent (if not downright hostile) attitudes. Stephen Heath describes the simultaneous attraction and repulsion of psychoanalysis in his own work:

> I find myself in fact continually defending and criticizing Freud and Lacan, psychoanalysis in their terms, rejecting and needing its descriptions, those terms. Which is where it is true that castration is the end, the final reality of this peculiar split, the original point to which it all comes down and from which, getting rid of the centrality of the concept of the phallus, it all has to be rethought, relived. ... It is as though psychoanalysis is there as a kind of necessary impasse today ...[12]

For Heath, the failure of psychoanalysis is directly linked to the centrality of castration and the concept of the phallus; its strength is in the accuracy of its delineation of psychical processes, of a linguistically structured unconscious. But since its linguistics is similar to if not the same as that informing the work of Barthes, what is the relation of psychoanalysis to the discourse of indifference or pure difference outlined by Schor?

Perhaps the aim should be not so much to explicate the position or non-position of sexual difference in the work of such influential male theorists as Barthes and Foucault and even Lacan, but rather to analyze the feminist transference in relation to such figures. Or what Michèle Le Doeuff, in the context of the philosophical institution, calls the erotico-theoretical transference.[13] For, as Schor points out, Barthes's prose is, precisely, seductive. And for many feminist theorists, the psychoanalytical framework is seductive as well. This is one of the reasons why the feminist fascination with psychoanalysis persists. And I would like to suggest that the aspects of psychoanalysis which are most appealing to the feminist have crucial links with what Schor refers to as Barthes's discourse of "pure difference" or "indifference."

I am going to put forward the fairly strange-sounding argument that the seductiveness of psychoanalytic theory, in its Lacanian formulation, stems from the fact that it is utopian without recognizing itself as such. I am thinking here of Jane Gallop's claim that Lacan's status as a prick somehow makes him less phallocentric or of Jacqueline Rose's belief that psychoanalysis exposes the phallus as a fraud. One only wishes ... But the thrust of my argument concerns the concept of identity. And since Rose's articulation of the importance of psycho-analysis for feminism is one of the most sophisticated and, for me at any rate, the most seductive, I will simply point out the vicissitudes of the concept of identity in some of her work. It is clear that what is crucial for Rose is the psychoanalytic insistence not upon the regularization or normalization of sexuality but upon the constant failure of sexual identity, its instability or even its impos-sibility: "The phallus can only take up its place by indicating the precariousness of any identity assumed by the subject on the basis of its token."[14] Any attempts to theorize a female sexuality—whether those of the 1920s and 1930s (Ernest Jones, Karen Horney, etc.) or those of more recent analysts such as Luce Irigaray and Michèle Montrelay—are resisted on the grounds of the precariousness and problematic nature of sexuality itself—its incompatibility with the very notion of identity. The division in the subject reflects a division in language and occasions an inevitable disphasure in the relation between the subject and the other. Identity is fictional and suspect—echoing Heath's "No doubt it's comforting at times to be a sex and have a relation with the other." But I would add to that—"No doubt it's comforting at times to be a divided, multiple, or plural subject and have no possibility of a relation with the other." Perhaps even more comforting. Yet this is of course deceptive since the choice of a comfortable or uncomfortable position is not up to the subject.

I am sure that most people would not agree to view the discourse of psycho-analysis as Utopian—whether it is situated as a misrecognized utopia or not. But I see the utopian tendency in the desire to annihilate an identity which has been oppressive—to annihilate it by fiat, simply declaring it non-operational at the level of an indisputable psychical reality. Identity in the realm of the social may be oppressive but insofar as patriarchy seems to work—and to have worked for a long time—it cannot be seen as either a failure or an impossibility. No doubt the difficulty emerges from the fact that psychoanalysis has never managed to successfully articulate relations between not only the biological and the psychical, but between the psychical and the social as well. An autonomy of the psychical, which can ultimately be just as restrictive and essentializing in its effects, has displaced the autonomy of the biological usually associated with essentialism. Rather than emphasizing the failure or dissolution of identity, it might be more productive to investigate closely the moments, temporary though they may be, and the processes of the formulation, solidification, and emplacement of identity, particularly in relation to a feminist politics. A politicization of desire. Identity at the level of the social may be oppressive, and identity at the level of the psychical may be fictional, but what about identity at the level of the political? One's identity as a feminist, for instance.

For it is in relation to a political discourse that Naomi Schor's call for more work on feminine specificity takes on its greatest meaning and force. Unlike Schor, however, I would support the idea that the elaboration of a feminine specificity or sexuality has only tactical or strategic value—but this "only" is not a "merely." This strategy is necessitated by a history of discourses which *are* indifferent and in their indifference erect and maintain a standard of masculinity, effectively effacing the woman. The history cannot be undone by reinserting indifference at another level. Strategy can be formulated only from a position. Identities must be assumed if only temporarily. Yet, the utopia this strategy has in view is not a utopia where woman will finally achieve an identity or specificity but where this type of identity will no longer be a problem. More akin to Barthes's utopia of pluralities. From this point of view, the opposition between homosexuality and heterosexuality should falter as well. Heath's meditation upon Guy Hocquenghem's theory of desire demonstrates the constraints of this particular binarism.

> What does Hocquenghem say? That there is no homosexual desire strictly speaking, that the hetero/homo system is a limiting identification, that there is just desire, multiple differences, possibilities, moments, that it is in the definitions assigned that desire turns out as "homo" or "hetero," that everything hinges on representations.[15]

Nevertheless, because the concepts of homosexuality and heterosexuality do exist and insist quite forcefully in the social field-fixing identities, this type of desire in its social formulation can only be viewed as, precisely, utopian. Hence, Findlay quite appropriately insists upon the necessity of delineating a specifically "lesbian theory" as a first stage in dismantling the hegemonic heterosexual regime. To pretend that desire operates in the limitless manner suggested by Hocquenghem— as constant displacement without fixity of any kind, is to imply that desire is a pure psychical force, absolutely independent of the social and political realms. It is, in effect, to destroy any explanatory power that psychoanalysis may have for feminism. Yet, while Findlay calls for a specificity of lesbian theory which challenges the given heterosexual dominant, that theory activates an identity which is already marked for destruction. The concept of "difference within difference," with its echoes of Barthes's gesture of multiplying differences, is designed to break down the monolithic category of "woman" which is often the result of demands for a "feminine specificity."

My critique of psychoanalysis is not a critique of utopian thinking—to the contrary—but of its misrecognition (as authoritative science). Insofar as Barthes links the notion of a pure dispersal (or anti-binarism) of difference to the idea of utopia, his discourse is in some ways more useful to feminist theory than that of a psychoanalysis which claims that dispersal as the real of the psychical. Utopias open up a space for non-essentialized identities—they authorize certain positions rather than others, certain politics rather than others. A utopia is the sighting (in terms of the gaze) and siting (in terms of emplacement) of another possibility. The chance of escaping the same. A refusal of utopian thinking is also a denial of the operation of fantasy and desire in the work of theory, leading us to the issue of pleasure—which is another question altogether.

Writing History

7

Gender: A Useful Category of Historical Analysis

Joan W. Scott

> Gender. n. a grammatical term only. To talk of persons or creatures
> of the masculine or feminine gender, meaning of the male or female
> sex, is either a jocularity (permissible or not according to context) or
> a blunder.
>
> (Fowler's *Dictionary of Modern English Usage,* Oxford, 1940)

Those who would codify the meanings of words fight a losing battle, for words, like the ideas and things they are meant to signify, have a history. Neither Oxford dons nor the Académie Française has been entirely able to stem the tide, to capture and fix meanings free of the play of human invention and imagination. Mary Wortley Montagu added bite to her witty denunciation "of the fair sex" ("my only consolation for being of that gender has been the assurance of never being married to any one among them") by deliberately misusing the grammatical reference.[1] Through the ages, people have made figurative allusions by employing grammatical terms to evoke traits of character or sexuality. For example, the usage offered by the *Dictionnaire de la langue française* in 1876 was: "On ne sait de quel genre il est, s'il est mâle ou femelle, se dit d'un homme très-caché, dont on ne connait pas les sentiments."[2] And Gladstone made this distinction in 1878: "Athene has nothing of sex except the gender, nothing of the woman except the form."[3] Most recently—too recently to find its way into dictionaries or the *Encyclopedia of the Social Sciences*—feminists have in a more literal and serious vein begun to use "gender" as a way of referring to the social organization of the relationship between the sexes. The connection to grammar is both explicit and full of unexamined possibilities. Explicit because the grammatical usage involves formal rules that follow from the masculine or feminine designation; full of unexamined possibilities because in many Indo-European languages there is a third category—unsexed or neuter. In grammar, gender is understood to be a way of classifying phenomena, a socially agreed upon system of distinctions rather than an objective description of inherent traits. In addition, classifications suggest a relationship among categories which makes possible distinctions or separate groupings.

In its most recent usage, "gender" seems to have first appeared among American feminists who wanted to insist on the fundamentally social quality of distinctions based on sex. The word denoted a rejection of the biological determinism implicit in the use of such terms as "sex" or "sexual difference." "Gender" also stressed the relational aspect of normative definitions of femininity. Those who worried that women's studies scholarship focused too narrowly and separately on women used the term "gender" to introduce a relational notion into our analytic vocabulary. According to this view, women and men were defined in terms of one another, and no understanding of either could be achieved by entirely separate study. Thus Natalie Davis suggested in 1975, "It seems to me that we should be interested in the history of both women and men, that we should not be working only on the subjected sex any more than an historian of class can focus entirely on peasants. Our goal is to understand the significance of the *sexes,* of gender groups in the historical past. Our goal is to discover the range in sex roles and in sexual symbolism in different societies and periods, to find out what meaning they had and how they functioned to maintain the social order or to promote its change."[4]

In addition, and perhaps most important, "gender" was a term offered by those who claimed that women's scholarship would fundamentally transform disciplinary paradigms. Feminist scholars pointed out early on that the study of women would not only add new subject matter but would also force a critical reexamination of the premises and standards of existing scholarly work. "We are learning," wrote three feminist historians, "that the writing of women into history necessarily involves redefining and enlarging traditional notions of historical significance, to encompass personal, subjective experience as well as public and political activities. It is not too much to suggest that however hesitant the actual beginnings, such a methodology implies not only a new history of women, but also a new history."[5] The way in which this new history would both include and account for women's experience rested on the extent to which gender could be developed as a category of analysis. Here the analogies to class and race were explicit; indeed, the most politically inclusive of scholars of women's studies regularly invoked all three categories as crucial to the writing of a new history.[6] An interest in class, race, and gender signaled, first, a scholar's commitment to a history that included stories of the oppressed and an analysis of the meaning and nature of their oppression and, second, scholarly understanding that inequalities of power are organized along at least three axes.

The litany of class, race, and gender suggests a parity for each term, but, in fact, that is not at all the case. While "class" most often rests on Marx's elaborate (and since elaborated) theory of economic determination and historical change, "race" and "gender" carry no such associations. No unanimity exists among those who employ concepts of class. Some scholars employ Weberian notions, others use class as a temporary heuristic device. Still, when we invoke class, we are working with or against a set of definitions that, in the case of Marxism, involve an idea of economic causality and a vision of the path along which history has moved dialectically. There is no such clarity or coherence for either race or gender. In the case of gender, the usage has involved a range of theoretical positions as well as simple descriptive references to the relationships between the sexes.

Feminist historians, trained as most historians are to be more comfortable with description than theory, have nonetheless increasingly looked for usable theoretical formulations. They have done so for at least two reasons. First, the proliferation of case studies in women's history seems to call for some synthesizing perspective that can explain continuities and discontinuities and account for persisting inequalities as well as radically different social experiences. Second, the discrepancy between the high quality of recent work in women's history and its continuing marginal status in the field as a whole (as measured by textbooks, syllabi, and monographic work) points up the limits of descriptive approaches that do not address dominant disciplinary concepts, or at least that do not address these concepts in terms that can shake their power and perhaps transform them. It has not been enough for historians of women to prove either that women had a history or that women participated in the major political upheavals of Western civilization. In the case of women's history, the response of most non-feminist historians has been acknowledgment and then separation or dismissal ("women had a history separate from men's, therefore let feminists do women's history which need not concern us."; or "women's history is about sex and the family and should be done separately from political and economic history"). In the case of women's participation, the response has been minimal interest at best ("my understanding of the French Revolution is not changed by knowing that women participated in it"). The challenge posed by these responses is, in the end, a theoretical one. It requires analysis not only of the relationship between male and female experience in the past but also of the connection between past history and current historical practice. How does gender work in human social relationships? How does gender give meaning to the organization and perception of historical knowledge? The answers depend on gender as an analytic category.

For the most part, the attempts of historians to theorize about gender have remained within traditional social scientific frameworks, using longstanding formulations that provide universal causal explanations. These theories have been limited at best because they tend to contain reductive or overly simple generalizations that undercut not only history's disciplinary sense of the complexity of social causation but also feminist commitments to analyses that will lead to change. A review of these theories will expose their limits and make it possible to propose an alternative approach.

I

The approaches used by most historians fall into two distinct categories. The first is essentially descriptive; that is, it refers to the existence of phenomena or realities without interpreting, explaining, or attributing causality. The second usage is causal; it theorizes about the nature of phenomena or realities, seeking an understanding of how and why these take the form they do.

In its simplest recent usage, "gender" is a synonym for "women." Any number of books and articles whose subject is women's history have, in the past few years, substituted "gender" for "women" in their titles. In some cases, this usage, though vaguely referring to certain analytic concepts, is actually about the political acceptability of the field. In these instances, the use of "gender" is meant to denote the scholarly seriousness of a work, for "gender" has a more neutral and objective sound than does "women." "Gender" seems to fit within the scientific terminology of social science and thus dissociates itself from the (supposedly strident) politics of feminism. In this usage, "gender" does not carry with it a necessary statement about inequality or power nor does it name the aggrieved (and hitherto invisible) party. Whereas the term "women's history" proclaims its politics by asserting (contrary to customary practice) that women are valid historical subjects, "gender" includes, but does not name women, and so seems to pose no critical threat. This use of "gender" is one facet of what might be called the quest of feminist scholarship for academic legitimacy in the 1980s.

But only one facet. "Gender" as a substitute for "women" is also used to suggest that information about women is necessarily information about men, that one implies the study of the other. This usage insists that the world of women is part of the world of men, created in and by it. This usage rejects the interpretive utility of the idea of separate spheres, maintaining that to study women in isolation perpetuates the fiction that one sphere, the experience of one sex, has little or nothing to do with the other. In addition, gender is also used to designate social relations between the sexes. Its use explicitly rejects biological explanations, such as those that find a common denominator for diverse forms of female subordination in the facts that women have the capacity to give birth and men have greater muscular strength. Instead, gender becomes a way of denoting "cultural constructions"—the entirely social creation of ideas about appropriate roles for women and men. It is a way of referring to the exclusively social origins of the subjective identities of men and women. Gender is, in this definition, a social category imposed on a sexed body.[7] Gender seems to have become a particularly useful word as studies of sex and sexuality have proliferated, for it offers a way of differentiating sexual practice from the social roles assigned to women and men. Although scholars acknowledge the connection between sex and (what the sociologists of the family called) "sex roles," these scholars do not assume a simple or direct linkage. The use of gender emphasizes an entire system of relationships that may include sex, but is not directly determined by sex nor directly determining of sexuality.

These descriptive usages of gender have been employed by historians most often to map out a new terrain. As social historians turned to new objects of study, gender was relevant for such topics as women, children, families, and gender ideologies. This usage of gender, in other words, refers only to those areas— both structural and ideological—involving relations between the sexes. Because, on the face of it, war, diplomacy, and high politics have not been explicitly about those relationships, gender seems not to apply and so continues to be irrelevant to the thinking of historians concerned with issues of politics and power. The effect is to endorse a certain functionalist view ultimately rooted in biology and to perpetuate the idea of separate spheres (sex or politics, family or nation, women or men) in the writing of history. Although gender in this usage asserts that relationships between the sexes are social, it says nothing about why these re- lationships are constructed as they are, how they work, or how they change. In its descriptive usage, then, gender is a concept associated with the study of things related to women. Gender is a new topic, a new department of historical inves- tigation, but it does not have the analytic power to address (and change) existing historical paradigms.

Some historians were, of course, aware of this problem, hence the efforts to employ theories that might explain the concept of gender and account for historical change. Indeed, the challenge was to reconcile theory, which was framed in general or universal terms, and history, which was committed to the study of contextual specificity and fundamental change. The result has been extremely eclectic: partial borrowings that vitiate the analytic power of a particular theory or, worse, employ its precepts without awareness of their implications; or accounts of change that, because they embed universal theories, only illustrate unchanging themes; or wonderfully imaginative studies in which theory is nonetheless so hidden that these studies cannot serve as models for other investigations. Because the theories on which historians have drawn are often not spelled out in all their implications, it seems worthwhile to spend some time doing that. Only through such an exercise can we evaluate the usefulness of these theories and begin to articulate a more powerful theoretical approach.

Feminist historians have employed a variety of approaches to the analysis of gender, but the approaches come down to a choice among three theoretical positions.[8] The first, an entirely feminist effort, attempts to explain the origins of patriarchy. The second locates itself within a Marxian tradition and seeks there an accommodation with feminist critiques. The third, fundamentally divided be- tween French post-structuralist and Anglo-American object-relations theorists, draws on these different schools of psychoanalysis to explain the production and reproduction of the subject's gendered identity.

Theorists of patriarchy have directed their attention to the subordination of women and found their explanation for it in the male "need" to dominate the female. In Mary O'Brien's ingenious adaptation of Hegel, she defined male domination as the effect of men's desire to transcend their alienation from the means of the reproduction of the species. The principle of generational continuity restores the primacy of paternity and obscures the real labor and the social reality of women's work in childbirth. The source of women's liberation lies in "an adequate understanding of the process of reproduction," an appreciation of the contradiction between the nature of women's reproductive labor and (male) ideological mystifications of it.[9] For Shulamith Firestone, reproduction was also the "bitter trap" for women. In her more materialist analysis, however, liberation would come with transformations in reproductive technology, which might in some not too distant future eliminate the need for women's bodies as the agents of species reproduction.[10]

If reproduction was the key to patriarchy for some, sexuality itself was the answer for others. Catherine MacKinnon's bold formulations were at once her own and characteristic of a certain approach: "Sexuality is to feminism what work is to marxism: that which is most one's own, yet most taken away." "Sexual objectification is the primary process of the subjection of women. It unites act with word, construction with expression, perception with enforcement, myth with reality. Man fucks woman; subject verb object."[11] Continuing her analogy to Marx, MacKinnon offered, in the place of dialectical materialism, consciousness-raising as feminism's method of analysis. By expressing the shared experience of objectification, she argued, women come to understand their common identity and so are moved to political action. Although sexual relations are defined in MacKinnon's analysis as social, there is nothing except the inherent inequality of the sexual relation itself to explain why the system of power operates as it does. The source of unequal relations between the sexes is, in the end, unequal relations between the sexes. Although the inequality of which sexuality is the source is said to be embodied in a "whole system of social relationships," how this system works is not explained.[12]

Theorists of patriarchy have addressed the inequality of males and females in important ways, but, for historians, their theories pose problems. First, while they offer an analysis internal to the gender system itself, they also assert the primacy of that system in all social organization. But theories of patriarchy do not show what gender inequality has to do with other inequalities. Second, whether domination comes in the form of the male appropriation of the female's reproductive labor or in the sexual objectification of women by men, the analysis rests on physical difference. Any physical difference takes on a universal and unchanging aspect, even if theorists of patriarchy take into account the existence of changing forms and systems of gender inequality.[13] A theory that rests on the single variable of physical difference poses problems for historians: it assumes a consistent or inherent meaning for the human body—outside social or cultural construction—

and thus the ahistoricity of gender itself. History becomes, in a sense, epiphenomenal, providing endless variations on the unchanging theme of a fixed gender inequality.

Marxist feminists have a more historical approach, guided as they are by a theory of history. But, whatever the variations and adaptations have been, the self-imposed requirement that there be a "material" explanation for gender has limited or at least slowed the development of new lines of analysis. Whether a so-called dual-systems solution is proferred (one that posits the separate but interacting realms of capitalism and patriarchy) or an analysis based more firmly in orthodox Marxist discussions of modes of production is developed, the explanation for the origins of and changes in gender systems is found outside the sexual division of labor. Families, households, and sexuality are all, finally, products of changing modes of production. That is how Engels concludes his explorations of the *Origins of the Family;*[14] that is where economist Heidi Hartmann's analysis ultimately rests. Hartmann insists on the importance of taking into account patriarchy and capitalism as separate but interacting systems. Yet, as her argument unfolds, economic causality takes precedence, and patriarchy always develops and changes as a function of relations of production.[15]

Early discussions among Marxist feminists circled around the same set of problems: a rejection of the essentialism of those who would argue that the "exigencies of biological reproduction" determine the sexual division of labor under capitalism; the futility of inserting "modes of reproduction" into discussions of modes of production (it remains an oppositional category and does not assume equal status with modes of production); the recognition that economic systems do not directly determine gender relationships, indeed, that the subordination of women pre-dates capitalism and continues under socialism; the search nonetheless for a materialist explanation that excludes natural physical differences.[16] An important attempt to break out of this circle of problems came from Joan Kelly in her essay, "The Doubled Vision of Feminist Theory," where she argued that economic and gender systems interact to produce social and historical experiences; that neither system was causal, but both "operate simultaneously to reproduce the socioeconomic and male-dominant structures of . . . [a] particular social order." Kelly's suggestion that gender systems have an independent existence provided a crucial conceptual opening, but her commitment to remain within a Marxist framework led her to emphasize the causal role of economic factors even in the determination of the gender system. "The relation of the sexes operates in accordance with, and through, socioeconomic structures, as well as sex/gender ones."[17] Kelly introduced the idea of a "sexually based social reality," but she tended to emphasize the social rather than the sexual nature of that reality, and, most often, "social," in her usage, was conceived in terms of economic relations of production.

The most far-reaching exploration of sexuality by American Marxist feminists is in *Powers of Desire,* a volume of essays published in 1983.[18] Influenced by increasing attention to sexuality among political activists and scholars, by French philosopher Michel Foucault's insistence that sexuality is produced in historical contexts, and by the conviction that the current "sexual revolution" requires serious analysis, the authors make "sexual politics" the focus of their inquiry. In so doing, they open the question of causality and offer a variety of solutions to it; indeed, the real excitement of this volume is its lack of analytic unanimity, its sense of analytic tension. If individual authors tend to stress the causality of social (by which is often meant "economic") contexts, they nonetheless include suggestions about the importance of studying "the psychic structuring of gender identity." If "gender ideology" is sometimes said to "reflect" economic and social structures, there is also a crucial recognition of the need to understand the complex "link between society and enduring psychic structure."[19] On the one hand, the editors endorse Jessica Benjamin's point that politics must include attention to "the erotic, fantastic components of human life," but, on the other, no essays besides Benjamin's deal fully or seriously with the theoretical issues she raises.[20] Instead, a tacit assumption runs through the volume that Marxism can be expanded to include discussions of ideology, culture, and psychology and that this expansion will happen through the kind of concrete examination of evidence undertaken in most of the articles. The advantage of such an approach lies in its avoidance of sharp differences of position, the disadvantage in its leaving in place an already fully articulated theory that leads back from relations of the sexes to relations of production.

A comparison of American Marxist-feminist efforts, exploratory and relatively wide-ranging, to those of their English counterparts, tied more closely to the politics of a strong and viable Marxist tradition, reveals that the English have had greater difficulty in challenging the constraints of strictly determinist explanations. This difficulty can be seen most dramatically in the debates in the *New Left Review* between Michèle Barrett and her critics, who charge her with abandoning a materialist analysis of the sexual division of labor under capitalism.[21] It can be seen as well in the replacement of an initial feminist attempt to reconcile psychoanalysis and Marxism with a choice of one or another of these theoretical positions by scholars who earlier insisted that some fusion of the two was possible.[22] The difficulty for both English and American feminists working within Marxism is apparent in the work I have mentioned here. The problem they face is the opposite of the one posed by patriarchal theory. For within Marxism, the concept of gender has long been treated as the by-product of changing economic structures; gender has had no independent analytic status of its own.

A review of psychoanalytic theory requires a specification of schools, since the various approaches have tended to be classified by the national origins of the founders and the majority of the practitioners. There is the Anglo-American school, working within the terms of theories of object-relations. In the U.S., Nancy Chodorow is the name most readily associated with this approach. In addition, the work of Carol Gilligan has had a far-reaching impact on American scholarship, including history. Gilligan's work draws on Chodorow's, although it is concerned less with the construction of the subject than with moral development and behavior. In contrast to the Anglo-American school, the French school is based on structuralist and post-structuralist readings of Freud in terms of theories of language (for feminists, the key figure is Jacques Lacan).

Both schools are concerned with the processes by which the subject's identity is created; both focus on the early stages of child development for clues to the formation of gender identity. Object-relations theorists stress the influence of actual experience (the child sees, hears, relates to those who care for it, particularly, of course, to its parents), while the post-structuralists emphasize the centrality of language in communicating, interpreting, and representing gender. (By "language," post-structuralists do not mean words but systems of meaning—symbolic orders—that precede the actual mastery of speech, reading, and writing.) Another difference between the two schools of thought focuses on the unconscious, which for Chodorow is ultimately subject to conscious understanding and for Lacan is not. For Lacanians, the unconscious is a critical factor in the construction of the subject; it is the location, moreover, of sexual division and, for that reason, of continuing instability for the gendered subject.

In recent years, feminist historians have been drawn to these theories either because they serve to endorse specific findings with general observations or because they seem to offer an important theoretical formulation about gender. Increasingly, those historians working with a concept of "women's culture" cite Chodorow's or Gilligan's work as both proof of and explanation for their interpretations; those wrestling with feminist theory look to Lacan. In the end, neither of these theories seems to me entirely workable for historians; a closer look at each may help explain why.

My reservation about object-relations theory concerns its literalism, its reliance on relatively small structures of interaction to produce gender identity and to generate change. Both the family division of labor and the actual assignment of tasks to each parent play a crucial role in Chodorow's theory. The outcome of prevailing Western systems is a clear division between male and female: "The basic feminine sense of self is connected to the world, the basic masculine sense of self is separate."[23] According to Chodorow, if fathers were more involved in parenting and present more often in domestic situations, the outcome of the oedipal drama might be different.[24]

This interpretation limits the concept of gender to family and household experience and, for the historian, leaves no way to connect the concept (or the individual) to other social systems of economy, politics, or power. Of course, it is implicit that social arrangements requiring fathers to work and mothers to perform most child-rearing tasks structure family organization. Where such arrangements come from and why they are articulated in terms of a sexual division of labor is not clear. Neither is the issue of inequality, as opposed to that of asymmetry, addressed. How can we account within this theory for persistent associations of masculinity with power, for the higher value placed on manhood than on womanhood, for the way children seem to learn these associations and evaluations even when they live outside nuclear households or in households where parenting is equally divided between husband and wife? I do not think we can without some attention to signifying systems, that is, to the ways societies represent gender, use it to articulate the rules of social relationships, or construct the meaning of experience. Without meaning, there is no experience; without processes of signification, there is no meaning.

Language is the center of Lacanian theory; it is the key to the child's induction into the symbolic order. Through language, gendered identity is constructed. According to Lacan, the phallus is the central signifier of sexual difference. But the meaning of the phallus must be read metaphorically. For the child, the oedipal drama sets forth the terms of cultural interaction, since the threat of castration embodies the power, the rules of (the Father's) law. The child's relationship to the law depends on sexual difference, on its imaginative (or fantastic) identification with masculinity or femininity. The imposition, in other words, of the rules of social interaction is inherently and specifically gendered, for the female necessarily has a different relationship to the phallus than the male does. But gender identification, although it always appears coherent and fixed, is, in fact, highly unstable. As meaning systems, subjective identities are processes of differentiation and distinction, requiring the suppression of ambiguities and opposite elements in order to ensure (create the illusion of) coherence and common understanding. The principle of masculinity rests on the necessary repression of feminine aspects— of the subject's potential for bisexuality—and introduces conflict into the opposition of masculine and feminine. Repressed desires are present in the unconscious and are constantly a threat to the stability of gender identification, denying its unity, subverting its need for security. In addition, conscious ideas of masculine or feminine are not fixed, since they vary according to contextual usage. Conflict always exists, then, between the subject's need for the appearance of wholeness and the imprecision of terminology, its relative meaning, its dependence on repression.[25] This kind of interpretation makes the categories of "man" and "woman" problematic by suggesting that masculine and feminine are not inherent characteristics but subjective (or fictional) constructs. This interpretation also implies that the subject is in a constant process of construction, and it offers a systematic way of interpreting conscious and unconscious desire by pointing to language as the appropriate place for analysis. As such, I find it instructive.

I am troubled, nonetheless, by the exclusive fixation on questions of the individual subject and by the tendency to reify subjectively originating antagonism between males and females as the central fact of gender. In addition, although there is openness in the concept of how "the subject" is constructed, the theory tends to universalize the categories and relationship of male and female. The outcome for historians is a reductive reading of evidence from the past. Even though this theory takes social relationships into account by linking castration to prohibition and law, it does not permit the introduction of a notion of historical specificity and variability. The phallus is the only signifier; the process of constructing the gendered subject is, in the end, predictable because always the same. If, as film theorist Teresa de Lauretis suggests, we need to think in terms of the construction of subjectivity in social and historical contexts, there is no way to specify those contexts within the terms offered by Lacan. Indeed, even in de Lauretis's attempt, social reality (that is, "material, economic and interpersonal [relations] which are in fact social, and in a larger perspective historical") seems to lie outside, apart from the subject.[26] A way to conceive of "social reality" in terms of gender is lacking.

The problem of sexual antagonism in this theory has two aspects. First, it projects a certain timeless quality, even when it is historicized as well as it has been by Sally Alexander. Alexander's reading of Lacan lead her to conclude that "antagonism between the sexes is an unavoidable aspect of the acquisition of sexual identity. . . . If antagonism is always latent, it is possible that history offers no final resolution, only the constant reshaping, reorganizing of the symbolization of difference, and the sexual division of labor."[27] It may be my hopeless utopianism that gives me pause before this formulation, or it may be that I have not yet shed the episteme of what Foucault called the Classical Age. Whatever the explanation, Alexander's formulation contributes to the fixing of the binary opposition of male and female as the only possible relationship and as a permanent aspect of the human condition. It perpetuates rather than questions what Denise Riley refers to as "the dreadful air of constancy of sexual polarity." She writes: "The historically constructed nature of the opposition [between male and female] produces as one of its effects just that air of an invariant and monotonous men/women opposition."[28]

It is precisely that opposition, in all its tedium and monotony, that (to return to the Anglo-American side) Carol Gilligan's work has promoted. Gilligan explains the divergent paths of moral development followed by boys and girls in terms of differences of "experience" (lived reality). It is not surprising that historians of women have picked up her ideas and used them to explain the "different voices" their work has enabled them to hear. The problems with these borrowings are manifold, and they are logically connected.[29] The first is a slippage that often happens in the attribution of causality: the argument moves from a statement such as "women's experience leads them to make moral choices contingent on contexts and relationships" to "women think and choose this way because they are women." Implied in this line of reasoning is the ahistorical, if not essentialist, notion of woman. Gilligan and others have extrapolated her description, based on a small sample of late twentieth-century American schoolchildren, into a statement about all women. This extrapolation is evident especially, but not exclusively, in the discussions by some historians of "women's culture" that take evidence from early saints to modern militant labor activists and reduce it to proof of Gilligan's hypothesis about a universal female preference for relatedness.[30] This use of Gilligan's ideas provides sharp contrast to the more complicated and historicized conceptions of "women's culture" evident in the *Feminist Studies* 1980 symposium.[31] Indeed, a comparison of that set of articles with Gilligan's formulations reveals the extent to which her notion is ahistorical, defining woman/ man as a universal, self-reproducing binary opposition—fixed always in the same way. By insisting on fixed differences (in Gilligan's case, by simplifying data with more mixed results about sex and moral reasoning to underscore sexual difference), feminists contribute to the kind of thinking they want to oppose. Although they insist on the revaluation of the category "female" (Gilligan suggests that women's moral choices may be more humane than men's), they do not examine the binary opposition itself.

We need a refusal of the fixed and permanent quality of the binary opposition, a genuine historicization and deconstruction of the terms of sexual difference. We must become more self-conscious about distinguishing between our analytic vocabulary and the material we want to analyze. We must find ways (however imperfect) to continually subject our categories to criticism, our analyses to self-criticism. If we employ Jacques Derrida's definition of deconstruction, this criticism means analyzing in context the way any binary opposition operates, reversing and displacing its hierarchical construction, rather than accepting it as real or self-evident or in the nature of things.[32] In a sense, of course, feminists have been doing this for years. The history of feminist thought is a history of the refusal of the hierarchical construction of the relationship between male and female in its specific contexts and an attempt to reverse or displace its operations. Feminist historians are now in a position to theorize their practice and to develop gender as an analytic category.

II

Concern with gender as an analytic category has emerged only in the late twentieth century. It is absent from the major bodies of social theory articulated from the eighteenth to the early twentieth centuries. To be sure, some of those theories built their logic on analogies to the opposition of male and female, others acknowledged a "woman question," still others addressed the formation of subjective sexual identity, but gender as a way of talking about systems of social or sexual relations did not appear. This neglect may in part explain the difficulty that contemporary feminists have had incorporating the term gender into existing bodies of theory and convincing adherents of one or another theoretical school that gender belongs in their vocabulary. The term gender is part of the attempt by contemporary feminists to stake claim to a certain definitional ground, to insist on the inadequacy of existing bodies of theory for explaining persistent inequalities between women and men. It seems to me significant that the use of the word gender has emerged at a moment of great epistemological turmoil which takes the form, in some cases, of a shift from scientific to literary paradigms among social scientists (from an emphasis on cause to one on meaning, blurring genres of inquiry, in anthropologist Clifford Geertz's phrase)[33] and, in other cases, the form of debates about theory between those who assert the transparency of facts and those who insist that all reality is construed or constructed, between those who defend and those who question the idea that "man" is the rational master of his own destiny. In the space opened by this debate and on the side of the critique science developed by the humanities, and of empiricism and humanism by post-stucturalists, feminists have not only begun to find a theoretical voice of their own but have found scholarly and political allies as well. It is within this space that we must articulate gender as an analytic category.

What should be done by historians who, after all, have seen their discipline dismissed by some recent theorists as a relic of humanist thought? I do not think we should quit the archives or abandon the study of the past, but we do have to change some of the ways we've gone about working, some of the questions we have asked. We need to scrutinize our methods of analysis, clarify our operative assumptions, and explain how we think change occurs. Instead of a search for single origins, we have to conceive of processes so interconnected that they cannot be disentangled. Of course, we identify problems to study, and these constitute beginnings or points of entry into complex processes. But it is the processes we must continually keep in mind. We must ask more often how things happened in order to find out why they happened; in anthropologist Michelle Rosaldo's formulation, we must pursue not universal, general causality but meaningful explanation: "It now appears to me that women's place in human social life is not in any direct sense a product of the things she does, but of the meaning her activities acquire through concrete social interaction."[34] To pursue meaning, we need to deal with the individual subject as well as social organization and to articulate the nature of their interrelationships, for both are crucial to understanding how gender works, how change occurs. Finally, we need to replace the notion that social power is unified, coherent, and centralized with something like Michel Foucault's concept of power as dispersed constellations of unequal relationships, discursively constituted in social "fields of force."[35] Within these processes and structures, there is room for a concept of human agency as the attempt (at least partially rational) to construct an identity, a life, a set of relationships, a society within certain limits and with language—conceptual language that at once sets boundaries and contains the possibility for negation, resistance, reinterpretation, the play of metaphoric invention and imagination.

My definition of gender has two parts and several subsets. They are interrelated but must be analytically distinct. The core of the definition rests on an integral connection between two propositions: gender is a constitutive element of social relationships based on perceived differences between the sexes, and gender is a primary way of signifying relationships of power. Changes in the organization of social relationships always correspond to changes in representations of power, but the direction of change is not necessarily one way. As a constitutive element of social relationships based on perceived differences between the sexes, gender involves four interrelated elements: first, culturally available symbols that evoke multiple (and often contradictory) representations—Eve and Mary as symbols of woman, for example, in the Western Christian tradition—but also, myths of light and dark, purification and pollution, innocence and corruption. For historians, the interesting questions are, which symbolic representations are invoked, how, and in what contexts? Second, normative concepts that set forth interpretations of the meanings of the symbols, that attempt to limit and contain their metaphoric possibilities. These concepts are expressed in religious, educational, scientific, legal, and political doctrines and typically take the form of a fixed binary opposition, categorically and unequivocally asserting the meaning of male and female, masculine and feminine. In fact, these normative statements depend on the refusal or repression of alternative possibilities, and sometimes, overt contests about them take place (at what moments and under what circumstances ought to be a concern of historians). The position that emerges as dominant, however, is stated as the only possible one. Subsequent history is written as if these normative positions were the product of social consensus rather than of conflict. An example of this kind of history is the treatment of the Victorian ideology of domesticity as if it were created whole and only afterwards reacted to instead of being the constant subject of great differences of opinion. Another kind of example comes from contemporary fundamentalist religious groups that have forcibly linked their practice to a restoration of women's supposedly more authentic "traditional" role, when, in fact, there is little historical precedent for the unquestioned performance of such a role. The point of new historical investigation is to disrupt the notion of fixity, to discover the nature of the debate or repression that leads to the appearance of timeless permanence in binary gender representation. This kind of analysis must include a notion of politics and reference to social institutions and organizations—the third aspect of gender relationships.

Some scholars, notably anthropologists, have restricted the use of gender to the kinship system (focusing on household and family as the basis for social organization). We need a broader view that includes not only kinship but also (especially for complex modern societies) the labor market (a sex-segregated labor market is a part of the process of gender construction), education (all-male, single-sex, or coeducational institutions are part of the same process), and the polity (universal male suffrage is part of the process of gender construction). It makes little sense to force these institutions back to functional utility in the kinship system, or to argue that contemporary relationships between men and women are artifacts of older kinship systems based on the exchange of women.[36] Gender is constructed through kinship, but not exclusively; it is constructed as well in the economy and the polity, which, in our society at least, now operate largely independently of kinship.

The fourth aspect of gender is subjective identity. I agree with anthropologist Gayle Rubin's formulation that psychoanalysis offers an important theory about the reproduction of gender, a description of the "transformation of the biological sexuality of individuals as they are enculturated."[37] But the universal claim of psychoanalysis gives me pause. Even though Lacanian theory may be helpful for thinking about the construction of gendered identity, historians need to work in a more historical way. If gender identity is based only and universally on fear of castration, the point of historical inquiry is denied. Moreover, real men and women do not always or literally fulfill the terms either of their society's prescriptions or of our analytic categories. Historians need instead to examine the ways in which gendered identities are substantively constructed and relate their findings to a range of activities, social organizations, and historically specific cultural representations. The best efforts in this area so far have been, not surprisingly, biographies: Biddy Martin's interpretation of Lou Andreas Salomé, Kathryn Sklar's depiction of Catharine Beecher, Jacqueline Hall's life of Jessie Daniel Ames, and Mary Hill's discussion of Charlotte Perkins Gilman.[38] But collective treatments are also possible, as Mrinalina Sinha and Lou Ratté have shown in their respective studies of the terms of construction of gender identity for British colonial administrators in India and for British-educated Indians who emerged as anti-imperialist, nationalist leaders.[39]

The first part of my definition of gender consists, then, of all four of these elements, and no one of them operates without the others. Yet they do not operate simultaneously, with one simply reflecting the others. A question for historical research is, in fact, what the relationships among the four aspects are. The sketch I have offered of the process of constructing gender relationships could be used to discuss class, race, ethnicity, or, for that matter, any social process. My point was to clarify and specify how one needs to think about the effect of gender in social and institutional relationships, because this thinking is often not done precisely or systematically. The theorizing of gender, however, is developed in my second proposition: gender is a primary way of signifying relationships of power. It might be better to say, gender is a primary field within which or by means of which power is articulated. Gender is not the only field, but it seems to have been a persistent and recurrent way of enabling the signification of power in the West, in Judeo-Christian as well as Islamic traditions. As such, this part of the definition might seem to belong in the normative section of the argument, yet it does not, for concepts of power, though they may build on gender, are not always literally about gender itself. French sociologist Pierre

Bourdieu has written about how the "di-vision du monde," based on references to "biological differences and notably those that refer to the division of the labor of procreation and reproduction," operates as "the best founded of collective illusions." Established as an objective set of references, concepts of gender structure perception and the concrete and symbolic organization of all social life.[40] To the extent that these references establish distributions of power (differential control over or access to material and symbolic resources), gender becomes implicated in the conception and construction of power itself. The French anthropologist Maurice Godelier has put it this way: "It is not sexuality which haunts society, but society which haunts the body's sexuality. Sex-related differences between bodies are continually summoned as testimony to social relations and phenomena that have nothing to do with sexuality. Not only as testimony to, but also testimony for—in other words, as legitimation."[41]

The legitimizing function of gender works in many ways. Bourdieu, for example, showed how, in certain cultures, agricultural exploitation was organized according to concepts of time and season that rested on specific definitions of the opposition between masculine and feminine. Gayatri Spivak has done a pointed analysis of the uses of gender and colonialism in certain texts of British and American women writers.[42] Natalie Davis has shown how concepts of masculine and feminine related to understandings and criticisms of the rules of social order in early modern France.[43] Historian Caroline Bynum has thrown new light on medieval spirituality through her attention to the relationships between concepts of masculine and feminine and religious behavior. Her work gives us important insight into the ways in which these concepts informed the politics of monastic institutions as well as of individual believers.[44] Art historians have opened a new territory by reading social implications from literal depictions of women and men.[45] These interpretations are based on the idea that conceptual languages employ differentiation to establish meaning and that sexual difference is a primary way of signifying differentiation.[46] Gender, then, provides a way to decode meaning and to understand the complex connections among various forms of human interaction. When historians look for the ways in which the concept of gender legitimizes and constructs social relationships, they develop insight into the reciprocal nature of gender and society and into the particular and contextually specific ways in which politics constructs gender and gender constructs politics.

Politics is only one of the areas in which gender can be used for historical analysis. I have chosen the following examples relating to politics and power in their most traditionally construed sense, that is, as they pertain to government and the nation-state, for two reasons. First, the territory is virtually uncharted, since gender has been seen as antithetical to the real business of politics. Second, political history—still the dominant mode of historical inquiry—has been the stronghold of resistance to the inclusion of material or even questions about women and gender.

Gender has been employed literally or analogically in political theory to justify or criticize the reign of monarchs and to express the relationship between ruler and ruled. One might have expected that the debates of contemporaries over the reigns of Elizabeth I in England and Catherine de Medici in France would dwell on the issue of women's suitability for political rule, but, in the period when kinship and kingship were integrally related, discussions about male kings were equally preoccupied with masculinity and femininity.[47] Analogies to the marital relationship provide structure for the arguments of Jean Bodin, Robert Filmer, and John Locke. Edmund Burke's attack on the French Revolution is built around a contrast between ugly, murderous *sans-culottes* hags ("the furies of hell, in the abused shape of the vilest of women") and the soft femininity of Marie-Antoinette, who escaped the crowd to "seek refuge at the feet of a king and husband" and whose beauty once inspired national pride. (It was in reference to the appropriate role for the feminine in the political order that Burke wrote, "To make us love our country, our country ought to be lovely.")[48] But the analogy is not always to marriage or even to heterosexuality. In medieval Islamic political theory, the symbols of political power alluded most often to sex between man and boy, suggesting not only forms of acceptable sexuality akin to those that Foucault's last work described in classical Greece but also the irrelevance of women to any notion of politics and public life.[49]

Lest this last comment suggest that political theory simply reflects social organization, it seems important to note that changes in gender relationships can be set off by views of the needs of state. A striking example is Louis de Bonald's argument in 1816 about why the divorce legislation of the French Revolution had to be repealed:

> Just as political democracy, "allows the people, the weak part of political society, to rise against the established power," so divorce, "veritable domestic democracy," allows the wife, "the weak part, to rebel against marital authority" . . . "in order to keep the state out of the hands of the people, it is necessary to keep the family out of the hands of wives and children."[50]

Bonald begins with an analogy and then establishes a direct correspondence between divorce and democracy. Harking back to much earlier arguments about the well-ordered family as the foundation of the well-ordered state, the legislation that implemented this view redefined the limits of the marital relationship. Similarly, in our own time, conservative political ideologues would like to pass a series of laws about the organization and behavior of the family that would alter current practices. The connection between authoritarian regimes and the control of women has been noted but not thoroughly studied. Whether at a crucial moment for Jacobin hegemony in the French Revolution, at the point of Stalin's bid for controlling authority, the implementation of Nazi policy in Germany, or with the triumph in Iran of the Ayatollah Khomeini, emergent rulers have legitimized domination, strength, central authority, and ruling power as masculine (enemies, outsiders, subversives, weakness as feminine) and made that code literal in laws (forbidding women's political participation, outlawing abortion, prohibiting wage-earning by mothers, imposing female dress codes) that put women in their place.[51] These actions and their timing make little sense in themselves; in most instances, the state had nothing immediate or material to gain from the control of women. The actions can only be made sense of as part of an analysis of the construction and consolidation of power. An assertion of control or strength was given form as a policy about women. In these examples, sexual difference was conceived in terms of the domination or control of women. These examples provide some insight into the kinds of power relationships being constructed in modern history, but this particular type of relationship is not a universal political theme. In different ways, for example, the democratic regimes of the twentieth century have also constructed their political ideologies with gendered concepts and translated them into policy; the welfare state, for example, demonstrated its protective paternalism in laws directed at women and children.[52] Historically, some socialist and anarchist movements have refused metaphors of domination entirely, imaginatively presenting their critiques of particular regimes or social organizations in terms of transformations of gender identities. Utopian socialists in France and England in the 1830s and 1840s conceived their dreams for a harmonious future in terms of the complementary natures of individuals as exemplified in the union of man and woman, "the social individual."[53] European anarchists were long known not only for refusing the conventions of bourgeois marriage, but for their visions of a world in which sexual difference did not imply hierarchy.

These examples are of explicit connections between gender and power, but they are only a part of my definition of gender as a primary way of signifying relationships of power. Attention to gender is often not explicit, but it is nonetheless a crucial part of the organization of equality or inequality. Hierarchical structures rely on generalized understandings of the so-called natural relationships between male and female. The concept of class in the nineteenth century relied on gender for its articulation. While middle-class reformers in France, for example, depicted workers in terms coded as feminine (subordinated, weak, sexually exploited like prostitutes), labor and socialist leaders replied by insisting on the masculine position of the working class (producers, strong, protectors of their women and children). The terms of this discourse were not explicitly about gender, but they were strengthened by references to it. The gendered "coding" of certain terms established and "naturalized" their meanings. In the process, historically specific, normative definitions of gender (which were taken as givens) were reproduced and embedded in the culture of the French working class.[54]

The subject of war, diplomacy, and high politics frequently comes up when traditional political historians question the utility of gender in their work. But here, too, we need to look beyond the actors and the literal import of their words. Power relations among nations and the status of colonial subjects have been made comprehensible (and thus legitimate) in terms of relations between male and female. The legitimizing of war—of expending young lives to protect the state—has variously taken the forms of explicit appeals to manhood (to the need to defend otherwise vulnerable women and children), of implicit reliance on belief in the duty of sons to serve their leaders or their (father the) king, and of associations between masculinity and national strength.[55] High politics itself is a gendered concept, for it establishes its crucial importance and public power, the reasons for and the fact of its highest authority, precisely in its exclusion of women from its work. Gender is one of the recurrent references by which political power has been conceived, legitimated, and criticized. It refers to but also establishes the meaning of the male/female opposition. To vindicate political power, the reference must seem sure and fixed, outside human construction, part of the natural or divine order. In that way, the binary opposition and the social process of gender relationships both become part of the meaning of power itself; to question or alter any aspect threatens the entire system.

If significations of gender and power construct one another, how do things change? The answer in a general sense is that change may be initiated in many places. Massive political upheavals that throw old orders into chaos and bring new ones into being may revise the terms (and so the organization) of gender in the search for new forms of legitimation. But they may not; old notions of gender have also served to validate new regimes.[56] Demographic crises, occasioned by food shortages, plagues, or wars, may have called into question normative visions of heterosexual marriage (as happened in some circles, in some countries in the 1920s), but they have also spawned pro-natalist policies that insist on the exclusive importance of women's maternal and reproductive functions.[57] Shifting patterns of employment may lead to altered marital strategies and to different possibilities for the construction of subjectivity, but they can also be experienced as new arenas of activity for dutiful daughters and wives.[58] The emergence of new kinds of cultural symbols may make possible the reinterpreting or, indeed, rewriting of the oedipal story, but it can also serve to reinscribe that terrible drama in even more telling terms. Political processes will determine which outcome prevails— political in the sense that different actors and different meanings are contending with one another for control. The nature of that process, of the actors and their actions, can only be determined specifically, in the context of time and place. We can write the history of that process only if we recognize that "man" and "woman" are at once empty and overflowing categories. Empty because they have no ultimate, transcendent meaning. Overflowing because even when they appear to be fixed, they still contain within them alternative, denied, or suppressed definitions.

Political history has, in a sense, been enacted on the field of gender. It is a field that seems fixed yet whose meaning is contested and in flux. If we treat the opposition between male and female as problematic rather than known, as something contextually defined, repeatedly constructed, then we must constantly ask not only what is at stake in proclamations or debates that invoke gender to explain or justify their positions but also how implicit understandings of gender are being invoked and reinscribed. What is the relationship between laws about women and the power of the state? Why (and since when) have women been invisible as historical subjects, when we know they participated in the great and small events of human history? Has gender legitimated the emergence of professional careers?[59] Is (to quote the title of a recent article by French feminist Luce Irigaray) the subject of science sexed?[60] What is the relationship between state politics and the discovery of the crime of homosexuality?[61] How have social institutions incorporated gender into their assumptions and organizations? Have there ever been genuinely egalitarian concepts of gender in terms of which political systems were projected, if not built?

Investigation of these issues will yield a history that will provide new perspectives on old questions (about how, for example, political rule is imposed, or what the impact of war on society is), redefine the old questions in new terms (introducing considerations of family and sexuality, for example, in the study of economics or war), make women visible as active participants, and create analytic distance between the seemingly fixed language of the past and our own terminology. In addition, this new history will leave open possibilities for thinking about current feminist political strategies and the (utopian) future, for it suggests that gender must be redefined and restructured in conjunction with a vision of political and social equality that includes not only sex, but class and race.

8

The Body Politic[1]

Carroll Smith-Rosenberg

This essay is concerned with "words and things," with the ways language forms and refracts human experience and action.[2] It explores the processes by which our passions and desires—indeed our sense of self—assume meaning within historically specific discourses and ideologies.

A post-structuralist fascination with the power and opacity of language is relatively new to historians. Only recently have we begun to read language as a dense web of metaphors, displacements, and silences, as the embodiment of difference and the source of meaning. But if we accept the post-structuralist argument that it is language that endows the social with meaning, we must also insist that language, itself, acquires meaning and authority only within specific social and historical settings. While linguistic differences structure society, social differences structure language. Social heterogeneity produces heteroglossia. Conflicting social dialects battle one another, forming and re-forming meanings, exemplifying change.

The historian's contribution to the post-modernist discourse is to insist upon the simultaneous separateness and inseparability of material and discursive practices, of "actions in the world" and symbolic gestures. By meticulously tracing the ways they weave in and out of one another, powerful yet mutually dependent, we can throw significant light on processes by which they construct one another, the realm of the social, indeed, meaning, itself. In doing so, we will gain a far more precise understanding of the ways social and linguistic differences take shape and power is deployed.

Human sexuality is emblematic of the interconnectedness of the material and discursive. Discourse constructs our perceptions of the body and the erotic at the same time as discourses themselves borrow from the body and the erotic to render themselves evocative and expressive. But is it only the discursively constructed body that language can draw upon? Or can our experience of the body transcend discourse, as when pain explodes beyond the expressive ability of words? More radically, can desire appear within a discourse that has not named it?

Considerations of power are central to the interaction of the physical body and the body of language. Sexuality produces power, at the same time as the

101

discourse of the powerful constructs sexuality. We must not collapse sexuality, power, and discourse upon each other. It is their interpenetration not their interchangeability that is critical within the abstractions of post-structural debate, within the affective world of the emotions—and within the political arena.

Certainly we live in a world that sexualizes discourse and politicizes sexuality. Slogans such as "Our Bodies, Ourselves," "The Right to Choose," signal the fusion of sexual and political subjectivity at the same time as they make sexual liberation a metaphor for social and economic empowerment. Sexuality represents social danger as well as social empowerment. For countless conservative Americans, the dismembered bodies of dead fetuses, the sexually assertive bodies of aborting feminists, of lesbians and gays, symbolize their own vulnerability in a frightening and disjointed world.

Bitter as these current debates may be, they are not new. The very issues— women's right to abortions, "the lesbian threat"—go back over a hundred years to middle-class women's first efforts to construct themselves as legitimate public and political subjects. During the 1850s, 1860s, and 1870s, conservative men successfully challenged the legality of abortions in state courts and legislatures. Only a few years later, homosexuality emerged as a critical political issue. By the 1920s, publicly assertive and politically powerful women had been labeled Mannish Lesbians, and women's educational and reform institutions were attacked as the breeding grounds of an unnatural female subjectivity.

Two concerns—a need to understand the origins of our present political debates, a desire to explore the interweaving of the discursive and the material, the sexual and the political—inform this essay. Texts, textuality, derived from *texto* (Latin, to weave), constitute the locus where bodies discursive and material weave fabrics of the self. The body of each text contains two other bodies which shape the text as it shapes them: the physical body, and the body politic whose materiality the physical body symbolically represents.

Post-structuralist theory and social history, together, have fractured these bodies making them multiple, diverse, decentered, ever changing. If this is true of the social and physical bodies, it is even more true of the body of discourse. Each discourse is an amalgam of earlier discourses, the vocabulary it chooses, the meanings it assigns to words, its very grammar, the result of repeated conflicts and compromises. The muted voices of defeated discourses and lost meanings haunt present usage. Only by seeking out those lost discourses, filling in the silences, accounting for disjunctures and discontinuities in the meanings assigned words, can we begin to understand how our own bodies and desires are constructed and how the power that constructs the body politic is deployed.

Language embodies past discursive complexities. Language also represents present social diversity. A cacophony of social dialects representing different classes, ethnicities, generations, professions, and genders characterizes every heterogeneous society, a cacophony reproduced differently within the consciousness of different social speakers. In this way, the structure of discourse is like the structure of the fugue, each voice, each strand, pursuing its own line, yet touching the other voices, harmoniously, at times, at times, discordantly. Tension and release follow, the one upon the other. In this same way are the discursive patterns of heterogeneous societies evanescently embodied, and like sound, fugitive, die away.

Power colors these fugitive discourses. The languages of the economically and politically dominant struggle to deny the legitimacy of more marginal social discourses. During periods of social transformation, when social forms crack open, social dialects proliferate, blending and conflicting with one another, challenging the dominant discourses. At such times, ideological conflict fractures discourse. At such times, as well, sexuality and the physical body emerge as particularly evocative political symbols. Those aspects of human sexuality considered most disorderly are evoked to represent social atomization, the overthrow of hierarchies, the uncontrollability of change. Within this discursive field, those fearful of change define the socially disorderly as sexually deviant, dangerous infections within the body politic. In this way the fearful project onto the bodies of those they have named social misfits their own desires for social control. But the marginal and the oppressed also fuse sexual and social disorder, defiantly displaying their own sexuality as a symbol of social resistance. Social disarray, discursive discord, warring bodies merge, reinforcing one another; the dismemberment of the symbolic body speaks of the dismemberment of the body politic—and of meaning.

Making generalizations concrete, let us turn now to the first of the two nineteenth-century sexual debates we have already mentioned, the abortion debate that engaged American men between the 1850s and the 1880s. Until those years, the American legal system, informed by British common law, had recognized first trimester abortions as legitimate medical procedures. Beginning in the 1860s, the American Medical Association, the newly formed political and professional arm of the allopathic school of American medicine—the "regulars," they called themselves—declared war on abortion. By the 1880s, Congress and virtually every state government had passed legislation making the performance of abortion and the dissemination of birth control and abortion information felonies.[5]

The A.M.A. campaign took place in a world rent by social and demographic transformations. Few of these changes struck contemporaries more forcefully than the emergence of visible and non-domestic roles for affluent, urban women. With fewer children and more servants, surrounded by a host of new urban institutions (schools, libraries, museums, clubs, philanthropic agencies) these women devoted less and less of their time to maternal tasks. Substituting education, intellectual sophistication, and social experience for the more traditional female virtues of docility, dependence, and domesticity, they joined women's clubs and urban charities by the thousands. They became experts on issues of public housing, infant mortality, and the under-employment of working-class women. In city halls and state legislatures, they battled for social purity, temperance, and social services.

But as upper middle-class women, they also frequented plays and the opera, collected art and traveled in Europe—in short ruled a social world that grew ever more affluent and sophisticated. In both these ways, as moral conscience and as social arbiters, affluent women constituted themselves public subjects.[4]

Husbands and fathers abetted these women, making their wives and daughters symbols of their own wealth and sophistication. A low birth rate was essential to the existence of such women and such families—a birth rate both the middle-class matron and the middle-class husband undoubtedly desired. Historical and sociological evidence suggests that family limitation is a family decision. Bourgeois husbands and wives responded to the demographic and economic realities of the new commercial cities and the new capitalist class structure. They responded, as well, to the commercialization of the American drug industry and of abortion practices. Beginning in the 1850's, physicians and midwives who performed abortions opened clinics and hospitals, sent agents to rural areas soliciting trade, advertised in the burgeoning tabloid press of the cities. So did drug companies, newly industrialized and concerned with expanding both sales and production. Abortifacients were popular and profitable drugs. Middle-class men as physicians, pharmacists, journalists, and husbands played a major role in the growth and visibility of abortion practices, practices which themselves reflected the growing commercialization of American society. In short, like the affluent woman herself, abortion practices were no longer private female (and familial) affairs. They had become public and commercial, transacted over the counters of numberless pharmacies, in the offices of countless physicians, on the pages of the tabloid press.[5]

Abortion, as represented in the A.M.A. rhetoric, bore little resemblance to actual abortion practices. Within the A.M.A. narrative the bourgeois matron emerged as a powerful, self-conscious, and autonomous subject. Motivated by a selfish love of luxury, a distaste for the inconveniences which motherhood entailed, an intoxication with the world of urban fashion which, unencumbered by children, she would govern, she, alone, chose to abort her helpless infant. The A.M.A.'s rhetoric, completely effacing husbands, transformed the real world of mid-century cities, of the ruthlessly competitive male medical profession, the male-controlled mass circulation newspapers, and the commercialized drug industry into a fantasy land of balls and dinner parties governed by affluent women, who, at ease within the consumer economy, purchased luxuries, including abortions.[6] "By some women abortion is demanded and paid a large price for," a fashionable Boston physician charged in 1859, "merely because of the annoyance of pregnancy and the duties involved by the newborn helpless child."[7] "Women," another abortion opponent argued, "have become altogether immersed in the pursuit of mere pleasure and fashion. Nothing must stand in the way of those objects."[8]

Ignoring doctor, lawyer, and clergyman, the A.M.A. narrative continued, these women cast caution to the winds. Facing pain and the possibility of death, they insisted on having their way, and their way was not that of traditional domesticity.

In constructing these women, mid-Victorian physicians conflated their own fears of the middle-class woman's public presence and social eminence with those women's equally troublesome refusal to accept traditional sexual responsibilities. By purchasing abortions, the women had publicly declared themselves sexual—and not reproductive. The cover illustration of a popular male magazine, *The National Police Gazette,* graphically merged these varied rhetorical strands in a single condensed symbol or mythic figure. Dis-covered to the gaze of the male readers of this sensationalist tabloid, a well-dressed woman, boldly stared out into the world. Her arms, transformed into devil's wings, exposed her pelvis, itself transformed into a devil's head with fang teeth gnawing the plump body of her innocent baby.[9]

The A.M.A. scripted social anxieties onto the physical and into the text. But the historian must ask, which anxieties? To un-cover the socially specific, Mary Douglas suggests asking three questions: who is the dangerous actor? who or what is endangered? what is the dangerous act?[10]

The urbane married woman constituted the dangerous actor. An A.M.A.-created caricature of the declining middle-class birth rate and the new wealth and customs of the cities, she sought to please herself in the public and urban arena, not to serve others in the cloistered home. The A.M.A.'s endangered figure was, of course, the innocent and vulnerable fetus. But the fetus itself served the A.M.A. as a condensed symbol for the traditional family, the polarization of female and male roles, of private and public worlds—a family and social order which the urban and commercial revolutions had only just created and which the creature of those revolutions, the newly visible and affluent bourgeois matron now, ironically, threatened to destroy. She threatened to destroy the Aryan world as well. Permitting immigrant women to outbreed her, the urbane matron endangered Anglo-Saxon survival.

The dangerous act, her decision to terminate her pregnancy, was multi-focal as well. By deciding, on her own, to abort, which the A.M.A. represented as the height of *self*ishness, the middle-class woman declared her *self*hood and her *will*fulness against the determinism of biology and class myths. Not only did she reject the philosophical and social assumptions of medical orthodoxy, she challenged its economic hegemony as well. Insisting on her right to choose her own physician, she turned to the regular physicians' professional competitors—homeopaths, eclectic physicians, midwives—to secure her abortion and then, maintaining them as her family physicians, she challenged the privileged economic position of the allopathic doctor.[11]

Having projected the problematic aspects of the bourgeois revolution (the declining birth rate and the sexual restraints birth control necessitated; the breakdown of old customs; the frightening ways of the new cities; the influx of new immigrants; conflicts within the medical world; the bourgeois matron's increasingly public persona; the pervasive sense of change out of control) onto the mystified figure of the aborting matron, mid-Victorian male physicians counterpoised her to another discursive sexual and medical construction—the True Woman who accepted her biological destiny and gloried in her reproductive sexuality. The aborting matron (not the complicitous husband nor the deceiving lover) served as the scapegoat for all that was problematic in the new social order. The dependent and domestic True Woman asserted that, despite its emerging problems, the bourgeois order, rooted in women's biology, was natural and God-ordained. The True Woman evoked a pre-commercial Eden where women were unproblematically reproductive and men public and productive, the Aborting Matron, an urban industrial hell where women sacrificed their young on the altars of Mammon and Fashion. Janus-faced, these two women, male-constructed symbols of order and disorder, guarded the bourgeois male order. If the object of bourgeois discourse is to make the bourgeois order seem natural, A.M.A. had constructed a complex and classic bourgeois myth.

To read in this way, however, is to discern only one of the many layers of meanings which informed the A.M.A. rhetoric. The True Woman counterpoised a mystified past to an anxious present in a sexual rhetoric that bespoke the discursive compulsions and ideological conflicts of an actual past. Mid-Victorian male doctors had not constructed the True Woman out of the whole cloth of their imaginations. Rather they inherited her, an amalgam of late eighteenth-century political discourses. The privatization of woman and of her sexuality was very much an ideological construction of the mid- and late eighteenth century and, I would argue, a central component in the construction of the male political subject. The Age of Revolution necessitated the conceptualization of a virtuous political subject, desiring and deserving the liberty of rational self-government. Political discourses going back at least as far as the Augustan Age associated him with military service and land holding, with Spartan and early Roman virtues. They made him rational, self-reliant, and virile. Of course, he had his mirror image—the effeminate, sybaritic man of court and fashion. A mirror man in many ways, the courtier, the man of fashion was driven by pride and "ardent passions," corrupted by luxury, dependent on the favor of the more powerful. He evoked the feminine and the impure.[12] Eighteenth-century political discourses, by so sexualizing the public and the political, banished middle-class women to domestic space and reproductive sexuality. The virtuous woman had now to deny all sexual, political, and public desires.[13]

The eighteenth century's discursive fusion of political virtue with male sexuality colored mid-Victorian perceptions of female sexuality and lent a political urgency to the A.M.A.'s attacks upon the public and aborting matron. Civic humanist fears of effeminate dependents, liberal humanist condemnations of corrupt court privileges constituted the unconscious heritage of these doctors' discourse. Eighteenth-century alarms reinforced nineteenth-century confusions. Together, they shaped legislative policies and court decisions that affected sexual feelings and behavior far into the twentieth century.

Social dialects also exist in dialogic interaction. The A.M.A.'s abortion rhetoric constituted a decidedly male discourse. Male physicians spoke primarily to each other and to male politicians, but rarely to women (women, after all, did not have to acquiesce in the legislative regulation of their own bodies). But the disseminators of this male medico-political language did have to share discursive space with a second, equally politicized sexual speaker—the middle-class matron. Responding to their own perceptions of economic and institutional change and to female/male power relations within the home, responding, as well, to the influences of earlier female- and male-generated discourses, middle-class women developed their own distinctive sexual vocabulary that paralleled and opposed the male abortion rhetoric. On the pages of female-authored sexual and marital advice books, images of marital rape, of unwanted pregnancies, of marriage as legalized prostitution, replaced male images of unnatural, aborting mothers. To purify America, the authors insisted, women must develop their own sexual power within the home, control the frequency of intercourse, dominate the sexual act.[14] Men's unrestrained sexual desires, not women's demands for social autonomy endangered the American family and the American nation.

Significantly, these women condemned abortion as bitterly as the A.M.A. had. For the women, however, the husband who forced unwanted pregnancies upon his wife, not the willful and fashionable matron, constituted the dangerous actor. Abortion did not symbolize an increase in personal and sexual freedom for these women, but the reverse. Within the women's narrative, the sexual (and often painful) penetration (the dangerous act) of the male abortionist replicated the sexual (and often unwanted) penetration of the husband. Sex, as told by these women, became an unending series of male violations of women's physical integrity. Women's rhetoric allied mothers and children, both physiologically weakened by man's uncontrolled sexuality, making them the endangered subjects.

Expressing what may well have been the actual sexual concerns of many of their readers (fear of pregnancy, fear of venereal infection, fear of intercourse), the authors transposed those concerns into an elaborate metaphoric construction in which male sexual power within the home came to symbolize male economic and political power without the home—the raped wife, the economic and legal powerlessness of women, the wife weighed down by children and domestic chores, the constraints and discontents of women's social roles.[15]

During the 1860s, 1870s, and 1880s, two warring mythic figures, the lustful and uncontrollable husband and the unnatural aborting wife, expressed middle-class women's and men's radically disparate social alarms and angers in words that expressed different sexual experiences as well. At times it seemed as if the disputants' voices drowned out one another. Despite their shared class identities and agendas, neither women nor men appeared able to hear or respond to the others' fears and complaints. Their discourses followed parallel but never-crossing paths.

One common thread, or mythic figure, however, did unite these two disparate discourses. She was the True Woman. Like their male physicians, middle-class women were heirs of the Revolutionary political discourses of the eighteenth century and their sexualization of the public and the political. Victorian men embraced this sexualization. Victorian women battled against it. Turning to millennial Evangelicalism (but note, not to the radical implications of liberal or Republican ideology), middle-class women claimed the public and the political for God and reforming women. Male appetites and passions, lust, greed, drunkenness, not the feminine or even the effeminate, threatened civic virtue. Sexuality must be banished from the political arena, sexual and political subjectivities severed. Within the women's reforming discourses, the sexual man was always the political enemy.

Indeed, throughout the nineteenth century, reforming women repeatedly identified public disorder with uncontrolled male sexuality; a pure America demanded the repression of the male animal. Female abolitionists' rhetoric, for example, had made the slave owners' sexual exploitation of Afro-American women represent all the evils of slavery. For pre-Civil War women urban reformers, prostitution served as a condensed symbol for the economic exploitation of working-class women in America's early industrial cities. Following the Civil War, the Women's Christian Temperance Union represented an industrial and urban America brought low by unrestrained male appetites and the corrupting influence of the liquor lobby. All proclaimed the middle-class woman the embodiment of civic virtue for she had renounced an active public sexual subjectivity. She alone could purify American politics of the taint of sexual corruption. It was in the language of female sexual purity and male sexual corruption that women waged their final *and successful* battle for political subjectivity, the Suffrage Movement of the second decade of this century.[16]

By turning to Millennial Christianity rather than to the egalitarian or radical components of late eighteenth-century political ideology, nineteenth-century middle-class women gained their public and political subjectivity at the cost of losing any claim to an active sexual subjectivity. This meant that they accepted the radical polarization of gender roles which male discourses had originated. It meant, as well, that they lost the discursive and ideological ground upon which to defend women's right to abortions or to participate, as feminists, in the sexual revolution of the early twentieth century.

Which brings us to our second major politico-sexual battle—the sexologists' attack upon the New Woman as an unnatural woman and a sexual pervert.[17]

Who was the New Woman? I use the term, borrowed, I must confess, from

Henry James, to refer to a cohort of middle and upper middle-class American women born between the late 1850s and the early 1900s, who were educated, ambitious, and, most frequently, single. In their own minds and the minds of their contemporaries, the New Women were most immediately associated with the new women's colleges. Education constituted their most salient characteristic and their first self-conscious demand. They linked college education to intellectual self-fulfillment, to autonomous roles outside the family, to glorious achievements.[18] Graduating from college, the New Women more frequently than not refused to return to their mothers' world of reproduction and domesticity. Rather, boldly asserting their right to a public voice and visible power, they laid claim to rights and privileges customarily accorded only to white middle-class men. They moved into the public sphere, not as religious, reforming matrons but as independent women trained in the new professions. As lawyers, doctors, writers, or social reformers, they created new roles for themselves as experts in urban problems, as political lobbyists, union organizers, publishers, and creative artists. In radical flight from the patriarchal home and heterosexual marriage, they created a variety of alternative female institutions. Living with (frequently espousing love for) other women within the separatist environment of women's colleges, settlement houses, and reform organizations, dedicating their lives to securing social justice for middle-class and working-class women, the New Women amassed greater political power and visibility than any other group of women in American experience.[19] Repudiating the Cult of True Womanhood in ways earlier middle-class matrons never could, these New Women threatened men in ways those matrons never did.

Radically unlike those matrons in so many ways, the New Women did preserve two key aspects of those matron's political and sexual world: the, by now, traditional female association of political corruption with male sexuality; their conflation of civic and female sexual virtue; and the equally traditional female assumption of the "naturalness" of women's passionate involvement with one another.[20] Indeed, it was only by insisting on the asexuality of their relations with other women, that the New Women could lay claim to a full-fledged public subjectivity as pure and asexual women. They were abetted in doing so by the Victorian assumption that sex in the absence of men was inconceivable. Not only were men essential to women's primary sexual act, the generation of babies, they were considered essential to the generation of female sexual desire. Victorian male medical and sexual discourses in America and England simply did not recognize sexual desire unless it was directed towards men. Thus school girls found in one another's arms were seen as loving friends. Even those discovered to have been genitally involved with one another were designated masturbators, that is, sexually active but lacking an object of desire.[21] (As a brief aside, it seems a tribute to the power of desire that, in their letters and diaries, the New Women were able to express such highly sensual, indeed erotic, feelings for one another. The erotic did not simply lurk as the unconscious of their letters or their lives. Time and again, it burst through all restraints and boldly claimed the name desire. But, note carefully, not the name sex.)

For half a century, middle-class American women and men bitterly debated the social and sexual legitimacy of the New Woman. Through her, they argued about the "naturalness" of gender and the legitimacy of the bourgeois social order. They agreed on only one point: the New Woman challenged existing gender relations and the distribution of power. By defining her as physiologically "unnatural," the symptom of a diseased society, those whom she threatened reaffirmed the legitimacy and the "naturalness" of the bourgeois order. By insisting on their own social and sexual legitimacy, the New Women repudiated that order.

The emergence of institutions of higher education for women elicited bourgeois men's first hostile and frightened response. Not only would higher education open new roles for bourgeois women, it challenged the West's traditional basis for gender differentiation. Since classical Greece, men had insisted that man represented the mind, woman the body, man the creative principle, woman the reproductive impulse, man the heaven-born aspect of human nature, woman its earth-bound component. Put must succinctly, man was the creator and representative of culture, woman of nature. Not only would the education of women deny the primacy of the sexual both in the sphere of public education and in women's lives. It would also violate this chain of binary oppositions, making woman, not man, the mediating figure. Alarmed by the real and the philosophical implications of equal education for women and men, Victorian educators and physicians launched an attack which combined some of the most ancient principles of medicine with the nineteenth-century's increasingly deterministic vision. In this battle, the old female body and the New Women's mind became the contested loci of female subjectivity, men insisting on the former, the New Women on the latter.

The human body, Victorian male physicians insisted and male educators readily concurred, was both hierarchical and fragile, its delicate balances easily destroyed by external forces. A closed energy system, the body allocated scarce energy resources governed by rigid, biologically determined and gender-linked priorities. Within the male body, the higher organs, the brain and heart, dominated. Predictably, the reproductive organs dominated woman's body. So far nature had created a balanced physical and social order. The rational man embodied the coherent, unified subject of liberal ideology, the reproductive woman, his equally unified and ordered mate. But the woman who favored her mind at the expense of her ovaries, especially the woman who spent her adolescence and early adulthood in college and graduate school, would not only disorder her delicate physiological balance.[22] She would become the unstable, incoherent subject, the embodiment of disorder, the fearful Other of western ideology. Physicians and asylum directors, college regents and male professors stridently and repeatedly warned young women and their mothers: the educated woman's brain would be over-stimulated. She would become morbidly introspective. Neurasthenia, hysteria, insanity would follow.[23] Her ovaries, robbed of energy rightfully theirs, would atrophy, her menses become irregular, sterility and cancer ensue. No longer reproductive, she would begin to look like a man. Her breasts would shrivel, facial hair develop. Many such women, one highly influential and well-published physician reported, began to wear heavy boots.[25].

It is easy to read this rhetoric as simply the scripting of public policy onto the female body. Nature, not individual caprice, determined woman's nature as emotional and reproductive, man's as cerebral and creative. Nature, thwarted, would wreak physiological and emotional havoc on the individual and disorder and decay upon the nation. But behind these male efforts to limit women's access to higher education lay a far more complicated emotional and symbolic message, one which expressed small-town America's fear of and resistance to social changes that extended far beyond the possibility of new roles for a female elite. Victorian male physicians had projected the principal characteristics of small-town America onto the human body. The human body, as described by male physicians, and the American small town were both hierarchical systems, composed of a myriad of interdependent parts. Physical and social health rested on the harmonious acceptance of that hierarchy. The brain must not steal energy from the ovaries, just as women must not alter their roles or the immigrant aspire to political or social dominance. The physical body's closed energy system paralleled the small town's limited market and capital resources. Each was frighteningly vulnerable to external forces which could disorder its delicate balances. Railroads, finance capitalism, the burgeoning industrial cities threatened small-town America. Stimulation associated with that new world—college, new urban opportunities—would destroy the delicate physiological balance of America's youth. Predictably, the male medical argument followed, physiological disorder would parallel social disorder when small-town America's daughters abandoned the old sureties and fled to the college and the city.

But devoid of literal power, small-town America could only resort to discursive weapons in its battle against change. The timeless and unambiguous social categories rooted in absolute physiological laws, which Victorian doctors had constructed, could rob change of its legitimacy— but not of its power. Finance capitalism did render small-town America economically and culturally marginal. No physiological force kept young women out of college no matter how vociferously physicians and educators warned that exhaustion and disease would destroy them. Mid-Victorian biology could only threaten sinners. It could neither prevent sin nor curtail change.

The New Women, bold in their claims to a place in the public arena and a voice in public debates, were unaffected by these impotent warnings. Rather they constructed a uniquely female discourse and an alternative mythic female figure and identity, one that drew upon liberal humanist and Progressive beliefs in the active and (sexually) virtuous individual citizen. Education, a sense of personal fulfillment, an active life, they argued, strengthened women physically and mentally. The sexual would not bind such women who would easily elevate reason above the passions and devote themselves to furthering the common good. Within a bourgeois social structure where both the birth rate and the marriage rate were steadily declining and the new urban values had triumphed, and within a political milieu where progressive liberalism countered the darker vision of biological determinism, the New Woman, product and espouser of these new arrangements and this bright vision, easily won this first "scientific" debate. Their brave New Woman, a sexually pure Female Warrior for social justice, brimming with energy and health, defending exploited child laborers, challenging corrupt politicians and callous capitalists, triumphed easily over the male physicians' caricature—the neurasthenic and sterile college woman.[26]

The New Woman's claim to a legitimate public subjectivity rested on her separation of the political and the sexual and on her denial of her own sexuality. Men, committed to the fusion of the political and the sexual, resentful of the New Women's political and professional successes, did not remain silent for long. Indeed, they had already begun to construct a second mythic figure in order to condemn the politically disruptive New Woman as sexually dangerous to her nation, her class, and her race. By 1900, male physicians, sex reformers, and educators had unveiled their new construction. The New Woman who stood outside of conventional institutions and socially acceptable roles was a secretly, but innately, sexualized subject. Belonging to an "intermediate sex," her physical body bespoke her social liminality. Her sexual inversion embodied her social disorder. She was the Mannish Lesbian, a social and sexual hermaphrodite.

While male homosexuality had been recognized throughout western history, within the Anglo-American world, few discussions of lesbianism predate the late nineteenth century. Although legal, medical, and pornographic literature on the continent contained graphic descriptions of lesbian behavior, few bourgeois American women (and apparently, few American physicians) were familiar with those descriptions. Neither these women nor their families and their physicians perceived passion between two women as either disturbing or deviant.

The arguments of the sexologists destroyed this vision. By mid-century, medical and scientific discussions of male homosexuality had begun to increase in number, forming one facet of the overall explosion of sexual and scientific discourse that marked the late nineteenth century. This was the golden age of scientific determinism, of social Darwinism and of eugenics, of an autochthonous vision which rooted the social in the material and the physical. Taxonomy assumed unquestioned scientific centrality as Victorian men traced the precise evolution of their social as well as their natural world. Grammar and political institutions, man, birds, and fish were all placed within a grand evolutionary schema of progressive development or degenerative decay. The sexologists' fascination with human sexual variations exemplifies this pattern. Specific sexual acts, fantasies, fetishes, sensations, became the subject of taxonomical scrutiny. Genus and species were assigned. Degrees of abnormality and perversion were carefully charted in much the same spirit as that with which the evolution of the horse and of the dative case were traced.

And with the same goal: the reassertion of order in a conflicting and changing world. This—not the control of actual literal sexual behavior—obsessed the sexologists. Within the sexologist's categorical elaborations, perverted behavior did not have to cease. Quite the contrary. A proxy, it existed to be railed against. It gave the sexologists a sense of power. It reaffirmed their faith in their ability to restore order. Just as the male Victorian imagination fused the social and the sexual, it fused the sexual and the political. The object of the discourse was the deployment of power—the regulation and control of the New Woman. By constituting her an avowedly sexual subject, they made her subject to the political regulation of the state.

While early medical students of the perverse had focused almost exclusively upon male homosexuality, by the mid-1880s case studies of lesbianism appeared with increasing regularity and occupied a prominent position within Richard von Krafft-Ebing's highly influential *Psychopathia Sexualis.*[27] Krafft-Ebing did not focus on the sexual behavior of the women he categorized as lesbian but, rather, on their social behavior and physical appearance. In every case study, Krafft-Ebing linked lesbianism to the rejection of conventional female roles, to cross-dressing, and to "masculine" physiological traits. The following statement exemplifies his approach:

> Uranism [a term that pre-dated "homosexuality"] may nearly always be suspected in females wearing their hair short, or who dress in the fashion of men, or pursue the sports and pastimes of their male acquaintances; also in opera singers and actresses who appear in male attire on the stage by preference. . . . The female urning may chiefly be found in the haunt of boys. She is the rival of their play, preferring the rocking-horse, playing at soldiers, etc., to dolls and other girlish occupations. The toilet is neglected, and rough boyish manners affected. Love for art finds a substitute in the pursuits of the sciences. . . . Perfumes and sweetmeats are disdained. The consciousness of being a woman and thus to be deprived of the gay college life, or to be barred from the military career, produces painful reflections. The masculine soul, heaving in the female bosom, finds pleasure in the pursuit of manly sports, and in manifestations of courage and bravado.[28]

Krafft-Ebing's lesbians seemed to desire male privileges and power as ardently as, perhaps more ardently than, they sexually desired women. As in yet another case study, Krafft-Ebing tells us: "She was quite conscious of her pathological condition," Krafft-Ebing reported of one woman: "Masculine features, deep voice, manly gait, without beard, small breasts; cropped her hair short and gave the impression of a man in women's clothes."[29] In this way, Krafft-Ebing, through the creation of a new medico-sexual subject—the Mannish Lesbian—linked women's rejection of traditional gender roles and their demands for social and economic equality to cross-dressing, sexual perversion, and borderline herma-phroditism.

Krafft-Ebing had constructed a condensed and multifocal symbol of social disorder.[30] His "Mannish Lesbian," her male soul trapped in her female form, literally embodied the New Women's rejection of gender polarities, at the same time that she affirmed the naturalness of those polarities—male as soul or mind, female as body. Translations of Krafft-Ebing's *Psychopathia Sexualis* also introduced into the Anglo-American medical discourse the phrase "sexual invert," a phrase which calls forth images of hierarchies inverted, of "the World Upside Down."[31] Linked to transvestism and women's assumptions of male roles, as Krafft-Ebing always linked it, the "sexual invert" suggests the medieval imagery of "The Woman On Top," a classic use of sexual and gender disarray to symbolize social disorder.[32] "The intermediate sex" stands between sexual categories, thus suggesting the possibility of existing outside socially acceptable categories of sexual and/or social behavior. Significantly none of these three metaphors conjures up literal sexual images. They are social and hierarchical, concerned with issues of order, structure, and location. Inverting traditional social and cultural distinctions, they link charges of irregular sexuality to the New Woman's challenge to social and domestic order.

Krafft-Ebing's fusion of a woman's love of other women with a masculine physiognomy, and with feminist demands for education and new roles remained an alien concept for this first generation of New Women. Their conceptual systems, their definitions of the natural and the abnormal, their understanding of sexuality, still reflected the beliefs and language of their mother's and father's generation. At the height of Progressive romanticism, it seemed to them equally laudable to re-form the world, to re-form gender, and to love women. Even the rejection of heterosexual marriage did not transform these genteel Edwardian women into "unnatural inverts"—in their own eyes or in those of the men of their generation

Their innocence would not survive the sexual revolution of the twentieth century. The male sexologist who most directly broke into this female world of love and intimacy, defining it as both actively sexual and as sexually perverted, was Havelock Ellis. More clearly than any other writer before Freud, Ellis insisted that a woman's love for other women was in itself sexual and "inverted."[33] Genteel, educated women, thoroughly feminine in appearance, thought, and behavior, Ellis insisted, might well be active lesbians.[34] Divorcing sexual inversion from cross-dressing and suspicions of transsexuality, Ellis tore from them their cloak of gentility—and transformed them into sexual predators. Lesbian inverts, Ellis warned, preyed on other women who, while possessing a predisposition for homosexuality, would have remained heterosexual women had they not been seduced by unnatural and aggressive lesbian inverts while resident in women's colleges or settlement houses or active in feminist politics. Separatist feminist institutions must be avoided.[35]

Havelock Ellis thus turned the new sexual rhetoric into a direct political attack upon the New Women, linking women's love for other women with female criminality and insanity and associating all with women's demands for a political voice and political power. "The modern movement of emancipation," Ellis warned,

> —the movement to obtain the same rights and duties, the same freedom and responsibility, the same education and the same work ... carries with it certain disadvantages. It has involved an increase in feminine criminality and feminine insanity. ... In connection with these, we can scarcely be surprised to find an increase in homosexuality, which has always been regarded as belonging to an allied, if not the same group of phenomena.[36]

Citing Ellis as an unimpeachable scientific expert, American physicians and educators launched an explicit political campaign against the New Woman, the institutions that nurtured her, and her feminist and reform programs. "Female boarding schools and colleges are the great breeding grounds of artificial [acquired] homosexuality," R.N. Shufeldt wrote in the *Pacific Medical Journal* in 1902.[37] William Lee Howard, in the respectable *New York Medical Journal* of 1900 commented acidly:

> The female possessed of masculine ideas of independence, the virago who would sit in the public highways and lift up her pseudo-virile voice, proclaiming her sole right to decide questions of war or religion or the value of celibacy and the curse of woman's impurity, and that disgusting antisocial being, the female sexual pervert, are simply different degrees of the same class—degenerates.[38]

As Progressive women reformers increased their political power in the years immediately preceding the First World War, and as the suffrage movement reached its crescendo, articles complaining of lesbianism in women's colleges, clubs, prisons, and reformatories—wherever women gathered—became common. By the 1920s, charges of lesbianism had become a common way to discredit women professionals, reformers, and educators.[39]

Ideology affects public policies, which in turn affect sexual behaviors. College administrators, wary of changing political attitudes, adopted restrictive dormitory policies. Warning young women of the danger inherent in intense female friendships, they prohibited women from spending the night in one another's rooms. Accusations of lesbianism now became grounds for expulsion from college. Sex reformers and psychoanalysts elaborated this ideology of the unnatural. Physicians as well as educators began to counsel women whom they considered to be "latent homosexuals." Forcefully drawing the young women's attention to their dangerous predispositions for "inversion," doctors pressed them to marry quickly and have children.[40]

By the 1920s, the male sex reformers portrayed the lesbian in one of two ways. As in earlier medical texts, she could surface within their literature as a "Mannish Lesbian," the aggressive seducer of other women, the ruthless, perverted competitor of the male suitor. Or she could assume the alternative persona of the aging Lady in Lavender, who preyed upon the innocence of young girls, teaching them to fear men and their own sexual impulses. The New Men were able to portray the New Woman as the enemy of liberated women because they had redefined the issue of female autonomy in sexual terms. They had divorced women's rights from their political and economic context. They made the daughter's quest for heterosexual pleasures, not the mother's demand for political power, personify female freedom. Linking orgasms to chic fashion and planned motherhood, male sex reformers, psychologists, and physicians promised a future of emotional support and sexual delights to women who accepted heterosexual marriage—and male political and economic hegemony. Offered such an alternative, only the "unnatural" woman, they argued, would continue to struggle with men for economic independence and political power.[41]

The extent to which these new public pressures changed women's sexual behavior, we as historians may never know. What we do know is that women's language altered radically during the 1920s and 1930s. An entire female vocabulary of passion and desire disappeared. Women's words, resonant with meaning throughout the nineteenth century, became meaningless to twentieth-century hearers. New words intervened. Male words, of course, those of nineteenth-century sexologists and twentieth-century sex reformers. But women's words as well. By the 1930s, the younger New Women had constructed a novel sexual dialect, one that fused male forms with feminist intent.

A striking generational disruption within the ranks of the New Women was central to these discursive changes. Those New Women who came to political and sexual maturity during the nineteenth century, women such as Jane Addams, Lillian Wald, Florence Kelley—the very women who had so resoundingly repudiated earlier male attacks upon the New Women—remained silent in the face of the sexologists' attacks. They had few political options. To have publicly responded to Krafft-Ebing's and Havelock Ellis's redefinitions of their loving relations as sexually perverted would have violated their political commitment, as heirs of earlier feminist reformers, to the privatization of the sexual. Publicly debating their sexual emotions and behavior would have transformed the politically active New Women into public sexual actors. In their own eyes, it would have polluted them and in so doing made them the polluters of the political sphere whose purity they were determined to defend.

In contrast to the first generation New Women, the New Women who came to maturity in the first three decades of the twentieth century evinced no such commitment to the separation of the political and the sexual. Daughters of the sexual revolution, since 1920 full political subjects, they boldly claimed a sexual subjectivity the older women had refused. Sexually and politically they lived within a radically different discursive world, a world they sought to contribute to.[42] Indeed, claiming full political, sexual, and economic equality with men, they boldly seized the very discursive devices male sexologists and sex reformers had created. Aggressively investing male images with feminist political intent, they sought to use male myths to repudiate male power.

Let us look at the literary debates of the 1920s and 1930s to trace this process. Men, from the sexologists in the 1880s through the sexual reformers of the 1920s, depicted the Mannish Lesbian as a freak of nature, a logical impossibility. The woman who would be a man does not appear in male writing as a powerful androgyne but only as the ludicrous hermaphrodite, symbol of chaos and decay. The fusion of genders, Havelock Ellis no less than Krafft-Ebing argued, constituted an atavistic throwback to primitive development—a diseased state. Sandra Gilbert, in her brilliant essay, "Costumes of the Mind," argues that male modernist writers rooted gender distinctions in genital differences. The genitals were biological, observable, unchangeable, incontestable. To protest gender, was to deny the genitals and war with nature. [43] In this way, the male literary giants of the 1920s, assuming the sexologists' metaphors, became the last great spokesmen for biological determinism. And also for a belief in the coherent consistent subject, at home in his body and his social world.

In contrast to male denunciations of the Mannish Lesbian as an unnatural hermaphrodite, Gilbert argues, the women insisted that gender distinctions, not the New Woman, were artificial, deforming both men and women. Lampooning the sexologists' obsession with cross-dressing, feminists caustically reproved male rapture with biological determinism. Insisting on the artificiality of gender, they proceeded to insist that nothing social or political was "natural." Institutional structures, values, behavior, all were artifact, all relative, all reflective not of nature but of power.

Feminist modernists spoke the political language of post-modernism. Repudiating a mimetic transparency between the sexual and social bodies, they constructed a female subjectivity that was decentered, intentionally incoherent and unstable. It violated gender, problematized the body and escaped the restraints of lineal time. To explore the feminist modernists' post-modern vision, let us look at two critical "lesbian" novels of the 1920s and 1930s, Virginia Woolf's *Orlando* and Djuna Barnes's *Nightwood*.[44]

In *Orlando,* gender is amorphous and time irrelevant. Centuries pass like days. Orlando, a man become a woman, a shimmering creature, layers the social characteristics of a woman on those he had displayed as a man, much as if she/ he were simply donning layers of new clothing. Indeed, through *Orlando,* clothes, not genitals or personality, symbolize gender change. The body remains amorphous, Orlando's character beyond gender. To become female is merely to add ironic distance to an already surrealistic life. If Orlando exists beyond gender so does her/his husband, Marmaduke Bonthrop Shelmerdine, who, as Sandra Gilbert points out, proves to be "as strange and subtle as a woman."[45] Both glory in the confusion of categories, the options that extend beyond social proprieties. Tying gender to dress rather than dress to gender, Woolf inverts Krafft-Ebing's dark vision of the "Mannish Lesbian." Her joyous and unstable androgyne counterpoises his decadent and physiologically centered hermaphrodite.

Repudiating the "natural," feminist modernists set their novels in "unnatural" worlds and unstructured situations, beyond the threshold of conventional order. Their plots violate the restrictions of time (*Orlando*), of day and night (*Nightwood*), of conventional literary forms (Gertrude Stein's novels), of national loyalties (Radclyffe Hall's *The Well of Loneliness*).[46] In surrealistic and expatriate worlds, New Women float between genders and violate divisions between appearance and reality.

Barnes's title, *Nightwood,* tells all, for a wood at night is a world without structure, a haunted place, invested with primitive magic. The epitome of disordered nature, the night wood inverts the ordered "natural world" of Darwinian evolution and of Social Darwinism. Barnes signals the "un-naturalness" of the night wood in her opening scene: the death of a widowed mother in childbirth. Basic natural processes have been disrupted in this scene. Fatherless, a newborn infant kills its mother; the mother, through death, abandons her child; a child in need of parents, is orphaned. These events depict the inhumanity of nature and the uncertainty of human existence. They also signal the demise of the family and of woman as mother. Barnes leads us ever further into her surrealistic night world. Everyone in *Nightwood* is homeless, afloat between expatriate Paris and Berlin and a dreamlike America. Not one can claim a certain identity, few a clear gender. Their existence denies the inevitability of all structure and categories. They are liminal. They are Tricksters, the breakers of taboos, the violators of categories, the defiers of structure. Disorder defines the Trickster, as does power and creativity. The Trickster continually alters her/his body, creates and re-creates a personality, personifies the unfettered.[47] She/he constitutes the ideal feminist hero.

Certainly, Orlando is a trickster par excellence. She floats across time, through unbelievable settings. Creating her/himself out of fancy, farce, and finery, she tricks us into abandoning all that we know: that sex is unchangeable, gender distinctions "natural," time confining, and patriarchy invincible. For a brief moment, as Orlando frees us, we revel in the headiness of what might be.

Barnes's *Nightwood* is filled with tricksters who have draped their lives in borrowed fancies and wear the whole cloth of illusion. Take Frau Mann, for instance: her name, an oxymoron that calls forth both the androgyne and Krafft-Ebing's "Mannish Lesbian." A trapeze artist, Frau Mann escapes the confines of earth (society). The single, autonomous woman, she violates all social categories and gender restraints. Yet to do so she must live in a circus night world beyond the "natural" order of day, gender, propriety. Indeed, her very body denies distinctions between reality and illusion. She seemed, Barnes tells us, "to have a skin that was the pattern of her costume. . . . The stuff of the tights was no longer a covering, it was herself." Illusion freed her from gender restraints. At the same time it robbed her of her sexuality. "The span of the tightly stitched crotch was so much her own flesh that she was as unsexed as a doll. The needle that had made one the property of the child made the other the property of no man."[48]

Sexuality was the critical issue for this generation of New Women. They linked it with a new, powerful identity, with social and political freedom. Yet to do so they had to adopt a sexual language whose original intent had been to confine their sexuality and condemn their political desires. Slippage and ambiguity mark their imagery. The repressed condemnations of conservative men lurk just below the surface of their texts. Let us return to Frau Mann. Had the defiance of gender restrictions made Frau Mann (and by extension all women who defined themselves as beyond conventional gender) "as unsexed as a doll," that is, within the new discourse of the New Women, without a true identity? Or is Barnes's suggestion more positive: that the woman beyond gender is beyond being owned? Frau Mann embodies one of the critical questions of modern feminism: in rejecting gender as an artificial construction, does one lose one's identity as a woman? Beyond gender, what is one? Frau Mann remains enigmatic.

Classically, the Trickster is a comic character, a joke that momentarily turns the world upside down. But the joke is not serious. Its inversion of order is transitory. It suggests but does not affect an alternative order. Woolf uses Orlando to expose the absurdity of rigid gender rules and the pomposity of the male literary canon. But Orlando changes neither England nor literature. She/he merely suggests what might be.

Not all Tricksters are comic, certainly not those in *Nightwood*. Having declared war against social convention, they live out the consequences of their actions. Sadly, in defeat, they retreat to a mad night wood of inversion and pain. They speak to a critical new aspect of the New Women's experiences—the cost paid by those who literally use their bodies and their emotions to invert received order. They depicted the pain of social ostracism and of legal censorship.

The New Women's discursive strategy raises significant questions for feminist scholars. Symbols and metaphors emerge out of and assume specific meanings within the relational and political world of their speakers. That being the case, could male-constructed metaphors (no matter how transposed) fully express women's perceptions and desires? By adopting male imagery had the New Women both curtailed their own expressive powers and relinquished a critical source of identity and political strength—the power to create language? Can embattled social and political groups survive if shorn of that power? As the New Women of the 1920s and 1930s developed their new discourse, they divested themselves of older female-rooted discourses, those of Victorian matrons and of the first generation of New Women. The older discourses, by their specific attacks upon male power and by their very separateness, had affirmed women's political solidarity and the uniqueness of women's experiences. Ceasing to speak with these older female words, the New Women of the 1920s lost their ability to speak with the older women. The political solidarity of the successive generations of New Women slipped away. And so did the New Women's ability to reach out to the succeeding generations. The women of the 1930s, 1940s, and 1950s often did not realize that the feminist modernists, inverting male symbols, had created a new female political language. These later women heard only the male metaphors. They felt they lived in a world devoid of women's words—in a world of female isolation and of gender restraints. Until, that is, the rebirth of the women's movement in the 1960s again emphasized the importance of women's distinctive discourses.

The New Woman is critically important to new feminist scholars. In her twin incarnations—as a social and political actor and as the condensed symbol of disorder and rebellion—she forces us to examine the way language forms and re-forms sexual and political identities and repositions power. Still more importantly, she depicts for us a convoluted and tortuous pattern of trans-generational relations among women. She makes it possible for us to see how feminisms and allegiances among feminists fracture at points of generational difference, how the language and victories of one generation of women can radically reposition the women who follow, making them speak different languages, avow different goals. The political, the discursive, and the psychological fuse. In the generational differences that fractured the New Women and robbed them of their political power, we see fictive daughters struggle for independence from mothers who would not respond to their new voices. We hear fictive mothers morn the loss of daughters who seem neither to understand nor appreciate the women who preceded them. The personal and political losses of those individuals were irreparable. Is their pattern inevitable?

For feminist historians pondering the challenges and opportunities of post-structuralism, the conflicts among successive generations of New Women suggest still further parallels with our own situation. The new sexual discourses of the 1920s and 1930s (a fusion of sexology, psychoanalysis, and companionate marriage liberalism) offered the New Women a sexual subjectivity earlier discourses had not provided, access to *au courant* scientific knowledge, and a way to distinguish themselves from both their real and fictive mothers. In adopting it, however, they adopted another's discourse. They problematized their identity as women and rejected political alliances based on that identity. Neither Orlando nor Robin Vote struggled for women's rights. Decentered and ambiguous figures, they neither can, nor do they seek to inspire other women to battle for those rights.

Inhabitants of a world in which man's inhumanity to man has fractured meaning, destroyed values, and reduced the bodies of Hiroshima to shadows on dry rocks, we find in post-structuralism a language for our times. But in speaking post-structuralism, what do we give up? An identity as women? A sense that acts are not the shadows of words but possess a substance in their own right, can transcend discourse, surprise it with the unexpected, exert power? In giving up these concepts, we must ask ourselves, as feminists, if we have forfeited our ability to act politically? We must ascertain if we, as historians, have renounced the subjects that we study, the historical practices we have struggled to master and thus made ourselves agents of another discourse? By relativizing difference, have we made difference meaningless?

Ours is a world of deadly politics. In this world is there a way in which we can preserve substance (the substance of being female, the substance of Hiroshima) and so remain political agents?

9

The Problem of Race in Women's History

Evelyn Brooks-Higginbotham

Elizabeth Hyde Botume, in her fascinating account of the first days of black freedom, presents a vivid image of black women:

> It was not an unusual thing to meet a woman coming from the fields, where she had been hoeing cotton, with a small bucket or cup on her head, and a hoe over her shoulder, contentedly smoking a pipe and briskly knitting as she strode along. I have seen added to all these, a baby strapped to her back. The patient devotion of these negro women was most admirable.[1]

Not an "unusual thing" for black women, this image stands in stark contrast to the usual one for most nineteenth-century white women. In fact, Botume's depiction of the black woman signals several dualities. The black woman labored in the cotton fields just like her man. A native of the American South, she had retained the African woman's custom of carrying items on her head. Oblivious to feminine etiquette, she smoked a pipe while knitting a garment. She was simultaneously breadwinner and mother, self-reliant and devoted.

Writing black women into history demands an understanding of a number of dualities. Black women's history, an identifiable field of inquiry in its own right, is equally part of Afro-American, American, and women's history. By addressing the problem of race in the history of American womanhood, scholars will more clearly illuminate the dialectical relation of women's history to American, as well as that of Afro-American to American history.

Both Afro-Americans and women reflect the complicated dialectic of being integrally part of American history, while also being quite distinguishable and apart from it. Both Afro-Americans and women find meaning and self-identity in the American past and in American culture, and yet they each claim a cultural uniqueness and separate consciousness. Afro-American history and women's history have shared similar historiographic trends throughout the twentieth century. Each has depended heavily upon the conventional subdisciplines—e.g., political, economic, and social history—for periodization, conceptual frameworks, and methodologies. Yet each has made its own unique methodological contribution. Both have suffered from the weakness of omission. Afro-American history has failed to address the problem of gender adequately, while women's history has likewise failed to address the problem of race.

Afro-American history enjoys a long tradition in American historiography. Harvard-trained historians, William Edward Burghardt Du Bois and Carter G. Woodson, pioneered in the professionalization and popularization of black history during the earliest decades of the twentieth century. By the time of his death in 1950, Woodson had come to be known as the Father of Black History. Even prior to the surge in black publications after 1960, the Woodson-founded Association for the Study of Negro Life and History, as well as his Journal of Negro History and Associated Publishers had long promoted a rich collection of monographs by black and white scholars. John Hope Franklin, in tribute to Woodson upon his death, remarked that his work served as an important source for the revision of American history, since "despite the precepts enunciated in the seminars and the rigorous subscription to truth and accuracy, the large majority of American historians were careless with the truth when dealing with Negroes."[2] At its best, American history had simply rendered the black experience invisible. At its worst, it had explicitly denied blacks a positive role in the development and welfare of this nation.

In the 1950s and 1960s the civil rights movement and later the black power revolt brought high visibility to America's black population and dramatized the need for greater understanding of the Afro-American past. In an effort to address the problem of race in American society, an unprecedented body of research proliferated on the nation's racial system and race relations. Studies on the black contribution and a host of revisionist interpretations integrated blacks into mainstream political history, while Marxist scholarship drew attention to the nexus of race and class.

In the 1960s black history also found expression in the new social history emerging at the time. Historians of the Afro-American past adopted its conceptual models and techniques and studied the masses of anonymous blacks in the slave quarters, in their family and household structures, and in their urban settings. The black nationalist movement of the late sixties and early seventies inspired still a more unique methodological contribution. Dispensing with the conceptual frameworks and periodization found in the conventional subdisciplines, the new trend resurrected and revised the African survivals argument of anthropologist Melville Herskovits and uncovered a black culture and consciousness separate from white.[3] Despite these historiographic trends, black history suffered from an overwhelmingly androcentric bias. By the mid–1970s black women were as invisible within its growing body of research as black people had previously been within most of American history.

Women's history, like black history, came to life during the early twentieth century, but it came of age during the politically charged 1960s and early 1970s. In certain respects, the study of women has followed a historiographic course similar to that of black history. It has striven to fill the female gaps in the American story by integrating women into political and social histories. It has devoted entire textbooks to the subject of women's achievements. It has revised misconceptions and chronicled woman's struggle for equality. Women's history has benefited especially from social history's focus on the invisible and anonymous masses in society and has exploited its quantitative and interdisciplinary methods via life cycles, workforce participation rates, and family reconstruction.[4]

Influenced by the conceptual principle of "cultural separatism"—especially as utilized in studies on slave culture—historians of women have sought to identify a female culture and consciousness divorced from the male point of reference, and they have explored hitherto unimagined, much less uninvestigated topics and sources related to the private world of women. Most important, in its formulation of the gender system as a set of social relations that interact and intersect with class and race relations, women's history has distinguished itself from all the other subdisciplines and has made a valuable and unique methodological contribution. These varied historiographic trends notwithstanding, women's history has suffered from a racial bias. Criticized for its largely white, middle-class, and northeastern emphasis, it has just begun to write black women into its blossoming field of literature.[5]

Although published work on black women remains sparse, articles and books increase and even now exist in sufficient number to suggest the paradoxical essence of black womanhood—of being black and female, black and American, and American and female. By focusing on black women within the Afro-American context and including them in studies on American womanhood, historians will discover the importance of black women to both black and women's history. By addressing the triple paradox of black womanhood, historians will also unveil the too-often obscured dialectical relationship between women's and American history and also that between Afro-American and American history.

The theme of double jeopardy marks the starting point for all literature on black women. To be black and female carries the dual burden of racial and sexist oppression. Most histories assert the primacy of race as opposed to gender in identifying objective conditions of the black female experience and subjective perceptions of these conditions. Rosalyn Terborg-Penn, Angela Davis, and Bettina Aptheker among others have enriched our knowledge of the contribution of black women to the nineteenth-century women's rights movement, and they have also convincingly argued that black women's organizations evolved as a reaction to racism, on the one hand, and as a race-conscious desire for a united black sisterhood on the other.[6] Histories of black women leaders and their organizations often play a double revisionist role inasmuch as they reinterpret the revisionist works of white feminist historians. Studies on black women recast the research of such historians as Eleanor Flexner, Aileen Kraditor, and Ellen DuBois in a new and different light.[7] While the aforementioned authors challenged the male-bias in traditional American history by drawing attention to the overlooked struggle for women's rights against male oppression, studies on black women stress the racist nature of the white women's movement. The white studies certainly do not disregard class and racial bias, but histories of black women examine racial conflict in much more detail and explore the resultant, separate development and character of black women's organizational work.

These histories call into question the concept of a universal womanhood by underscoring the unity of white men and women in determining American racial thought and policy. The white suffragists' vision of representative government excluded black women as well as black men. Their discrimination against black suffragists, along with their vascillation between silence and vocal support for the southern states' disfranchisement of black male voters, exposed their goal for equality with white men only.[8] In this regard, the white suffragists remain very much an integral part of the dominant American culture.

Social histories provide another source for observing racial differences among women. Again, black women defy dominant American patterns. These studies employ an arsenal of statistics to disclose racial disparities in household structures, workforce participation rates, and types of occupation. The more sophisticated social histories place black women against the backdrop of contrasting patterns among various white ethnic groups and introduce cultural factors to explain differences further.[9]

Suzanne Lebsock's inclusion of black women within her social history of antebellum free women in Petersburg employs census schedules, tax records, deeds, and wills in order to chart woman's status and culture between 1784 and 1860. Lebsock's study adds more proof to the discussion of divergent socio-economic patterns by race. The majority of Petersburg free black households were female-headed, with the majority of black children living therein. A high proportion of black women were gainfully employed. Little discrepancy existed between the percentage of black male and female property holders. If indicative of greater female autonomy, these patterns just as keenly portray the oppression and vulnerability of black women. They were the poorest group in Petersburg free society. The small differential in the number of black male and female property holders reflected the extreme poverty of the city's black population. For 1860, Lebsock found among taxable property owners: 6.1% free black women; 7.9% free black men; 19% white women; and 67% white men.[10]

Despite the divergent racial patterns, Lebsock notes parallels between the position of black women and the overall one of women. Like black women, white Petersburg women who did enter the workforce did so out of economic necessity, and their earnings were small. Women property owners exercised limited power in their community, and their ownership represented "small stakes."[11]

Another orientation in the history of black women raises cultural difference to illustrate the race-specific context of gender systems. Proponents of cultural difference have made us sensitive to the unique culture and consciousness of black women by first establishing a cultural identity for Afro-Americans as a people. Shaped by African traditions and American socio-economic forces, black women are described as perceiving and experiencing womanhood in many ways distinctly different from white women.[12]

Deborah White's research on slave women exemplifies this orientation. In asserting the black woman's self-reliance during slavery and her centrality within the slave family, she challenges interpretations by such noted historians as John Blassingame, Eugene Genovese, and Herbert Gutman who concentrate on the importance of the male figure within the dual-headed slave household.[13] White rejects their scant treatment of slave women and also their implicit equating of the female-headed household with deviance or pathology. She finds no argument with the typicality of the two-headed slave family, but she describes its specific form of gender relations as quite different from that of white families. She observes that the slave community, unlike white society, attached no intrinsic superiority to men's work, since plantation slavery forced male and female into field labor. Nor did black women feel dependent upon their husbands. Slavery undermined the role of husband as provider. Slave man and woman alike depended upon the master for food, clothing, and other necessities. The slave woman, White posits, worked just as often as her man to supplement the family's food rations.[14]

Under slavery, the mother rather than the father served as the focal point of the family. The significance of the mother-child bond transcended that of husband and wife and all other relationships. The African heritage is important to Deborah White's analysis of slave women. Rooted in the African past was the tradition of the matrifocal family in which women were independent and played needed economic roles. Most important, the role of mother, specifically her childbearing capability, was highly valued in African societies, while matrilineal descent was common to African kinship systems.[15]

The operation of the slave system encouraged African predilections toward fecundity and childbearing. Pregnant slaves recognized their value to the master. They received lighter workloads and more rations, while barren women were more likely to be sold. White maintains that the black community's respect for the mother-child bond weighed heavily in its acceptance of births out-of-wedlock. Although such births involved only a minority percentage of the slave population, no stigma was placed on either mother or child. This cultural pattern differed sharply from white perceptions of "legitimate" and "illegitimate" births.[16]

In highlighting cultural difference, the research of both Deborah White and Jacqueline Jones proposes the existence of a private female world separate not only from white women, but also from black men. White and Jones single out the work reality of black women as the primary factor directly responsible for the existence of a black female culture and consciousness.

Black women worked, for the most part, either in gender-specific employment or in female-segregated groups within types of employment that engaged both sexes. Deborah White illustrates the latter for slave field labor. Except for harvesting time, when male and female worked side by side, male gangs commonly plowed and female ones hoed. Under slavery, women were not unknown to perform physically arduous tasks associated with masculine strength. On the other hand, the positions of cook, mid-wife, and seamstress—in addition to being female jobs—commanded respect in the quarters. Since slave women worked largely in sexually segregated groups during the course of the day, they shared a world in which they developed their own criteria and value system for ranking and ordering themselves. The private world of slave women afforded, too, a sense of interdependence and cooperation that encouraged female self-esteem both individually and collectively and helped mitigate the dehumanizing aspects of slavery.[17]

Jacqueline Jones's *Labor of Love, Labor of Sorrow,* a history of black women's work and family roles from slavery to the 1980s, also identifies a "unique subculture" among black women—a culture "not shared entirely by either black men or white women." While part of the workforce, black women experienced forms of sexual discrimination unknown to white women regardless of class. Race and sex discrimination, along with structural changes in the economy over time, combined to make the labor participation and domestic expectations of black women different from all other groups. Jones argues that the racist dimension of the sexual division of labor evoked responses and strategies peculiar to black women, who consciously sought to fashion an orderly world for themselves and their families. Racism, therefore, thwarted the development of a female world and sensibility capable of uniting black and white women:

> But if black women sought solace and support in the company of their sisters, if they took pride in a family well fed, a congregation led joyfully in song, or a child graduated from high school, they nonetheless maintained a racial self-consciousness and loyalty to their kin (reinforced by white hostility) that precluded any interracial bonds of womanhood.[18]

The preponderant emphasis on differences between black and white women testifies to the overarching historical reality of racist oppression and the exclusion of blacks from a large part of American life. The acknowledgment of this reality notwithstanding, the singular focus on racial differences misses the bicultural aspects of the black woman's existence.[19] It avoids understanding her as black and American.

Black women have historically lived in a community whose collective behavior derived not only from the Afro-American group, but also from the values and social behavior of the dominant American society. The case for cultural difference is strongest, although not beyond challenge for the slave period as the slave narratives themselves reveal. Dorothy Sterling's beautiful anthology of the voices of black women in slavery and freedom speaks of cultural dualism when describing the North's impact on black female abolitionists:

> Only a generation or two removed from slavery themselves, hemmed in by the same discriminatory laws that poor blacks faced, they nevertheless strove to live up to the standards of their white associates. No one's curtains were as starched, gloves as white, or behavior as correct as black women's in the anti-slavery societies. Yet the pinch of poverty was always there.[20]

The bicultural process heightened dramatically after Emancipation. Lawrence Levine's excellent study of black culture observes that the "cultural self-containment" of the slave community gave way to cultural marginality in freedom. Although slavery prescribed the black community to a "cultural world whose dictates and values were accepted with a minimum of ambivalence and questioning, or inhibiting self-consciousness," freedom introduced new and alternate cultural standards, namely those of the dominant American society. The new standards, promoted by Yankee missionaries, black schools and colleges, and the black churches, set the process of biculturation in motion. The schools and churches taught that individual advancement, as well as the advancement of the entire black community demanded a lifestyle that stood at odds with many of the older black cultural traditions.[21] Gaining respect, even justice from white America required changes in religious beliefs, speech patterns, and also in gender roles and relations.

In the self-conscious and also sub-conscious acceptance of dominant American values, many blacks experienced cultural marginality. They increasingly linked the new values with upward mobility and the old with backwardness. Even the masses, held down by poverty and racial oppression, deemed certain mainstream values and behavior as proper and correct, albeit their inability to manifest them in practice. The cultural marginality Levine describes is the same dual consciousness of which Du Bois wrote so eloquently at the dawn of the twentieth century—the duality of being black and American, of having "two warring ideals in one dark body."[22]

My work on the women's movement in the black Baptist church between 1880 and 1920 exposes the class dimension of biculturation and the decisive participation of women missionaries in the dissemination and internalization of middle-class values among and by countless poor and uneducated blacks. Within the Jim Crow

South of the late nineteenth century, women's societies—called conventions by black Baptists—influenced some blacks to aspire to and even achieve upward mobility, but they influenced many more to make financial sacrifices, limit personal consumption, and channel their meager resources to the support of the educational and other self-help institutions of their race. Elizabeth Pleck, contrasting blacks with poor immigrant groups, argues that the former's unswerving faith in education often translated into a mother's decision to work rather than remove an older child from school to earn needed family income.[23]

Through the home mission and educational efforts of their own state and national conventions, black churchwomen organized independently of men and implemented programs for the social and economic uplift of the black masses. These programs represented the black woman's contribution to racial self-help in an era of diminishing civil and political rights for blacks, but they represented something more. They both reflected and contributed to the movement of social Christianity that marked American Protestantism during the late nineteenth and early twentieth centuries.

Both black and white Protestants strove to alleviate the social ills caused by industrialization and urbanization. John McDowell's study of white southern Methodist women places their efforts within the larger American context of social reform.[24] The convention movement among black Baptist women constitutes another segment of this unfolding drama. Between 1900 and 1920 the women's response to increasing black urbanization was directly influenced by the Social Gospel, the secular orientation of such black organizations as the NAACP and the National Urban League, and the general interest in sociology that characterized the Progressive era. The women's movement among black Baptists is an American story, no less than an Afro-American one.[25]

If the concept of biculturation informs the black woman's identity as a black American, it simultaneously shapes her identity as an American woman. Genovese and others interpret the withdrawal of married black women from the workforce in the immediate post-Civil War South as the freed people's desire to replicate the gender roles prevalent in white families. Economic necessity soon returned these women to the fields and kitchens of the South, but this reversal does not imply a rejection of their preference for domesticity. E. Franklin Frazier's pioneering study of the black church observed that the postbellum church gave support to the patriarchal family—to the position of the father in authority. Jacqueline Jones's work on Yankee missionary women in Georgia and my own on black and white Baptist women reveals the influential role of women missionaries in fostering the domestic ideal in the minds of southern blacks during the late nineteenth century.[26]

The ex-slaves were quick to idealize the role of man as provider and woman as homemaker, even though both were forced to work. Charles Valentine's analysis of biculturation asserts: "The structural conditions of poverty, discrimination, and segregation prevent people from achieving many mainstream middle-class values and aspirations, and role models to which they nevertheless give psychologically deep-rooted allegiance."[27] Indeed, Afro-Americans protested the racist reality that forced so many of their women into the full-time jobs of cleaning and caring for white women's homes and children. This reality served as a constant reminder of the inability of black men to earn a "man's" wage. Racial restrictions and job ceilings denied them the same "breadwinner" self-image that white husbands enjoyed. Implicit in their idealization of domesticity seemed to be the reinstatement of dignity to black manhood and womanhood.

The visible assimilation or, at least, psychological allegiance to the sexual behavior and attitudes of white middle-class America conveys the class-specific context of gender relations within the black community. Unquestioningly, discussions of class differences among blacks become inherently problematic, because of the difficulty in establishing objective definitions that are useful beyond the slavery period. Until recently racism and poverty skewed income and occupational levels so drastically that sociologists relied heavily upon values and behavior as additional criteria for discerning blacks who maintained or aspired to middle-class status from those who practiced alternative lifestyles. Thus social scientists and also members of the black community itself focused on adherence to bourgeois standards of respectability and morality in designating classes.[28]

Gender relations constitute one of the important variables, although not the only one, traditionally used to establish value and behavioral criteria for class differences among blacks. Nineteenth-century leaders rarely alluded to income or occupation when referring, as they frequently did, to the "better class of Negroes." Domestic servants could be included, and some were cited in this category, for it comprised all who were hardworking, religious, clean, and so far as sex was concerned, respectful of the dominant society's manners and morals.

Baptist women's organizations in the late nineteenth century directed much of their racial uplift efforts toward members of their own sex as they preached the gospel of education, cleanliness, and Victorian morality. They conducted mothers' training schools, women's meetings, and mothers' conferences among poor ex-slave women, in order to teach "proper" childrearing and marital duties. Black colleges, besides providing academic and industrial training, charged their female students with the special responsibility of maintaining clean and cultured homes despite the poverty of their households. Given the economic realities, many black women sought to emulate mainstream female roles, codes of dress, and public behavior as best they could, for they linked them with self-respect and racial progress. It is not uncommon for oppressed peoples to adopt the values of their oppressors for reasons of their own. The shared acceptance of the dominant society's normative gender roles forged the link between black and white missionary women and permitted their cooperative work through religious and educational institutions.[29]

The image of the black woman as "superwoman" arose from her constant, yet rather successful struggle to adapt mainstream gender roles to the socio-economic realities of black life. But her struggle does not end here. As American women, the names of antebellum leaders Maria Stewart, Sarah Remond, and Sojourner Truth combine with Mary Church Terrell, Nannie Burroughs, and Ida Wells Barnett of the late nineteenth and early twentieth centuries to testify to the black woman's struggle for woman's equality with man. At particular historical moments, black women have borne discrimination more so because of gender. The ratification of the Fifteenth Amendment accentuates discrimination against the black woman as an American woman. During Reconstruction black women shared their men's ecstasy and optimism, but not their right to wield the ballot. Like all American women, they stood as spectators, not as recipients of an expanding democracy. Black women rejoiced to hear the voices of their men resound from the lowest local offices in the South to the halls of the United States Congress, and yet they, as women, remained on the margins of representative government.[30]

Black clubwomen and countless numbers in church societies championed woman's suffrage in the early twentieth century. Studies by Rosalyn Terborg-Penn and others reveal the racism that divided white and black suffragists, but they also clearly exhibit the importance of the vote to black women. Divisions in women's political and reform work reflected the very real barrier of white racism; however, parallels and cooperative efforts, which also existed between black and white women's organizations, reflected commonalities and shared interests among women regardless of race.

Writing black women into history proves that the Afro-American past cannot be exempted from the important effort to identify and study gender relations and gender consciousness. For many years, race and, to a lesser extent, class provided the only reference points for analyzing the black community. If the overwhelming reality of racism has tended to obscure the class differences in the black community, it has obscured the system of gender relations even more. The convention movement among black Baptists mirrored the racial, gender, and class interests of the larger Afro-American community. The movement sought to establish a black leadership, a black bourgeoisie that would articulate and advance the cause of the inarticulate masses. Black women perceived themselves as part of the black Baptist family and as part of an evangelical sisterhood that cut across racial lines. They echoed the racial concerns of the larger male-dominated movement that spoke for all blacks, but they also struggled for separate spheres of power through which to fight for women's rights in the church and broader American society.

Sharon Harley explores the interaction of gender, race, and class in her study of black women in Washington, D.C. between 1890 and 1920. Black women in the District did not benefit from the feminization of clerical work in the late nineteenth century as did white women. The new sexual division of labor caused women to outnumber men among whites in clerical jobs, although the reverse held true for blacks. Racism retained black men in an increasingly female occupation by restricting their access to male-prescribed employment that was white collar or well-paying. By excluding black women from clerical work, however, racism confined the great majority to domestic service and thus presented them with fewer options than black men for upgrading their class position or working conditions.[31]

Writing black women into history holds the key to a better understanding of the interaction and intersection of gender, race, and class, and their roles—as sets of social relations—in both determining and being determined by power relations. Arguing the case for recognizing the intersection of class and gender systems, Elizabeth Fox-Genovese writes: "The domination of women by men figures at the core of the domination of specific classes, races, ethnic groups, and people. It intersects with all forms of subordination and superordination and cannot be understood apart from them."[32]

By addressing the problem of race, women's history will more clearly see how race and class give meaning to gender. Delores Janiewski's article on white and black women's paid and unpaid work in the South between 1880 and 1950 illustrates how racism determined gender and class consciousness. The southern racial system gave form to the sexual division of labor by observing rigid distinctions between black and white female work. The gender system prescribed domestic service as female work; the racial system determined that it be black female work. Systemic racism, according to Janiewski, afforded "white men greater power and white women greater privilege." Within the southern economy, the interaction of gender, race, and class relegated black women to the very bottom, subordinated all women, and subverted any potential for collective worker consciousness on the part of black and white women in the same objective class position.[33]

In her biography of Jessie Daniel Ames, a white crusader against lynching in the 1930s, Jacquelyn Dowd Hall admirably connects this heinous form of racial oppression to class and gender oppression. Lynching, rationalized by the white South as the defense of its womanhood, served more often to maintain racial etiquette and the socio-economic status quo. It was used to enforce labor contracts and crop lien laws. Once known, consenting and loving relationships between black men and white women were certain to end in the death of the men. Lynching was rooted, Hall asserts, in a double sexual standard that contained enormous gender-role presumptions. It presupposed white male protection of white women, but it exacted her obedience to ladyhood—to chastity, frailty, and dependence. The white South's double standard presumed it the white woman's duty to preserve the purity of the race, while it gave white men free license to insult and assault black women. It deemed all white women pure and worthy of respect. It assumed the exact opposite for all black women. The double sexual standard and its weapon of lynching left the black woman vulnerable and the black man powerless to protect her. "As the ritualistic affirmation of white authority," mob violence kept the black community in fear and submission. In 1892 a woman, Ida Wells Barnett, was the first Afro-American to speak openly and militantly against lynching. When white women mobilized in the 1930s under Jessie Daniel Ames, they implicitly rejected the paternalism of southern chivalry and their image as fragile sexual objects in need of protection.[34]

The relation of gender to power figures at the core of women's history, and yet factors of class and race make any generalization of womanhood's common oppression impossible. The relation of race to power remains central to Afro-American history, but gender and class preclude a monolithic black community. Studies of black women help to correct imbalances in both Afro-American and women's history. Most of all they help explain the contradictory relationship of women and blacks to the American experience.

10

Commentary: Feminism and the Consolidations of "Women" in History

Denise Riley

The essays here act as witnesses to a development: there is now no way for a feminist history to sidestep some serious engagement with questions of language, broadly conceived, especially with the proliferations and densities of designations of "women." What do all these often excessive addresses to categories of women have to do with a contemporary feminist politics which is also caught up with speaking for, as, women? It's clear that simply to amass the many "languages of" gender cannot by itself illuminate much, in the same way that a new historical sociology of language alone cannot serve social historians well. For the relations between these "words," "language," and "languages," let alone the fundamental question of how the linguistic and extra-linguistic realms are to be thought, tend to vanish under the dazzling proliferation of detail. The rhetoric of domesticity, the language of female conservatism—such fresh objects of investigation will only be fruitful if they are pursued with a boldness which overshoots tabulation. All three essays below have their own persuasions here.

Carroll Smith-Rosenberg's study leads us straight to the key question of what sense we can give to the idea of a "female language" or the slightly different "female voice," as an echo or a resonance to be caught in history—or as also charged with historically fluctuating political weightings. She reflects on those New Women of the 1920s who, "armed with androgynous images and male words, could not permanently alter society's insistence on gender distinctions."* No, indeed: here she is on the critical ground: what is to say that voices, languages, images have a sex, a gender, and what are the political repercussions and sources of differing convictions here; what histories emerge, differently, in the common name of feminism?

For there is the awkward problem of origins of "sexed" languages, in that what some might confidently identify as the distinctive languages of women, taking that to be a commendatory description, might be viewed less confidently by other

---

* A phrase Smith-Rosenberg uses in an earlier version of her essay. (ed. note).

historians—as representing, rather, the triumph of a history of attribution and assignation followed by adoption; as with descriptions of female virtues which are then assumed and flourished by (some) women. Indeed this kind of process may secure and demonstrably has secured degrees of political visibility for "women," and it cannot be denied that a great part of the history of modern feminism does rest on the underwriting of particular categorizations of "women," while challenging others. Nevertheless, it is necessary to avoid collapsing the metaphorically female, with its sources in old fissions of Nature and Reason along the lines of sex, into the sociologically female—"women" is above all an overcrowded category—and one means of avoidance is to look at the vicissitudes of the idea of a female language, in or against the armory of feminism. If we take up I.A. Richards's suggestion that all language is radically metaphoric, then however that is qualified, speech and writing naming women are at least heavy with metaphoric proximity.[1] These too have their histories of formation and alignments, which stand in need of an analysis which won't be seduced by their claims for themselves.

The significance of generational shifts within feminism itself, as it alternately refuses and adopts conceptions of a gendered language in its political thinking, emerges clearly in Carroll Smith-Rosenberg's work on the effects of the New Women's espousal of androgyny. As she illustrates it, the drive to assert a female language in the multiple ways this can be understood, has been intimately associated with the will to a female identity as the heart of a feminist politics. And yet this, which is so self-evident to certain feminisms now as well as "then," is itself a historical problem and phenomenon of great complexity. The "identities" of women—so close to their "natures" although natures have been transparently disgraced—have elaborate histories of assignation which stem from a sexualized social order whose very sexualization alters and, from the 1790s on, stiffens into the shapes of gendered attributions which we inherit. It is, I think, true that these are both the working raw material of a modern, post 1790s feminism and the foundations of that excess of identifications under which women so frequently labor as "women." Not that this business of identification is an even matter. And surely some concept of identity essential for stating a feminist politics can without too great difficulty be distinguished from the evidently conservative forms of *identification* of women? Mary Ann Doane puts the same question in her commentary, and concludes that it might be preferable, rather than endlessly brooding over the annoying fixity of social identity or the wavering, perhaps reassuringly wavering, nature of psychical identity as a woman, to examine this identity "at the level of the political[.] One's identity as a feminist, for instance."

Yes, and yet this very identity as a feminist can perfectly well be both passionately maintained *and* drive one into querying the history of the identity of women in relation to feminist politics in their developments and recessions. For to claim that even one's identity as a feminist has a history (in a more profound sense than that of an autobiographical conversion or adherence, that is) is not in itself at war with politics. Modern post-Enlightenment feminism is built on a fluctuation between "being a woman" and "being a person" or "human being" and its lineaments *are* these movements. As women flicker in and out of the general category of humanity in different discursive namings, so the trajectories of feminism have changed either to insist on their inclusion or snatch them back from drowning in the impossible generality, the indifferences of the broadly human. Sometimes "human beings" are historically designated as men-and-women, sometimes as men-and-others, sometimes as "people"; and the constant challenge to feminism has been the necessary alacrity of response—when and how is "woman" related to "human"? The political problem isn't so much one of identities but of when women take on the identities of "women" or of "humans," and how. It is a question of the *temporalities* of women. "Identities," says Mary Ann Doane, "must be assumed if only temporarily." This is indeed strategically the case; but I would go farther to suggest that identities *can* only be held for a time, both individually and collectively, and both the history of feminism and the semantic logic of "women" bear witness to this founding temporality. Such a deep volatility may be awkward, but there it is. It is a volatility shared—differently shared—by other emancipationist political groupings which demand entry to, but the also simultaneous overhauling of, the general category of humanity; movements for racial and economic as well as sexual equality, or revolution.

Evelyn Brooks-Higginbotham takes on the relations of "black women" to the illusory generality of "women," the gaps and elisions in both "women's history" and "Afro-American history." Her work goes beyond breaking down that universalized "womanhood" which forgets the history of racism, for she is preoccupied with the multiplicity of interlockings at work: "by addressing the problem of race, women's history will more clearly see how race and class give meaning to gender." And her essay also illustrates ways in which sexualized metaphorical structures affect the very formulations of race and class. No universalizing accounts can be adequate, she insists: "The relation of gender to power figures at the core of women's history, and yet factors of class and race make any generalization of womanhood's common oppression impossible. The relation of race to power remains central to Afro-American history, but gender and class preclude a monolithic black community."

Is there, though, anything paradoxical about a history which is alert to gender but which refuses the generality of women? On the contrary, it could be argued that the very universality of womanhood which Evelyn Brooks-Higginbotham rightly takes to pieces is itself a product of those massive consolidations of the sexes which have a slow yet nevertheless discernible history. And if gender, as Joan Scott writes is "one of the recurrent references by which political power has been conceived, legitimated, and criticized"—if power is somehow thought through gender, broadly conceived, it does not follow that there is any hegemonic oppression of women. The attributes which are bestowed on both "women" and "black women" possess their own political histories and should not be venerated as if they offered a reliable quintessence of femininity because developed and sanctified by women themselves, desert gardens tended and brightening in remote and uncontaminated air. Again, it is a necessary step to insist on the inclusion, the writing-in as Evelyn Brooks-Higginbotham puts it for American historians, of black women's history, with the many illuminations that sheds on both "women's" and "Afro-American history." Yet this is more than a writing-in, for it involves a shaking-out and refashioning of the entire fields. The processes she advocates aren't cosmetic but reconstitutive in the terms of our understanding, in the same way that the relations of "feminist history" to "history" cannot be merely additive (and must fight against being isolated).

"Hierarchical structures rely on generalized understandings of the so-called natural relationship between male and female" proposes Joan Scott, and one can speculate as to how far this is borne out in racial metaphor. How does power-thought-through gender work within, for instance, colonial speech? Certainly metaphors of sexual anxiety in racialist as well as homophobic attributions—contamination, emasculation, sensuality, promiscuity—have long been noted, not least by Franz Fanon,[2] let alone sometimes defensively-aggressively adopted. Is the phenomenon of feminization as a vehicle for contempt not consonant with the bipartite theory of gender which Joan Scott's essay advances? She aims at the vector of two overlapping propositions; that "gender" is a system which constitutes social relationships and that it is crucial for conceptualizing power hierarchies. "Political history," she writes succinctly, "has, in a sense, been enacted on the field of gender." It is this attempt to develop an understanding of the conjugating powers of the "system of gender"— its capacities to infiltrate *and* construe outside the seemingly obvious boundaries of its own self-referring dominions—which overrides one possible objection here. That is, that we are only being offered an analogy for class (and differently, for race) in this double proposition: that gender is being tossed in the ring with race and class to do battle for the epistemological ascendancy, in such a way perhaps, that the more discreetly democratic tactic for a feminist historian might be to retreat to the corner of gender, which is roped off for "women."

On the contrary: it is the thoroughgoing implication of this gender in the "concept of class in the nineteenth century" which Joan Scott is determined to elaborate. That implication is at a constitutive level and not merely or exclusively at the metaphoric level (only where metaphor, that is, is understood as an essentially decorative overlay, an assumption open to challenge). Power, she suggests, declines itself in part, though not exclusively, by means of the binary opposition of man to woman—an opposition which has its histories at many different pitches including the institutional, and can be differently deployed. So that one problem for historical tracking would be the very volatility of these pitches of sexual opposition and the many forms of political services in which they may function.

For the deep veins of gender—declensions in the breadth of their distributions make it impossible for a feminist history to be restricted to the surface equations: equations, say, of gender with the body and with the home, with children, households, kin, or "sexuality." Not that these are not hugely important questions, which have suffered from gross neglect in the past. But rather that if we do tacitly accept the equation of "gender" with the familial, the domestic, and the scars of the domestic across the division of labor, then—still fully allowing for the need for research to be strong, as it is, in these areas—we have accepted a historical formation which itself needs to be interrogated. That's the very assignation of "women" to the familial which slips into that amorphous "social," which from the early nineteenth century is defined as a realm distinct from the "political." For if Woman is placed outside History[3] she is at the same time thoroughly embedded in and also constitutive of the newer "social," as both investigator and object of the peculiar continuum between philanthropy and a rising sociology. It is in the separations between what counts as the social and the political that we can trace one modern origin *and* function of the "gender system," in Joan Scott's phrase.

Any "women's history" will also need to be a history of feminization: of the processes of naming, characterizing, assigning "women" whether done in the name of conservatism, socialism, feminism, or any other; but also of a less obvious kind of feminization which may be more voluble about, say, political institutions than it is about "women." For neither a heavy concentration on naming "women" in political speech nor a silence here are by themselves sufficiently legible. Neither, alone, reveals anything about the backdrop of sexual oppositions through which political conceptions themselves may be ordered. This is one reason why a feminist history can't afford to validate characterizations of "women," however flattering these may look. "Women" always has a prehistory, such that it is always risky to congratulate women for being women, or to import psycho-sociologies (such as Nancy Chodorow's or Carol Gilligan's work) into history. Such moves simply aren't historical enough, and moreover are innocently congruent with the kind of omissions which Evelyn Brooks-Higginbotham describes below as leading to an impossible generalization of womanhood's common oppression. And to trace the sexualized metaphoric constructions of the body politic and its political effects, one object of Carroll Smith-Rosenberg's study, becomes impracticable if the "female" as a historically weighted attribution slips by unchallenged, to re-enter triumphantly as the level of "language."

If, to return to I.A. Richards, language is essentially metaphoric, and the "gender system" tunnels beneath so many conventionally ungendered historical fields (as all three preceding essays differently detail) then how can its attacks be distinguished and indeed resisted? This is analogous to the question for the concept of "power," and certainly there are serious problems in delimiting and specifying what may risk becoming a hopelessly overarching concept which inherits the amorphous drawbacks of the modern usage of "society." Indeed distinguishing the libertarian from the juridical senses of power in Michel Foucault's work has informed critical exegeses.[4] The edges of power as well as the edges of metaphor and of language are the common questions which the contributions here entail.

They are generated in the course of feminist history's inescapable engagement with the category of "women" in history. To admit, forced by the archives, the historical as well as the semantic vacillations of "women," needn't mean any abandonment of the political incisiveness for which a feminist history longs. On the contrary, as it is the lot of women as historical subjects to fight their way in and out of sexually indifferent categories of being like race or class, so the tracks of slow and powerful consolidations which name and characterize the sexes and their relations must also be pursued, and through many possible indirections, interruptions, displacements, oversaturation, silences.

Discourses of Domination

11

Feminism and Cross-Cultural Inquiry: The Terms of the Discourse in Islam

Leila Ahmed

Like the idea of "human rights" and of other political and civil "rights" which today are the common currency of international political thought, "feminism" or "women's rights" is an idea which has its origin in Western democratic societies. In fact the Western ideas of nationhood (and, in particular, of citizenry involving rights and obligations) and of feminism (in the sense of a more equal treatment of women and of women as contributory citizens alongside men to the wealth of the nation) both began to be articulated in Arab societies at about the same time, and in conjunction with each other. Indeed one particular work, *Takhlis al-ibriz ila talkhis Bariz* (1834) by the Egyptian intellectual Al-Tahtawi, who accompanied a student mission to France in the 1820s and wrote an account of French society on his return, is credited with being the first to have launched both ideas, at least on the intellectual plane, in the Arab world. It was also at this time that these ideas of national renovation and of rethinking the role of women began to make their appearance on the plane of social experimentation—in the opening of new, secular type schools for men, and the opening of schools for women.

The emergence of initial feminist and nationalist ideas and of social experimentation in these matters at this point (early to mid-nineteenth century) was part of the Middle East's broad response to the historical process then under way: Western capitalist penetration of the Middle East and Arab exposure to Western society and thought, including Western political ideas. Both feminism and the demand for new political structures reflecting the rights of citizens were socio-political ideas that steadily gained ground through the nineteenth century and into the early twentieth century. However, while the idea of political rights was embraced, and Arabicized and Islamicized without difficulty, feminism began to have opponents as well as proponents, and to be attacked as a "Western" and "un-Islamic" import whose consequences would be to weaken or destroy the fabric of Islamic society. (Why these two politico-intellectual imports fared so differently is a complex inquiry, which I have pursued elsewhere.[1] Having touched on the subject, though, it is necessary to note that the "paranoid" suspiciousness in the Islamic world with regard to the combination women, feminism, and Western influence, did have considerable justification at the time it first began to be expressed—in the late nineteenth and early twentieth centuries. That is, in that period the colonial powers and their agents, and in particular the missionaries through the schools they founded did indeed explicitly set out to undermine Islam through the training and remolding of women.)

Today, in the context of a rising "Islamic fundamentalism" that vein of criticism—the alienness of feminism and the incumbency therefore on Muslim women of rejecting it—has become more strident. This essay was written as an attempt, in 1985, to address that question, and to suggest that while the idiom of contemporary feminism, like that of political rights generally is indeed Western, the beliefs on which it rests and which it is dedicated to realizing socially—social justice for all and the full and equal humanity of men and women—are an endemic part of Islamic civilization (just as they are an endemic part of Western civilization before the development of the political idiom of democracy). In 1988 the gains made by Islamic political movements on the governmental level have had indubitably negative consequences for women—as the laws instituted by the "Islamic" governments of Iran and Pakistan, for example, illustrate. Paradoxically, though, the new dynamism of Islamic thought also has positive potential for women. The intellectual revitalization of Islam is leading to the rethinking of Islamic history and a questioning of received views about orthodox Islam, including those about the sacredness of Islamic law as traditionally constituted—the domain in which, above all, the social inferiority of women is inscribed and through which it is perpetuated. Students, including feminists, are asking who compiled the edifice of the law, why they formulated Koranic dicta into these particular laws, and whether these laws do not, in fact, reflect the classbound masculinist ideology of a particular segment of post-Koranic society at a particular moment in history, rather than capture the Koranic intention.

In fact, what today constitutes orthodox Islam—its laws, its traditions, and its view of history—is the product in the main of the middle and upper classes of the early and Classical epoch (632–1250), and represents their values, culture, and interests. From the start, however, what constituted the correct interpretation of Islam was contested territory, and from the start the orthodox hegemonic view of the politically dominant was vigorously challenged. The Sufi and the Qarmati movements, for example, along with other oppositional movements evolved over the same period as that in which orthodoxy established its hegemony, and like other oppositional movements they challenged the dominant group's right to political power, and their definition of what constituted Islam. Both were working-class movements in origin and drew most of their adherents from the lower classes. Both movements espoused versions of Islam that differed radically from orthodox Islam in their visions of social organization, including, by implication at least, with respect to proper sexual roles; and both the Qarmati movement (c. ninth to twelfth centuries) and, in its early days and in its socially radical phase (which came to an end c. 1100), Sufism were declared heretical, and were outlawed and savagely persecuted.[2] Once eradicated, they were erased or all but erased from history. (The Sufism that was to survive and to be permitted to some degree to flourish within orthodoxy was a tamed variety—a spiritual and mystical movement that had been shorn largely of its socially radical dimensions.)

To open up such avenues of thought, avenues that place in question the hegemonic claims of orthodox Islam as the only "true" version of Islam, leads to a reclaiming of the resistance and dissent that have been erased from history by the version of the past put forward by a hegemonic orthodoxy, and restores historicity to "Islam" and the version of it that lays claim to uncontested authority. The restoration of historical complexity shows incontrovertibly that the hegemonic version of Islam has always been contested, and makes clear also that the challenge and debate between versions of Islam is not about a transcendant and "God-given" Islam but about the clashing ideologies of different classes and about who, historically, had the power to make the laws and construct the edifice of official belief and culture. The fact that some of the movements contesting orthodoxy's vision also challenged its understanding of the significance of gender furthermore enables women to dismiss the myth perpetuated by orthodox Islam that the inferiority of women has never been questioned in Islamic societies, and that only the evil influence of Westernization prompted Muslim men and women to question that "God-given" order. The consequences of such a reclaiming of resistance and dissent in Islamic history may also have some practical application, at any rate for women living in societies that lay claim in their rhetoric to the wish or intention to return to Islam as a political or social vehicle. Even if Islam is adopted as government policy, reclaiming challenge and resistance in history makes it possible to point out that a return to Islam in no way forecloses the quest for an equitable society, in matters of gender as in everything else. What "Islam" means is not the uncontested system that those in power claim it to be but is, today as always in Middle Eastern history, open to redefinition in fundamental ways.

The following pages primarily explore the ways that Sufism—or certain strands within early Sufi thought—handled the concept of gender. Focusing principally on the figure of Rabi'a—an 8th century female mystic—I examine the literary representations of her life and activities (and much of the material relating to Rabi'a is essentially legend and fiction) with a view to analyzing what those representations declare, imaginatively and symbolically as well as literally, about Sufi perception of gender.

Rabi'a was born in 717 C.E. and lived into her eighties. Her life therefore falls in the 'Abbasid or Classical age of Islam. This was the age which saw, following Islam's rapid expansion, the inflow of vast wealth into the capital cities, and, in particular, into the imperial city of Bagdad. Rabi'a was from Basra which, like Bagdad, is in Iraq. The lifestyles of the elite and royalty of this age in Bagdad are fictionally represented in *The Arabian Nights:* the monarch Harun al-Rashid and his vizir Ja'afar, historical figures of this age, are among the characters whose fictional exploits the *Arabian Nights* recounts. The tales around these characters depict a world of lavish consumption: of jewels, feasts, eunuchs, and women (as wives, slaves, or concubines). Historical accounts of the life of al-Rashid and other 'Abbasid monarchs fully match the fictional accounts for the luxury and the lavish consumption they portray, of goods and of people, and, in particular, of women as objects. Caliphs and their elite companions and cohorts are depicted in works of history as well as in fiction as sexually relating to women in hordes—they generally enjoyed not merely the full quota of four legal wives, but also owned concubines by the dozens or hundreds.[3] The Caliph al-Mutawakkil, for example, reputedly had sexual intercourse with over 4,000 women.[4] Thus among royalty and elites, in terms even of numerical ratio alone, men related to women in ways which experientially signaled women's inferior, object-like status, their status as consumable entities. This was further reinforced by the fact that men of this class—in that they had numerous concubines (slave women) and generally no more than four wives (free women) related to women predominantly as masters to slaves. Obviously such lifestyles could only be indulged in by the very wealthy, but they were nevertheless the mores and values of the elite and hence constituted the visible and dominant values in society.

This was the background of mores among the upper classes against which early Sufism developed, and it is the background which constituted the context of Rabi'a's development.

Rabi'a's personal background is not precisely known. However, such information as we do have suggests that she was either a slave or a servant from a very poor family. According to her earliest—13th century—biographer, Rabi'a's master released the young Rabi'a from his service as a house servant when he woke one night to see a light shining over her head and illuminating the whole house—a light that denoted her special saintliness. Rabi'a then retired to the desert, and returned after a time and followed the profession of a flute player. (The profession of music it may be noted, as instrumentalist or singer, was one that was frequently followed by slave girls, as skill in music enhanced their status.) For the following few years the material we have about Rabi'a is clearly legendary, nevertheless, says Rabi'a's major twentieth-century biographer, Margaret Smith, these stories do give us "a clear idea of a woman renouncing this world and its attractions and giving up her life to the service of God—the first step on the mystic way trodden by Sufi the saint."[5]

But such a reading—to see Rabi'a as a woman "renouncing this world and its attractions"—seems, in view of the elite mores of the world in which she lived and what the options of a slave or servant woman might have been in it, both to ignore material reality and to romanticize Rabi'a's mysticism. Surely it would be reading that mysticism more accurately to see it as a path, and probably the only path for a woman in that age, and particularly a woman of Rabi'a's class, through which she might be permitted to live a life of autonomy and self-definition. In Rabi'a's case it was, in addition—since she was among the earliest of leading female mystics—a path which she in large part forged for herself and thereby created for other women. To say this is not in any way to disparage her mysticism, or to deny its genuineness and its spiritual dimension—rather it is to suggest that her "mysticism" represented a richer, denser, more complex and total response to her society and its mores, to the world in which she lived in its every realm and level than is generally allowed by the term "mysticism"; and to suggest that it was not merely a response to some narrow view of life and experience in which, conventionally, we often tend to place and see mysticism as something otherworldly and of relevance only to that dimension of experience generally connoted by words like "spirituality" and "God."

In fact the Sufi movement as a whole, which developed with remarkable vigor during this age, itself should be read in this way. Given some of its major and fundamental tenets and those which received particular stress during this age— the enormous importance for example of poverty and celibacy (i.e. the renunciation of money and sex) and the prohibiting of food not earned by the labor of one's own hands or provided by a fellow-Sufi who would have similarly earned it— it would be difficult and reductive to read the movement as being merely about "God" and spirituality, rather than as a movement which, even as it affirmed a particular perception as to the nature and significance of human life, expressed also a vehement and comprehensive rejection of the values of the dominant society.

Sufi traditions around the figure of Rabi'a furthermore distinctly suggest that Sufis rejected the dominant society's perception of women as completely as they rejected its high valuation of material possessions and unbridled sexuality. Biology and gender, Sufi tales about Rabi'a implicitly declare, are neither the only nor the chief basis of male/female relations; nor is gender to any degree a significant human qualifier. One tale for example has Hasan al-Basri, one of the most esteemed Sufi figures, declare:

"I passed one whole night and day with Rabi'a speaking of the Way and the Truth, and it never passed through my mind that I was a man nor did it occur to her that she was a woman, and at the end when I looked at her I saw myself a bankrupt (i.e. spiritually worth nothing), and Rabi'a as truly sincere."[6]

The fact that Hasan al-Basri died when Rabi'a was in her youth and therefore was unlikely to have had such a relation with her is obviously neither here nor there as to what such stories declare about Sufi thought and ideals.

The reversal of the dominant society's valuation of male over female that this tale also implies—it is *he* who is spiritually bankrupt compared to her—is also a theme that is amplified in numerous Sufi tales. Many stories show Rabi'a surpassing her male colleagues in intellectual forthrightness and percipience as well as in spiritual powers. For example, in one story she makes the pilgrimage to Mecca, and when she is halfway there the Ka'aba (the holiest shrine in Mecca) rises up and goes forward to meet her. Seeing this, Rabi'a, unimpressed, says, "What have I to do with the house, it is the Lord of the house I need." Meanwhile, an eminent fellow Sufi, Ibrahim ibn Adham, has also been making the pilgrimage— having taken fourteen years over it, as he had piously stopped at every spot to perform the ritual prayers. Arriving at Mecca and not seeing the Ka'aba, he is concluding that his eyes are at fault when a voice informs him that the Ka'aba has gone forth to meet a woman. When Rabi'a and the Ka'aba later both arrive, Rabi'a points out to Ibrahim (who is consumed with jealousy that the Ka'aba has so honored her) that while he crossed the desert with the formal ritual prayers, she came in inward prayer.[7]

Intellectual forthrightness, the ability to question the validity of even the most sacred rituals and institutions (as implied in her response to the approaching Ka'aba and in her attitude to Ibrahim's adherence to formal prayer), are hallmarks of Rabi'a's thought—as is her ironic and gently (if penetratingly) chiding stance towards those aspects of Islam the orthodox invest with inordinate reverence: the facilely dazzling and the mystifying. She laments, for example, with respect to Sufyan al-Thawri (represented in Sufi tales as a friend and frequent companion of hers), that he is devoted to studying and expounding the Hadith or Traditions (which are regarded by the orthodox with deep reverence, as are those who study them): "Sufyan would be a (good) man," she said, "if only he did not love the Traditions." In another tale, Hasan al-Basri approaches Rabi'a who is sitting on a bank with a number of contemplators. Throwing his prayer carpet on the water, he sits on it and calls to her to come and converse with him. Rabi'a, understanding that he wanted to impress people with his spiritual powers, threw her prayer carpet into the air and flew up to it and sitting there said, "Oh Hasan, come up here where people will see us." Hasan was silent, as it was beyond his power to fly: "Oh Hasan," Rabi'a then said, "that which you did a fish can do . . . and that which I did a fly can do. The real work (for the saints of God) lies beyond both of these . . ."[8]

Rabi'a's special and original contribution to Sufi thought is generally considered to be her introducing into it the notion that the mystic's prime and fundamental relation to God is that of love—not desire for reward or fear of punishment. "O God," one of her famous prayers reads, "if I worship Thee for fear of Hell, burn me in Hell, and if I worship Thee in hope of Paradise, exclude me from Paradise; but if I worship Thee for Thy own sake, grudge me not Thy everlasting beauty."[9] In her insistence on the primacy of love, and her rejection of the desire for reward or punishment as a spiritually valid motive she was again departing from orthodox Islamic doctrine and developing an independent approach.

One other topic is recurringly treated in Sufi accounts of Rabi'a's life: she is represented as being repeatedly sought in marriage for her outstanding spiritual qualities—sometimes by secular figures (such as the governor of Basra), but more particularly by her fellow Sufis, especially the most revered and eminent ones. Rabi'a rejects all her suitors, sometimes by setting them conundrums the answers to which demonstrate that spiritually she would have nothing whatever to gain by marriage, and sometimes by rebuking them for their sensuality and declaring that she herself knows neither love nor desire for anyone but God. In sum, then, Sufi presentations of Rabi'a portray a woman pursuing spiritually and socially a life other than that prescribed or permitted for women in the dominant society. She follows her own understanding of the nature of God and spirituality and not that decreed by religious orthodoxy; she pursues her intellectual and spiritual life in free discussions with men, as well as with women, and is subject to none in making her decisions as to the degree of intimacy or otherwise in which she relates to men or women; she retains full control and legal autonomy with respect to herself in that she is neither wife, nor slave, nor under any male authority, in a way that was actually impossible at the time within the world of orthodox Islam—and which would have been impossible for her as well had she not withdrawn to the alternative mental and spiritual space of Sufism.

In addition to indicating all this, Sufi accounts of Rabi'a convey a further message. They convey not only that Rabi'a was able to find and, in part, to create for herself a space in which to pursue her own development, but also that Sufism itself made, or was amenable to making such a space available to her, that is to making it available to women; and not only was Sufism amenable to making such a space available, but it also—in that it prominently incorporated Rabi'a into the heart of Sufi tradition, where she is counted as an "elect of the elect"—cherished and projected as ideal the example of a woman leader, a woman in free and open interchange with other men and women, an interchange regulated only by her own will and not by the enforced segregation of orthodox society, and cherished and projected as ideal individuals, women and men, not as embodiments of biological urges but as creatures needing resourcefully and thoughtfully to balance, as Rabi'a does, spiritual, biological, and social dimensions.

Much less is known regarding Qarmati views about women, but they too appear to have departed fundamentally from the prescriptions pertaining in orthodox Islamic society with respect to the proper relations between men and women. Qarmati writings have not survived so that one cannot base investigations of their beliefs or practices on their own accounts; the movement, which challenged the

'Abbasid regime militarily and, for a time, even succeeded in establishing an independent republic, was eventually eradicated and its writings destroyed or lost. Nearly all the available information about their activities and society comes from the pens of unsympathetic observers who were supporters of the 'Abbasid regime.

The Qarmati movement saw itself, like the Sufi movement, as representing the true realization of the Islamic message, as against the corruptions practiced by the dominant society. Accounts of their society describe them as practicing communism of property. Qarmati missionaries are described, for example, as organizing villagers and inviting them to bring to a central place all they owned by way of "cattle, sheep, jewelry, provisions," after which no one owned anything, and the goods were redistributed according to people's needs. "Every man worked with diligence and emulation at his task in order to deserve high rank by the benefit he brought. The woman brought what she earned by weaving, the child brought his wages for scaring away birds."[10] In the republic they established, property was communal and was administered by a central committee which insured that all had their housing, clothing, and food needs taken care of. Some writers went on to assert that the Qarmatis (who incidentally further offended the orthodox because they preached the irrelevance of religious difference and abolished state religion) also practiced communism of women. Contemporary scholars, however, suggest that this view represented a misperception of the practices the writers witnessed, practices which differed strikingly from the practices with respect to women of their own orthodox societies. For instance, the evidence they adduced in support of this accusation was that Qarmati women were not veiled, that both sexes practiced monogamy, and that women and men socialized together.[11] It was apparently these and similar practices that led the writers to assert that the Qarmatis were "debauched" and "obscene," themselves coming from societies in which the "unobscene" norm among the elite was for men to keep, and relate sexually to, women in droves.

This brief review of Sufi ideas on gender as expressed in the legends relating to Rabi'a, and of elements in the Qarmati movement affecting women, makes clear that even as the laws and structure of Classical Islam were being established, their validity and authority were being disputed, including in the area in which orthodox Islam is and has always been most rigidly prescriptive, that of gender relations (though disputed, to be sure, in terms of the idiom of the day, that of religious discourse). This brief review suggests further that orthodox Islam, the Islam that "Islamic" governments of the eighties are establishing and asserting to be the only Islam, represents the reinterpretation and reassertion in modern terms of the solidified culture, mores, and interests of the elite of a particular past age, a culture and values which won out by virtue of this group's power to impose their culture over those without power—in particular, over the lower classes. Even if Islamic republics were to build cultural walls and outlaw the political idioms of human rights that originated in the West (idioms now the common currency in all societies) resourceful women and men living in such societies would still have the intellectual means to contest—using the idiom and rhetoric of "Islam" and Islamic history—the injustices against women (and other groups) that governments are imposing in the name of "Islam."

12

"It's you, and not me": Domination and "Othering" in Theorizing the "Third World"

Rey Chow

1

In Lu Xun's "The New Year's Sacrifice,"[1] we find one of the most compelling encounters between a member of the dominating class and a downtrodden "other" in twentieth-century literature. A short story that forms part of the collection *Panghuang* (*Wandering,* 1926), it is a first-person account of the narrator's visit to his hometown, Luzhen, just before the New Year, when he happens to see Xianglin Sao, an old beggar woman who used to work for his Fourth Uncle. While he is still disturbed by the riddle-like questions that Xianglin Sao posed to him about life after death, she dies during the night of New Year's Eve. The rest of the story takes the form of a recollection of Xianglin Sao's life. A widow, she first came to Fourth Uncle's house as a servant. As she was strong, quiet, and hard-working, she soon won the favor of her master and mistress. One day, her dead husband's family came and took her home by force to be remarried, so that they would have money to buy a wife for their younger son. Xianglin Sao "gave in" after many protests and an attempt at suicide. She became happily married and gave birth to a boy. But her second husband suddenly died of typhoid fever. As she tried to make a living by gathering firewood, picking tea, and raising silkworms, her son was carried off by a wolf. She was soon asking for work again at Fourth Uncle's; only she had become slow, dazed, and gloomy. Because she was twice a widow and thus an ominous figure, she was no longer allowed to have anything to do with ancestral sacrifices. She now tirelessly repeated the story of how her little son was snatched away, which turned her into a laughing stock. Meanwhile, fearful about being punished in her afterlife for having had two husbands, she spent all her savings on buying a threshold in the local temple, which she believed would take her place in being "trampled upon" and free her of her sins. Psychotic,

152

aging, and losing her memory, Xianglin Sao was dismissed by her master and became a beggar.

From the beginning, the process of "othering" in this story is inseparable from the contradictions of the narrator's position. By the early twentieth century, Chinese intellectuals had more or less accepted China's need to modernize. This surrender to a long-resisted change meant the submission to China's "othering," that is, to the image of "China" as given back to it by the West in their multiple intercourses throughout the nineteenth century—China as backward, corrupt, filthy, weak, etc. And yet this acceptance was complicated by the very different conceptions of "power" in Chinese culture, in which being powerful, when it is the result of a high social status, can mean non-assertion and privileges won without effort.

To the extent that it is the subservient who perform tasks, which often amounts to some kind of decision-making, domination in the Confucian East Asian context is arguably through "indirection"—a non-coincidence between power and visible action.[2] In pre-modern China, the non-assertive functioning of power was perhaps best demonstrated by the intellectual, whose literary talents had long been institutionalized for the purposes of state administration. As the cross-breed between the thinker and the bureaucrat, the traditional Chinese intellectual therefore occupied the peculiar position of one who exercised political power through literature or "writing." In this sense, it would be difficult, if not impossible, to give to literature the subversive critical value that is at the heart of so many contemporary Western deconstructive practices, precisely because the inherent capacity to deconstruct that is attributed to language-as-structure—a capacity which we might reinterpret as a kind of disruptive but redemptive *nature*—has for so long been systematically tamed in China through bureaucracy. In other words, in Lu Xun's intellectual narrator, we encounter a kind of cultural "subject" whose access to society was, by tradition, through a thorough political subjugation of himself. The acquisition of a particular consciousness through the Confucian literary education made him at once the privileged beneficiary and the custodian of "culture."[3] With the arrival of imperialism, however, this traditional structure of power-as-subjugation was disrupted. The Chinese intellectual was oppressed by two kinds of impotence—first, the realization that "literature" as he used to understand it no longer worked in sustaining his power; second, that as a "Chinese national" he witnessed the fragmentation of his civilization vis-à-vis the West in an utterly helpless manner.

It is against the background of such impotence that the many figures of the "other" make their first entries into modern Chinese literature, figures in which an otherwise inexplicable excess of emotion is invested to the point of sentimentalism. One thinks of the children and mothers in Bing Xin and You Shi, the house servants in Ba Jin, the neurotic young women in Ding Ling and Mao Dun, the illiterate rural people in Lu Xun and Wu Zuxiang, the sold wives and

154 / Rey Chow

polyandrous scrap-paper collector in Xu Dishan, among others. These oppressed "others" provide the stage onto which a total sense of collapse is projected. Against this background of impotence, also, the unprecedented literary "presence" of these "others" gives to modern Chinese literature a consciously political meaning. But persisting in the writings of the 1920s and 1930s were the questions of how these others could be genuinely released and the implications their presence had for the "dominating" position of the narrating subject.

In Lu Xun's story, there is a general, if mild, sense of dislocation from the time the narrator arrives "home." Not only is he ill at ease; he also quickly decides he has to leave. But what exactly does this urge for departure mean? When he realizes that his Fourth Uncle and he are clearly opposed on the question of reform and modernization, he "departs" by withdrawing to the study, and into the traditional scholastic mode of contemplation. This departure sets the tone for the rest of the narrative. While the narrator cannot forget his encounter with Xianglin Sao, his engagement with her is at the same time an evasion that takes the most convoluted and indecisive turns:

"You have come back?" she asked me first.

"Yes."

"That is very good. You are a scholar, and have traveled too and seen a lot. I just want to ask you something." Her lusterless eyes suddenly gleamed.

I never would have guessed she would say something like this. I stood there in amazement.

"It is this." She drew two paces nearer, and lowered her voice, and said very confidentially: "After a person dies, is there really a soul that lives on?"

As she fixed her eyes on me I was seized with foreboding. A shiver ran down my spine and I felt more nervous than during an unexpected examination at school, when unfortunately the teacher stands by one's side. Personally, I had never given the least thought to the existence of spirits. In this instance how should I answer her? Hesitating for a moment, I reflected: "It is the tradition here to believe in spirits, yet she seems to be skeptical—perhaps it would be better to say she hopes: hopes that there is immortality and yet hopes that there is not. Why increase the worries of people nearing the end of their lives? To give her something to look forward to, it would be better to say there is."

"There may be, I think," I told her hesitantly.

"Then, there must also be a Hell?"

"What, Hell?" Greatly startled, I could only try to evade the question. "Hell? According to reason there should be one too—but not necessarily. Who cares about it anyway?"

"Then will all the people of one family who have died see each other again?"

"Well, as to whether they will see each other again or not—" I realized now that I was a complete fool; for all my hesitation and reflection I had been unable to answer her three questions. Immediately I lost confidence and wanted to say the exact opposite of what I had previously said. "In this case . . . as a matter of fact, I am not sure. Actually, regarding the question of ghosts, I am not sure either."

Taking advantage of the pause in her questioning, I walked off, and beat a hasty retreat to my uncle's house, feeling exceedingly uncomfortable. I thought to myself: "I'm afraid my answer will prove dangerous to her. Probably it's just that when other people are celebrating she feels lonely all by herself, but could there be another reason? Could she have had some premonition? If there is another reason, I shall be held responsible to a certain extent." Finally, however, I ended by laughing at myself, thinking that such a chance meeting could have no great significance, and yet here I was pondering it so carefully; no wonder certain educators call me a neurotic. Moreover I had distinctly said, "I am not sure," contradicting my previous answer; so that even if anything did happen, it would have nothing at all to do with me.

"I am not sure" is a most useful phrase.

Inexperienced and rash young men often take it upon themselves to solve people's problems for them or choose doctors for them, and if by any chance things turn out badly, they are probably held to blame; but simply by concluding with this phrase "I am not sure," one can free oneself of all responsibility. At this time I felt even more strongly the necessity for such a phrase, since even in speaking with a beggar woman there was no getting along without it.

No commentary can recapture sufficiently the deconstructive quality of the above passage. Evidently troubled by a figure like Xianglin Sao and yet incapable of locating the sources of his feelings, the narrator is beset by a terror which doubles back on the narrative as a constant flight from his own position. Indeterminacy here becomes an indispensable means of self-defense. But defense against what? Why is the narrator, like so many of Lu Xun's narrators when faced with their socially oppressed "others," so terrified? What constitutes neurosis here? The ironic language of the story does not provide an answer.

Instead, this narrative blank is elaborated through a completely different treatment of Xianglin Sao. While the narrator is a "mind" with which we become acquainted through its contradictions, Xianglin Sao remains someone we observe from without, like an animal: she has "big strong feet and hands" and "would eat anything." She is not called by her own name but by "Xianglin's wife." She is sold by her first husband's family exactly as a commodity. Her perplexity over life and death is not entertained nor articulated collectively to form a larger experience; her obsession with her dead child dwindles into a ridiculous psychosis which no one bothers to investigate; her inability to comprehend her own life prevents it from being transcended to any teleological perspective, including that of sacrifice. All the representational channels that could have given her a kind of "subjectivity" are carefully blocked. This hardened "object" which we do not "understand" becomes in this way the projection of the narrator's fleeting subjectivity, a subjectivity that is felt in the form of elliptic shifts in narrative mood, which is now melancholy, now hopeful.

In a brilliant article, Marston Anderson points out the peculiar reputation Lu Xun has among his critics. As modern China's most famous writer, Lu Xun has been described alternately as "satiric realist" and "predominantly reminiscent and lyrical."[4] The conflict between these two perspectives, whereby the mood of a progressive orientation toward modernization is annulled by the involved narration of childhood and country life with their pathetic characters, and by a sadness over the immobile habits of a long civilization, suggests that Lu Xun's work must be considered primarily as an exploration of the fundamental problematic of writing in modern China.[5] The question that his work as a whole poses for an understanding of "Third World" politics is this: if writing has always been the possession of the educated classes, how might it be justified for social revolution? While Lu Xun's fiction remarkably demonstrates one of the most powerful formal effects of writing—that is, the effect of representation as distancing—for him that effect was also indistinguishable from a complicity with the existing political order at a time when "complicity" could not be supported by the kind of leisure that would allow it to be read as its opposite, as the resistance-in-silence that "literature" theoretically provides. If the process of "othering" in "The New Year's Sacrifice" is a process of cognition, it is also cognition as disability. A strangely light-hearted ending indicates once again the readily "departing" state of the narrator in the form of a peaceful obliviousness:

> I was woken by the noisy explosion of crackers close at hand and, from the faint glow shed by the yellow oil lamp and the bangs of fireworks as my uncle's household celebrated the sacrifice, I knew that it must be clearly dawn. Listening drowsily I heard vaguely the ceaseless explosion of crackers in the distance. It seemed to me that the whole town was enveloped by the dense cloud of noise in the sky, mingling with the whirling snowflakes. Enveloped in this medley of sound I relaxed; the doubt which had preyed on my mind from dawn till night was swept clean away by the festive atmosphere, and I felt only that the saints of heaven and earth had accepted the sacrifice and incense and were reeling with intoxication in the sky, preparing to give Luzhen's people a boundless good fortune.

This ending must be understood as a double disappearance. Not only does the spectacle of Xianglin Sao's suffering disappear as a mere disturbing dream which now gives way to the relaxed atmosphere of the New Year's celebration, but the narrator, too, disappears with the feelings of "boundless good fortune." As the convolutions of cognition on the preceding pages fade, he becomes "enveloped" like the whole town in the ritualized respects that are paid to the saints of heaven and earth. A return to normality-as-intoxication thus puts an end to both "subject" and "object."

The process of "othering" in which the "other" is opposed, in the form of an impenetrable spectacle, to a contradictory "subjective" narrative position is a self-defeating one. The polarization of "self" and "other" as such blocks any perception of inequality, however genuine, from being able to change the existing reality as it potentially should. In order for such perception not to be blocked and impoverished in this way, it needs to be supported by a radically reorganized division and distribution of intellectual labor: not only should "inequality" be approached through the concentration of intellectual complexities such as ellipses and undecidabilities in the "dominating subject," but the "dominated object," too, has to be liberated precisely in its contradictions, its specific structurations.

2

My arguments would become clearer if we turn to another set of texts—the debate between Jacques Derrida and Anne McClintock and Rob Nixon on South African apartheid.[6] As Elizabeth Weed puts it, the debate "enacts an intense struggle going on in critical theory between deconstruction and the critical left— a struggle that often leaves the 'left' out of deconstruction."[7] On the one hand, we have the perception of the inseparability between overt politics and the basic representational structures of "Western" discourse, a perception of which Derrida's way of invoking "apartheid" in "Racism's Last Word" is paradigmatic. On the other hand, we see the insistence on "history" as an attempt to refute the understanding of apartheid in a theoretical, because generalized, manner. What is unfortunate about the debate is that the interesting points of contention that should have together provided a formulation of the larger problem we face as participants in world politics are lost in an increasingly personalized quarrel. The quarrel is summarized in Derrida's phrase: "It's you, and not me, who . . . seem to be frightened by this work . . . " (p. 358). This polarization of positions is symptomatic of the contemporary theoretical scene to which Derrida also draws attention: "We have never met but . . . I have a sense of something familiar, as if our paths had often crossed at colloquia or in some other academic place" (p. 354). Clearly, the place where this exchange takes place—not South Africa but the coveted pages of one of the foremost academic journals in the United States—should alert us to the overdetermined nature of political struggles which cannot be reduced to a "choice" between the amplification of rhetorical rules and the chronicling of historical events?

One of the lessons we learn from this exchange is, as I said, a larger problem facing us as participants in cross-cultural inquiry. This problem is the asymmetrical structure between the "West" as dominating subject and the "non-West" or "Third World" as the oppressed "other." Derrida's main argument about apartheid should be understood as an attempt to articulate this asymmetry. The gist of his argument takes us back to post-Enlightenment theoreticians of human nature such as Hegel, for whom what distinguishes western man from the rest of the world is his ability to present himself to himself. Whereas in Asia, Africa, and elsewhere, human beings are still living in a sensuous continuity with Nature, in Europe man has risen out of this natural bond into a state of consciousness.[8] Hegel's construction of human self-consciousness as the precondition for "universality" received its parallel in language theory from the work of his older contemporary Johann Gottfried von Herder, a fellow philosopher. Herder's essay "On the Origin of Language" (1772)[9] lays down the ground-breaking definition of language as what separates human beings from the rest of the natural world *in kind,* not in degree. His theory thus represents a decisive break from earlier and later theories of language that show language to be derived from instinctual, "animal" emotions. For Herder, language begins with Man as an inner consciousness that *names* rather than mimics or responds to the rest of the world; the world literally begins and takes shape with Man "the talking animal."

These theoretical efforts to delineate the "human," be it in terms of language, reflection, or subjectivity, took place against a background of looming non-European "others." Conceivably, it would not be difficult for the distinction between the human and the non-human, which is argued by Hegel and Herder as a definitive and original break, to become also the distinction between Europe and the rest of the world. The fact that these non-European others were irreducibly present did not matter. As it is Man (hence Europe) that hails the world into being, what remains is how the non-European world can be depicted in such a way as to mark it off from European consciousness or universality. "Othering" for Hegel was a matter of placing: Africa "is no historical part of the World,"[10] and the East "is to be excluded from the history of philosophy."[11] The rationality of placing is a progressive one: while Africa is still in the state of sensuous nature, magic, and fetishism (i.e., the arbitrary bestowal of supernatural power on natural objects), the Oriental world, notably China whose documented cultural history cannot be written off as sensuous nature, is depicted in terms of "Oriental despotism." In the concept of despotism, Oriental culture is placed as a second-order nature that allows Hegel to retain all that he considers to be "natural" (i.e., non-differentiated sensuousness, unfree consciousness, etc.) in the analysis of an unmistakably developed culture. The notions of slavery and slavish consciousness are thus indispensable for Hegel's interpretation of China. The Chinese are unfree because they cannot represent themselves to themselves; they are liars who cheat whenever and whomever they can.

In the constructions of human freedom as self-consciousness—Man's first possession—lies the course of European cultural domination. For Derrida, it is the indelible effects inscribed by these constructions in human behavior—the effects of division and separation—that the term "apartheid" underscores. The currently topical or "political" meaning of apartheid, then, becomes the *setting apart* of separation as a basic human fact. Hence Derrida associates South African apartheid with "another regime of abstraction, that of confined separation": "The word concentrates separation, raises it to another power and sets separation itself *apart.*" The critical reminders of Hegel and Herder become clear when Derrida says, "there's no racism without a language. The point is not that acts of racial violence are only words but rather that they have to have a word. . . . racism always betrays the perversion of a man, the *'talking animal'*" (p. 331, my emphasis).

By calling racism "perversion," and by suggesting that that perversion lies in the talking, or linguistic, function of Man, Derrida offers a very powerful way of undoing the complacent constructions of "humanity" that we encounter in Hegel and Herder. Instead of showing "separation" to be definitive of human nature in a superior way, Derrida argues the reverse, namely, that yes, separation is definitive of human nature, but it's perverse. An even more crucial point is that this perverse way of constructing humanity is, alas for Hegel and Herder, European: "*Apartheid* constitutes, therefore, the first 'delivery of arms,' the first product of European exportation." It is something that "had to be possible and, what is more, durable." In other words, what is exported from Europe to the rest of the world, culminating in the scandal of South African apartheid, is a whole set of symbolic relations in its full play, including "its incoherences, its compromises, and its stabilization." These elements constitute "the occidental essence of the historical process" (p. 334). That essence is what we might safely call "contradiction."

However, the impasse created by this way of criticizing a particular cultural domination is precisely that the premise of contradiction from which Derrida proceeds—a premise which deconstructs the wholesome universal subject that we receive from Hegel—does not only implicate the "other" in such a way as to pre-neutralize the insurgency of the confrontation; it also foreseeably destroys its own critical import. This is the "double disappearance" of domination and othering that Lu Xun's story demonstrates. The two sides of this polarized debate converge, in fact, in the politics of "prescriptive" writing, of which both sides implicitly or explicitly accuse the other of not understanding. While McClintock and Nixon's point is to show the prescriptive nature of the South African authorities' manipulation of the word "apartheid," a manipulation which may be paraphrased as "Erase 'apartheid'—so that people will think it's gone"; Derrida insists that he, too, is writing in a prescriptive mode, a mode which may be paraphrased as "May 'apartheid' stay, the better for us to confront its cunning with." Between prescriptive speech as domination and prescriptive speech as resistance, the wheel of "European" language seems to have come full circle.

3

The resistance to—the "othering" of—domination that takes the forms of internal doublings of speech, silent parodies, and self-demolitions is familiar to all students of representation. But such forms of resistance, while offering the "First World" critic of imperialism so many ways of saying "Mea culpa," also tend to leave his "others" intact in their totally valorized and totally deprived state. An attempt to criticize this kind of asymmetry between subject and object, action and spectacle, lies behind every anti-imperialist discourse. And yet, in addressing this asymmetry, critics often elaborate on domination-as-structure in such a way as to repeat precisely this asymmetry. For instance, Raymond Williams (quoted by Edward Said) says, "however dominant a social system may be, the very meaning of its domination involves a limitation or selection of the activities it covers, so that by definition it cannot exhaust all social experience, which therefore always potentially contains space for alternative acts and alternative intentions which are not yet articulated as a social institution or even project."[12] Or, theorizing questions of ambivalence and authority, Homi Bhabha says, "the colonial discourse has reached that point when, faced with the hybridity of its objects, the *presence* of power is revealed as something other than what its rules of recognition assert."[13] While these nuanced ways of theorizing domination, which are not limited to deconstruction but can be extended to much post-colonialist criticism informed by Michel Foucault and by post-structuralist Marxism, make full use of the radical implications of structure and systematicity to produce the necessary awareness that domination contains its own undoing, they tend also to ontologize the overdetermined instances of domination in specific cultural contexts as *indeterminacy*, in a way that is perfectly in keeping with the indeterminacy between the "descriptive" and "prescriptive" modes of speech. The ontology of indeterminacy could thus be termed *"less than one and double,"*[14] in Homi Bhabha's otherwise enigmatic phrase. The inadequacy of this deconstructive—even though critical—approach to domination lies in its overconcentration of such notions as "activity," "movement," and "the capacity for contradiction" in the dominating stance, often at the expense of discourses which try to resist domination in other ways. In this asymmetrical structure of *anti*-imperialism, one is tempted to see a kind of uncanny repetition of the treatment of the "other" that was in Hegel—a treatment that privileges the eventfulness, the motility, and thus the "self-consciousness" of the "universal subject" to the detriment of the represented or colonized object, who, by implication, has not even begun to be contradictory.

In other words, insofar as it offers a means of showing the structural inevitability of "othering" in all acts of domination, deconstructive criticism has collaborated with anti-imperialism in the most abstract sense. But it is not enough to know this inevitability structurally, for that remains, precisely, "knowledge" from within the dominating stance. As we see in Lu Xun's story, this kind of knowledge leads not to change but to an oblivion of crises which is indistinguishable from a complicity with domination and oppression. The mysterious shifts in narrative mood in Lu Xun were perhaps symptomatic of his discomfort with this asymmetrical process of "othering," a process which haunted him as a legacy from his own scholarly background. The "double disappearance" in "The New Year Sacrifice" could therefore be understood in retrospect as a kind of sign that predicted his ultimate discontinuation of fiction-writing as the practice in which "others" could emerge with genuine significance. Lu Xun did not give up writing but turned instead to critical essays and stories that were conscious rewritings of the past, such as those collected in *Zhao hua xi shi* (Dawn flowers plucked at dusk) (1928) and *Gushi xin pian* (Old tales retold) (1935).

Contrary to the absolute difference that is often claimed *for* the "Third World," then, the work of a twentieth-century Chinese intellectual foretells much that is happening in the contemporary "Western" theoretical scene. Xianglin Sao, who is not only "Woman" or "native" or the "socially oppressed" but all of the above, is the kind of figure in whom contemporary theory, in an attempt to overcome its own limits, has barely begun to take an interest. But "othering" cannot simply be a process of earnest excavations of the forgotten. It means, more importantly, making way for "others" to come forth not as spectacles but in their contradictions, in which perhaps already lie a decipherment of "our" problems. If "China" is one such "other," the socialist realism that the Chinese Communist Government introduced after 1942 as a programmed correction to the kinds of impasse suggested by Lu Xun's story is extremely instructive. In the dogmatic efforts to empower the "lower classes" as content, we saw an insertion of "others" in all representations that became pure ideology. While full-fledged arguments about this over-compensatory process of "othering" in mainland China must be made on another occasion, my point is that this "other" historical trajectory of domination and othering is "ours" as well. The first thing it teaches us is that no genuine encounter can be based on the plaint that, after all, is only part of a more revealing idiom— "*I'm glad* it's you, and not me."

13

Commentary: "All That is Inside is not Center": Responses to the Discourses of Domination

Barbara Harlow

"In fact the inside/outside antithesis in relation to culture hides the fact that the inside is capitalism and that even the seemingly outside, as regards the international labor force of the Third World is very much inside, within the spheres of multinational capitalism, but that at the same time all that is inside is not center."[1] In her essay, "Ethnicity, Ideology and Academia," the Chicana writer and critic Rosaura Sánchez examines the ways in which a prevailing "discourse of boundaries" as practiced within the U.S. academy, as in other of its dominant institutions, from the Immigration and Naturalization Services to the Federal Bureau of Prisons, serves to underwrite the hegemonic cultural and political practices of the West generally, but of the United States in particular. The "discourse of boundaries" is at the same time continuous with what Sánchez refers to as a "discourse of opportunity" that renders the political boundaries as objective criteria of merit or standards of academic quality and scholarly excellence. As such it is complicit in the cooptive process of absorption, into the system, of counter-hegemonic cultural strategies which would otherwise demand a political, even partisan, interventionism into/from out of the conscientiously isolated preserves of culture: the academy. "The notion of pluralism," according to Sánchez, "of a multicultural society, points then to a type of heterogeneous cohesive whole while suppressing the reality of social fragmentation. Similarly, the talk of boundaries leaves us contemplating one plane, one dimension, rather than aware of a hierarchical structure, a class system, that establishes social constraints and creates antagonisms between groups" (p. 81). Sánchez goes on to locate the attendant issue of the "task of the [oppositional] intellectual" within the larger economic and institutional market nexus which sustains the very premises of the university complex: "The question is whether one can in fact ever represent a counter project while being funded, housed and incorporated within the system" (p. 84). Neither delicacy nor development have provided uncompromised, politically absolved answers to this positional aporia, posed again in the work of Lu Xun and

162

re-articulated by Rey Chow: "if writing has always been the possession of the educated classes, how might it be justified for social revolution?"

Both Leila Ahmed in "Feminism and Cross-Cultural Inquiry: The Terms of the Discourse in Islam" and Rey Chow in her essay, " 'It's you, and not me': Domination and 'Othering' in Theorizing the 'Third World'," challenge this "discourse of boundaries" as it is deployed in maintaining the geo-political divide between First and Third Worlds, West and East, North and South, core and periphery, metropolis and colony. While Ahmed focuses on "feminism" and its participation in the maintenance of these discretionary borders, Chow implicates a certain construction of "theory" in reconstituting the hierarchical divisions of labor and relations of power across the global arena. Each critic, however, elicits from a specific historical configuration and the material conditions that inform it—Islam in the 8th century A.D. and 20th-century Chinese "modernism"—the potential for an insurgent politics and its challenge to the tactics of containment which seek to obfuscate such opposition. Critical to both Ahmed and Chow's analyses is the displaced role of women in elaborating interventionary strategies.

Leila Ahmed, in an article entitled "Western Ethnocentrism and Perceptions of the Harem," has pointed out that the purported horror and fascination expressed on the part of early western travelers to the East at the harem life of "oriental" women was paralleled by no less a horror on the part of these women at what they saw as the corseted bodily imprisonment of European ladies behind stays and bars of bone and ivory.[2] These reciprocating but unrequited perceptions of "other" women by "other" women as oppressed by their respective cultural traditions and social strictures persist in the contemporary context as well, altered, however, by the intervening history of western expansion, imperialism, and global domination. The mutual responses have in the interim been distorted by the unequal power relationships which that historical narrative has produced, and western feminism, as part of that process, has at times assumed for itself the prerogative of the exemplary "civilizing mission" of its own colonial past, and this at the expense of a larger liberationist agenda.

These dominant distortions of historical power were evident at the three international conferences in Mexico City, Copenhagen, and Nairobi which marked the beginning, middle, and end of the United Nations "decade of women" from 1975 to 1985, landmark events in that they brought together women from all regions of the world in a collective discussion of their common struggles. These conferences, however, were significant not only for the show of solidarity that they elicited from women of different national, ethnic, religious, class, and political backgrounds, but for the critical differences in priorities and issues which came to divide the women in their debates, panels, and workshops. The disputes, described, for example, by the Bolivian representative from the Housewives Committee of the miners union, Domitila Barrios de Chungara, in *Let Me Speak* (1979) and *Aquí tambien, Domitila* (1985),[3] or by Nawal el-Saadawi, who saw her critical remarks in Copenhagen on Israel and the Camp David agreements as partial reason for her arrest by Sadat in 1981,[4] engaged Third World women against First World women, and divided too the government-sponsored delegations of women from those other women who represented non-governmental organizations (NGOs).

Geo-political issues divide as well the U.S. academy against itself. The "women's liberation movement" and its later developments in "feminism" have played a critical and decisive role in redefining the parameters of research in the western academic disciplines, from classics to economics. They have been central as well to the literary-critical debate over what has now been canonized as the "opening of the canon." The theoretical and immanently insurgent contribution of "third world women" to these debates has, however, been largely re-marginalized, if only because of their erstwhile homogenization within dominant theoretical constructions which disallows the complications raised by unsanctioned historical contradiction. The critique of the "British women's movement" proposed by Angela Weir and Elizabeth Wilson which points to the alteration in designation from "women's liberation movement" to "feminism" as indicative of a shift away from a commitment not only to sexual liberation but also to the national liberation movements in other parts of the world,[5] is reiterated by Jenny Bourne in her article "Homelands of the Mind":

> Today's feminism bears few hallmarks of such liberatory socialist principles. "The struggle for social change and the transformation of society" articulated as a primary purpose at the first British Women's Liberation Conference (1970) has been obscured by a feminism which is separatist, individualistic and inward-looking. The organic relationship we tried to forge between the personal and the political has been so degraded that now the only area of politics deemed to be legitimate *is* the personal.[6]

Both Leila Ahmed in her presentation of the biography and social circumstances of Rabi'a al-Awadiyyah, an early Islamic mystic and female saint, and Rey Chow, whose reading of Lu Xun's "The New Year's Sacrifice" questions the stratagems of domination in the "theorizing of the 'third world,' " and for all the crucial differences that mark their respective interventions, reassert the relevance of "liberation." They insist too on the significance of the historical conditions and material context of women's position within and against internally generated and externally imposed cultural norms in elaborating the parameters of a larger collective and emancipatory project. The very nature of such a project, as the papers themselves suggest, entails empirical work and research, the work of archivists, editors, anthologizers, translators, and journalists, no less than theoretical adjudications and speculation. What remains at issue, however, is the division of labor within this enterprise of what Gayatri Spivak has referred to as "information retrieval,"[7] its production and its consumption. Rey Chow, for example, insists on the need for a "radically reorganized division and distribution of intellectual labor" which must involve the specificity in all its contradictions of the "dominated object" as much as those of the "dominating subject." No less militantly, Leila Ahmed argues against the ascendancy of the West in its claim to be a promoter of progress in her contention that the terminology and categories of dissent, change, and appropriation are available already within the traditional or indigenous social, cultural, and political forms of Islam. As she writes in an earlier version of the paper, "the structures of gender and class can as readily and as radically be challenged in a terminology internal to Islamic civilization as in any other other." The elucidation of Rabi'a's mysticism and the Qarmatian movement in the early centuries of Islam are designed to outline the since suppressed possibilities of such a challenge.

In turning to the classical Islamic past to retrieve the biography of Rabi'a al-Awadiyyah, Leila Ahmed reminds us of the pernicious distortions of the present. The tendency in the West, and especially in the United States—and this not only in reaction to the fall of the Shah and Shiite resistance in southern Lebanon following the Israeli invasion in 1982 (resistance which turned subsequently, however, to internecine competition among militias and against the Palestinian refugee camps)—to view Islam in a monolithically manichean way has only obscured the various, often contradictory, directions within the religious tradition and the attendant heterogeneity within the Arab world today. Sufism itself, as Ahmed points out, has historically assumed an oppositional stance vis-à-vis orthodox and especially Sunni Islam. From the Qarmati movement in the 9th and 10th centuries, a branch of the Ismailis, or Assassins, *Hashishiyyin,* as they came to be called, to individual mystics such as Rabi'a in the 8th century or al-Hallaj in the 9th century, to popular veneration of saints by the urban lower classes and rural peasantry of present-day Egypt, Sufism has provided not only a kind of ecstatic escape from, but a very worldly criticism of, the oppression of state-institutionalized orthodoxy. Like Rabi'a, al-Hallaj too has been resuscitated in modern Arabic literature, in such dramas as *Masa'at al-Hallaj* by the late Egyptian writer and former Minister of Culture, Salah Abd al-Sabur, as an example of principled resistance to state tyranny. The 19th-century Mahdist movement of national liberation in the Sudan was similarly inspired.

Leila Ahmed has, however, as the background to her re-narrativizing of Rabi'a's significance, the "rising 'Islamic fundamentalism' " in the Arab world today, with the re-veiling of women as only one of its consequences. This re-veiling has, of course, been variously interpreted by some critics as evidence for the renewed repression of Arab-Muslim women, but it has also been justified by other apologists as a release of women from the economic coercions of "fashion" and "western chic" through a return to traditional dress. Like the veil used by Algerian women during the struggle for national liberation to conceal explosives destined by the resistance for French establishments in the occupied country, or the traditional white kerchiefs worn by the Mothers of the Plaza de Mayo in Argentina seeking their disappeared children, "knotted, implying a lack of freedom," and covering the hair, a "symbol of the repression within the ideology of women," the current Islamic revival of the veil must be examined within the historicized context of the multiple economic and socio-political factors which determine its use. As Marjorie Agosin points out, concerning the kerchief of the Mothers of the Plaza, it has been "changed, revised, and elaborated under a new canon: the kerchief is embroidered with the name of the disappeared child."[8]

In his article, "Religion and the Left: An Introduction," Cornel West speaks to the phenomenon of religious revival in maintaining that, "notwithstanding the secular sensibilities of most leftist intellectuals and activists, religion permeates and pervades the lives of the majority of people in the capitalist world."[9] West's concern, however, is with the role played by religious revivals and upsurges in the Third World and the contribution they have to make to the left movement in general. Such contradictions as that between the rearguard support for the anti-Sandinista "contras" by Nicaraguan Cardinal Obando y Bravo and the secular emancipatory vision of the assassinated archbishop of El Salvador, Monsignor Oscar Romero, are indicative of the dispute over dogma and authority, on the one hand, and resistance, on the other, waged between Pope John Paul and the representatives of liberation theology in Central and South America, a dispute which is reflected in the literature and cultural practices of these countries. Manlio Argueta's *One Day of Life,* an El Salvadoran novel, chronicles, for example, the coming to political consciousness of Lupe, a peasant woman whose husband is murdered by the death squads. Part of her evolution is catalyzed by the change in priests now coming to the village, priests who do not attempt to resolve the death of children through dehydration with promises of new angels in heaven to pray for those left behind. Given then, the increased influence of religion in the contemporary world, it is important to examine religions not only as abstract, transcendent dogma, but in terms of the specificity of their historical and ideological conditions of acceptance, as what Cornel West calls "popular responses to intense capitalist domination of more traditional societies" (p. 14). According to West, "the major contribution religious revivals can make to left strategy is to demand that Marxist thinkers and activists take seriously the culture of the oppressed" (pp. 16–17).

The historical blindness that Cornel West sees in the "European Enlightenment legacy—the inability to believe in the capacities of oppressed people to create cultural products of value—which stands between contemporary Marxism and oppressed people," (p. 17) can sometimes stand between contemporary feminism and "third world women" as well. The argument that "feminism" is a western or First World concept exported along with modernization and technology to Third World countries has been adduced by indigenous traditionalists and western feminists alike. Kumari Jayawardena describes the apparent contradiction:

The concept of feminism has also been the cause of much confusion in Third World countries. It has variously been alleged by traditionalists, political conservatives and even certain leftists, that feminism is a product of "decadent" Western capitalism; that it is based on a foreign culture of no relevance to women of the local bourgeoisie; and that it alienates or diverts women, from their culture, religion and family responsibilities on the one hand, and from the revolutionary struggles for national liberation and socialism on the other. In the West, too, there is a Eurocentric view that the movement for women's liberation is not indigenous to Asia or Africa, but has been a purely West European and North American phenomenon, and that where movements for women's emancipation or feminist struggles have arisen in the Third World, they have been merely imitative of Western models.[10]

For all the ostensible and ideological differences separating their respective positions, such an argument as to the western origins of women's struggle aligns nativists and feminists alike together within a linear stages of development narrative as this is legislated from the centers of economic and military power in First World capitals. According to such a narrative and the models for progress that it propagates, the Third World will forever remain underdeveloped and disadvantaged, trapped in a kind of Zeno's paradox, as it seeks to adopt and adapt to the cultural and socio-political paradigms developed primarily in the First World and only subsequently, if at all, disseminated to its Third World dependents. The contradictions inherent in the imperial espousal of "third world women's" rights and the nativist's defense of his women are displayed in Gayatri Spivak's analysis of *suttee* in colonial India, where they elicit from the analysis a counterhistory that would position differently the dependent's dissent: "Faced with the dialectically interlocking sentences that are constructible as 'White men are saving brown women from brown men' and 'The women wanted to die,' the postcolonial woman intellectual asks the question of simple semiosis—What does this mean?—and begins to plot a history" (p. 297).

The very terms of the traditionalism/modernism dichotomy which characterize much of the present debate in "developing" countries over their past and its resources and the future ends in whose service these will be enlisted are manipulated as historical necessity by the centers of "development" and their funding agencies. As the Palestinian critic Faysal Draj has pointed out, the distinction itself and the periodization of which it is a constitutive part are complicit with cultural dependency, and its deployment only serves to reinforce that dependency.[11] Similarly, Rey Chow's critical re-reading of Chinese "modernism" "from within" in "Rereading Mandarin Ducks and Butterflies"[12] argues through its focus on the specificity of Chinese socio-cultural conditions that "Chinese modernism was taking a rather different path from what its periodization in accordance with western historical developments has granted" (p. 83). Chow concludes her analysis of the popular Butterfly literature with a question and an admonition. "The question that keeps rearing its ugly head is that of history and, in this case, its related issue of ethnocentrism" (p. 92). The still immanent alternative seems, according to the critic, "to lie in the use of history as a continuous confrontation with precisely these two impossible ends of totality and difference" (p. 93).

" 'It's you, and not me': Domination and 'Othering' in Theorizing the 'Third World' " pursues that historical trajectory by reading Lu Xun's story "The New Year's Sacrifice" against both the multiple appropriations in recent Chinese political history of the writer as politically correct revolutionary and his rescue by literary critics as artiste. Focusing on Xianglin Sao, the old beggar woman whose questions confute, if only temporarily, the ideological security of the intellectual, Chow elicits the historical contradictions, and thus the active agency, of the suppressed figure of the marginalized peasant woman and displaces the self-centered critique of self which the story and its conventional readings have foregrounded. According to Irene Eber, "the reception accorded to Lu Xun's works often reflects the thaws and freezes in international relations.[13] The fluctuations of power complexes, however, within the history even of international relations, remains on the level of what Chow calls " 'knowledge' from within the dominating stance." Xianglin Sao's heterogeneously dissident refutation of the ascendancy of that stance argues for the potential for resistance in the "dominated other."

The "very notion of theory," as Armand Mattelart has pointed out, cannot "escape the contingency of the criteria of relevance which each culture elaborates, nor the blind spots which the culture maintains."[14] "Theory," however, or a regionalized construction of what constitutes theoretical work, has, like "feminism" in its more dominant modes, come to be legislated from out of the western capitals, thus giving rise to another "international division of labor" whereby the cultural raw materials are mined in the Third World and delivered to the manufacturing and processing centers of the First World where they are transformed into commodities consumed by an educated elite, a consumerism to which the "third world" is systematically denied access. This theoretical denial has its legitimizing basis in the propagation of an exclusive historical narrative. While riding the microbus to San Salvador, a young woman, alias Beatriz, nicknamed Ticha, a partisan in the Salvadoran resistance, reflects to herself, "If the [North American] advisers knew our history, would they still treat us the same? I don't know. Besides, our history is sad and boring. Maybe they're not interested in hearing about it. We're interested, though, because it gives us strength. It teaches us to survive. We've learned how to survive. That's why I use an alias."[15] Beatriz/Ticha is one of the main characters in Manlio Argueta's novel *Cuzcatlán Where the Southern Sea Beats*. Her reflections on the contending histories in El Salvador—the agenda of domination and control by the United States "advisers" with the collaboration of the Salvadoran government against a narrative of popular resistance—has further implications for a global itinerary, for the Middle East and southern Africa no less than for Central and South America.

In his 1972 response to the question put to him by a European reporter, "from the left no less," who asked, " 'does there exist a Latin American literature?'," the Cuban writer Roberto Fernandez Retamar insisted strongly on the significance of cultural production from within the Latin American context. *Caliban: Apuntes sobre la cultura en nuestra América* maintains furthermore that that cultural production must be understood, both in Latin America and in the western metropolises, in terms of its own theoretical and material conditions. According to Retamar, "Colonialism has penetrated so deeply within us that we read with real respect only those anti-colonialist authors who are *disseminated from the metropolis*" (emphasis in original).[16] He goes on to point out the need to rethink resistance through the intellectual and practical contributions of the Third World itself: "To be consistent with our anti-colonialist position, we have effectively to turn to our own people who in their conduct and their thinking have embodied and illuminated that position." This counter-hegemonic position raises important questions too for the theoretical ascendancy of western critical paradigms.

" 'Othering' for Hegel," according to Rey Chow, "was a matter of placing." This placing, which excluded Africa from the "historical part of the World," and the East from the "history of philosophy," has as its legacy in the contemporary geo-political context the "discourse of boundaries" which superintends national borders and disciplines academic practice. It further maintains the First World/ Third World distinction as a geographical demarcation, which displaces, indeed deports, in order to contain, insurgent practices onto the "other" side of those same territorial boundaries which it rhetorically polices. The unidimensional rhetoric of territoriality thus obscures, as Sánchez explained, a systemic oppression which itself knows no bounds. Laila al-Hamdani, a Palestinian woman, begins her notes on her experience in Israeli prisons with an account of how the prison authorities chose one day to chop down the jasmine tree growing in the prison courtyard, a tree that "had been here before the state—which had built this prison—was planted on our land."[17] Al-Hamdani's prison experience takes her from the Maskobiya prison in Jerusalem, to Neveh Tirtzah, the women's prison in Ramleh, to the military court in Nablus. In each prison and detention center, the story of the jasmine tree is refashioned, through songs, shared stories, literacy classes—as is that of the failed friendship with Ruth, an Israeli sociology student from the Hebrew University come to the prison as part of a study in criminology. The two women became acquaintances, even friends, until the day Ruth asks: " 'Suppose that one day we meet on opposite sides, me with an Uzi sub-machine gun, and you with a Kalashnikov rifle—would you be able to shoot me?' " The prisoner's insistence on a political account, not the personalized response the sociologist wants, of their relationship, produces silence.

We spoke no more. Suddenly I realized that there was always a barrier between us, like a glass wall, invisibly separating our positions. We pretended not to see it, we did not want to admit its existence, but we both felt it. Her question made both of us realize that as long as she was the occupier and I the occupied, as long as we were not equals we would never be able to transcend this invisible barrier. (p. 58)

Nancy Taylor Day grew up on the grounds, between the inside and outside walls, of Folsom Prison in California where her father was the chief resident medical officer. The stories in her collection *Represa*[18] are set in that peripheral space, on the edge between inside and outside, and in each of the stories that edge and the alternatives it offers are elaborated differently. In "Mooney," Dennis the prisoner reveals love to Mooney who delivers meat to the prison and news of the world outside to the prisoner. In the end, they each make good their combined escape—Dennis from prison and Mooney from his marriage. "Represa" in turn tells the story of Hooper, the son of a prison employee, who proves himself to his girlfriend by running the prison gate in his Chevrolet truck while Fireman, one of the prisoners, proves the vulnerability of the prison walls by riding underneath the truck during its run through the gate. "Hobbies" and "Wings of an Angel" each develop alternative strategies of escape, counter-projects which reverse the relations of power determining the inside/outside antithesis. Finally, in the stories "Wilma" and "Celia," high school senior Celia is educated into college and independence from her family by Robin, a prisoner, who leaves her notes and reading lists, titles and authors, in a potted plant at the door of her father's house and takes her with him when he is paroled. In *Represa*'s stories, it is the "other" who is cordoned off, held inside, by the authority of the state prison system. But it is this same "other" who poses the possibility of challenge to the authoritarian system and initiates another story, another narrative, of "all that is inside [that] is not center."

Rethinking Political Economy

14

A Manifesto for Cyborgs:
Science, Technology, and
Socialist Feminism in the 1980s

Donna Haraway

This paper was first published in Socialist Review, *no. 80, 1985. The essay originated as a response to a call for political thinking about the 1980s from socialist-feminist points of view, in hopes of deepening our political and cultural debates in order to renew commitments to fundamental social change in the face of the Reagan years. The "Cyborg Manifesto" tried to find a feminist place for connected thinking and acting in profoundly contradictory worlds. Since its publication, this bit of cyborgian writing has had a surprising half-life. It has proved impossible to rewrite the cyborg. Cyborg's daughter will have to find its own matrix in another essay, starting from the proposition that the immune system is the bio-technical body's chief system of differences in late capitalism, where feminists might find provocative extra-terrestrial maps of the networks of embodied power·marked by race, sex, and class. The essay below is substantially the same as the 1985 version, with minor revisions and correction of notes.*

An Ironic Dream of a Common Language for Women in the Integrated Circuit

This essay is an effort to build an ironic political myth faithful to feminism, socialism, and materialism. Perhaps more faithful as blasphemy is faithful, than as reverent worship and identification. Blasphemy has always seemed to require taking things very seriously. I know no better stance to adopt from within the secular-religious, evangelical traditions of United States politics, including the politics of socialist feminism. Blasphemy protects one from the moral majority within, while still insisting on the need for community. Blasphemy is not apostasy. Irony is about contradictions that do not resolve into larger wholes, even dia-lectically, about the tension of holding incompatible things together because both or all are necessary and true. Irony is about humor and serious play. It is also a rhetorical strategy and a political method, one I would like to see more honored

173

within socialist feminism. At the center of my ironic faith, my blasphemy, is the image of the cyborg.

A cyborg is a cybernetic organism, a hybrid of machine and organism, a creature of social reality as well as a creature of fiction. Social reality is lived social relations, our most important political construction, a world-changing fiction. The international women's movements have constructed "women's experience," as well as uncovered or discovered this crucial collective object. This experience is a fiction and fact of the most crucial, political kind. Liberation rests on the construction of the consciousness, the imaginative apprehension, of oppression, and so of possibility. The cyborg is a matter of fiction and lived experience that changes what counts as women's experience in the late twentieth century. This is a struggle over life and death, but the boundary between science fiction and social reality is an optical illusion.

Contemporary science fiction is full of cyborgs—creatures simultaneously animal and machine, who populate worlds ambiguously natural and crafted. Modern medicine is also full of cyborgs, of couplings between organism and machine, each conceived as coded devices, in an intimacy and with a power that was not generated in the history of sexuality. Cyborg "sex" restores some of the lovely replicative baroque of ferns and invertebrates (such nice organic prophylactics against heterosexism). Cyborg replication is uncoupled from organic reproduction. Modern production seems like a dream of cyborg colonization of work, a dream that makes the nightmare of Taylorism seem idyllic. And modern war is a cyborg orgy, coded by C^3I, command-control-communication-intelligence, an $84 billion item in 1984's U.S. defense budget. I am making an argument for the cyborg as a fiction mapping our social and bodily reality and as an imaginative resource suggesting some very fruitful couplings. Michel Foucault's biopolitics is a flaccid premonition of cyborg politics, a very open field.

By the late twentieth century, our time, a mythic time, we are all chimeras, theorized and fabricated hybrids of machine and organism; in short, we are cyborgs. The cyborg is our ontology; it gives us our politics. The cyborg is a condensed image of both imagination and material reality, the two joined centers structuring any possibility of historical transformation. In the traditions of "Western" science and politics—the tradition of racist, male-dominant capitalism; the tradition of progress; the tradition of the appropriation of nature as resource for the productions of culture; the tradition of reproduction of the self from the reflections of the other—the relation between organism and machine has been a border war. The stakes in the border war have been the territories of production, reproduction, and imagination. This essay is an argument for *pleasure* in the confusion of boundaries and for *responsibility* in their construction. It is also an effort to contribute to socialist-feminist culture and theory in a post-modernist, non-naturalist mode and in the utopian tradition of imagining a world without gender, which is perhaps a world without genesis, but maybe also a world without end. The cyborg incarnation is outside salvation history. Nor does it mark time on an Oedipal calendar, attempting to heal the terrible cleavages of gender in oral symbiotic utopia or post-Oedipal apocalypse. As Zoe Sofoulis argues in her unpublished manuscript on Jacques Lacan, Melanie Klein, and nuclear culture, *Lacklein,* the most terrible and perhaps the most promising monsters in cyborg worlds are embodied in non-Oedipal narratives with a different logic of repression, which we need to understand for our survival.

The cyborg is a creature in a post-gender world; it has no truck with bisexuality, pre-Oedipal symbiosis, unalienated labor, or other seductions to organic wholeness through a final appropriation of all the powers of the parts into a higher unity. In a sense, the cyborg has no origin story in the Western sense; a "final" irony since the cyborg is also the awful apocalyptic *telos* of the "West's" escalating dominations of abstract individuation, an ultimate self untied at last from all dependency, a man in space. An origin story in the "Western," humanist sense depends on the myth of original unity, fullness, bliss and terror, represented by the phallic mother from whom all humans must separate, the task of individual development and of history, the twin potent myths inscribed most powerfully for us in psychoanalysis and Marxism. Hilary Klein has argued that both Marxism and psychoanalysis, in their concepts of labor and of individuation and gender formation, depend on the plot of original unity out of which difference must be produced and enlisted in a drama of escalating domination of woman/nature. The cyborg skips the step of original unity, of identification with nature in the Western sense. This is its illegitimate promise that might lead to subversion of its teleology as star wars.

The cyborg is resolutely committed to partiality, irony, intimacy, and perversity. It is oppositional, utopian, and completely without innocence. No longer structured by the polarity of public and private, the cyborg defines a technological polis based partly on a revolution of social relations in the *oikos,* the household. Nature and culture are reworked; the one can no longer be the resource for appropriation or incorporation by the other. The relationships for forming wholes from parts, including those of polarity and hierarchical domination, are at issue in the cyborg world. Unlike the hopes of Frankenstein's monster, the cyborg does not expect its father to save it through a restoration of the garden; i.e., through the fabrication of a heterosexual mate, through its completion in a finished whole, a city and cosmos. The cyborg does not dream of community on the model of the organic family, this time without the Oedipal project. The cyborg would not recognize the Garden of Eden; it is not made of mud and cannot dream of returning to dust. Perhaps that is why I want to see if cyborgs can subvert the apocalypse of returning to nuclear dust in the manic compulsion to name the Enemy. Cyborgs are not reverent; they do not re-member the cosmos. They are wary of holism, but needy for connection—they seem to have a natural feel for united front politics, but without the vanguard party. The main trouble with cyborgs, of course, is that they are the illegitimate offspring of militarism and patriarchal capitalism, not to mention state socialism. But illegitimate offspring are often exceedingly unfaithful to their origins. Their fathers, after all, are inessential.

I will return to the science fiction of cyborgs at the end of this essay, but now I want to signal three crucial boundary breakdowns that make the following political-fictional (political-scientific) analysis possible. By the late twentieth century in United States scientific culture, the boundary between human and animal is thoroughly breached. The last beachheads of uniqueness have been polluted if not turned into amusement parks—language, tool use, social behavior, mental events, nothing really convincingly settles the separation of human and animal. And many people no longer feel the need of such a separation; indeed, many branches of feminist culture affirm the pleasure of connection of human and other living creatures. Movements for animal rights are not irrational denials of human uniqueness; they are clear-sighted recognition of connection across the discredited breach of nature and culture. Biology and evolutionary theory over the last two centuries have simultaneously produced modern organisms as objects of knowledge and reduced the line between humans and animals to a faint trace re-etched in ideological struggle or professional disputes between life and social science. Within this framework, teaching modern Christian creationism should be fought as a form of child abuse.

Biological-determinist ideology is only one position opened up in scientific culture for arguing the meanings of human animality. There is much room for radical political people to contest for the meanings of the breached boundary.[1] The cyborg appears in myth precisely where the boundary between human and animal is transgressed. Far from signaling a walling off of people from other living beings, cyborgs signal disturbingly and pleasurably tight coupling. Bestiality has a new status in this cycle of marriage exchange.

The second leaky distinction is between animal-human (organism) and machine. Pre-cybernetic machines could be haunted; there was always the specter of the ghost in the machine. This dualism structured the dialogue between materialism and idealism that was settled by a dialectical progeny, called spirit or history, according to taste. But basically machines were not self-moving, self-designing, autonomous. They could not achieve man's dream, only mock it. They were not man, an author to himself, but only a caricature of that masculinist reproductive dream. To think they were otherwise was paranoid. Now we are not so sure. Late twentieth-century machines have made thoroughly ambiguous the difference between natural and artificial, mind and body, self-developing and externally designed, and many other distinctions that used to apply to organisms and machines. Our machines are disturbingly lively, and we ourselves frighteningly inert.

Technological determination is only one ideological space opened up by the reconceptions of machine and organism as coded texts through which we engage in the play of writing and reading the world.[2] "Textualization" of everything in post-structuralist, post-modernist theory has been damned by Marxists and socialist feminists for its utopian disregard for lived relations of domination that ground the "play" of arbitrary reading.[3]* It is certainly true that post-modernist strategies, like my cyborg myth, subvert myriad organic wholes (e.g., the poem, the primitive culture, the biological organism). In short, the certainty of what counts as nature—a source of insight and a promise of innocence—is undermined, probably fatally. The transcendent authorization of interpretation is lost, and with it the ontology grounding "Western" epistemology. But the alternative is not cynicism or faithlessness, i.e., some version of abstract existence, like the accounts of technological determinism destroying "man" by the "machine" or "meaningful political action" by the "text." Who cyborgs will be is a radical question; the answers are a matter of survival. Both chimpanzees and artifacts have politics, so why shouldn't we?[4]

The third distinction is a subset of the second: the boundary between physical and non-physical is very imprecise for us. Pop physics books on the consequences of quantum theory and the indeterminacy principle are a kind of popular scientific equivalent to the Harlequin romances as a marker of radical change in American white heterosexuality: they get it wrong, but they are on the right subject. Modern machines are quintessentially microelectronic devices: they are everywhere and they are invisible. Modern machinery is an irreverent upstart god, mocking the Father's ubiquity and spirituality. The silicon chip is a surface for writing; it is etched in molecular scales disturbed only by atomic noise, the ultimate interference for nuclear scores. Writing, power, and technology are old partners in Western

---

*A provocative, comprehensive argument about the politics and theories of "post-modernism" is made by Fredric Jameson, who argues that post modernism is not an option, a style among others, but a cultural dominant requiring radical reinvention of left politics from within; there is no longer any place from without that gives meaning to the comforting fiction of critical distance. Jameson also makes clear why one cannot be for or against post-modernism, an essentially moralist move. My position is that feminists (and others) need continuous cultural reinvention, post-modernist critique, and historical materialism; only a cyborg would have a chance. The old dominations of white capitalist patriarchy seem nostalgically innocent now: they normalized heterogeneity, e.g., into man and woman, white and black. "Advanced capitalism" and post-modernism release heterogeneity without a norm, and we are flattened, without subjectivity, which requires depth, even unfriendly and drowning depths. It is time to write *The Death of the Clinic.* The clinic's methods required bodies and works; we have texts and surfaces. Our dominations don't work by medicalization and normalization anymore; they work by networking, communications redesign, stress management. Normalization gives way to automation, utter redundancy. Michel Foucault's *Birth of the Clinic, History of Sexuality,* and *Discipline and Punish* name a form of power at its moment of implosion. The discourse of biopolitics gives way to technobabble, the language of the spliced substantive; no noun is left whole by the multinationals. These are their names, listed from one issue of *Science:* Tech-Knowledge, Genentech, Allergen, Hybritech, Compupro, Genen-cor, Syntex, Allelix, Agrigenetics Corp., Syntro, Codon, Repligen, MicroAngelo from Scion Corp., Percom Data, Inter Systems, Cyborg Corp., Statcom Corp., Intertec. If we are imprisoned by language, then escape from that prison house requires language poets, a kind of cultural restriction enzyme to cut the code; cyborg heteroglossia is one form of radical cultural politics.

stories of the origin of civilization, but miniaturization has changed our experience of mechanism. Miniaturization has turned out to be about power; small is not so much beautiful as pre-eminently dangerous, as in cruise missiles. Contrast the TV sets of the 1950s or the news cameras of the 1970s with the TV wrist bands or hand-sized video cameras now advertised. Our best machines are made of sunshine; they are all light and clean because they are nothing but signals, electromagnetic waves, a section of a spectrum, and these machines are eminently portable, mobile—a matter of immense human pain in Detroit and Singapore. People are nowhere near so fluid, being both material and opaque. Cyborgs are ether, quintessence.

The ubiquity and invisibility of cyborgs is precisely why these sunshine-belt machines are so deadly. They are as hard to see politically as materially. They are about consciousness—or its simulation.[5] They are floating signifiers moving in pickup trucks across Europe, blocked more effectively by the witch-weavings of the displaced and so unnatural Greenham women, who read the cyborg webs of power very well, than by the militant labor of older masculinist politics, whose natural constituency needs defense jobs. Ultimately the "hardest" science is about the realm of greatest boundary confusion, the realm of pure number, pure spirit, C^3I, cryptography, and the preservation of potent secrets. The new machines are so clean and light. Their engineers are sun-worshipers mediating a new scientific revolution associated with the night dream of post-industrial society. The diseases evoked by these clean machines are "no more" than the miniscule coding changes of an antigen in the immune system, "no more" than the experience of stress. The nimble fingers of "Oriental" women, the old fascination of little Anglo-Saxon Victorian girls with doll houses, women's enforced attention to the small take on quite new dimensions in this world. There might be a cyborg Alice taking account of these new dimensions. Ironically, it might be the unnatural cyborg women making chips in Asia and spiral dancing in Santa Rita jail whose constructed unities will guide effective oppositional strategies.

So my cyborg myth is about transgressed boundaries, potent fusions, and dangerous possibilities which progressive people might explore as one part of needed political work. One of my premises is that most American socialists and feminists see deepened dualisms of mind and body, animal and machine, idealism and materialism in the social practices, symbolic formulations, and physical artifacts associated with "high technology" and scientific culture. From *One-Dimensional Man* to *The Death of Nature*,[6] the analytic resources developed by progressives have insisted on the necessary domination of technics and recalled us to an imagined organic body to integrate our resistance. Another of my premises is that the need for unity of people trying to resist worldwide intensification of domination has never been more acute. But a slightly perverse shift of perspective might better enable us to contest for meanings, as well as for other forms of power and pleasure in technologically mediated societies.

From one perspective, a cyborg world is about the final imposition of a grid of control on the planet, about the final abstraction embodied in a Star War apocalypse waged in the name of defense, about the final appropriation of women's bodies in a masculinist orgy of war.[7] From another perspective, a cyborg world might be about lived social and bodily realities in which people are not afraid of their joint kinship with animals and machines, not afraid of permanently partial identities and contradictory standpoints. The political struggle is to see from both perspectives at once because each reveals both dominations and possibilities unimaginable from the other vantage point. Single vision produces worse illusions that double vision or many-headed monsters. Cyborg unities are monstrous and illegitimate; in our present political circumstances, we could hardly hope for more potent myths for resistance and recoupling. I like to imagine LAG, the Livermore Action Group, as a kind of cyborg society, dedicated to realistically converting the laboratories that most fiercely embody and spew out the tools of technological apocalypse, and committed to building a political form that actually manages to hold together witches, engineers, elders, perverts, Christians, mothers, and Leninists long enough to disarm the state. Fission Impossible is the name of the affinity group in my town. (Affinity: related not by blood but by choice, the appeal of one chemical nuclear group for another, avidity.)[8]

Fractured Identities

It has become difficult to name one's feminism by a single adjective—or even to insist in every circumstance upon the noun. Consciousness of exclusion through naming is acute. Identities seem contradictory, partial, and strategic. With the hard-won recognition of their social and historical constitution, gender, race, and class cannot provide the basis for belief in "essential" unity. There is nothing about being "female" that naturally binds women. There is not even such a state as "being" female, itself a highly complex category constructed in contested sexual scientific discourses and other social practices. Gender, race, or class consciousness is an achievement forced on us by the terrible historical experience of the contradictory social realities of patriarchy, colonialism, and capitalism. And who counts as "us" in my own rhetoric? Which identities are available to ground such a potent political myth called "us," and what could motivate enlistment in this collectivity? Painful fragmentation among feminists (not to mention among women) along every possible fault line has made the concept of *woman* elusive, an excuse for the matrix of women's dominations of each other. For me—and for many who share a similar historical location in white, professional middle class, female, radical, North American, mid-adult bodies—the sources of a crisis in political identity are legion. The recent history for much of the U.S. left and U.S. feminism has been a response to this kind of crisis by endless splitting and searches for a new essential unity. But there has also been a growing recognition of another response through coalition—affinity, not identity.[9]

Chela Sandoval, from a consideration of specific historical moments in the formation of the new political voice called women of color, has theorized a hopeful model of political identity called "oppositional consciousness," born of the skills for reading webs of power by those refused stable membership in the social categories of race, sex, or class.[10] "Women of color," a name contested at its origins by those whom it would incorporate, as well as a historical consciousness marking systematic breakdown of all the signs of Man in "Western" traditions, constructs a kind of post-modernist identity out of otherness, difference, and specificity. This post-modernist identity is fully political, whatever might be said about other possible post-modernisms. Sandoval's oppositional consciousness is about contradictory locations and heterochronic calendars, not about relativisms and pluralisms.

Sandoval emphasizes the lack of any essential criterion for identifying who is a woman of color. She notes that the definition of the group has been by conscious appropriation of negation. For example, a Chicana or U.S. black woman has not been able to speak as a woman or as a black person or as a Chicano. Thus, she was at the bottom of a cascade of negative identities, left out of even the privileged oppressed authorial categories called "women and blacks," who claimed to make the important revolutions. The category "woman" negated all non-white women; "black" negated all non-black people, as well as all black women. But there was also no "she," no singularity, but a sea of differences among U.S. women who have affirmed their historical identity as U.S. women of color. This identity marks out a self-consciously constructed space that cannot affirm the capacity to act on the basis of natural identification, but only on the basis of conscious coalition, of affinity, of political kinship.[11] Unlike the "woman" of some streams of the white women's movement in the United States, there is no naturalization of the matrix, or at least this is what Sandoval argues is uniquely available through the power of oppositional consciousness.

Sandoval's argument has to be seen as one potent formulation for feminists out of the worldwide development of anti-colonialist discourse; i.e., discourse dissolving the "West" and its highest product—the one who is not animal, barbarian, or woman; i.e., man, the author of a cosmos called history. As orientalism is deconstructed politically and semiotically, the identities of the occident de-stabilize, including those of feminists.[12] Sandoval argues that "women of color" have a chance to build an effective unity that does not replicate the imperializing, totalizing revolutionary subjects of previous Marxisms and feminisms which had not faced the consequences of the disorderly polyphony emerging from decolonization.

Katie King has emphasized the limits of identification and the political/poetic mechanics of identification built into reading "the poem," that generative core of cultural feminism. King criticizes the persistent tendency among contemporary feminists from different "moments" or "conversations" in feminist practice to taxonomize the women's movement to make one's own political tendencies appear to be the *telos* of the whole. These taxonomies tend to remake feminist history to appear to be ideological struggle among coherent types persisting over time, especially those typical units called radical, liberal, and socialist feminism. Literally, all other feminisms are either incorporated or marginalized, usually by building an explicit ontology and epistemology.[13] Taxonomies of feminism produce epistemologies to police deviation from official women's experience. And of course, "women's culture," like women of color, is consciously created by mechanisms inducing affinity. The rituals of poetry, music, and certain forms of academic practice have been pre-eminent. The politics of race and culture in the U.S. women's movements are intimately interwoven. The common achievement of King and Sandoval is learning how to craft a poetic/political unity without relying on a logic of appropriation, incorporation, and taxonomic identification.

The theoretical and practical struggle against unity-through-domination or unity-through-incorporation ironically not only undermines the justifications for patriarchy, colonialism, humanism, positivism, essentialism, scientism, and other unlamented -isms, but *all* claims for an organic or natural standpoint. I think that radical and socialist/Marxist feminisms have also undermined their/our own epistemological strategies and that this is a crucially valuable step in imagining possible unities. It remains to be seen whether all "epistemologies" as Western political people have known them fail us in the task to build effective affinities.

It is important to note that the effort to construct revolutionary standpoints, epistemologies as achievements of people committed to changing the world, has been part of the process showing the limits of identification. The acid tools of post-modernist theory and the constructive tools of ontological discourse about revolutionary subjects might be seen as ironic allies in dissolving Western selves in the interests of survival. We are excruciatingly conscious of what it means to have a historically constituted body. But with the loss of innocence in our origin, there is no expulsion from the Garden either. Our politics lose the indulgence of guilt with the naïveté of innocence. But what would another political myth for socialist feminism look like? What kind of politics could embrace partial, contradictory, permanently unclosed constructions of personal and collective selves and still be faithful, effective—and, ironically, socialist feminist?

I do not know of any other time in history when there was greater need for political unity to confront effectively the dominations of "race," "gender," "sexuality," and "class." I also do not know of any other time when the kind of unity we might help build could have been possible. None of "us" have any longer the symbolic or material capability of dictating the shape of reality to any of "them." Or at least "we" cannot claim innocence from practicing such dominations. White women, including socialist feminists, discovered (i.e., were forced kicking and screaming to notice) the non-innocence of the category "woman." That consciousness changes the geography of all previous categories; it denatures them as heat denatures a fragile protein. Cyborg feminists have to argue that "we" do not want any more natural matrix of unity and that no construction is whole. Innocence, and the corollary insistence on victimhood as the only ground for insight, has done enough damage. But the constructed revolutionary subject must give late twentieth-century people pause as well. In the fraying of identities and in the reflexive strategies for constructing them, the possibility opens up for weaving something other than a shroud for the day after the apocalypse that so prophetically ends salvation history.

Both Marxist/socialist feminisms and radical feminisms have simultaneously naturalized and denatured the category "woman" and consciousness of the social lives of "women." Perhaps a schematic caricature can highlight both kinds of moves. Marxian socialism is rooted in an analysis of wage labor which reveals class structure. The consequence of the wage relationship is systematic alienation, as the worker is dissociated from his (sic) product. Abstraction and illusion rule in knowledge, domination rules in practice. Labor is the pre-eminently privileged category enabling the Marxist to overcome illusion and find that point of view which is necessary for changing the world. Labor is the humanizing activity that makes man; labor is an ontological category permitting the knowledge of a subject, and so the knowledge of subjugation and alienation.

In faithful filiation, socialist feminism advanced by allying itself with the basic analytic strategies of Marxism. The main achievement of both Marxist feminists and socialist feminists was to expand the category of labor to accommodate what (some) women did, even when the wage relation was subordinated to a more comprehensive view of labor under capitalist patriarchy. In particular, women's labor in the household and women's activity as mothers generally (i.e., reproduction in the socialist feminist sense), entered theory on the authority of analogy to the Marxian concept of labor. The unity of women here rests on an epistemology based on the ontological structure of "labor." Marxist/socialist feminism does not "naturalize" unity; it is a possible achievement based on a possible standpoint rooted in social relations. The essentializing move is in the ontological structure of labor or of its analogue, women's activity.[14]* The inheritance of Marxian humanism, with its pre-eminently Western self, is the difficulty for me. The contribution from these formulations has been the emphasis on the daily responsibility of real women to build unities, rather than to naturalize them.

* The central role of object-relations versions of psychoanalyses and related strong universalizing moves in discussing reproduction, caring work, and mothering in many approaches to epistemology underline their authors' resistance to what I am calling post-modernism. For me, both the universalizing moves and these versions of psychoanalysis make analysis of "women's place in the integrated circuit" difficult and lead to systematic difficulties in accounting for or even seeing major aspects of the construction of gender and gendered social life.

Catherine MacKinnon's version of radical feminism is itself a caricature of the appropriating, incorporating, totalizing tendencies of Western theories of identity grounding action.[15] It is factually and politically wrong to assimilate all of the diverse "moments" or "conversations" in recent women's politics named radical feminism to MacKinnon's version. But the teleological logic of her theory shows how an epistemology and ontology—including their negations—erase or police difference. Only one of the effects of MacKinnon's theory is the rewriting of the history of the polymorphous field called radical feminism. The major effect is the production of a theory of experience, of women's identity, that is a kind of apocalypse for all revolutionary standpoints. That is, the totalization built into this tale of radical feminism achieves its end—the unity of women—by enforcing the experience of and testimony to radical non-being. As for the Marxist/socialist feminist, consciousness is an achievement, not a natural fact. And MacKinnon's theory eliminates some of the difficulties built into humanist revolutionary subjects, but at the cost of radical reductionism.

MacKinnon argues that feminism necessarily adopted a different analytical strategy from Marxism, looking first not at the structure of class, but at the structure of sex/gender and its generative relationship, men's constitution and appropriation of women sexually. Ironically, MacKinnon's "ontology" constructs a non-subject, a non-being. Another's desire, not the self's labor, is the origin of "woman." She therefore develops a theory of consciousness that enforces what can count as "women's" experience—anything that names sexual violation, indeed, sex itself as far as "women" can be concerned. Feminist practice is the construction of this form of consciousness; i.e., the self-knowledge of a self-who-is-not.

Perversely, sexual appropriation in this feminism still has the epistemological status of labor; i.e., the point from which analysis able to contribute to changing the world must flow. But sexual objectification, not alienation, is the consequence of the structure of sex/gender. In the realm of knowledge, the result of sexual objectification is illusion and abstraction. However, a woman is not simply alienated from her product, but in a deep sense does not exist as a subject, or even potential subject, since she owes her existence as a woman to sexual appropriation. To be constituted by another's desire is not the same thing as to be alienated in the violent separation of the laborer from his product.

MacKinnon's radical theory of experience is totalizing in the extreme; it does not so much marginalize as obliterate the authority of any other women's political speech and action. It is a totalization producing what Western patriarchy itself never succeeded in doing—feminists' consciousness of the non-existence of women, except as products of men's desire. I think MacKinnon correctly argues that no Marxian version of identity can firmly ground women's unity. But in solving the problem of the contradictions of any Western revolutionary subject for feminist purposes, she develops an even more authoritarian doctrine of experience. If my complaint about socialist/Marxian standpoints is their unintended erasure of polyvocal, unassimilable, radical difference made visible in anti-colonial discourse and practice, MacKinnon's intentional erasure of all difference through the device of the "essential" non-existence of women is not reassuring.

In my taxonomy, which like any other taxonomy is a reinscription of history, radical feminism can accommodate all the activities of women named by socialist feminists as forms of labor only if the activity can somehow be sexualized. Reproduction had different tones of meanings for the two tendencies, one rooted in labor, one in sex, both calling the consequences of domination and ignorance of social and personal reality "false consciousness."

Beyond either the difficulties or the contributions in the argument of any one author, neither Marxist nor radical feminist points of view have tended to embrace the status of a partial explanation; both were regularly constituted as totalities. Western explanation has demanded as much; how else could the "Western" author incorporate its others? Each tried to annex other forms of domination by expanding its basic categories through analogy, simple listing, or addition. Embarrassed silence about race among white radical and socialist feminists was one major, devastating political consequence. History and polyvocality disappear into political taxonomies that try to establish genealogies. There was no structural room for race (or for much else) in theory claiming to reveal the construction of the category woman and social group women as a unified or totalizable whole. The structure of my caricature looks like this:

Socialist Feminism—structure of class//wage labor//alienation
labor, by analogy reproduction, by extension sex, by addition race

Radical Feminism—structure of gender//sexual appropriation//objectification
sex, by analogy labor, by extension reproduction, by addition race

In another context, the French theorist Julia Kristeva claimed women appeared as a historical group after World War II, along with groups like youth. Her dates are doubtful; but we are now accustomed to remembering that as objects of knowledge and as historical actors, "race" did not always exist, "class" has a historical genesis, and "homosexuals" are quite junior. It is no accident that the symbolic system of the family of man—and so the essence of woman—breaks up at the same moment that networks of connection among people on the planet are unprecedentedly multiple, pregnant, and complex. "Advanced capitalism" is inadequate to convey the structure of this historical moment. In the "Western" sense, the end of man is at stake. It is no accident that woman disintegrates into women in our time. Perhaps socialist feminists were not substantially guilty of producing essentialist theory that suppressed women's particularity and contradictory interests. I think we have been, at least through unreflective participation in the logics, languages, and practices of white humanism and through searching for a single ground of domination to secure our revolutionary voice. Now we have less excuse. But in the consciousness of our failures, we risk lapsing into boundless difference and giving up on the confusing task of making partial, real connection. Some differences are playful; some are poles of world historical systems of domination. "Epistemology" is about knowing the difference.

The Informatics of Domination

In this attempt at an epistemological and political position, I would like to sketch a picture of possible unity, a picture indebted to socialist and feminist principles of design. The frame for my sketch is set by the extent and importance of rearrangements in worldwide social relations tied to science and technology. I argue for a politics rooted in claims about fundamental changes in the nature of class, race, and gender in an emerging system of world order analogous in its novelty and scope to that created by industrial capitalism; we are living through a movement from an organic, industrial society to a polymorphous, information system—from all work to all play, a deadly game. Simultaneously material and ideological, the dichotomies may be expressed in the following chart of transitions from the comfortable old hierarchical dominations to the scary new networks I have called the informatics of domination:

Representation	Simulation
Bourgeois novel, realism	Science fiction, post-modernism
Organism	Biotic component
Depth, integrity	Surface, boundary
Heat	Noise
Biology as clinical practice	Biology as inscription
Physiology	Communications engineering
Small group	Subsystem
Perfection	Optimization
Eugenics	Population Control
Decadence, *Magic Mountain*	Obsolescence, *Future Shock*
Hygiene	Stress Management
Microbiology, tuberculosis	Immunology, AIDS
Organic division of labor	Ergonomics/cybernetics of labor
Functional specialization	Modular construction
Reproduction	Replication
Organic sex role specialization	Optimal genetic strategies
Biological determinism	Evolutionary inertia, constraints
Community ecology	Ecosystem
Racial chain of being	Neo-imperialism, United Nations humanism

Scientific management in home/factory	Global factory/Electronic cottage
Family/Market/Factory	Women in the Integrated Circuit
Family wage	Comparable worth
Public/Private	Cyborg citizenship
Nature/Culture	Fields of difference
Cooperation	Communications enhancement
Freud	Lacan
Sex	Genetic engineering
Labor	Robotics
Mind	Artificial Intelligence
World War II	Star Wars
White Capitalist Patriarchy	Informatics of Domination

This list suggests several interesting things.[16] First, the objects on the right-hand side cannot be coded as "natural," a realization that subverts naturalistic coding for the left-hand side as well. We cannot go back ideologically or materially. It's not just that "god" is dead; so is the "goddess." Or both are revivified in the worlds charged with microelectronic and biotechnological politics. In relation to objects like biotic components, one must think not in terms of essential properties, but in terms of design, boundary constraints, rates of flows, systems logics, costs of lowering constraints. Sexual reproduction is one kind of reproductive strategy among many, with costs and benefits as a function of the system environment. Ideologies of sexual reproduction can no longer reasonably call on notions of sex and sex role as organic aspects in natural objects like organisms and families. Such reasoning will be unmasked as irrational, and ironically corporate executives reading *Playboy* and anti-porn radical feminists will make strange bedfellows in jointly unmasking the irrationalism.

Likewise for race, ideologies about human diversity have to be formulated in terms of frequencies of parameters, like blood groups or intelligence scores. It is "irrational" to invoke concepts like primitive and civilized. For liberals and radicals, the search for integrated social systems gives way to a new practice called "experimental ethnography" in which an organic object dissipates in attention to the play of writing. At the level of ideology, we see translations of racism and colonialism into languages of development and underdevelopment, rates and constraints of modernization. Any objects or persons can be reasonably thought of in terms of disassembly and reassembly; no "natural" architectures constrain system design. The financial districts in all the world's cities, as well as the export-processing and free-trade zones, proclaim this elementary fact of "late capitalism." The entire universe of objects that can be known scientifically must be formulated as problems in communications engineering (for the managers) or theories of the text (for those who would resist). Both are cyborg semiologies.

One should expect control strategies to concentrate on boundary conditions and interfaces, on rates of flow across boundaries—and not on the integrity of natural objects. "Integrity" or "sincerity" of the Western self gives way to decision procedures and expert systems. For example, control strategies applied to women's capacities to give birth to new human beings will be developed in the languages of population control and maximization of goal achievement for individual decision-makers. Control strategies will be formulated in terms of rates, costs of constraints, degrees of freedom. Human beings, like any other component or subsystem, must be localized in a system architecture whose basic modes of operation are probabilistic, statistical. No objects, spaces, or bodies are sacred in themselves; any component can be interfaced with any other if the proper standard, the proper code, can be constructed for processing signals in a common language. Exchange in this world transcends the universal translation effected by capitalist markets that Marx analyzed so well. The privileged pathology affecting all kinds of components in this universe is stress—communications breakdown.[17] The cyborg is not subject to Foucault's biopolitics; the cyborg simulates politics, a much more potent field of operations.

This kind of analysis of scientific and cultural objects of knowledge which have appeared historically since World War II prepares us to notice some important inadequacies in feminist analysis which has proceeded as if the organic, hierarchical dualisms ordering discourse in "the West" since Aristotle still ruled. They have been cannibalized, or as Zoe Sofia (Sofoulis) might put it, they have been "techno-digested." The dichotomies between mind and body, animal and human, organism and machine, public and private, nature and culture, men and women, primitive and civilized are all in question ideologically. The actual situation of women is their integration/exploitation into a world system of production/reproduction and communication called the informatics of domination. The home, workplace, market, public arena, the body itself—all can be dispersed and interfaced in nearly infinite, polymorphous ways, with large consequences for women and others— consequences that themselves are very different for different people and which make potent oppositional international movements difficult to imagine and essential for survival. One important route for reconstructing socialist-feminist politics is through theory and practice addressed to the social relations of science and technology, including crucially the systems of myth and meanings structuring our imaginations. The cyborg is a kind of disassembled and reassembled, post-modern collective and personal self. This is the self feminists must code.

Communications technologies and biotechnologies are the crucial tools recrafting our bodies. These tools embody and enforce new social relations for women worldwide. Technologies and scientific discourses can be partially understood as formalizations, i.e., as frozen moments, of the fluid social interactions constituting them, but they should also be viewed as instruments for enforcing meanings. The boundary is permeable between tool and myth, instrument and concept, historical systems of social relations and historical anatomies of possible bodies, including objects of knowledge. Indeed, myth and tool mutually constitute each other.

Furthermore, communications sciences and modern biologies are constructed by a common move—*the translation of the world into a problem of coding,* a search for a common language in which all resistance to instrumental control disappears and all heterogeneity can be submitted to disassembly, reassembly, investment, and exchange.

In communications sciences, the translation of the world into a problem in coding can be illustrated by looking at cybernetic (feedback controlled) systems theories applied to telephone technology, computer design, weapons deployment, or data base construction and maintenance. In each case, solution to the key questions rests on a theory of language and control; the key operation is determining the rates, directions, and probabilities of flow of a quantity called information. The world is subdivided by boundaries differentially permeable to information. Information is just that kind of quantifiable element (unit, basis of unity) which allows universal translation, and so unhindered instrumental power (called effective communication). The biggest threat to such power is interruption of communication. Any system breakdown is a function of stress. The fundamentals of this technology can be condensed into the metaphor C^3I, command-control-communication-intelligence, the military's symbol for its operations theory.

In modern biologies, the translation of the world into a problem in coding can be illustrated by molecular genetics, ecology, sociobiological evolutionary theory, and immunobiology. The organism has been translated into problems of genetic coding and read-out. Biotechnology, a writing technology, informs research broadly.[18] In a sense, organisms have ceased to exist as objects of knowledge, giving way to biotic components, i.e., special kinds of information-processing devices. The analogous moves in ecology could be examined by probing the history and utility of the concept of the ecosystem. Immunobiology and associated medical practices are rich exemplars of the privilege of coding and recognition systems as objects of knowledge, as constructions of bodily reality for us. Biology here is a kind of cryptography. Research is necessarily a kind of intelligence activity. Ironies abound. A stressed system goes awry; its communication processes break down; it fails to recognize the difference between self and other. Human babies with baboon hearts evoke national ethical perplexity—for animal-rights activists at least as much as for the guardians of human purity. In the U.S. gay men and intravenous drug users are the "privileged" victims of an awful immune-system disease that marks (inscribes on the body) confusion of boundaries and moral pollution.[19]

But these excursions into communications sciences and biology have been at a rarefied level; there is a mundane, largely economic reality to support my claim that these sciences and technologies indicate fundamental transformations in the structure of the world for us. Communications technologies depend on electronics. Modern states, multinational corporations, military power, welfare-state apparatuses, satellite systems, political processes, fabrication of our imaginations, labor-control systems, medical constructions of our bodies, commercial pornography, the international division of labor, and religious evangelism depend intimately upon electronics. Microelectronics is the technical basis of simulacra; i.e., of copies without originals.

Microelectronics mediates the translations of labor into robotics and word processing; sex into genetic engineering and reproductive technologies; and mind into artificial intelligence and decision procedures. The new biotechnologies concern more than human reproduction. Biology as a powerful engineering science for redesigning materials and processes has revolutionary implications for industry, perhaps most obvious today in areas of fermentation, agriculture, and energy. Communications sciences and biology are constructions of natural-technical objects of knowledge in which the difference between machine and organism is thoroughly blurred; mind, body, and tool are on very intimate terms. The "multinational" material organization of the production and reproduction of daily life and the symbolic organization of the production and reproduction of culture and imagination seem equally implicated. The boundary-maintaining images of base and superstructure, public and private, or material and ideal never seemed more feeble.

I have used Rachel Grossman's image of women in the integrated circuit to name the situation of women in a world so intimately restructured through the social relations of science and technology.[20] I use the odd circumlocution, "the social relations of science and technology," to indicate that we are not dealing with a technological determinism, but with a historical system depending upon structured relations among people. But the phrase should also indicate that science and technology provide fresh sources of power, that we need fresh sources of analysis and political action.[21] Some of the rearrangements of race, sex, and class rooted in high tech-facilitated social relations can make socialist feminism more relevant to effective progressive politics.

The Homework Economy

The "New Industrial Revolution" is producing a new worldwide working class, as well new sexualities and ethnicities. The extreme mobility of capital and the emerging international division of labor are intertwined with the emergence of new collectivities, and the weakening of familiar groupings. These developments are neither gender- nor race-neutral. White men in advanced industrial societies have become newly vulnerable to permanent job loss, and women are not disappearing from the job rolls at the same rates as men. It is not simply that women in third world countries are the preferred labor force for the science-based multinationals in the export-processing sectors, particularly in electronics. The picture is more systematic and involves reproduction, sexuality, culture, consumption, and production. In the prototypical Silicon Valley, many women's lives have been structured around employment in electronics-dependent jobs, and their intimate realities include serial heterosexual monogamy, negotiating childcare, distance from extended kin or most other forms of traditional community, a high likelihood of loneliness and extreme economic vulnerability as they age. The ethnic and racial diversity of women in Silicon Valley structures a microcosm of conflicting differences in culture, family, religion, education, language.

Richard Gordon has called this new situation the homework economy.[22] Although he includes the phenomenon of literal homework emerging in connection with electronics assembly, Gordon intends "homework economy" to name a restructuring of work that broadly has the characteristics formerly ascribed to female jobs, jobs literally done only by women. Work is being redefined as both literally female and feminized, whether performed by men or women. To be feminized means to be made extremely vulnerable; able to be disassembled, reassembled, exploited as a reserve labor force; seen less as workers than as servers; subjected to time arrangements on and off the paid job that make a mockery of a limited work day; leading an existence that always borders on being obscene, out of place, and reducible to sex. Deskilling is an old strategy newly applicable to formerly privileged workers. However, the homework economy does not refer only to large-scale deskilling, nor does it deny that new areas of high skill are emerging, even for women and men previously excluded from skilled employment. Rather, the concept indicates that factory, home, and market are integrated on a new scale and that the places of women are crucial—and need to be analyzed for differences among women and for meanings for relations between men and women in various situations.

The homework economy as a world capitalist organizational structure is made possible by (not caused by) the new technologies. The success of the attack on relatively privileged, mostly white, men's unionized jobs is tied to the power of the new communications technologies to integrate and control labor despite extensive dispersion and decentralization. The consequences of the new technologies are felt by women both in the loss of the family (male) wage (if they ever had access to this white privilege) and in the character of their own jobs, which are becoming capital-intensive; e.g., office work and nursing.

The new economic and technological arrangements are also related to the collapsing welfare state and the ensuing intensification of demands on women to sustain daily life for themselves as well as for men, children, and old people. The feminization of poverty—generated by dismantling the welfare state, by the homework economy where stable jobs become the exception, and sustained by the expectation that women's wages will not be matched by a male income for the support of children—has become an urgent focus. The causes of various women-headed households are a function of race, class, or sexuality; but their increasing generality is a ground for coalitions of women on many issues. That women regularly sustain daily life partly as a function of their enforced status as mothers is hardly new; the kind of integration with the overall capitalist and progressively war-based economy is new. The particular pressure, for example, on U.S. black women, who have achieved an escape from (barely) paid domestic service and who now hold clerical and similar jobs in large numbers, has large implications for continued enforced black poverty *with* employment. Teenage women in industrializing areas of the third world increasingly find themselves the sole or major source of a cash wage for their families, while access to land is ever more problematic. These developments must have major consequences in the psychodynamics and politics of gender and race.

Within the framework of three major stages of capitalism (commercial/early industrial, monopoly, multinational)—tied to nationalism, imperialism, and multinationalism, and related to Jameson's three dominant aesthetic periods of realism, modernism, and post-modernism—I would argue that specific forms of families dialectically relate to forms of capital and to its political and cultural concomitants. Although lived problematically and unequally, ideal forms of these families might be schematized as (1) the patriarchal nuclear family, structured by the dichotomy between public and private and accompanied by the white bourgeois ideology of separate spheres and nineteenth-century Anglo-American bourgeois feminism; (2) the modern family mediated (or enforced) by the welfare state and institutions like the family wage, with a flowering of a-feminist heterosexual ideologies, including their radical versions represented in Greenwich Village around World War I; and (3) the "family" of the homework economy with its oxymoronic structure of women-headed households and its explosion of feminisms and the paradoxical intensification and erosion of gender itself.

This is the context in which the projections for worldwide structural unemployment stemming from the new technologies are part of the picture of the homework economy. As robotics and related technologies put men out of work in "developed" countries and exacerbate failure to generate male jobs in third-world "development," and as the automated office becomes the rule even in labor-surplus countries, the feminization of work intensifies. Black women in the United States have long known what it looks like to face the structural underemployment ("feminization") of black men, as well as their own highly vulnerable position in the wage economy. It is no longer a secret that sexuality, reproduction, family, and community life are interwoven with this economic structure in myriad ways which have also differentiated the situations of white and black women. Many more women and men will contend with similar situations, which will make cross-gender and race alliances on issues of basic life support (with or without jobs) necessary, not just nice.

The new technologies also have a profound effect on hunger and on food production for subsistence worldwide. Rae Lessor Blumberg estimates that women produce about 50 per cent of the world's subsistence food.[23]* Women are excluded generally from benefiting from the increased high-tech commodification of food and energy crops, their days are made more arduous because their responsibilities to provide food do not diminish, and their reproductive situations are made more complex. Green Revolution technologies interact with other high-tech industrial production to alter gender divisions of labor and differential gender migration patterns.

The new technologies seem deeply involved in the forms of "privatization" that Ros Petchesky has analyzed, in which militarization, right-wing family ideologies and policies, and intensified definitions of corporate property as private synergistically interact.[24] The new communications technologies are fundamental to the eradication of "public life" for everyone. This facilitates the mushrooming of a permanent high-tech military establishment at the cultural and economic expense of most people, but especially of women. Technologies like video games and highly miniaturized televisions seem crucial to production of modern forms of "private life." The culture of video games is heavily oriented to individual competition and extraterrestrial warfare. High-tech, gendered imaginations are produced here, imaginations that can contemplate destruction of the planet and a sci-fi escape from its consequences. More than our imaginations is militarized; and the other realities of electronic and nuclear warfare are inescapable. These are the technologies that promise ultimate mobility and perfect exchange—and incidentally enable tourism, that perfect practice of mobility and exchange, to emerge as one of the world's largest single industries.

The new technologies affect the social relations of both sexuality and of reproduction, and not always in the same ways. The close ties of sexuality and instrumentality, of views of the body as a kind of private satisfaction- and utility-maximizing machine, are described nicely in sociobiological origin stories that stress a genetic calculus and explain the inevitable dialectic of domination of male and female gender roles.[25] These sociobiological stories depend on a high-tech

---

* The conjunction of the Green Revolution's social relations with biotechnologies like plant genetic engineering makes the pressures on land in the Third World increasingly intense. AID's estimates (New York Times, 14 October 1984) used at the 1984 World Food Day are that in Africa, women produce about 90 per cent of rural food supplies, about 60–80 per cent in Asia, and provide 40 per cent of agricultural labor in the Near East and Latin America. Blumberg charges that world organizations' agricultural politics, as well as those of multinationals and national governments in the third world, generally ignore fundamental issues in the sexual division of labor. The present tragedy of famine in Africa might owe as much to male supremacy as to capitalism, colonialism, and rain patterns. More accurately, capitalism and racism are usually structurally male dominant.

view of the body as a biotic component or cybernetic communications system. Among the many transformations of reproductive situations is the medical one, where women's bodies have boundaries newly permeable to both "visualization" and "intervention." Of course, who controls the interpretation of bodily boundaries in medical hermeneutics is a major feminist issue. The speculum served as an icon of women's claiming their bodies in the 1970s; that hand-craft tool is inadequate to express our needed body politics in the negotiation of reality in the practices of cyborg reproduction. Self-help is not enough. The technologies of visualization recall the important cultural practice of hunting with the camera and the deeply predatory nature of a photographic consciousness.[26] Sex, sexuality, and reproduction are central actors in high-tech myth systems structuring our imaginations of personal and social possibility.

Another critical aspect of the social relations of the new technologies is the reformulation of expectations, culture, work, and reproduction for the large scientific and technical work force. A major social and political danger is the formation of a strongly bimodal social structure, with the masses of women and men of all ethnic groups, but especially people of color, confined to a homework economy, illiteracy of several varieties, and general redundancy and impotence, controlled by high-tech repressive apparatuses ranging from entertainment to surveillance and disappearance. An adequate socialist-feminist politics should address women in the privileged occupational categories, and particularly in the production of science and technology that constructs scientific-technical discourses, processes, and objects.[27]

This issue is only one aspect of inquiry into the possibility of a feminist science, but it is important. What kind of constitutive role in the production of knowledge, imagination, and practice can new groups doing science have? How can these groups be allied with progressive social and political movements? What kind of political accountability can be constructed to tie women together across the scientific-technical hierarchies separating us? Might there be ways of developing feminist science/technology politics in alliance with anti-military science facility conversion action groups? Many scientific and technical workers in Silicon Valley, the high-tech cowboys included, do not want to work on military science.[28] Can these personal preferences and cultural tendencies be welded into progressive politics among this professional middle class in which women, including women of color, are coming to be fairly numerous?

Women in the Integrated Circuit

Let me summarize the picture of women's historical locations in advanced industrial societies, as these positions have been restructured partly through the social relations of science and technology. If it was ever possible ideologically to

characterize women's lives by the distinction of public and private domains—
suggested by images of the division of working-class life into factory and home,
of bourgeois life into market and home, and of gender existence into personal
and political realms—it is now a totally misleading ideology, even to show how
both terms of these dichotomies construct each other in practice and in theory.
I prefer a network ideological image, suggesting the profusion of spaces and
identities and the permeability of boundaries in the personal body and in the
body politic. "Networking" is both a feminist practice and a multinational corporate
strategy—weaving is for oppositional cyborgs.

So let me return to the earlier image of the informatics of domination and
trace one vision of women's "place" in the integrated circuit, touching only a
few idealized social locations seen primarily from the point of view of advanced
capitalist societies: Home, Market, Paid Work Place, State, School, Clinic-Hospital,
and Church. Each of these idealized spaces is logically and practically implied in
every other locus, perhaps analogous to a holographic photograph. I want to
suggest the impact of the social relations mediated and enforced by the new
technologies in order to help formulate needed analysis and practical work.
However, there is no "place" for women in these networks, only geometrics of
difference and contradiction crucial to women's cyborg identities. If we learn how
to read these webs of power and social life, we might learn new couplings, new
coalitions. There is no way to read the following list from a standpoint of
"identification," of a unitary self. The issue is dispersion. The task is to survive
in the diaspora.

Home: Women-headed households, serial monogamy, flight of men, old women alone,
technology of domestic work, paid homework, reemergence of home sweat shops,
home-based businesses and telecommuting, electronic cottage, urban homelessness,
migration, module architecture, reinforced (simulated) nuclear family, intense domestic violence.

Market: Women's continuing consumption work, newly targeted to buy the profusion
of new production from the new technologies (especially as the competitive race
among industrialized and industrializing nations to avoid dangerous mass unemployment necessitates finding ever bigger new markets for ever less clearly needed
commodities); bimodal buying power, coupled with advertising targeting of the
numerous affluent groups and neglect of the previous mass markets; growing importance of informal markets in labor and commodities parallel to high-tech, affluent
market structures; surveillance systems through electronic funds transfer; intensified
market abstraction (commodification) of experience, resulting in ineffective utopian
or equivalent cynical theories of community; extreme mobility (abstraction) of mar-
keting/financing systems; interpenetration of sexual and labor markets; intensified
sexualization of abstracted and alienated consumption.

Paid Work Place: Continued intense sexual and racial division of labor, but considerable growth of membership in privileged occupational categories for many white women and people of color; impact of new technologies on women's work in clerical, service, manufacturing (especially textiles), agriculture, electronics; international restructuring of the working classes; development of new time arrangements to facilitate the homework economy (flex time, part time, over time, no time); homework and out work; increased pressures for two-tiered wage structures; significant numbers of people in cash-dependent populations worldwide with no experience or no further hope of stable employment; most labor "marginal" or "feminized."

State: Continued erosion of the welfare state; decentralizations with increased surveillance and control; citizenship by telematics; imperialism and political power broadly in the form of information rich/information poor differentiation; increased high-tech militarization increasingly opposed by many social groups; reduction of civil service jobs as a result of the growing capital intensification of office work, with implications for occupational mobility for women of color; growing privatization of material and ideological life and culture; close integration of privatization and militarization, the high-tech forms of bourgeois capitalist personal and public life; invisibility of different social groups to each other, linked to psychological mechanisms of belief in abstract enemies.

School: Deepening coupling of high-tech capital needs and public education at all levels, differentiated by race, class, and gender; managerial classes involved in educational reform and refunding at the cost of remaining progressive educational democratic structures for children and teachers; education for mass ignorance and repression in technocratic and militarized culture; growing anti-science mystery cults in dissenting and radical political movements; continued relative scientific illiteracy among white women and people of color; growing industrial direction of education (especially higher education) by science-based multinationals (particularly in electronics- and biotechnology-dependent companies); highly educated, numerous elites in a progressively bimodal society.

Clinic-hospital: Intensified machine-body relations; renegotiations of public metaphors which channel personal experience of the body, particularly in relation to reproduction, immune system functions, and "stress" phenomena; intensification of reproductive politics in response to world historical implications of women's unrealized, potential control of their relation to reproduction; emergence of new, historically specific diseases; struggles over meanings and means of health in environments pervaded by high technology products and processes; continuing feminization of health work; intensified struggle over state responsibility for health; continued ideological role of popular health movements as a major form of American politics.

Church: Electronic fundamentalist "super-saver" preachers solemnizing the union of electronic capital and automated fetish gods; intensified importance of churches in resisting the militarized state; central struggle over women's meanings and authority in religion; continued relevance of spirituality, intertwined with sex and health, in political struggle.

The only way to characterize the informatics of domination is as a massive intensification of insecurity and cultural impoverishment, with common failure of subsistence networks for the most vulnerable. Since much of this picture interweaves with the social relations of science and technology, the urgency of a socialist-feminist politics addressed to science and technology is plain. There is much now being done, and the grounds for political work are rich. For example, the efforts to develop forms of collective struggle for women in paid work, like SEIU's District 925, should be a high priority for all of us. These efforts are profoundly tied to technical restructuring of labor processes and reformations of working classes. These efforts also are providing understanding of a more comprehensive kind of labor organization, involving community, sexuality, and family issues never privileged in the largely white male industrial unions.

The structural rearrangements related to the social relations of science and technology evoke strong ambivalence. But it is not necessary to be ultimately depressed by the implications of late twentieth-century women's relation to all aspects of work, culture, production of knowledge, sexuality, and reproduction. For excellent reasons, most Marxisms see domination best and have trouble understanding what can only look like false consciousness and people's complicity in their own domination in late capitalism. It is crucial to remember that what is lost, perhaps especially from women's points of view, is often virulent forms of oppression, nostalgically naturalized in the face of current violation. Ambivalence toward the disrupted unities mediated by high-tech culture requires not sorting consciousness into categories of "clear-sighted critique grounding a solid political epistemology" versus "manipulated false consciousness," but subtle understanding of emerging pleasures, experiences, and powers with serious potential for changing the rules of the game.

There are grounds for hope in the emerging bases for new kinds of unity across race, gender, and class, as these elementary units of socialist-feminist analysis themselves suffer protean transformations. Intensifications of hardship experienced worldwide in connection with the social relations of science and technology are severe. But what people are experiencing is not transparently clear, and we lack sufficiently subtle connections for collectively building effective theories of experience. Present efforts—Marxist, psychoanalytic, feminist, anthropological—to clarify even "our" experience are rudimentary.

I am conscious of the odd perspective provided by my historical position—a Ph.D. in biology for an Irish Catholic girl was made possible by Sputnik's impact on U.S. national science-education policy. I have a body and mind as much constructed by the post-World War II arms race and cold war as by the women's movements. There are more grounds for hope by focusing on the contradictory effects of politics designed to produce loyal American technocrats, which as well produced large numbers of dissidents, rather than by focusing on the present defeats.

The permanent partiality of feminist points of view has consequences for our expectations of forms of political organization and participation. We do not need a totality in order to work well. The feminist dream of a common language, like all dreams for a perfectly true language, of perfectly faithful naming of experience, is a totalizing and imperialist one. In that sense, dialectics too is a dream language, longing to resolve contradiction. Perhaps, ironically, we can learn from our fusions with animals and machines how not to be Man, the embodiment of Western logos. From the point of view of pleasure in these potent and taboo fusions, made inevitable by the social relations of science and technology, there might indeed be a feminist science.

Cyborgs: A Myth of Political Identity

I want to conclude with a myth about identity and boundaries which might inform late twentieth-century political imaginations. I am indebted in this story to writers like Joanna Russ, Samuel Delany, John Varley, James Tiptree, Jr., Octavia Butler, Monique Wittig, and Vonda McIntyre.[29] These are our storytellers exploring what it means to be embodied in high-tech worlds. They are theorists for cyborgs. Exploring conceptions of bodily boundaries and social order, the anthropologist Mary Douglas should be credited with helping us to consciousness about how fundamental body imagery is to world view, and so to political language.[30] French feminists like Luce Irigaray and Monique Wittig, for all their differences, know how to write the body; how to weave eroticism, cosmology, and politics from imagery of embodiment, and especially for Wittig, from imagery of fragmentation and reconstitution of bodies.[31]

American radical feminists like Susan Griffin, Audre Lorde, and Adrienne Rich have profoundly affected our political imaginations—and perhaps restricted too much what we allow as a friendly body and political language.[32] They insist on the organic, opposing it to the technological. But their symbolic systems and the related positions of ecofeminism and feminist paganism, replete with organicisms, can only be understood in Sandoval's terms as oppositional ideologies fitting the late twentieth century. They would simply bewilder anyone not preoccupied with the machines and consciousness of late capitalism. In that sense they are part of the cyborg world. But there are also great riches for feminists in explicitly embracing the possibilities inherent in the breakdown of clean distinctions between organism and machine and similar distinctions structuring the Western self. It is the simultaneity of breakdowns that cracks the matrices of domination and opens geometric possibilities. What might be learned from personal and political "technological" pollution? I will look briefly at two overlapping groups of texts for their insight into the construction of a potentially helpful cyborg myth: constructions of women of color and monstrous selves in feminist science fiction.

Earlier I suggested that "women of color" might be understood as a cyborg identity, a potent subjectivity synthesized from fusions of outsider identities and in the complex political-historical layerings of her "biomythography," *Zami*.[33] There are material and cultural grids mapping this potential. Audre Lorde captures the tone in the title of her *Sister Outsider*. In my political myth, Sister Outsider is the offshore woman, whom U.S. workers, female and feminized, are supposed to regard as the enemy preventing their solidarity, threatening their security. Onshore, inside the boundary of the United States, Sister Outsider is a potential amidst the races and ethnic identities of women manipulated for division, competition, and exploitation in the same industries. "Women of color" are the preferred labor force for the science-based industries, the real women for whom the worldwide sexual market, labor market, and politics of reproduction kaleidoscope into daily life. Young Korean women hired in the sex industry and in electronics assembly are recruited from high schools, educated for the integrated circuit. Literacy, especially in English, distinguishes the "cheap" female labor so attractive to the multinationals.

Contrary to orientalist stereotypes of the "oral primitive," literacy is a special mark of women of color, acquired by U.S. black women as well as men through a history of risking death to learn and to teach reading and writing. Writing has a special significance for all colonized groups. Writing has been crucial to the Western myth of the distinction of oral and written cultures, primitive and civilized mentalities, and more recently to the erosion of that distinction in "post-modernist" theories attacking the phallogocentrism of the West, with its worship of the monotheistic, phallic, authoritative, and singular work, the unique and perfect name.[34] Contests for the meanings of writing are a major form of contemporary political struggle. Releasing the play of writing is deadly serious. The poetry and stories of U.S. women of color are repeatedly about writing, about access to the power to signify; but this time that power must be neither phallic nor innocent. Cyborg writing must not be about the Fall, the imagination of a once-upon-a-time wholeness before language, before writing, before Man. Cyborg writing is about the power to survive, not on the basis of original innocence, but on the basis of seizing the tools to mark the world that marked them as other.

The tools are often stories, retold stories, versions that reverse and displace the hierarchical dualisms of naturalized identities. In retelling origin stories, cyborg authors subvert the central myths of origin of Western culture. We have all been colonized by those origin myths, with their longing for fulfillment in apocalypse. The phallogocentric origin stories most crucial for feminist cyborgs are built into the literal technologies—technologies that write the world, biotechnology and microelectronics—that have recently textualized our bodies as code problems on the grid of C³I. Feminist cyborg stories have the task of recoding communication and intelligence to subvert command and control.

Figuratively and literally, language politics pervade the struggles of women of color; and stories about language have a special power in the rich contemporary writing by U.S. women of color. For example, retellings of the story of the indigenous woman Malinche, mother of the mestizo "bastard" race of the new world, master of languages, and mistress of Cortés, carry special meaning for Chicana constructions of identity. Cherríe Moraga in *Loving in the War Years* explores the themes of identity when one never possessed the original language, never told the original story, never resided in the harmony of legitimate heterosexuality in the garden of culture, and so cannot base identity on a myth or a fall from innocence and right to natural names, mother's or father's.[35] Moraga's writing, her superb literacy, is presented in her poetry as the same kind of violation as Malinche's mastery of the conquerer's language—a violation, an illegitimate production, that allows survival. Moraga's language is not "whole"; it is self-consciously spliced, a chimera of English and Spanish, both conquerer's languages. But it is this chimeric monster, without claim to an original language before violation, that crafts the erotic, competent, potent identities of women of color. Sister Outsider hints at the possibility of world survival not because of her innocence, but because of her ability to live on the boundaries, to write without the founding myth of original wholeness, with its inescapable apocalypse of final return to a deathly oneness that Man has imagined to be the innocent and all-powerful Mother, freed at the End from another spiral of appropriation by her son. Writing marks Moraga's body, affirms it as the body of a woman of color, against the possibility of passing into the unmarked category of the Anglo father or into the orientalist myth of "original illiteracy" of a mother that never was. Malinche was mother here, not Eve before eating the forbidden fruit. Writing affirms Sister Outsider, not the Woman-before-the-Fall-into-Writing needed by the phallogocentric Family of Man.

Writing is pre-eminently the technology of cyborgs, etched surfaces of the late twentieth century. Cyborg politics is the struggle for language and the struggle against perfect communication, against the one code that translates all meaning perfectly, the central dogma of phallogocentrism. That is why cyborg politics insist on noise and advocate pollution, rejoicing in the illegitimate fusions of animal and machine. These are the couplings which make Man and Woman so problematic, subverting the structure of desire, the force imagined to generate language and gender, and so subverting the structure and modes of reproduction of "Western" identity, of nature and culture, of mirror and eye, slave and master, body and mind. "We" did not originally choose to be cyborgs, but choice grounds a liberal politics and epistemology that imagines the reproduction of individuals before the wider replications of "texts."

From the perspective of cyborgs, freed of the need to ground politics in "our" privileged position of the oppression that incorporates all other dominations, the innocence of the merely violated, the ground of those closer to nature, we can see powerful possibilities. Feminisms and Marxisms have run aground on Western epistemological imperatives to construct a revolutionary subject from the perspective of a hierarchy of oppressions and/or a latent position of moral superiority, innocence, and greater closeness to nature. With no available original dream of a common language or original symbiosis promising protection from hostile "masculine" separation, but written into the play of a text that has no finally privileged reading or salvation history, to recognize "oneself" as fully implicated in the world, frees us of the need to root politics in identification, vanguard parties, purity, and mothering. Stripped of identity, the bastard race teaches about the power of the margins and the importance of a mother like Malinche. Women of color have transformed her from the evil mother of masculinist fear into the originally literate mother who teaches survival.

This is not just literary deconstruction, but liminal transformation. Every story that begins with original innocence and privileges the return to wholeness imagines the drama of life to be individuation, separation, the birth of the self, the tragedy of autonomy, the fall into writing, alienation; i.e., war, tempered by imaginary respite in the bosom of the Other. These plots are ruled by a reproductive politics—rebirth without flaw, perfection, abstraction. In this plot women are imagined either better or worse off, but all agree they have less selfhood, weaker individuation, more fusion to the oral, to Mother, less at stake in masculine autonomy. But there is another route to having less at stake in masculine autonomy, a route that does not pass through Woman, Primitive, Zero, the Mirror Stage and its imaginary. It passes through women and other present-tense, illegitimate cyborgs, not of Woman born, who refuse the ideological resources of victimization so as to have a real life. These cyborgs are the people who refuse to disappear on cue, no matter how many times a "Western" commentator remarks on the sad passing of another primitive, another organic group done in by "Western" technology, by writing.[36] These real-life cyborgs (e.g., the Southeast Asian village women workers in Japanese and U.S. electronics firms described by Aihwa Ong), are actively rewriting the texts of their bodies and societies. Survival is the stakes in this play of readings.

To recapitulate, certain dualisms have been persistent in Western traditions; they have all been systemic to the logics and practices of domination of women, people of color, nature, workers, animals—in short, domination of all constituted as others, whose task is to mirror the self. Chief among these troubling dualisms are self/other, mind/body, culture/nature, male/female, civilized/primitive, reality/appearance, whole/part, agent/resource, maker/made, active/passive, right/wrong, truth/illusion, total/partial, God/man. The self is the One who is not dominated, who knows that by the service of the other; the other is the one who holds the future, who knows that by the experience of domination, which gives the lie to the autonomy of the self. To be One is to be autonomous, to be powerful, to be God; but to be One is to be an illusion, and so to be involved in a dialectic of apocalypse with the other. Yet to be other is to be multiple, without clear boundary, frayed, insubstantial. One is too few, but two are too many.

High-tech culture challenges these dualisms in intriguing ways. It is not clear who makes and who is made in the relation between human and machine. It is not clear what is mind and what body in machines that resolve into coding practices. Insofar as we know ourselves in both formal discourse (e.g., biology) and in daily practice (e.g., the homework economy in the integrated circuit), we find ourselves to be cyborgs, hybrids, mosaics, chimeras. Biological organisms have become biotic systems, communications devices like others. There is no fundamental, ontological separation in our formal knowledge of machine and organism, of technical and organic. The replicant Rachel in the Ridley Scott film *Blade Runner* stands as the image of a cyborg culture's fear, love, and confusion.

One consequence is that our sense of connection to our tools is heightened. The trance state experienced by many computer users has become a staple of science-fiction film and cultural jokes. Perhaps paraplegics and other severely handicapped people can (and sometimes do) have the most intense experiences of complex hybridization with other communication devices.[37] Anne McCaffrey's pre-feminist *The Ship Who Sang* explored the consciousness of a cyborg, hybrid of girl's brain and complex machinery, formed after the birth of a severely handicapped child. Gender, sexuality, embodiment, skill: all were reconstituted in the story. Why should our bodies end at the skin, or include at best other beings encapsulated by skin? From the seventeenth century till now, machines could be animated— given ghostly souls to make them speak or move or to account for their orderly development and mental capacities. Or organisms could be mechanized—reduced to body understood as resource of mind. These machine/organism relationships are obsolete, unnecessary. For us, in imagination and in other practice, machines can be prosthetic devices, intimate components, friendly selves. We don't need organic holism to give impermeable wholeness, the total woman and her feminist variants (mutants?). Let me conclude this point by a very partial reading of the logic of the cyborg monsters of my second group of texts, feminist science fiction.

The cyborgs populating feminist science fiction make very problematic the statuses of man or woman, human, artifact, member of a race, individual identity, or body. Katie King clarifies how pleasure in reading these fictions is not largely based on identification. Students facing Joanna Russ for the first time, students who have learned to take modernist writers like James Joyce or Virginia Woolf without flinching, do not know what to make of *The Adventures of Alyx* or *The Female Man,* where characters refuse the reader's search for innocent wholeness while granting the wish for heroic quests, exuberant eroticism, and serious politics. *The Female Man* is the story of four versions of one genotype, all of whom meet, but even taken together do not make a whole, resolve the dilemmas of violent moral action, or remove the growing scandal of gender. The feminist science

202 / Donna Haraway

fiction of Samuel Delany, especially *Tales of Neveryon,* mocks stories of origin by redoing the neolithic revolution, replaying the founding moves of Western civilization to subvert their plausibility. James Tiptree, Jr., an author whose fiction was regarded as particularly manly until her "true" gender was revealed, tells tales of reproduction based on non-mammalian technologies like alternation of generations of male brood pouches and male nurturing. John Varley constructs a supreme cyborg in his arch-feminist exploration of Gaea, a mad goddess-planet-trickster-old woman-technological device on whose surface an extraordinary array of post-cyborg symbioses are spawned. Octavia Butler writes of an African sorceress pitting her powers of transformation against the genetic manipulations of her rival (*Wild Seed*), of time warps that bring a modern U.S. black woman into slavery where her actions in relation to her white master-ancestor determine the possibility of her own birth (*Kindred*), and of the illegitimate insights into identity and community of an adopted cross-species child who came to know the enemy as self (*Survivor*). In her latest novel, *Dawn* (1987), the first installment of a series called *Xenogenesis,* Butler tells the story of Lilith Iyapo, whose personal name recalls Adam's first and repudiated wife and whose family name marks her status as the widow of the son of Nigerian immigrants to the U.S. A Black woman and a mother whose child is dead, Lilith mediates the transformation of humanity through genetic exchange with extraterrestrial lovers/rescuers/destroyers/genetic engineers, who reform earth's habitats after the nuclear holocaust and coerce surviving humans into intimate fusion with them. It is a novel that interrogates reproductive, linguistic, and nuclear politics in a mythic field structured by late twentieth-century race and gender.

Because it is particularly rich in boundary transgressions, Vonda McIntyre's *Superluminal* can close this truncated catalogue of promising and dangerous monsters who help redefine the pleasures and politics of embodiment and feminist writing. In a fiction where no character is "simply" human, human status is highly problematic. Orca, a genetically altered diver, can speak with killer whales and survive deep ocean conditions, but she longs to explore space as a pilot, necessitating bionic implants jeopardizing her kinship with the divers and cetaceans. Transformations are effected by virus vectors carrying a new developmental code, by transplant surgery, by implants of microelectronic devices, by analogue doubles, and other means. Laenea becomes a pilot by accepting a heart implant and a host of other alterations allowing survival in transit at speeds exceeding that of light. Radu Dracul survives a virus-caused plague in his outerworld planet to find himself with a time sense that changes the boundaries of spatial perception for the whole species. All the characters explore the limits of language; the dream of communicating experience; and the necessity of limitation, partiality, and intimacy even in this world of protean transformation and connection. *Superluminal* stands also for the defining contradictions of a cyborg world in another sense; it embodies textually the intersection of feminist theory and colonial discourse in the science fiction I have alluded to in this essay. This is a conjunction with a long history that many "First World" feminists have tried to repress, including myself in my readings of *Superluminal* before being called to account by Zoe Sofoulis, whose different location in the world system's informatics of domination made her acutely alert to the imperialist moment of all science fiction cultures, including women's science fiction. From an Australian feminist sensitivity, Sofoulis remembered more readily McIntyre's role as writer of the adventures of Captain Kirk and Spock in TV's *Star Trek* series than her rewriting the romance in *Superluminal*.

Monsters have always defined the limits of community in Western imaginations. The Centaurs and Amazons of ancient Greece established the limits of the centered polis of the Greek male human by their disruption of marriage and boundary pollutions of the warrior with animality and woman. Unseparated twins and hermaphrodites were the confused human material in early modern France who grounded discourse on the natural and supernatural, medical and legal, portents and diseases—all crucial to establishing modern identity.[38] The evolutionary and behavioral sciences of monkeys and apes have marked the multiple boundaries of late twentieth-century industrial identities. Cyborg monsters in feminist science fiction define quite different political possibilities and limits from those proposed by the mundane fiction of Man and Woman.

There are several consequences to taking seriously the imagery of cyborgs as other than our enemies. Our bodies, ourselves; bodies are maps of power and identity. Cyborgs are no exception. A cyborg body is not innocent; it was not born in a garden; it does not seek unitary identity and so generate antagonistic dualisms without end (or until the world ends); it takes irony for granted. One is too few, and two is only one possibility. Intense pleasure in skill, machine skill, ceases to be a sin, but an aspect of embodiment. The machine is not an *it* to be animated, worshiped, and dominated. The machine is us, our processes, an aspect of our embodiment. We can be responsible for machines; *they* do not dominate or threaten us. We are responsible for boundaries; we are they. Up till now (once upon a time), female embodiment seemed to be given, organic, necessary; and female embodiment seemed to mean skill in mothering and its metaphoric extensions. Only by being out of place could we take intense pleasure in machines, and then with excuses that this was organic activity after all, appropriate to females. Cyborgs might consider more seriously the partial, fluid, sometimes aspect of sex and sexual embodiment. Gender might not be global identity after all, even if it has profound historical breadth and depth.

The ideologically charged question of what counts as daily activity, as experience, can be approached by exploiting the cyborg image. Feminists have recently claimed that women are given to dailiness, that women more than men somehow sustain daily life, and so have a privileged epistemological position potentially. There is a compelling aspect to this claim, one that makes visible unvalued female acitvity and names it as the ground of life. But *the* ground of life? What about all the ignorance of women, all the exclusions and failures of knowledge and skill? What about men's access to daily competence, to knowing how to build things, to take them apart, to play? What about other embodiments? Cyborg gender is a local possibility taking a global vengeance. Race, gender, and capital require a cyborg theory of wholes and parts. There is no drive in cyborgs to produce total theory, but there is an intimate experience of boundaries, their construction and deconstruction. There is a myth system waiting to become a political language to ground one way of looking at science and technology and challenging the informatics of domination—in order to act potently.

One last image: organisms and organismic, holistic politics depend on metaphors of rebirth and invariably call on the resources of reproductive sex. I would suggest that cyborgs have more to do with regeneration and are suspicious of the reproductive matrix and of most birthing. For salamanders, regeneration after injury, such as the loss of a limb, involves regrowth of structure and restoration of function with the constant possibility of twinning or other odd topographical productions at the site of former injury. The regrown limb can be monstrous, duplicated, potent. We have all been injured, profoundly. We require regeneration, not rebirth, and the possibilities for our reconstitution include the utopian dream of the hope for a monstrous world without gender.

Cyborg imagery can help express two crucial arguments in this essay: (1) the production of universal, totalizing theory is a major mistake that misses most of reality, probably always, but certainly now; (2) taking responsibility for the social relations of science and technology means refusing an anti-science metaphysics, a demonology of technology, and so means embracing the skillful task of reconstructing the boundaries of daily life, in partial connection with others, in communication with all of our parts. It is not just that science and technology are possible means of great human satisfaction, as well as a matrix of complex dominations. Cyborg imagery can suggest a way out of the maze of dualisms in which we have explained our bodies and our tools to ourselves. This is a dream not of a common language, but of a powerful infidel heteroglossia. It is an imagination of a feminist speaking in tongues to strike fear into the circuits of the super-savers of the new right. It means both building and destroying machines, identities, categories, relationships, space stories. Though both are bound in the spiral dance, I would rather be a cyborg than a goddess.

15

Commentary: Allies and Enemies

Christina Crosby

"A Manifesto for Cyborgs" is, as Donna Haraway writes in the first sentence of the essay, "an effort to build an ironic political myth faithful to feminism, socialism, and materialism." I would characterize it as ironic and political and apocalyptic—an ironic political apocalypse. Of course, these terms don't "fit," but then, much of the pleasure of this text and its power, too, come from its unexpected conjunctions and energetic connections. I would like briefly to consider how this essay is apocalyptic, how it is ironic, and how an ironic apocalypse might be political.

An apocalypse is a revelation, a disclosure. Jewish and Christian apocalyptic texts, like the Book of Daniel and Revelations, prophesy the end of the world "as we have known it," the end of human history, and the beginning of a new era when man is one with God. The apocalypse reveals man redeemed from sin, no longer alienated from his Creator. The apocalypse is thus a call and a promise—come listen to the word, hear before it is too late, I will reveal to you what has been revealed to me, a world in which God and Man are one. As Donna Haraway points out, the great Western narratives of liberation, marxism, and psychoanalysis, are apocalyptic in design, revealing how human being is alienated from itself and promising future wholeness. For marxism, human being is constituted through labor, for psychoanalysis, through lack; and on these ontological bases each can envision a union of subject and object, though that union may be interminably deferred.

Of course, ever since Hiroshima the apocalypse may be no revelation at all, but simply the end of history. This nuclear apocalypse would seem to be nothing but a threat with no promise whatsoever, the horrifying end of the micro-electronic nuclear post-modern era. But in a strategic move which is key to her project, Donna Haraway finds in the nuclear apocalypse—if not a promise—at least a possibility, the possibility of theorizing a politics not based on alienation from a human essence, not organized teleologically from beginning to end. This is the possibility of developing a theory which can articulate the workings of late twentieth-century relations of power and a politics adequate to oppose certain effects of those power relations. The question is whether any apocalypse, even an ironic one, can be anything other than totalizing at some point.

So how is the "Manifesto" apocalyptic? It is above all a disclosure, revealing the truth of the "informatics of domination," as Haraway calls the new network of power. This "polymorphous" information system has indeed brought an end to life as we have known it, that is, to life organized around what she calls "the comfortable old hierarchical dominations" of industrial capitalism. Haraway reveals that we are already, cyborgs whether we know it or not, that we are worked up, caught up in a global system of domination in which the classic boundaries have been breached—human and animal, organism and machine, the physical and non-physical intermingle, are indistinguishable. So, too, the oppositions with which we are so familiar have been displaced—subject/object, self/other, inside/outside, man/woman—these relatively stable hierarchies are no longer in place. And Haraway's revelation shows that the end is at hand. In the apocalyptic tone, she declares that "it is time to write *The Death of the Clinic*" since normalization has given way to automations and subjects have become cyborgs, "the awful apocalyptic telos of the West's escalating dominations of abstract individuation ... a man in space."

But if the cyborg which (as Haraway says) "is our ontology" and "gives us our politics" is the end product of a system of domination that is leading to the explosive end of Star Wars, it is also, simultaneously, an artificial construct that need not naturally, necessarily lead in any one direction. It's dynamic, mobile, programmable, which makes the cyborg incalculably dangerous in the form of a cruise missile, but also offers opportunities that haven't yet been calculated for forming new alliances, new affinity groups, new coalitions. Thus Haraway's is an ironic apocalypse, for the networks of the informatics of domination which cover the globe are both a grid through which power is exercised and the pathways along which resistance runs. The exercise of power produces the conditions for new kinds of resistance, the alliance between U.S. labor, for instance, and the new working class in the Philippines, or in Hong Kong. The system can be worked back against itself, making noise and stress where the engineers strive to achieve stress-free, smooth communication and exchange.

Haraway's apocalyptic revelation is ironic in another way, too, for the cyborg, while it may have an ontological status, is no natural or essential being. So there is no prophecy of a final union in the "Manifesto," only of partial identities, momentary conjunctions, multiple connections. This is an apocalypse without end, which is what Haraway wants, considering that the end, in this case, would be The End.

The irony of the "Manifesto" is, I believe, the pleasure of the text, the pleasure of the unexpected turn, of finding oneself elsewhere than expected, of seeing surprising openings where there seemed to be a dead end. For those readers who have been active in socialist and feminist politics, there's the pleasure too, of the politically "incorrect," the break with the solemnities of left politics and the reductive dualisms which are all too familiar. The pleasures of this text are, as Haraway herself says, perverse, not only in the sense of being turned away from what the Left has taken to be right and true, and not just in the sense of being stubbornly oppositional to the informatics of domination. "A Manifesto for Cyborgs" is also perverse in finding pleasure in pain, in celebrating the death of the subject as the birth—or assembling—of the cyborg, a distinctly disturbing construct. This perverse and ironic text refuses nineteenth-century consolations for twenty-first century conditions, and searches instead for the points of stress in the command-control-communications-intelligence system, turning C^{3}I against itself.

The turns of the text are thus ironic, pleasurable, perverse—and powerful. Indeed, the powerful inclusiveness of the "Manifesto" is one of its most stunning turns—for Haraway enlists everything that might make noise, anything that might cause stress in the system, whatever might help to disrupt smooth communication. This inclusiveness is a great pleasure for a reader like myself (intellectually engaged with theoretical questions, politically committed to radical change), for it brings together Jacques Derrida, Maria Patricia Fernandez-Kelly, Linda Gordon, Luce Irigaray; philosophy, science fiction, primatology, discussions of labor organizing; Greenham Common women and Julia Kristeva. The principle of inclusion is explicitly political, for the "Manifesto" is above all a political essay dedicated to furthering the possibilities for effective organizing against the informatics of domination. But I wonder whether this inclusiveness, which contributes significantly to the prophetic, revelatory, apocalyptic tone of the text—I wonder whether this inclusiveness is as powerful politically as it is intellectually pleasurable.

My concern is this. Haraway brings together theories in her text—most clearly evident in the extensive footnotes—theories that don't fit together. I agree with her that "fitting" or coherence is by no means a virtue necessarily to be upheld, but the inclusiveness of the "Manifesto" tends to juxtapose theoretical positions rather than make the connections Haraway recognizes are so necessary. I think of the final section of the essay, an effort to construct "a myth of political identity" by bringing together the "stories about language" told by U.S. women of color and deconstructive theories of writing. In her brief discussion, Haraway finds in Cherríe Moraga's writing themes which are deconstructive in import and a use of language that isn't natural, that is neither Spanish nor English but both. But deconstruction loses much of its force when rendered thematically, and I wonder whether Moraga's work might lose some of its power, too, by being interpreted in these terms. I'm not objecting to the "unnatural" joining of French theory with Chicana writing—indeed, I wish for more such illegitimate unions—but as this part of the "Manifesto" stands, the edge seems to have been taken off both deconstruction (which can open a text beyond any thematic coherence) and Moraga's writing (the specificity of which is obscured in reading it as the deconstructive story).

The superinclusiveness of the text, then, is managed at the cost of some specificity, a loss which is particularly important when one thinks of the repeated—and important—call Haraway makes for alliances, for coalition politics. I wonder how a cyborg, which has multiple points of connection, knows how to say no. How can we determine the proper (although not natural, not necessary, not essential) limits and boundaries of coalitions? Haraway notes that politics makes strange bedfellows or cyborg interfaces, giving as one example the "ironic" (as she says) alliance between "corporate executives reading *Playboy* and anti-porn radical feminists," both of whom find it irrational to assume that sex is natural or necessarily linked to reproduction. Now I see the logic—and the irony—of this alliance, but I want a politics of exclusion as well as inclusion, a politics that enables me to say that the porn industry in general as it is now constituted, and *Playboy* in particular (whoever its readers are) are (how can I put it?) the enemy. That's awfully strong for this instance, I know, but the principle is important, for we need a principle of exclusion that's not just a nostalgic return to the clarities of bygone binaries—which were always more complicated than they seemed, anyway.

I don't mean to suggest that Donna Haraway hasn't thought of these problems. Indeed, she writes of "the confusing task of making partial, real connection," and goes on to say, "Some differences are playful; some are poles of world historical systems of domination. 'Epistemology' is about knowing the difference." But I'm not sure what a cyborg epistemology would look like, although I have a good idea of what the failures of other epistemologies have been, the essentialism of both marxism and radical feminism. So I don't want to be the revolutionary subject and I don't want to be a goddess—I want to be a cyborg— I *am* a cyborg whether I want to be or not. But I want to be a cyborg that knows how to make the right connections and block the wrong ones so as to make as much "noise" as possible.

16

Commentary: Cyborgs, Origins, and Subjectivity

Mary Ann Doane

A manifesto is a public declaration of intentions, motives, or views, usually associated with a person, a group, a government—in short, an identifiable entity. An entity with an identity, if only for the temporary duration of the utterance. Is "A Manifesto for Cyborgs" written by a cyborg, on behalf of cyborgs, or addressed to cyborgs? Of these possibilities, only the final one seems out of the question since cyborgs, by their very nature as it were, always already embrace the postmodernist strategy advocated by Haraway. The mode of address, instead, seems to involve a curious turning back on itself. It's not at all clear what a cyborg's analysis would be. "A Manifesto for Cyborgs" is, above all, a performative utterance—a staging of an uninhabitable feminist position. This is not necessarily in itself a criticism. It may ultimately be the case that all feminist positions are in some sense uninhabitable or only uncomfortably inhabitable. But this is to be desired. Haraway's analysis quite appropriately shatters the monism of *one* comfortable and secure feminism, dispersing it into partial views. But the question remains: what is the status of her own discourse? Haraway claims that she is attempting to construct an "ironic political myth" at the center of which is the image of the cyborg. What constitutes a myth here?

We have come to understand mythical language, via Claude Lévi-Strauss and Roland Barthes, as entirely dominated by the logic of the binary opposition (according to Lévi-Strauss, "Mythical thought always progresses from awareness of oppositions toward their resolution"[1] and "the purpose of myth is to provide a logical model capable of overcoming a contradiction" [p. 229]). Irony, however, is—according to Haraway—"about contradictions that do not resolve into larger wholes, even dialectically, about the tension of holding incompatible things together because both or all are necessary and true." From this perspective, the phrase "ironic political myth" is oxymoronic. Furthermore, the cyborg represents, above all, the dismantling of binary oppositions, the collapse of boundaries, and the failure of a stable identity previously safeguarded by the oppositions animal/human, organism/machine, physical/non-physical. In addition, Lévi-Strauss's notion of mythical thought stipulates that it involves an obsession with origins. A myth is the repetitive telling of a story about origins and Haraway's " 'Western,' humanist sense depends on the myth of original unity, fullness, bliss and terror, represented by the phallic mother from whom all humans must separate. . . ." Origin stories anchor the nostalgic desire to return to a natural identity and "The cyborg skips the step of original unity, of identification with nature in the Western sense." I will return later to the question of Haraway's activation of an anti-originary, deconstructive myth but, for now, I would like to focus on some of the implications of her critique of originary narratives in theory.

The cyborg is born all at once, fully developed, a full-fledged member of the work force. Cyborgs don't need the couch or the talking cure, for they have no unconscious. What is missing in this account—and seemingly unnecessary in the advanced technological society described here—is a theory of subjectivity. The cyborg has no mother and it certainly has no father: "The main trouble with cyborgs, of course, is that they are the illegitimate offspring of militarism and patriarchal capitalism, not to mention state socialism. But illegitimate offspring are often exceedingly unfaithful to their origins. Their fathers, after all, are inessential." Are we dealing with transgression here? Can Oedipus be far behind? But Haraway's aim is to detach the cyborg from a past and an origin—effectively, to dehistoricize it. In this orientation toward the future, we witness the annihilation of history—both the history of the subject and the history of culture. A high-tech society somehow marks a complete break with the societies which preceded it—and their dualisms. The cyborg, emerging from nowhere, is indeed the representation of a kind of innocence. The cyborg has no complicity with the mechanisms of its own society; it floats through that network intact. Hence it is conceived either as pure resistance or as the purely submissive exemplification of the military's command-control-communication-intelligence nexus. From this point of view—which in fact juggles two—the possibility of mixture seems unthinkable. This is what allows Haraway to criticize other feminisms which stress sexuality, describing them as theories of victimization (one is either a victim or a hero), when what is really at issue—and demands a theory of subjectivity and sexuality—is the question of complicity.

What is lost in Haraway's rejection of theories which circulate obsessively around representations of an origin are the very categories of loss, of absence, and even of difference. The cyborg—without a history, without an unconscious—is present to itself. It must be in order to counter what Haraway refers to as the two most potent myths of original unity and identity we have—Marxism and psychoanalysis. In her account, Marxism—through its conceptualization of labor as the privileged ontological category and as the "humanizing activity that makes man"—and psychoanalysis—by positioning an originary maternal unity preceding individuation—promise the end of alienation in a return to a unitary and grounding identity. In order to make this argument, Haraway must reduce Marxism and psychoanalysis to their humanist versions and must consistently ignore the steady gains of anti-humanist tendencies in contemporary feminism. What about anti-humanist Marxisms (such as that of Louis Althusser) which do not privilege the categories of labor or alienation but rather those of ideology and the interpellation of subjectivity? And what happens to the stabilizing tale of origins when division and splitting in psychoanalysis do not signal a fall away from a healthy unity but a fundamental condition of the psyche? Originary narratives are not the only way of conceiving of history. On the other hand, Haraway is quite right to imply that these theories along with the ones she explicitly discusses, appear to leave no structural room for race—or perhaps more accurately, can conceive of the other only within the bind of the Western episteme's construction of subjectivity. But if this is the case, it is certainly not due to complicity with either essentialism or humanism. The totalizing tendency cannot be countered by a fragmentation or dispersal which it already envisages.

This is precisely where the issue of identity would seem to be most crucial. Perhaps it is Haraway's concentration on feminist theories informed by humanism which leads her to a position assuming that identity cannot be thought outside of processes of naturalization. The opposition between identity and affinity (the latter—espoused by Haraway) is subtended by that between nature and choice: one is condemned by nature to an identity but one chooses an affinity. Her privileged example is "women of color," theorized by Chela Sandoval as "oppositional consciousness." As a fusion of outsider identities, this is a fractured postmodernist "identity," characterized by the "conscious appropriation of negation." Again, identity is either natural or chosen (in which case it becomes affinity)—a polar opposition which curiously echoes that between determinism and free will. But I would argue that there are identities—crucially important identities—which are neither natural nor chosen but constructed, mapped. In Freudian psychoanalysis, for instance, one is not born with a sexual identity. It is laboriously constructed and constantly subject to failure. And it would be a grave mistake to over-emphasize either the construction or the process of its failure—held in tension, both are always in play.

It is my understanding that this is something of what Haraway has in mind in activating the image of the cyborg which holds in tension two different perspectives on technology. On the one hand, the cyborg points to "the final imposition of a grid of control on the planet," an invidious network of invisible power relationships made possible through high technology. On the other hand, the image of the cyborg reveals the human kinship with animals and machines, the necessity of assuming "permanently partial identities" and "contradictory standpoints." Yet, while there is clearly an attempt to hold the two in balance, the radical cyborg seems ultimately to win out. This is due to Haraway's repeated insistence upon refusing a "demonology of technology" or an anti-science metaphysics which would view technology as the primary mode of our exploitation. She strongly criticizes feminists who re-activate the opposition between the organic and the technological in order to authorize their nostalgia for an imagined and originary organic unity and their consequent anti-science and anti-technology positions. In contrast to theorists such as Luce Irigaray for whom technology, or *technē*, is always the tool of a phallocentrically designed project aimed at conquering and controlling nature as maternal origin, Haraway's work represents an attempt to envisage a "happy technology" which would constitute yet another sign of our alleged postmodernism.

Here, I would like to shift my focus to what would also seem to be an exemplary text of the cyborg, although it certainly does not fit within the category of feminist science fictions outlined by Haraway. The fact that the union of body and machine has been anticipated and theorized with both anxiety and pleasure produces a combination of affects which makes the theme a perfect field of play for the genre of the horror film. I am thinking here especially of David Cronenberg's 1982 film, *Videodrome,* in which the protagonist, Max Renn, is literally transformed into a VCR through the effect of a video signal deployed by a malevolent conspiratorial organization. He can thus be repeatedly programmed by various characters in the fiction. For Cronenberg, in an advanced technological society, the body really does become something else—extended, mutated, endowed with the new organs required by a televisual culture. *Videodrome* specifies contemporary cultural experience as a mass of technologically produced images and sounds which penetrate and transform the body. The film clearly represents its protagonist's feminization by the television discourse and his consequent vulnerability to a kind of rape by pulsating video cassettes and furthermore elaborates an intricate thematics linking the opposition hardware/software to that between masculinity and femininity. But, I am primarily interested in its discourse on what happens to power in a technologically advanced society and the relation of this discourse to Haraway's argument. In *Videodrome,* the notion of power is shifted, displaced from the axis of vision (the perceptual) to that of the invisible ray—a video signal which penetrates the body and induces a brain tumor. The electronic is thus associated with the unfelt, the unseen, and terror is attached to the unperceived.

The exemplary disease in this context—and one which consistently recurs in Cronenberg's work—is cancer. The alleged causes of cancer include radiation, chemicals in the air we breathe or the food we eat, X-rays, emanations from the television set or the word processor—in short, the enemy is that which cannot be readily detected. Electronic technology is characterized by its ability to penetrate every space, to invade anywhere without respect to barriers or boundaries so that nothing can remain concealed, hidden. Aligning itself with the paranoid conspiracy films of the 1970s, *Videodrome* participates in the tendency to fantasize about huge corporations which exercise a total deployment of an almost intangible power over every aspect of life. This is a new kind of horror film in which horror no longer resides in the domestic, the familial, or the psychological, but in institutions.

Institutions become monstrous insofar as they assimilate or cover vast territories. Television via satellite overcomes limitations of space and time and becomes all-encompassing. This is a totalizing power—everything is exposed; nothing can be hidden in the cellar any longer. Technology is a tool of this monstrous lateral extension and the television image is paradigmatic; it infiltrates everywhere—even the body is invaded.

Haraway certainly has a sense of the consequences of such a reorganization of power particularly insofar as it demolishes the oppositions between public and private space, surface and depth. As she points out, we are no longer dealing with a single source of domination but with its dispersal in the Informatics of Domination. From this point of view, it would be a mistake to over-simplify power by situating it as a hierarchical ordering of the "old dualisms"—mind/body, organism/machine, public/private, nature/culture, man/woman. And according to Haraway, feminist analysis "has proceeded as if the organic, hierarchical dualisms ordering discourse in 'the West' since Aristotle still ruled." The seductiveness of these previous dualisms lies in our ability to isolate the enemy—to figure out where domination is located. Power as a function of the Informatics of Domination, on the other hand, due to its very invisibility and dispersal, is in fact more difficult to resist, or even to describe. Who or what dominates in the Informatics of Domination? Where is power? How can we conceive of power let alone resistance in this kind of system? This image of power is reminiscent of Michel Foucault's—effervescent, everywhere and nowhere, generating localized sectors of resistance, the property of no-one.

Here, it is important to return to and re-examine the figure of the cyborg. The specificity of the cyborg's resistance, its pleasure and potency, lies in its territorial transgression of the boundaries between nature and culture, body and mind, the organic and the technological.

But according to Haraway, these dualisms are already anachronistic. How can the collapse of oppositions represented by the cyborg be liberating or potentially productive if oppression is no longer organized through dualisms? Within the Informatics of Domination, the collapse of these oppositions—i.e. the cyborg—will be the norm. The cyborg will not be enough. And it will be even more necessary to understand how technology is made complicit with the dispersal of power, its invisibility. The sheer complexity of the reorganization of technologically maintained powers will require new modes of analysis and images of something other than transgression.

On the other hand, the cyborg does have a limited efficacy—in relation to the extent to which we are still haunted by the old dualisms. These dualisms have not simply disappeared, much as theories of postmodernism would like them to. The postmodernist culture described by Haraway is still resisted on the grounds of the old dualisms and their maintenance. It would be more appropriate to speak of the overlap and strategies which might be appropriate to such an overlap. There is no clean break.

And in this sense Haraway's image of the cyborg does retain a certain force— particularly in light of the desire to articulate imagination and the real. It is important not to ignore her discourse's status as a kind of utopian fantasy, and here the stress on fiction is crucial. Who would *not* want to be rid of its unconscious? By holding in balance two contradictory readings of the cyborg, two visions both pleasurable and horrible of high technology, Haraway's discourse does indeed constitute a myth for feminists. And it also comes quite close to the structural anthropologist's description of the function of myth. For the myth works toward the resolution of a contradiction even if that contradiction is not resolvable at the level of the real. And at this point there is a slippage whereby myth no longer allays the terror of the real but becomes the real. In a kind of simulation-effect. So I would like to end by quoting—more accurately tearing out of its context (which is, ironically, an analysis of the Oedipus myth)—the comments by Lévi-Strauss which embody this slippage and which seem also to denote something of the appeal and fascination of Haraway's project:

> Although experience contradicts theory, social life validates cosmology by its similarity of structure. Hence cosmology is true. (p. 216)

17

Commentary: Cyborgian Socialists?

Joan W. Scott

The "Manifesto for Cyborgs" is an oppositional utopian myth for socialist-feminists. I must begin by saying that I love its ringing, declarative phrases, its brilliant formulations, its incredibly comprehensive scope and its optimism. Sentences like the following are simply wonderful to read for they recombine ideas and allusions in highly original ways. The essay, Haraway writes, is "an effort to contribute to socialist-feminist culture and theory in a post-modernist, non-naturalist mode and in the utopian tradition of imagining a world without gender, which is perhaps a world without genesis, but maybe also a world without end. The cyborg incarnation is outside salvation history."

My comments on this piece are small ones and they come in threes. First I offer a quick summary of what seem to me to be its three major points in order to then express what I can only call three small nagging doubts.

1.   The essay refuses tired nineteenth-century dualisms of man/animal, organism/machine, physical/non-physical, nature/culture, production/reproduction, in the name of a new post-modern order based in a technological revolution the expression of which is electronics. It argues that feminists must adjust their politics to the "realities" of the late twentieth century. The Industrial Revolution, rooted in steam and steel, has been displaced by the integrated circuit. Information is the product of this new technological revolution and its means of exchange.

2.   Since the "informatics of domination" has made the world a coded text, the analytic strategies appropriate for cyborg politics involve attention to language, to meanings, to the forms and methods by which everything is textualized. There is no alternative to "deconstruction" in this brave new world. Particularly important for those who would articulate political oppositions is the ability to read the new texts in order to detect fissures, permeable boundaries, and point out fault lines in seemingly intact categories. Opposition consists in the transgression of boundaries, the confusion of categories, and the invention of new languages. "If we are imprisoned by language, then escape from that prison house requires language poets, a kind of cultural restriction enzyme to cut the code; cyborg heteroglossia is one form of radical cultural politics."

3.   Cyborg politics substitute a notion of affinity as a basis for collective action

rather than shared identity—which is a naturalized or essentialized construction. The politics Haraway projects in her utopian vision involve strategic combinations of individuals who do not claim that their consciousness inheres in their being; do not claim as women, for example, a shared "natural" experience of sexual subjugation, or as male workers, alienation from the "essential" life activity that Marx defined as labor. Rather, collective affinities play on identifications that have been attributed to individuals by their societies, and that have served to exclude them or subordinate them. "Women of color" is an example of the kind of affinal politics Haraway wants to encourage.

These three points have to do with the new order science and technology have created, with the analytic strategies appropriate for those who would resist its new forms of domination, and with the kind of changing political alliances, shifting and multiple affinities among individuals that might follow from such analyses. Perhaps even in my arrangement of the list I have expressed my reservations or hesitations. These all have to do with what seem to me to be traces of an older mode of analysis not entirely displaced, and contained in the label socialist-feminist.

1. I know this article is meant to be a redefinition of socialist-feminist politics, but can those two words be used unproblematically? Can their humanist histories be transformed? The essay centrally espouses post-modernism and the dissolution of oppositions and boundaries, on the one hand, but, on the other, retains traces of the philosophical and political languages of socialism. In the usages of this essay, what is socialist-feminist? What are "progressive" politics? Why aren't those terms made more problematic?

2. There is a kind of scientific/technological determinism in the essay which echoes back to arguments about base and superstructure. "I would argue," Haraway writes, "that specific forms of families dialectially relate to forms of capital and to its political and cultural concomitants." And later on, "The new technologies affect the social relations of both sexuality and of reproduction, and not always in the same ways." To be sure, neither of these statements is starkly deterministic, but they harken me back to an implication of monocausality that gives me pause. And they raise another question about Haraway's rhetorical strategy—which is to grant certain positions to her audience of socialist-feminists in order to get them to consider the importance of the kinds of analyses she is proposing. Yet, we must ask what are the boundaries between such rhetorical gestures and the endorsement of technological determinism in this essay?

3. The examples of exemplary cyborg politics are "women of color," whose identity is strategically constructed out of existing principles of exclusion. "These real-life cyborgs (e.g., the Southeast Asian village women workers in Japanese and U.S. electronics firms described by Aihwa Ong), [who] are actively rewriting the texts of their bodies and societies. Survival is the stakes in this play of readings." What is the difference between Haraway's looking to these groups for the politics of the future and (the association such a gesture has for me with) the romantic

attribution by white liberal or socialist women to minority or working-class women of the appropriate (if not authentic) socialist or feminist politics? One difference, I know, is that Haraway is looking at *how* resistance is improvised not at the objective conditions that give rise to it. Still, there are some things that need to be explained: Why are Southeast Asian women "real-life" cyborgs? How have "women of color" been able to claim affinity without evoking a "natural" identity?

I think my three points boil down to a single question: Is this paper, aimed at disrupting socialist-feminist discourse, still argued too much with its terms?

Still, a manifesto is not a political program, it is a statement of theory and purpose; a utopian manifesto is meant always to be as much a critical take on current politics as a blueprint for the future new society. A post-structuralist utopian manifesto is even more unsettling for it sets us loose to improvise temporary affinities, strategically aimed at targets whose shape constantly changes and which also change our shapes. We are left still to ponder and to try to answer a question Donna Haraway poses, but does not, cannot perhaps answer: "What kind of politics. . .?"

18

The Political Economy of Women as Seen by a Literary Critic

Gayatri Chakravorty Spivak

Headnote (1988)

If I were to revise the following pages, I would have to sharpen them so much and weigh them down with such detail of documentation, that they should lose their naive passion, which I still endorse. Please read them as the first stirrings of a work that remains in progress with no end in sight.

Introduction

Here is the project for my paper. The condition of women is fractured by the international division of labor. How does a literary critic read a paper at a Feminist Conference in the light of this? My method will be to offer repetitive generalizations. Although nothing I have to *say* is new, I believe there is something new in what I *want*. I want both the so-called "theoretical" contingent and the so-called "empiricists" in the audience to hear me. This is in response to something Heleieth Saffioti describes in the following way: "It is as difficult to set feminism as a social movement aside from feminism as a intellectual production as it is to gather these two levels of the phenomenon in one."[1]

Why I want to speak to so-called empiricists is perhaps the burden of the entire paper. Let me at the outset state why I want the so-called theoretical contingent to be patient with generalizations: When we are dealing with the international division of labor—the general relationship between advanced and comprador capitalisms—we are in the arena of economy in the narrow sense. To beg that question as merely empirical and to shift immediately into economy in the general sense—either of the "libidinal economy"-variety or the "absolute heterogeneity"-variety—is paradoxically, a positivist gesture that claims to know where the narrow and the general break, and also claims that economy in general

218

can be an object of presentation at a Conference. They do not thereby *avoid* the generalizing moment. They fall, in fact, into an "anti-economism" for which other narrative-historical clues can be found.

If this excursus is already appearing incomprehensible and abstract to the "empiricist" sisters in the audience, I will ask them to ignore it. This particular request was not meant for them, but for an equally important segment of our group. Let me set us back to where I began: How does a literary critic read a paper at a Feminist Conference, given that the condition of women is fractured by the international division of labor? My method will be to offer repetitive generalizations.

I   The Field

In the West, writes Francis Mulhern, the greatest challenge to traditional strategic thought comes today from feminism and ecology.[2] No comparable claim can be made for the so-called developing nations. It may even be said that the developing nations challenge this claim. What are the nature and place of feminism on the other side of the international division of labor? Four generalizations can be offered: I. the worsening condition of women in the urban sub-proletariat and in peasant labor in the so-called developing nations is a function of the complicity between multinational and comprador capitalism on the one hand, and patriarchal structures of desire and power on the other; II. the ideological framework of feminist leadership in the Third World is of necessity constituted by the history of the bourgeois indigenous nationalist elite; III. feminist theory in the West is largely ethnocentric; often primitivist when broadly concerned with the "Third World," and when supposedly Marxist, often relating to no more than the mode-of-production narrative or recent debates within Western marxisms; IV. this ethnocentrism is nowhere more evident than in the cutting edge of Western feminist speculative theory (vaguely "French" in provenance), which deals with the inscriptions of the body and the constitution of the subject.

II   The Investigator

So much for generalizations about the field. Now let us offer three predictable generalizations about the *subject* of investigations, the capital "I" who investigates.

A. Historically, it is well known that we in this country take our model of militancy from the British nineteenth century. For feminist individualism in that age of imperialism, the stake was the making of human beings. That meant the constitution and interpellation of the subject, not only as individual, but as "individualist." It was represented on two registers: child-bearing (female/private) and soul-making (male/public). The first was domestic-society-through-sexual-reproduction cathected or fixed in desire as "companionate love." The second was the imperialist project cathected as civil-society-through-social-mission. As the female individualist articulated herself in shifting relationship to these stakes, fighting the male for a greater share of the public sphere, it was the "native female" as such (*within* discourse, *as* a signifier) who was excluded from any share in this emerging norm. If this account is read from the perspective of the "metropolitan" context, the reader sees nothing there but the history of the militant female subject. The literary critic contemplating or investigating the political economy of women is still liable to reproduce this structure, caught in the mesmerizing focus of the history of the female becoming individualist.

B. My second generalization in this area relates to our specific workplace. I hope no one in this crowd, at this panel where we are supposed to be considering the relationship between Marxism and feminism, under the auspices of an Institute that occupies itself with the cultural construction of gender, will disagree that there is something like a relationship between and among political economy, the nature of a movement, and its sustaining ideological production. In that context I ask, how, not in terms of the intellectual content of what is taught and written about, but *in terms of institutional behavior,* is an adult worker interpellated (or identified) as a "feminist" *in the U.S. academy?* In answer to this I offer my second generalization about the subject of investigation or the capital "I" who investigates:

I agree, of course, that "in every class society based on special caste oppression, the female members of the lowest caste constitute an even more downtrodden sub-caste which concentrates in more acute form all of the disabilities of class exploitation and caste oppression in that society."[3] But the classroom or the department in a University has a upwardly mobile energy that is at least two centuries old, by some reckoning much older. Its promise of freedom from class-labeling has to be investigated through the history of the place of "education" in our society. Suffice it to say that the class-liberating energy and promise contained in college and university teaching have not changed in contemporary United States. As feminist academics enter *this* arena of class-struggle, the invocation of the pervasive oppression of Woman in every class and race stratum, indeed in the lowest sub-caste, cannot help but justify the institutional interests of the (female) academic. In terms of the specific nature of the institution, it is quite appropriate that academic feminist activism should concentrate on tenure decisions regarding minority women whose own sense of caste and class is, willy-nilly, caught within the scenario of upward mobility. I think, however, that the invocation of the female members of the world's lowest sub-castes is disingenuous there. And it is on such invocations that *our* privileging of women's oppression rests. This privileging can work in the interest of yet another justification of upward mobility within the U.S. context. There are many stories I could tell you to prove this unhappy fact.

I hope, at this point, that the bare argument will be enough to make you suspect that the question of political economy does not just apply to corporate women, proletarian women, and Third World women. We as a group are not exempt from it and this, rather than genitalist notions of sexual difference, distinguishes us from non-female feminists.

C. My third generalization is about the post-colonial subject who investigates these problems within the U.S. academy. Here also the field of generalization must be made more specific. We must take into consideration such things as the more direct relationship of domination and exploitation between the United States and the Latin American countries; the shifting adversarial relationship between the United States and Japan; the embarrassing confusion between Africans and Afro-Americans (of which no feminist teaching in Atlanta, Georgia—as I do—should be unaware); not to mention the peculiar etheriality of literary work within U.S. Asian Studies Programs and departments. So much said, let me offer my third generalization about the investigating subject in this area:

Calls for cross-cultural exchange can be answered readily only by Third World women moving up in the First World. These answers do not consider the historical (rather than romantic or nostalgic) constitution of geography—how the world (geo) was written (graphy) in the last few centuries. Such considerations would not rule out the desire to cross cultures, but would reveal the difficulty of the task. The privileged Third World informant crosses cultures within the network made possible by socialized capital, or from the point of view of the indigenous intellectual or professional elite in actual Third World countries. Among the latter, the desire to "cross" cultures means accession, left *or* right, feminist *or* masculist, into the elite culture of the metropolis. This is done by the commodification of the particular "Third World culture" to which they belong. Here entry into consumerism and entry into "Feminism" (the proper named movement) have many things in common.

You may ask why, asked to speak on "The Political Economy of Women," I spend fully a third of my time on introductory generalizations. It is because my project is how a literary critic reads a paper on this topic at a Feminist Conference. As I have often remarked before, the history of the institutional study of literature is one of great permissiveness. (On this topic I could speak at great length at any time.) When a literary critic makes like a political economist or a psychoanalyst she is speaking as an insider of her discipline in terms of her fantasy about what kinds of social value those other disciplines carry (the structure of the formulation is Jonathan Réc's).[4] If she does not attend to the generalizations I have laid out before you, or dismisses them as only too obvious or positivistic, in the esoteric register of Heideggerian discourse, that would be to be "pre-comprehending" them. She then acts out the pretentious self-marginalization of the sanctioned ignorance of so-called interdisciplinary talk.

III   The Woman at the Other End

Let me now repeat a well-known fact about the international division of labor, that general relationship between advanced and comprador countries. It has changed since 1974. I want to offer here a fabulated and abstract account of it which anyone who attended my lucubrations on postmodernism at the *Social Text* soirée last year will, alas, have heard.

Marx wrote in the *Grundrisse:*

> The continuity of production presupposes that circulation time has been sublated [*aufgehoben*: destroyed but preserved on another level]. The nature of capital presupposes that it travels through the different phases of circulation not as it does in the idea [*Vorstellung*: literally idea-representation], where one concept turns into the other at the speed of thought [*mit Gedankenschnelle*], in no time [in English in the original], but rather as situations which are separated in terms of time.[5]

Marx's suggestion is that, if circulation were sublated into the speed of mind, production (of Value) as continuous totality would annul Value itself. This would be a crisis.

Has the circulation time of capital been sublated into the speed of mind under telecommunication? Here is Ted Levitt of the Harvard Business School: "Today money is simply electronic impulses. With the speed of light it moves effortlessly between distant centers (and even lesser places). A change of ten basic points in the price of a bank causes an instant˙ and massive shift of money from London to Tokyo. The system has profound impact on the way companies operate throughout the world."[6] Here is *The New York Times*: "The start of a solution of the market's major dilemma, *the management of time*, appeared in 1972 when the New York Stock Exchange, the American Stock Exchange and their member firms organized the Securities Industries Automation Corporation . . . Not long ago, the executives kept up with their investments on a monthly or weekly schedule; today, the reporting can be instantaneous because of the computer."[7]

Granted, then, that the circulation of capital has been sublated into the speed of light. How is this crisis being managed? A detailed answer would probably be boring and incomprehensible for the theoretical people. Since one of the foci of my paper is the useless division between empiricism and "theory" within feminism, I cannot resist the temptation here of producing a philosophical generalization that would be equally incomprehensible to both sides: As the subject as super-adequation in labor-power seems to negate itself under telecommunication, a negation of the negation is continually produced by the shifting lines of the international division of labor.

Some consequences of this "crisis" can fortunately be more soberly described in the following way. The next four quotations are from the Introduction to *Women, Men, and the International Division of Labor,* edited by June Nash and Maria Patricia Fernandez-Kelly:[8]

> The mode of integration of underdeveloped countries into the international economy has shifted from a base relying exclusively on the exploitation of primary resources and labor to one in which manufacturers have gained preponderance. This movement has paralleled the proliferation of export-processing zones (EPZ's) throughout the world. More than a uniformly defined or geographically delimited concept, the export-processing zone provides a series of incentives and loosened restrictions for multinational corporations by developing countries in their effort to attract foreign investment in export-oriented manufacturing. This has given rise to new ideas about development which *often question preexisting notions of national sovereignty.* (viii: italics mine)

In feminism, we often fasten upon culturalism when we think of culture studies as a way out of ethnocentricity. Concepts of culture have very interesting relationships with concepts of nationhood. Let us remark the fact that changes in the international division of labor *question notions of national sovereignty.* All investigations into culture must be complicated by this ideological shift. I will touch upon this in my concluding suggestions. To continue with my quotation: "Almost two million people employed in EPZs throughout the world and many more are directly or indirectly affected by their existence. In Asia alone more than three hundred thousand women labor in electronic plants located in EPZs" (viii).

In territorialist imperialism, the colonial subjects were more directly men. Women acceded to it indirectly and through class- and cast-privilege. But these hordes of women who, because of the patriarchal structures of parental and conjugal desire and power are the new army of "permanent casual" labor working below the minimum wage—these women represent the international neo-colonial subject paradigmatically. Their production is different from the production of the *colonial* subject. I want to quote two passages from Nash and Fernandez-Kelly and then draw out some of the consequences in my own way. For obvious reasons, I want, once again, to draw your attention to this little example of collaboration between two empiricists and a "theorist."

Anyhow, I am making the point that the production of this neo-colonial subject, women in the EPZs and comparable locations, is different from the production of the colonial subject in at least one way. Two passages from Nash and Fernandez-Kelly can be helpful in constructing my explanation. I will run them together. The first part might clarify how the sublation of circulation time is being negated by the exploitation of women's bodies.

The geographical dispersion of productive stages as part of a wholly integrated manufacturing process has been made possible, in many cases, by the reduction of operations to minute, repetitive, and monstrous manual tasks. By virtue of this fragmentation, training periods for workers have also been curtailed, affording maximum flexibility to industry but increasingly denying workers control over their labor . . . The case of Korea and that of the Philippines . . . vividly demonstrate the truncation of a developmental process that would integrate workers in an expanding economy. The redistribution of some profits through government or union action is nullified in both center and periphery. (viii, x)

In the great age of territorial imperialism, a certain effort at settling the country to make capital flow and thus to facilitate transportation as well as to codify the law and regularize education, was necessary. Thus the social mission-aspect of imperialism took on an ideological hold that for some people became its central task and justification. With this came the training into consumerism "introducing imperceptibly a gradual improvement in the habits and manners of the people," to quote an early 19th-century document of the East India Company. It is of significance that this was written of the so-called "aboriginals of various kinds" who, according to the writer, constituted the Indian "people."

Thus a new code of law, a new system of education, and a new perception of needs operated the epistemic violence—violently changing the shape of the mind and the person—which produced the old colonial subject who had a chance to enter the struggle for individualism.

This elaborate constitution of the subject is not necessary under international subcontracting in post-modern or electronic capitalism. No legal structure need be laid down for the army of "permanent casuals," only the circumventing of rudimentary labor and safety regulations is on the agenda. No consistent training into consumerism is any longer needed. The industries can move on. The markets are elsewhere, or, in classical Marxist language, the surplus-value is realized elsewhere and the proportion of fixed to variable capital is much lower.

Thus these women and men are moving further and further away from us. Electronic capitalism is not making them enter post-modern culture. They are re-entering what Partha Chatterjee has called "the feudal mode of power."[9] (Since we are speaking of post-industrial rather than pre-industrial feudalization, any extended consideration would ask for the phrase "physical force" to be re-defined):

The *feudal* mode of power is characterized fundamentally by sheer superiority of physical force, i.e. a relationship of domination. It is founded on *conquest or some other means of physical subordination* of a subject population. In our conception, it denotes not just the state formation which accompanies the feudal mode of production, but may in fact serve to describe political institutions corresponding to a whole range of forms of organization or production based on direct physical control over the life-processes of the producers. (317; italics mine)

And, unlike the case of European social relations under the feudal mode of production, it is the *woman* who confronts this structure doubly: at home and at work. Generalizing from Michel Foucault's discursive analysis of power, Chatterjee distinguishes among three modes of power: the communal, the feudal, and the bourgeois. Again, there is no doubt that the taxonomy—the systemic table—of these modes of power can never be exhaustive. It is also true that all micrological or minute-scale considerations of modes of power must account for heterogeneity—differences among people—discontinuity—lack of synch and gaps between, within, among, and beyond people, and libidinal economy. Yet, reminding ourselves, as before, that one ignores things in the narrow sense at one's peril, let us note that the woman is worst off under the feudal mode of power. In the communal mode of power notions of tribe, clan, kinship, affinity, consanguinity provide the sustaining underpinning (infrastructure) of the flow of power. There the importance of endogamy and exogamy (the inscription of the female) is crucial. It is in this unsentimental sense that the medieval poem *Beowulf* calls women "peace-weavers." In the bourgeois mode of power, as is abundantly clear, upward class mobility may mean woman's access to individualism.

In the case of the new feudalization under electronic capitalism there is a double whammy on both sides. Unlike in the classical context, where mode of production and mode of power go hand in hand, in this new feudalization the men are set against the women. The feudal mode of power cannot now be contested by invoking communal modes of power (utilizing inscription through the female) from *below*, as in cases of pre-capitalist insurgency. In addition, accession to the bourgeois mode of power, given "the truncation of development" that I have just described, is also made much more difficult for these women. Thus this new feudal mode of power cannot be easily resisted from *above* by these women or their representatives.

IV   Disciplinary Suggestions

If *this* is the constituency of feminism, what is a literary critic to say about such a fact at a feminist conference?

First, on a humble and banal level, she might point out that our daily distancing from these women is an unavoidable fact of everyday life. It is very well known that the worst theaters of international subcontracting are the electronics and the textile industries. All our pleasures over the liberating effect of computers and over our everyday wardrobe are mired by this fact. I am not advocating absurd pieties—or, to quote what Stanley Aronowitz said about me in a memorable line a couple of years ago—I am not denying the worker his cappuccino. I am just suggesting that our complicity in the international division of labor will not go away by boycotting Coors beer or iceberg lettuce. I have just read that computers are going to be used in Nicaragua in a politically correct way. I suppose that means that it will not involve the mediation of a million tiny manual movements by exploited and isolated women. I hope to be able to see how that happens.

Secondly, the literary critic might emphasize another truism. The situation of the subject(s) of post-modern neo-colonialism must be rigorously distinguished from the situation of immigrants, who are still caught in some way within structures of *colonial* subject-production; and, especially, from the historical problem of ethnic oppression on First World soil. This second point is less paralyzing than the suggestion above, which merely and sadly indicates the limits of our benevolence.

Marxist-feminist sociologists, economists, and Third World area specialists are not unaware of the need to make this obvious distinction between the Third World as such and varieties of ethnic oppression in the First World. As a literary critic attempting to come to grips with the problem of talking generally about the political economy of women, I feel that I must *read* the work in other disciplines, however quantified or "empiricist" their approach might be. I cannot open up my disciplinary expertise without studying them on their institutional home ground. It is only then, privileging the cornerstone of my own craft, that I can begin to feel that *their* researches have to be fleshed out with considerations of the Third World female sub-proletariat as *subject*. Here I would ask the sisters from the "empiricist" disciplines to hold their impatience.

The suggestions I give below are just as simplistic as all my generalizations have been so far.

The theories of subject-formation that we know are either psychoanalytic or counter-psychoanalytic. When these theories are used to describe the subject of power, male or colonial, these theories became what Paul de Man has called "allegories of reading." They then operate a slippage from the morphological (or epistemological) side of psychoanalysis to a diagnostic (or ethical) register by way of metaphors of (the male or colonialist) will (to power). (This previous sentence is a digest of de Man's *Allegories of Reading*.)[10] Within such a generalizing compass, it may be said that descriptions of *female* power work a mere reversal of such allegories of reading. How are we to get to the paradigmatic subject of post-modern neo-colonialism, the Third World female sub-proletarian beyond this game of psychoanalysis and its other?

If my earlier remarks about the academic feminists were *about* colleagues, here I am speaking *to* students.

I think we might begin by looking at the insertion of institutional psychoanalysis into these countries. For institutional psychoanalysis can be a latter-day support of what I have earlier called epistemic violence. And, if we want to do high theory, here we have not only the work of Frantz Fanon, but also the anti-Oedipal, anti-psychiatric, anti-psychoanalytic work of Gilles Deleuze, Félix Guattari, and Foucault, the geo-psychoanalytic work of Jacques Derrida. This study will not single women out, because men in Third World contexts are *also* the victims of strategic exclusions from psychoanalytic normativity. In the Indian context, for example, the works of V.S. Naipaul (*India: A Wounded Civilization*) and Sudhir Kakar are examples of this sorry state of affairs. This investigation will also not take you very close to the kind of women I am invoking but, in the case, for example, of Ashis Nandy's benevolent study of Indian widow-sacrifice,[11] it will tell you where the use of psychoanalytic categories might themselves become the mark of a foreclosure.

The next thing is a little harder but I think much more fun. It is to track the regulative psychobiographies that constitute the subject-effect of these women, give these women a sense of their "I." I have said many a thing today about not taking refuge in heterogeneity as a dodge against empiricism. But here you fall into irreducible heterogeneity.

Perhaps I should tell you what I mean by "regulative psychobiography." It is the model narratives that give "meaning" to our readings of ourselves and others. *We* are used to working with variations on, critiques of, and substitutions for, the narratives of Oedipus and Adam. What narratives produce the signifiers of the subject for other traditions? Always in a confrontation and complicity with the epistemic re-constitution of the subject-in-imperialism, traces of this psychobiography can be found in the indigenous legal tradition, in the scriptures, and of course, in myth. (I mention myth last because, structuralized or folklorized, it has become hard to use in the way I am describing.) However humble the woman or women you are considering, the grandeur of the regulative psychic narrative remains undiminished. (In fact, and here I'm stepping completely into the realm of probability, I would like to examine if and how these narratives are de-hegemonized and made the site of emergent power in the self- and situation-representation of the few female leaders within the Third World proletariat that I have heard of.)

At any rate, I have to end on a note that might make you a bit melancholy. You know how tremendously we in literature privilege language. Most of the recent ways of curtailing this privilege have in fact backfired. Discourse, text, semiosis have become tenor or vehicle of the metaphor of language. The kind of psychoanalysis that the literary-theoretical establishment favors is not immune to this privileging. Jacques Lacan's caution to Roman Jakobson—that he was only linguisticking (*linguistiquer*) in "The Instance of the Letter" has not been noticeably heeded. The allure of cryptonymic psychoanalysis—launched by Nicolas Abraham and Maria Torok—for literary-critical employers of psychoanalysis is that it sees the entire psychoanalytic enterprise in terms of words, their breakdown, and their recovery.[12] In fact, it is my belief that Abraham & Torok's notion of endopsychic incorporation will provide the next allegory for the diagnosis of masculine or colonial power. (If any of you do this, you must give me a footnote. My most jealous pride-of-achievement is in figuring out that Doris Lessing's *The Four-Gated City* is a roman à clef about E.P. Thompson and in making this prediction about endopsychic incorporation.)

Well, I have gone on about this because tracking regulative psychobiographies cannot be seriously undertaken without knowing the appropriate languages well. We cannot ask the economists and the sociologists to attend to our speculations about the subject-constitution of the woman in post-modern neo-colonialism if we do it as charming primitivists. Three obvious things can be said in this connection.

One, we cannot all hope to learn every language under the sun. We cannot even all be in the business of learning languages. It is here that we must envisage our work as collective. (The ambivalence of the enterprise of translation, brought to my attention by Barbara Harlow, should be considered in any extended discussion of this point.) The collective must embrace both so-called empirical research and serious work on subject-constitution. Otherwise, and I cannot say this often enough, Third Worldist theoretical feminism is merely making up its object in the tradition of benevolent imperialism.

Two, we are all justly proud to claim that the work of feminism is necessarily interdisciplinary. But uninstructed object-making drains political importance from the interdisciplinary work associated with Women's Studies. The existence in this country of places like the Pembroke Center, CROW, SIROW, the Rutgers Institute, and other newly emerging centers should make literary feminists aware of this.

Three, on the other side, the Army, the Foreign Service, the multi-nationals themselves, and intelligence and counter-intelligence take the necessity of language-learning with the utmost seriousness. We have something to learn from our enemies.

Summary

Because literary criticism is my home, the political economy of women my focus, and speaking to you the immediate occasion of production of my words—I have generalized the following problems:

    a)   in the field

    b)   in the workplace

    c)   with the post-colonial investigating subject

I have tried to outline the emerging subject of post-modernist neo-colonialism.

I have suggested that her "feudalization" be approached through empirical research and a serious collective study of subject-constitution.

As you know, politics and economics drag in a third word, ideology. As far as *I* could figure out, without something like the steps above, the title "Political Economy of Women" can become an ideological construct in the hands of a literary critic. *You* will tell me where I've gone right, where wrong.

19

Commentary: What is to be Done

Ellen Rooney

___

> It is no accident that the symbolic system of the family of man—and
> so the essence of women—breaks up at the same moment that
> networks of connection among people on the planet are unprece-
> dentedly multiple, pregnant, and complex. "Advanced capitalism" is
> inadequate to convey the structure of this historical moment. In the
> "Western" sense, the end of man is at stake. It is no accident that
> woman disintegrates into women in our time. Donna Haraway, "A
> Manifesto for Cyborgs: Science, Technology, and Socialist Feminism
> in the 1980s"

> These women and men are moving further and further away from us.
> Gayatri Spivak, "The Political Economy of Women as Seen By a Literary
> Critic"

In the closing passages of "The Political Economy of Women as Seen By a
Literary Critic," Gayatri Spivak sounds a note that she suspects may leave her
audience "a bit melancholy." Her theme is language, but she ignores the familiar
idioms of the linguistic turn. Spivak is concerned with the question of languages,
plural; specifically, with the natural languages that critics working in the national
literatures of the West tend not to read. She doesn't name them, but the women
and men laboring in the export-processing zones often speak Cantonese, Korean,
Tagalog.

The issue of languages emerges as Spivak presents her "Disciplinary Suggestions"
for feminist literary critics working within the effects (but "on the other side")
of the international division of labor. She asks: "How are we to *get to* the
paradigmatic subject of post-modern neo-colonialism, the Third World female
sub-proletarian?" and warns that many of the more obvious strategies will "not
take you very close to the kind of women [she is] invoking" (my emphases). To get
closer, Spivak suggests that we might "*track* the regulative psychobiographies . . .
of these women," investigating the "model narratives that give 'meaning' to [their]
readings of [themselves] and others" and thus constitute their own "sense of their

'I.' " Finally, recalling "how tremendously we in literature privilege language," she insists that to follow this path, we must know "the appropriate languages well." Otherwise, "Third Worldist theoretical feminism is merely making up its object in the tradition of benevolent imperialism" (my emphasis). Languages may enable us to close the distance that separates us from our objects.

Spivak's remarks inscribe for the last time in her essay the problem of discontinuity, of the fractures within the condition of women. Linguistic differences here figure the distance that separates a "Third Worldist theoretical feminism" and every Western feminist from the "subject of post-modern neo-colonialism," the "woman at the other end." The difficulty, if not the impossibility, of "getting to" these "paradigmatic" subjects, of even getting "close," energizes the whole of Spivak's polemic: "our daily distancing from these [sub-proletarian] women is an unavoidable fact of everyday life," a fact made more intractable as they move "further and further away from us." Her essay forces us to confront the "limits of our benevolence" in the form of this radical discontinuity, materially formidable and in many ways fed by our own practices and work as consumers and as intellectuals.

Distance, discontinuity, divisions, fractures; these are the pervasive topoi of Spivak's text. Her title announces the double focus of her project as a *literary critic* entering the terrain of *political economy* and signals that hers is a discourse already divided within: she seeks both to "read a paper at a Feminist Conference, given that the condition of women is fractured by the international division of labor" and to map the enabling conditions of that very reading, to make visible the means of its production and its limits. Addressing an audience she divides between the "so-called 'theoretical' contingent" and the "sisters from the 'empiricist' disciplines," Spivak approaches her disciplinary suggestions as to what is to be done by means of a description of who "we" are, both in terms of our distance from the neo-colonial subject and in relation to the fractures within the constituency of feminism *on this side* of the international division of labor: we are empiricists and theorists, political economists and literary critics, women who approach cross-cultural exchange from the first world and women who come to it from the third world, militants with a model of individualism inherited from the British (imperialist) tradition and privileged informants from the elites of the "Third World" developing countries.

Spivak's strategic multiplication of difference positions us as historical subjects within our disciplines, within the history of feminism and within the logic of late capitalism: she problematizes feminism's production of knowledge precisely by focusing on its subject(s), the "I who investigates," and thus registers the sense of limitation that is one response to an intensified consciousness of the fractures within the condition of women. Jenny Bourne has recently argued that the privileging of identity has undermined feminism's political practice: "Identity Politics is all the rage. Exploitation is out (it is intrinsically determinist). Oppression is in (it is intrinsically personal). What is to be done has been replaced by who am I."[1] Exploitation remains conceptually central to Spivak's analysis: the international division of labor defines the *exploitation* of women working in the export-processing zones. Yet her focus on the question "who are we?" ultimately overshadows the question of what we are to do.

Spivak is well known for her embrace of deconstruction's "greatest gift": "to question the authority of the investigating subject *without* paralyzing him, persistently transforming the conditions of impossibility into possibility."[2] But in this essay, perhaps even because of its unrelenting testimony to distance, difference, and boundaries, Spivak overestimates the power of our inherited languages; her analysis finds its own "mesmerizing focus" and thus its limits in the trope of discontinuity. Ultimately, she figures distance as the "incomprehensible" language of her own text; the body of her essay undertakes to describe the grounds for this cognitive failure by detailing her audience's *interest* in overlooking the consequences of the international division of labor. This disclosure of interests is essential; but it tempts Spivak to reproduce the discontinuity that separates her audience both from the women in the export-processing zones and from the language of marxism. The question of political practice is displaced by the question of identity, and Spivak's radical diagnosis of feminism's confrontation with the disintegration of woman is wed to a modest program for collective work under the sign of the interdisciplinary. The eloquent absence in her text marks the place of a collectivity that might exceed the boundaries of (inter)disciplinary power.

I Subjects

> ". . . this elaborate constitution of the subject . . ."

All the forms of feminist discourse are entangled with questions of subjectivity. Ideology must, as Althusser argues, produce subjects that "work all by themselves"; once resistance exposes femininity as an ideology, as artifice, the mechanism of ideological "interpellation" breaks down.[3] Thus, even those feminisms which seem most theoretically naive drive a wedge into the notion of the natural self, if only by stressing the lived stereotypes of femininity and masculinity. To make the artifice of an oppressive femininity visible is to suggest the remedy of self-fashioning, and thus to fall into the problem of the subject. "Changing the subject" is among the earliest of feminist programs.[4]

Spivak's essay introduces "subjects" of every kind: subjects as objects of study, speaking subjects—"the I who investigates"—and the problem of subjectivity itself, both as the privileged theme of certain forms of feminist agitation (individualism) and inquiry (French theory) and as an urgent political problem born of the discontinuities in capitalism's construction of subjects in the international division of labor. She is rightly suspicious of the process by which "the title 'Political Economy of Women' can become an ideological construct in the hands of a literary critic"; her overriding concern is to escape the specular process that elides the divisions among women, obscuring differences of race and class, oppression and exploitation, in favor of a homogenizing figure of Woman. Spivak attacks this figure by insisting on the specificity of our economic, historical, and institutional positions, disclosing the interest each of us has in her own innocence, in (what she elsewhere calls) our alibis.

Bell Hooks has analyzed the political effects of the longing for innocence as it was expressed in the concept of sisterhood. As she argues, sisterhood "was not viewed as a revolutionary accomplishment," but as a natural effect of "common oppression": "it was primarily bourgeois white women, both liberal and radical in perspective, who professed belief in the notion of common oppression. The idea . . . was a false and corrupt platform disguising and mystifying the true nature of women's varied and complex social reality."[5] As Hooks makes clear, sisterhood has been one of the alibis obscuring our "daily distancing" from other women; indeed, insofar as it distracts many feminists from the struggle to construct a practical political solidarity, sisterhood is one of the ideologies that moves us further and further apart.

Spivak derails every argument that rests on the alibi of common oppression. Thus she warns feminists in the United States, formed by a model of militancy taken from imperial Britain, that they will only reproduce the nineteenth-century feminist individualist's exclusion of the "native female" if they read uncritically "from the perspective of the 'metropolitan' context." Yet, to recognize this exclusion is not to privilege every strategy of inclusion. Previously excluded women have been included by academic feminists who invoke "the pervasive oppression of Woman in every class and race stratum, indeed in the lowest sub-caste," and identify with Third World women whose status " 'concentrates in more acute form all of the disabilities of class exploitation and caste oppression.' " Spivak argues that this "disingenuous" identification "cannot help but justify the institutional interests of the (female) academic." The privileging of (other) women's oppression "can work in the interest of yet another justification of upward mobility within the U.S. context," nourishing the illusion that Everywoman shares the status of the most oppressed.

These examples illustrate the central strategy of Spivak's essay: to multiply the articulations of discontinuity and distance among women, thus to underscore the particular interests served by specific feminists' interventions and to position the I who would investigate the political economy of women. In every case, the contradictory processes by which feminists of all kinds are "interpellated" are revealed as a knot of historical, economic, and institutional effects. Spivak's generalizations concerning the production of subjectivity are a rebuke to the ethnocentrism of "Western feminist speculative theory (vaguely 'French' in provenance)," which theorizes the subject according to "genitalist notions of sexual difference"; the Feminine may also function as an alibi. But she is wary of cross-cultural exchange as the sole antidote to ethnocentrism or to feminism as a strategy for upward mobility. Thus, she questions the authority of the "privileged Third World informant," who "crosses cultures within the network made possible by socialized capital" and· accedes to the "elite culture of the metropolis" by means of "the commodification of the particular 'Third World culture' " to which she belongs.

Spivak's elaborate examination of the constitution of the subject(s) of feminism underscores the difficulty of getting to the neo-colonial subject of late capitalism. "The production of this neo-colonial subject, women in the EPZ's and comparable locations, is different from the production of the colonial subject," who was continuously bombarded by the "epistemic violence" characteristic of the "social mission-aspect of imperialism"; new legal codes, educational practices, and training in the needs and stratagems of consumerism gave "the old colonial subject . . . a chance to enter the struggle for individualism." But "this elaborate constitution of the subject is not necessary under international subcontracting in post-modern or electronic capitalism." The apparatus that territorial imperialism evolved for "violently changing the shape of the mind and the person" is obsolete. In the export-processing zones, we find a "new army of 'permanent casual' labor working below the minimum wage." Spivak argues that "these women represent the international neo-colonial subject paradigmatically," but "electronic capitalism is not making them enter post-modern culture," where we reside; it transports them into a new feudalism.

In Spivak's view, the distances between us are rapidly increasing, even as "the circulation time of capital has been sublated into the speed of light [mind]," that is, as capital pulses from place to place instantaneously.[6] She argues that the crisis resulting from the "production (of Value) as continuous totality would annul Value itself" were capital not able to manage it by rapidly and continually shifting the international division of labor.

Ironically, in this account, "we," those of us "on the other side" of the international division of labor, resemble nothing less than we resemble capital. It zooms from place to place, oblivious to distance and " 'situations which are separated in terms of time,' " averting crisis with "runaway shops" that move production sites overnight, and blocking the resistance of its workforce from above and from below.[7] By contrast, "we" are weighed down by our militant and imperialist traditions, our nationalism and dreams of accession, our institutional investments, our languages, our comforts—our computers and clothing—and our privilege, our positions on this side of the international division of labor. With no universal equivalent, we seem rooted in our places, "mired" in "paralyzing" complicity.

II Discipline

"Because literary criticism is my home . . ."

Spivak's careful mapping of our places and of the distances between them exposes a bleak chasm; this is the most powerful effect of her text. Yet she is not without strategies for movement. The constraints of our subject-positions seem paralyzing, but our disciplines are more ambiguous: they may offer a partial solution. Spivak uses the word discipline to articulate a certain ideal—as a figure for knowledge, sober instructions, responsibility, and control, which she contrasts with self-indulgence, fantasy, ignorance, and permissiveness,[8] and she is quite harsh in her evaluation of intellectual strategies that are less respectful of "disciplinary expertise." She condemns "the pretentious self-marginalization of the sanctioned ignorance of so-called interdisciplinary talk," and mocks the literary critic who "makes like a political economist or a psychoanalyst" as a figure who speaks "as an insider of her discipline in terms of her fantasy about what kinds of social value those other disciplines carry." But Spivak does not dismiss "interdisciplinary talk" per se. (These remarks appear as she passes through the field of political economy proper.) On the contrary, she insists that "the work of feminism is necessarily interdisciplinary. But *uninstructed* object-making drains political importance from the interdisciplinary work associated with women's studies" (my emphasis). Finally, her suggestion for the feminist literary critic working this side of the international division of labor is precisely a *disciplinary* one, a literary critic's program for collaboration across disciplines.

Spivak is here uncharacteristically willing to speak for the disciplines, as a disciplinarian. Her notion of "pretentious self-marginalization" resembles that of the traditional defenders of disciplinary boundaries and seems to assume an unproblematic "insider," a figure she has undermined in her own "Marginalia."[9] She refers to "my home" in literary criticism and argues that we must visit the "institutional home ground" of other disciplines, before we can move on, "privileging the cornerstone of [our] own craft." Insofar as she urges us to abandon the "useless division" between theory and empiricism and to read across the disciplines, her suggestions are unexceptional. But Spivak encourages us to take instruction in "object-making" from the disciplines as they are currently constituted; she fails to remind us that these disciplines posit objects of inquiry that cannot be useful to oppositional critics without being fundamentally revised. As a literary critic reading this "literary critic attempting to come to grips with the problem of talking generally about the political economy of women," I am surprised that literary criticism itself retains so much of its traditional authority.

"Women's studies" exists to help erode the comforts and the clarity of the "home" that is now literary studies.[10] This is not a matter of fantasies of a transcendent discourse beyond the disciplines or of a wholesale abandonment of our disciplinary habits; but one of political practice. The question is to what extent we must stop being literary critics in any familiar sense of the word—while using all of our textual skills and historical knowledge, of course—if we hope to undermine the dominant modes of the production of knowledge. What place do the traditions of literary studies have in the kind of struggle that might put at least some of us in league with the women of the export-processing zones? Spivak's discourse on the subject makes this question seem naive. Yet in *Resistance Literature,* Barbara Harlow argues that "no less than the multinational corporations, . . . the cultural institutions and academies of higher learning which define and process information and cultural production participate not only in the dissemination of specific and hegemonic forms of social organization but also in determining the content of cultural commodities." If it is true that "not just anthropologists, economists, and political scientists, but students of literature too, with their theories of discourse, rhetoric, and textual criticism, provide the necessary information and tools of analysis for the propagation of cultural and even military domination,"[11] then we should be most cautious when the rhetoric of disciplinary order enters our theorizing. Perhaps the emphasis in our work should be *anti*-disciplinary rather than interdisciplinary, and our efforts directed towards deconstructing our traditional "disciplinary expertise" rather than employing it as the "cornerstone" of our endeavors.

Spivak's essay discloses the barriers our subject positions present to the work we imagine ourselves doing and the multiplicity of the alibis concealing the fractures in the condition of women. In the end, her tone, which is otherwise uncompromising, reconciles us to a modest program: she advises that the " 'feudalization' [of the neo-colonial subject] be approached through empirical research and a serious collective study of subject-constitution." But she asks too little when she suggests only that we "approach" with our disciplinary standards in place as protection against "uninstructed object-making." The disciplinary can also be an alibi, securing our positions as investigators approaching an object, confident that the appropriate languages—both disciplinary and natural—will get us closer. What Spivak fails to suggest is that we might position ourselves elsewhere, a little further from the disciplines where we feel so at home.

III   Languages, or Making Ourselves Too Much at Home

> ". . . there is something new in what I *want*. I want both the so-called 'theoretical' contingent and the so-called 'empiricists' in the audience to hear me."

The faint melancholy Spivak's disciplinary suggestions may induce has several undertones but she renders one in particular vividly. Her last words recall that "on the other side, the Army, the Foreign Service, the multi-nationals themselves, and intelligence and counter-intelligence take the necessity of language-learning with the utmost seriousness. We have something to learn from our enemies." The word "enemy" reminds us that language-learning functions for many as a weapon, an unabashed form of power-knowledge, which grounds military, economic, and political interventions. As Donna Haraway might suggest, the multi-nationals and the State Department view the differences among languages as a kind of "stress," a babble that threatens an "interruption of communication"; their "search for a common language" derives from their recognition of the link between communication and control and their "translation of the world into a problem of coding."[12] The painful irony here is that these "enemy" institutions may know the languages of *their* enemies better than we do those of our (potential) allies. The unspoken danger is that even as we learn those languages, we may further our opponents' projects. Spivak hints at this insidious complicity when she interrupts her call for collective work that employs translation to acknowledge the "ambivalence of the enterprise of translation." As Haraway notes, "universal translation" is the tool of "unhindered instrumental power (called effective communication)." Benevolent imperialism shadows our most rigorous efforts to elude it.

Languages thus have an ambiguous place among Spivak's suggestions. They figure the distance that separates us, but they are essential to work that hopes to negotiate those distances, however tentatively. They link us to our enemies, for they too recognize the importance of language-learning. This coincidence alerts us to the risk that our work on "the Third World female sub-proletariat as subject" may also have its uses in the files of the multi-nationals. Obviously, this threat doesn't mean we should fall silent or abandon our tools to our opponents. But these instructions from our enemies suggest that we might think again about what distinguishes "them" from "us." Spivak's presentation of languages is consistent with her account of disciplinary knowledge in general: they retain a certain disciplinary neutrality. What is finally at stake is who makes use of the language and to what ends.

Marxism, of course, is a language, perhaps the most crucial of those Spivak speaks in her essay; it is also notoriously indifferent to traditional disciplinary boundaries. The case of marxism suggests that the question of language can be understood as a question of solidarity; to share a language is to establish the grounds for the collective work Spivak ultimately advocates. But despite the significance of marxism in her own analysis, she avoids the demand that her readers take up the challenge of its language. One of Spivak's themes is her interpellation of her audience, which presents her with consistent problems. She voices her concern and her desire to be heard at the outset, worrying that the theorists should be "patient with generalizations," while the empiricists ought to ignore an "excursus" that may seem "incomprehensible and abstract." Indeed, Spivak warns each "segment of our group" to be sensitive to the question of whether a "particular request [is] meant for them." Her acknowledgment of the divisions within her audience and her decision to address them partially is an index of her awareness of the limits of her language.[13] At the same time, she attempts to bring the segments of her audience together, criticizing the clichés we use to discredit one another and calling for collective work. But when she invokes the "collective," Spivak refers to cooperation between empiricists and theorists of subjectivity, literary critics and sociologists—to the ideal of inter-disciplinarity. She defines the "collective" as collaboration across disciplines; marx-ism is not the ground of this collectivity.

Spivak's explicit references to "classical Marxist language" reflect her doubt about what it might mean to her audience. She patiently explains that academic feminists are "not exempt" from "the question of political economy," and she introduces her discussion of our place within it with a (melancholy?) remark: "I hope no one in this crowd, at this panel where we are supposed to be considering the relationship between Marxism and feminism . . . will disagree that there is something like a relationship between and among political economy, the nature of a movement, and its sustaining ideological production." She feels she must urge her audience away from an anti-reductionism which is really an anti-marxism that dismisses "economy in the narrow sense" as "merely empirical." When Spivak finally speaks of "Marxist-feminist sociologists, economists, and Third World area specialists," it is not to draw attention to the marxist component of their work, but to urge all of us to approach sociology, economics, and area studies on their "institutional home ground." She speaks here "as a literary critic" and refers to this material as "work in other disciplines"; the fact that it is specifically *marxist* work goes unremarked.

The most important and revealing appearance of marxism in Spivak's text is her analysis of the crisis of Value, the true "cornerstone" of her own inter-disciplinary study. This is the moment of greatest disciplinary transgression, when Spivak "makes like a political economist." It is also the point at which her anxiety about her audience, her language, and the possibility of being understood, is most intense. This analysis is at the heart of Spivak's argument, but she discusses it only very briefly, and she explains the terseness of her discussion in terms of her audience.[14] She cuts short her remarks with the suggestion that "a detailed answer" to the question of how this crisis is managed "would probably be boring and *incomprehensible* for the theoretical people." At the same time, she yields to the "temptation" of incomprehensibility with a "philosophical generalization" that she labels as "equally *incomprehensible* to *both sides*," theorists and empiricists (my emphases). This invocation of the incomprehensible effectively positions Spivak's audience beyond the reach of her language—whether detailed and empirical or philosophical and generalizing—at the very moment when the issues of value and exploitation are articulated in the vocabulary of marxism. This evaluation of her readers motivates her shift in emphasis toward the question of who we are.

The "permissive" moment immediately fades into more "sober" description. But it suggests a reason for Spivak's apparent unwillingness to demand that her audience move beyond interdisciplinary approaches to interpretation: she assumes that "we" cannot follow her into the language of marxism. Interdisciplinary study is a strategic substitute for marxism: if "we" read the work in "other disciplines" and from other parts of the world, we may be weaned from our resistance to "economy in the narrow sense" and acquire at least certain marxist conclusions, all under the sign of disciplinary authority, painlessly and without the difficult task of acquiring the particular politics or the language of marxism.

At this critical juncture, Spivak abandons her passionate concern with the fracture: she introduces a new homogeneity, taking the historically and politically constituted positions of her audience—outside marxism—as givens. Her powerful representation of the women on the other end makes any facile or sentimental "identification" with them unthinkable. But the intensity of her focus on her description of who we are here obscures the possibility of a political gesture that is not rooted in identity, in a coincidence of subject-positions. What is necessarily overlooked is the fact that there are *political* differences even among "us." Just as the condition of women is fractured by the international division of labor, so it is fractured—even in the U.S.—by the political commitments that divide women. Spivak's swerve away from marxism is hardly inexplicable; it is not a language many feminists in the United States have mastered, and the political culture of this country is infamously hostile to any form of anti-capitalist agitation. But her account of the many divisions among us makes it clear that the problems political economy presents to feminism can only be confronted by means of a politics that is more or other than an alibi of sisterhood. Spivak's displacement of this political demand feeds a misconception: that the impossibility of identification across the distances that separate us from the export-processing zones constitutes a political impasse and leaves us only disciplinary avenues for our work. She reserves for the disciplinary an authority not fundamentally disrupted by political questions and thus obscures the possibility of displacements in the arena of politics.

Isn't it necessary that we who are literary critics stop being simply literary critics (or anthropologists or economists) and perhaps even that we stop being simply (or complexly) feminists and become—this is an assumption never *stated* in Spivak's paper—marxists, socialists, active opponents of capitalism, whatever the label or venue we choose? Only defeatism argues that the consensus politics of the U.S. make this flatly impossible. And if we cannot bring ourselves to oppose capital in our local zones, don't we have to admit that insofar as feminism has an international constituency that encompasses the women of the export-processing zones, it also harbors a certain enemy within?

Notes

Introduction: Terms of Reference

1. Stephen Heath, *The Sexual Fix* (New York: Schocken Books, 1982), p. 85.

2. Joan Wallach Scott, *Gender and the Politics of History* (New York: Columbia University Press, 1988), p. 172.

3. Denise Riley, "Does Sex Have a History? 'Women' and Feminism," *New Formations,* 1 (Spring, 1987), 42.

4. Cf. Gayatri Spivak's discussion of the feminist reversal of the public/private (speaking, in fact, from the other side of the reversal): "if the fabric of the so-called public sector is woven of the so-called private, the definition of the private is marked by a public potential, since it *is* the weave, or texture, of public activity. The opposition is thus not merely reversed; it is displaced." *In Other Worlds: Essays in Cultural Politics* (New York and London: Methuen, 1987), p. 103.

5. Wlad Godzich in foreword to Paul de Man, *The Resistance to Theory* (Minneapolis: University of Minnesota Press, 1986), pp. xii–xiii.

6. Naomi Schor, *Reading in Detail: Aesthetics and the Feminine* (New York and London: Methuen, 1987), p. 97.

7. Hazel Carby, "White Women Listen! Black Feminism and the Boundaries of Sisterhood," in Carby, et al., eds., *The Empire Strikes Back: Race and Racism in 70s Britain* (London: Hutchinson, 1982), p. 213.

8. Riley, "Does Sex Have a History?" p. 35.

9. Cf. Gayatri Chakravorty Spivak, "Scattered Speculations on the Questions of Value," *Diacritics,* 15 (Winter, 1985), 90.

10. Spivak, *In Other Worlds,* p. 106.

11. Juliet Mitchell and Jacqueline Rose, eds., *Feminine Sexuality: Jacques Lacan and the école freudienne* (New York: Pantheon Books, 1982), p. 47.

12. Heath, *The Sexual Fix,* p. 85.

13. Teresa de Lauretis, "Strategies of Coherence," in her *Technologies of Gender: Essays on Theory, Film, and Fiction* (Bloomington and Indianapolis: Indiana University Press,

1987), pp. 107–26. In her essay, de Lauretis uses the term in a different but not entirely unrelated context.

14. De Lauretis, "Strategies of Coherence," p. 108. Again, de Lauretis's comment has a very different resonance in the context of her argument.

15. Paula Treichler, "Teaching Feminist Theory," in Cary Nelson, ed., *Theory in the Classroom* (Urbana and Chicago: University of Illinois Press, 1986), p. 76.

16. De Lauretis, *Alice Doesn't: Feminism, Semiotics, Cinema* (Bloomington: Indiana University Press, 1984), p. 186.

17. Mae Henderson, paper delivered at Rockefeller Foundation conference on "Women's Studies Research: Critical Issues Past, Present, and Future," Institute for Advanced Study, June, 1988. Henderson's discussion of Afro-American "testifying" refers to the work of Geneva Smitherman on the subject.

18. Gayatri Chakravorty Spivak, "Can the Subaltern Speak?," in Cary Nelson and Lawrence Grossberg, eds., *Marxism and the Interpretation of Culture* (Urbana and Chicago: University of Illinois Press, 1988), p. 306. Citation from Michel Foucault, *The History of Sexuality*, vol. I, trans. Robert Hurley (New York: Vintage Books, 1980), p. 4.

19. Riley, "Does Sex Have a History?," p. 44.

20. Cf., for example, Jacques Derrida, *Limited, Inc.* (Baltimore: The Johns Hopkins University Press, 1977).

21. I am indebted to Barbara Babcock's discussions of word play and linguistic marking in the Pembroke Seminar, 1987–88.

22. Comments made at Rockefeller Foundation conference, June, 1988.

Chapter 1 Changing the Subject

With the exception of the introductory remarks, which I read in slightly different form at Milwaukee, the material that appears in italics was written after the events of the paper as discursive endnotes; not so much as side issues, as asides pointing to the limits of the essay's rhetorical space. Its place here in dialogic relation to the main body of the text is the result of an experiment brought about by the always imaginative critical judgment of the editor of the volume in which it first appeared, *Feminist Studies/Critical Studies*, Teresa de Lauretis. Once I saw it in print, I decided to reproduce it here in that form, with a few editorial changes of my own.

1. The fox-trot is defined in Webster's Third as "a ballroom dance in duple time that includes slow walking steps, quick running steps, and two-steps." What appeals to me here is the change of pace, the doubleness of moves within the shape of the dance, and the collaborative requirement. The latter will reemerge at the end of this paper, but really runs through the argument: the deadendedness of the one-way street that bears the traffic (to mix a few metaphors) between feminist and dominant critics.

    This figuration of the problem bears a certain resemblance to my discussion of shoes and tropes in "The Text's Heroine." My current position has been reformulated for me by Biddy Martin, who said at the Milwaukee conference that indeterminacy (what I am thematizing here as the denegation and denigration of identity) is no excuse for not acting; that we must find a way to ground indeterminacy so that we can make political interventions. The question before us then becomes how to locate and allow for particularities within the collective.

2. Barthes's essay should be situated within the discussion of changing definitions of art in conjunction with the laws governing authorship in France, in particular a 1957 law which attempted to account for new kinds of artistic and authorial production not covered by the copyright law (droits d'auteur) of 1793. I am indebted to Molly Nesbit's "What is an Author," for an illuminating explanation of this material. Nesbit points out that the death of the author for Barthes seems to have meant "really the imprinting author of 1793"; she also describes the original occasion for the essay: "in 1967 in America for Aspen magazine, nos. 5 + 6 . . . dedicated to Stéphane Mallarmé." It is boxed (literally) along with all kinds of "authorial work, much of it technologically based" (241–43). See also "Le Droit d'auteur s'adapte à la nouvelle économie de la création," in Le Monde, August 3, 1985. These are pieces of a more contextual history of criticism.

3. At the Cerisy colloquium of which he was the "prétexte," this phrase drew a certain amount of attention. In his comments on the meaning of the phrase Barthes situated his own relation to the historical context of writing Sade, Fourier, Loyola: "It was the heyday of modernity and the text; we talked about the death of the author (I talked about it myself). We didn't use the word writer [écrivain]: writers were slightly ridiculous people like Gide, Claudel, Valéry, Malraux" (412–13).

4. In "Women's Time, Women's Space: Writing the History of Feminist Criticism," Showalter adopts Julia Kristeva's "genealogy" of subjectivity; of a space of generation which is both "European and trans-European" (15). In writing the history of American feminist criticism, she wants "to emphasize its specificity by narrating its development in terms of the internal relationship, continuities, friendships, and institutions that shaped the thinking and writing of the last fifteen years" (30). As examples of asymmetrical events in these non-parallel chronologies, Showalter contrasts the 1966 conference on "the Structuralist Controversy and the Sciences of Man" (Johns Hopkins University) with "the first feminist literary session at the Chicago MLA in 1970" (32), neither of which I attended. In 1971 I was reading Roland Barthes, not Adrienne Rich. The discovery of Rich, for me a belated one, comes from being involved with a Women's Studies Program; this trajectory, I think, figures an inverse relation to the reading habits of much mainstream American feminist criticism, while remaining outside the classical reading patterns of women in French; which may or may not explain the feeling people have had that I am mixing things— Barthes and Rich—that somehow don't belong together. What is worrisome to me is the way in which conferences in literary studies continue to follow their separate paths: though women are invited to English Institute (for which Showalter wrote this essay), Georgetown, etc., and men to Pembroke and Milwaukee, there is no evidence yet that feminist critical theory has affected dominant organizations and theorizations.

5. The stories of readers and writers emerge in both Rich and Barthes from a gendered

poetics of sexual difference and family romances. For Barthes, like Rich, the Author is male, and in his effects, patriarchal: "As an institution, the author is dead: . . . dispossessed, his [identity] no longer exerts the formidable paternity over his work that literary history, teaching, opinion had the responsibility of establishing . . . but in the text, in a certain way *I desire the author:* I need his figure (which is neither his representation, nor his projection)" (45–46). In Barthes's model of desire the reader and the writer participate in a system of associations that poses the masculine experience as central and universal. This "I" who desires the author, and desires to be desired by him, who worries about the return of the father (having banished him), who takes his pleasure in a fragmented subjectivity, desires, worries, enjoys within an economy as (he of course says it himself) a son. The failure to differentiate (the question, for example, of the daughter's desire) becomes more than a matter of philosophy, or style when allied with the authority—of the intellectual, writer, teacher—that supports the concept of indifference in the first place. On the politics of indifference, see Naomi Schor's "Dreaming Dissymmetry: Barthes, Foucault, and Sexual Difference," in this volume.

6. This move corresponds to Gayatri Spivak's insistence on "a simultaneous other focus: not merely who am I? but who is the other woman? How am I naming her? How does she name me?" "French Feminism in an International Frame," 179. On the "other woman," see also Jane Gallop's "Annie Leclerc Writing a Letter, with Vermeer."

7. Smith wrote in her 1977 essay, "Toward a Black Feminist Criticism," from which she read at the Milwaukee conference: "I finally want to express how much easier both my waking and sleeping hours would be if there were one book in existence that would tell me something specific about my life. One book based in Black feminist and Black lesbian experience, fiction or nonfiction. Just one work to reflect the reality that I and the Black women who I love are trying to create. When such a book exists then each of us will not only know better how to live, but how to dream" (184). For O'Neale's position, see her "Inhibiting Midwives, Usurping Creators: The Struggling Emergence of Black Women in American Fiction."

    In the *New York Times Book Review,* June 2, 1985, Gloria Naylor, in a survey of writers' favorite opening passages, comments on the beginning of Toni Morrison's *The Bluest Eye.* Naylor writes: "While the novel handles a weighty subject—the demoralization of black female beauty in a racist society [this was also the subject of O'Neale's paper]—it *whispers* in the mode of minimalist poetry, thus resulting in the least common denominator for all classics: the ability to haunt. It alerts my students to the fact that fiction should be about storytelling, the 'why' of things is best left to the sociologists, the 'how' is more than enough for writers to tackle . . ." (52). It seems to me that we are in desperate need of a specifically text-based discussion between black and white feminist critics and writers on the relations between the why and the how, between reference and representation. Without it we run the risk of a devastating repolarization of the sort that at times during the Milwaukee conference resulted in bitter asides and accusations of racism.

8. At the Milwaukee conference Jane Gallop asked about the implicit risk one runs that irony can misfire. In *A Handlist of Rhetorical Terms* Richard Lanham describes

this problem under the rubric of "rhetorical irony" (61). He points out that the "relationship of persuader and persuaded is almost always self-conscious to some degree," and goes on to make the claim that "every rhetorical posture except the most naive involves an ironical coloration, of some kind or another of the speaker's *Ethos.*" To the extent that the ethos (character, disposition) of feminism historically has refused the doubleness of "saying one thing while it tries to do another" (the mark of classical femininity one might argue), it may be that an ironic feminist discourse finds itself at odds both with itself (its identity to itself), and with the expectations its audience has of its position. If this is true, then irony, in the final analysis, may be a figure of limited effectiveness. On the other hand, since non-ironic, single, sincere, hortatory feminism is becoming ineffectual, it may be worth the risk of trying out this kind of duplicity on the road.

In "A Manifesto for Cyborgs," in this volume, Donna Haraway, calling for a greater use of irony "within socialist feminism," argues: "Irony is about contradictions that do not resolve into larger wholes, even dialectically, about the tension of holding incompatible things together because both or all are necessary and true."

9. The task of "dephallicizing the father," as Gallop puts it in *The Daughter's Seduction,* to succeed must break out of the limits of the family circle (xv).

10. If Lucy in the classroom writes her way out of humiliation and into agency, on stage the use of language becomes a question of voice. The difficulty, Lucy discovers, once she begins to speak, lies not in the audience but in her performance: "When my tongue got free, and my voice took its true pitch, and found its natural tone, I thought of nothing but the personage I represented" (210). In both instances, Lucy's performative subjectivity is structured through a text and in another language. I have a more sustained analysis of this phenomenon in the chapters on *Corinne* and *The Vagabond.*

11. In "A Man's Place," a talk she gave at the 1984 MLA session on "Men in Feminism," which has been published in the volume *Men in Feminism,* Elizabeth Weed brilliantly outlined many of the issues with which I struggle here.

Works Cited in "Changing the Subject"

Auerbach, Nina. "Why Communities of Women Aren't Enough." In *Feminist Issues in Literary Scholarship.* Ed. Shari Benstock, Bloomington: Indiana UP, 1987.

Barthes, Roland. *Sade, Fourier, Loyola.* Paris: Seuil, 1971.

————. *Sade-Fourier-Loyola.* Trans. Richard Miller. New York: Hill and Wang. 1976.

————. *Le Plaisir du texte.* Paris: Seuil, 1973.

————. *Roland Barthes par Roland Barthes.* Paris: Ecrivains de Toujours, Seuil, 1975.

————. *Prétexte: Roland Barthes, Colloque de Cerisy.* Paris: UGE, 10/18, 1978.

————. "The Death of the Author." in *Image-Music-Text.* Trans. Stephen Heath. New York: Hill and Wang, 1977.

Braidotti, Rosi. "Patterns of Dissonance: Women and/in Philosophy." unpublished ms.

Brontë, Charlotte. *Villette.* 1853. rpt. New York: Penguin, 1983.

Cixous, Hélène. "The Laugh of the Medusa." *Signs: Journal of Women in Culture and Society* 1,4 (Summer, 1976), 875–94.

Culler, Jonathan. *On Deconstruction.* Ithaca: Cornell UP, 1982.

De Lauretis, Teresa. *Alice Doesn't: Feminism, Semiotics, Cinema.* Bloomington: Indiana UP, 1984.

Foucault, Michel. "What is an Author?" In *Language, Counter-Memory, Practice: Selected Essays and Interviews by Michel Foucault.* Ed. Donald F. Bouchard. Ithaca: Cornell UP, 1980.

Gallop, Jane. *The Daughter's Seduction.* Ithaca: Cornell UP, 1982.

Haraway, Donna. "A Manifesto for Cyborgs: Science, Technology, and Socialist Feminism in the 1980s." *Socialist Review* 15, 2 (March–April 1985), 65–107.

Huyssen, Andreas. "Mapping the Postmodern." *New German Critique* 33 (Fall, 1984), 5–52.

Kristeva, Julia. "Women's Time." *Signs: Journal of Women in Culture and Society* 7,1 (Autumn 1981), 13–35.

Lanham, Richard A. *A Handlist of Rhetorical Terms.* Berkeley and Los Angeles: California UP, 1969.

Marcus, Jane. "Still Practice, A/Wrested Alphabet: Toward a Feminist Aesthetic." In *Feminist Issues in Literary Scholarship.* Ed. Shari Benstock. Bloomington: Indiana University Press, 1987.

Miller, Nancy K. "The Text's Heroine: A Feminist Critic and her Fictions." *Diacritics* 12,2 (Summer 1982), 48–53.

Mitchell, Juliet. "Femininity, Narrative and Psychoanalysis." *Women: The Longest Revolution.* New York, Pantheon, 1984.

Naylor, Gloria. "Famous First Words." *The New York Times Book Review.* June 2, 1985.

Nesbit, Molly. "What Was An Author?" *Yale French Studies* 73 (1987), 229–57. Special issue on "Everyday Life." Ed. Alice Kaplan and Kristin Ross.

Rich, Adrienne. "When We Dead Awaken: Writing as Re-Vision (1971)"; "Toward a Woman-Centered University (1973–74)." *On Lies, Secrets and Silence: Selected Prose, 1966–1978.* New York: Norton, 1979.

———. "Blood, Bread, and Poetry: The Location of the Poet." *Blood Bread and Poetry.* New York: Norton, 1986.

Schor, Naomi. *Breaking the Chain: Women, Theory, and French Realist Fiction.* New York: Columbia University Press, 1985.

Showalter, Elaine. "Women's Time, Women's Space: Writing the History of Feminist Criticism." In *Feminist Issues in Literary Scholarship.* Ed. Shari Benstock. Bloomington: Indiana University Press, 1987.

———. "Women Who Write Are Women." *The New York Times Book Review.* December 16, 1984.

Smith, Barbara. "Toward a Black Feminist Criticism." rpt. in *The New Feminist Criticism: Essays on Women, Literature, Theory*. Ed. Elaine Showalter. New York: Pantheon, 1985.

Spivak, Gayatri. "The Politics of Interpretations." *Critical Inquiry* 9,1 (September 1982), 259–78.

————. "French Feminism in an International Frame." *Yale French Studies* 62 (1981), 154–84.

Weed, Elizabeth. "A· Man's Place." In *Men In Feminism*. Ed. Alice Jardine and Paul Smith. New York: Methuen, 1987.

Chapter 2   Julia Kristeva: Take Two

1. Julia Kristeva, "Ellipse sur la frayeur et la séduction spéculaire," *Communications*, special issue *Psychanalyse et Cinéma*, 23 (1975), p. 77, (my italics) (tr. Dolores Burdick, "Ellipsis on Terror and The Specular Seduction," *Wide Angle*, 3:2 [1979]). This essay was written in part as a response to Ann Rosalind Jones, "Julia Kristeva on Femininity: The Limits of a Semiotic Politics," *Feminist Review* 15 (Winter 1984).

2. Sigmund Freud, *Group Psychology and the Analysis of the Ego*, (1921) *The Standard Edition of the Complete Psychological Works* (London: Hogarth), 18, pp. 111–116; PF 12, pp. 141–147.

3. Julia Kristeva, *Histoires d'amour*, Collection "Infini" (Paris: Denoël, 1983).

4. Kristeva, "Stabat Mater" in *Histoires d'amour*, p. 237; this chapter first appeared as "Héréthique d'amour," *Tel Quel* 77 (Winter 1974) (tr. in *The Kristeva Reader*, ed. Toril Moi [New York: Columbia University Press, 1986]).

5. Julia Kristeva, "Mémoires," *Infini* 1 (1983), p. 44.

6. Julia Kristeva, *La révolution du langage poétique*, Collection Tel Quel (Paris: Seuil, 1974), p. 130.

7. Julia Kristeva, *Desire in Language*, ed. Leon S. Roudiez, tr. Thomas Gora, Alice Jardine and L. Roudiez (London: Oxford University Press, 1984), preface, p.x.

8. Julia Kristeva, *Semioteke, Recherches pour une sémanalyse*, Collection Tel Quel (Paris: Seuil, 1969).

9. Julia Kristeva, *Pouvoirs de l'horreur: essai sur l'abjection*, Collection Tel Quel (Paris: Seuil, 1980) (tr. Leon Roudiez, *Powers of Horror* [New York: Columbia University Press, 1982]).

10. Kristeva, "Mémoires," pp. 45, 53.

11. Elisabeth Roudinesco, "Histoire de la psychanalyse en France," *Infini* 2 (1983), p. 66.

12. Kristeva, *La révolution du langage poétique*, p. 477.

13. Roman Jakobson, "Why Mama and Papa?" (1959), *Studies on Child Language and Aphasia* (Hague: Mouton, 1971).

14. Cit. in Kristeva, *La révolution du langage poétique*, p. 29.

15. Kristeva, *La révolution du langage poétique*, p. 270.

16. See, for example, Terry Eagleton, *Literary Theory* (Oxford: Basil Blackwell), pp. 190–191.

17. First manifesto of the Cubo-futurists issued in 1912 and signed by Mayakovsky, Burlyuk, Khlebnikov, and Kruchyonykh.

18. Julia Kristeva, "Un nouveau type d'intellectuel: le dissident," *Tel Quel* 74 (Winter 1977), p. 4 (tr. "A New Type of Intellectual: the Dissident" in *The Kristeva Reader*).

19. Kristeva, *La révolution du langage poétique,* p. 169.

20. Kristeva, *La révolution du langage poétique,* p. 616.

21. Jones, "Julia Kristeva on Feminity," p. 68.

22. Kristeva, *La révolution du langage poétique,* p. 148.

23. Kristeva, *La révolution du langage poétique,* p. 493; and her "Sujet dans le langage et pratique politique," *Tel Quel* 58 (Summer 1974), p. 27.

24. Kristeva, *La révolution du langage poétique,* pp. 386–387.

25. Sigmund Freud, "Negation" (1925), *Standard Edition* 19; PF 11.

26. Jones, "Julia Kristeva on Feminity," p. 61.

27. One of the clearest examples of this tendency is the article by Peter Dews, "The *Nouvelle Philosophie* and Foucault," *Economy and Society* 8:2 (May 1979).

28. Kristeva, *La révolution du langage poétique,* p. 80.

29. Julia Kristeva, "La littérature dissidente comme réfutation du discours de gauche," *Tel Quel* 76 (Summer 1978); and her "*Histoires d'amour*—Love Stories," in *Desire,* ed. Lisa Appignanesi, (London: Institute of Contemporary Arts Documents, 1983).

30. Sheila Rowbotham, Lynn Segal, and Hilary Wainwright, *Beyond the Fragments: Feminism and the Making of Socialism* (London: Merlin, 1979).

31. Julia Kristeva, "Le temps des femmes," 34/44: *Cahiers de recherche de science des textes et documents 5* (Winter 1979) (tr. Alice Jardine and Harry Blake, "Women's Time," in N.O. Keohane et al., *Feminist Theory: A Critique of Ideology* [Chicago: University of Chicago Press, 1981; Brighton: Harvester, 1982]; also in *The Kristeva Reader*).

32. James Joyce, cit. in Kristeva, *La révolution du langage poétique,* p. 504.

33. André Green, *Le discours vivant: le concept psychanalytique de l'affect* (Paris: Presses Universitaires de France, 1973).

34. Julia Kristeva, "Il n'y a pas de maître à langage," *Nouvelle Revue de Psychanalyse, Regards sur la psychanalyse en France,* 20 (Autumn 1979), pp. 130–131.

35. Julia Kristeva, with Philippe Sollers and Marcelin Pleynet, "Pourquoi les Etats Unis?," *Tel Quel* 71–73 (Autumn 1977), pp. 4, 19 (tr. "The US Now: A Conversation," *October* 6 [Fall 1978]; also in *The Kristeva Reader*).

36. Juliet Mitchell, "Introduction I," *Feminine Sexuality: Jacques Lacan and the "école freudienne,"* ed. Mitchell and Jacqueline Rose (London: Macmillan/New York: Pantheon, 1983).

37. Sigmund Freud, *Totem and Taboo* (1913), *Standard Edition* 13; PF 12.

38. Sigmund Freud, *Moses and Monotheism* (1938–39), *Standard Edition* 23, p. 118; PF 13, p. 365 (cit. in Kristeva *La révolution du langage poétique*, p. 445n).

39. Kristeva, *La révolution du langage poétique*, pp. 24–25, p. 579n.

40. Francis MacDonald Cornford, tr., *Plato's Cosmology, The Timaeus*, (London: Kegan Paul, Trench and Trubner/New York: Harcourt Brace, 1937), p. 187.

41. Stéphane Mallarmé, "Lettre à Cazalis," *Correspondance*, 1, (Paris: Gallimard, 1953–84), p. 77; cit. in Kristeva, *La révolution du langage poétique*, p. 453.

42. Kristeva, *Powers of Horror*.

43. Kristeva, *La révolution du langage poétique*, p. 545.

44. Kristeva, *La révolution du langage poétique*, pp. 468, 474.

45. Kristeva, *Powers of Horror*, pp. 158, 91, 100, 106 (translations modified).

46. Kristeva, *Powers of Horror*, p. 106.

47. Jennifer Stone, "The Horrors of Power: A Critique of Julia Kristeva," *The Politics of Theory*, Proceedings of the Essex Conference in the Sociology of Literature, July 1982 (Colchester: University of Essex, 1983); Peter Gidal, "On Julia Kristeva," *Undercut* (Journal of the London Filmmakers Cooperative) 12, (1984).

48. Kristeva, *Desire in Language*, preface, p. x.

49. Julia Kristeva, "D'une identité, l'autre," *Tel Quel* 62 (Summer 1975) (tr. "From One Identity to Another," *Desire in Language*).

50. Kristeva, *Histoires d'amour*, p. 242.

51. Juliet Mitchell, *Psychoanalysis and Feminism* (London: Allen Lane, 1974).

52. Kristeva, "Sujet dans le langage et pratique politique," p. 26; "La femme, ce n'est jamais ça," *Tel Quel* 59 (Autumn 1974), p. 24 (tr. Marilyn August, "Woman Can Never Be Defined," *New French Feminisms*, ed. Elaine Marks and Isabelle de Courtivron, [Brighton: Harvester, 1981] p. 141); *Powers of Horror*, p. 208.

53. Julia Kristeva, "Polylogue," *Tel Quel* 57 (Spring 1974); tr. in *Desire in Language*, p. 164, as "experience."

54. Kristeva, "Woman Can Never Be Defined."

55. Kristeva, "Woman Can Never Be Defined," p. 138 (tr. modified).

56. Jones, "Julia Kristeva on Femininity," p. 62.

57. Kristeva, *La révolution du langage poétique*, p. 102.

58. Kristeva, *Histoires d'amour*, p. 81.

59. Kristeva, *Histoires d'amour*, p. 349.

60. Kristeva, *Histoires d'amour*, pp. 242–244.

61. William Shakespeare, *Hamlet*, IV, iii, 26.

62. Kristeva, *Histoires d'amour*, p. 121.

63. Sigmund Freud, *The Ego and the Id*, (1923), *Standard Edition* 19, pp. 31–32; pp. 370–371; and *Group Psychology and the Analysis of the Ego*, (1921), *Standard Edition* 18, p. 105; pp. 134–135; Kristeva, *Histoires d'amour*, pp. 31–32.

64. Louise Burchill, "The Last Word of this Adventure: Interview with Julia Kristeva," *On the Beach* (1984), p. 26.

65. Maud Mannoni, *L'enfant, sa "maladie" et les autres,* Collection "le champ freudien" (Paris: Seuil, 1967) (tr. *The Child, its "Illness" and the Others* [London: Tavistock, 1970]).

66. Kristeva, *La révolution du langage poétique,* p. 452.

67. Rosalind Coward, *Patriarchal Precedents* (London: Routledge and Kegan Paul, 1982).

68. Kristeva, *Histoires d'amour,* p. 69.

69. Kristeva, *Powers of Horror,* p. 38 (tr. modified).

70. Kristeva, "Woman Can Never Be Defined," p. 139.

71. Kristeva, *Histoires d'amour,* p. 354.

72. Kristeva, *Histoires d'amour,* pp. 168, 348; *"Histoires d'amour*—Love Stories," p. 21.

73. Kristeva, "Mémoires," pp. 46–47.

Chapter 3 Commentary: Postponing Politics

1. Michel Foucault, *Power/Knowledge: Selected Interviews and Other Writings, 1972–77,* ed. Colin Gordon (New York: Pantheon, 1980) p. 117.

2. See Brian Street, *Literacy in Theory and Practice* (Cambridge: Cambridge University Press, 1984); and John Guillory, "Canonical and Non-canonical: A Critique of the Current Debate," *ELH* (Fall 1987): 483–527.

3. See Ariel Dorfman, *The Empire's Old Clothes,* trans. Clark Hanson (New York: Pantheon, 1983); and Ariel Dorfman and Armand Mattelart, *How to Read Donald Duck: Imperialist Ideology in the Disney Comic,* trans. David Kunzle (International General, 1984).

4. Julia Kristeva, "Interview" in *New French Feminisms,* ed. Elaine Marks and Isabelle de Courtivron (New York: Schocken, 1981), p. 137.

5. See Louis Althusser's "Ideology and ideological state apparatuses," in *Lenin and Philosophy and Other Essays* (London: New Left Books, 1971); and Annette Kuhn and AnnMarie Wolpe, eds., *Feminism and Materialism: Women and Modes of Production* (London: Routledge and Kegan Paul, 1978).

Chapter 4 Dreaming Dissymmetry: Barthes, Foucault, and Sexual Difference

1. Ann Snitow, Christine Stansell, and Sharon Thompson, eds., *Powers of Desire: The Politics of Sexuality* (New York: Monthly Review Press, 1983), p. 9.

2. Snitow et al., *Powers of Desire,* p. 10.

3. Snitow et al., *Powers of Desire.* As valuable as this point is, in her article, "Feminism, Criticism, and Foucault," *New German Critique* (Fall 1982), 27: 3–30, Biddy Martin reminds us that, "Foucault's deconstructive methodology provides an immanent critique of such a search for *the* authentic female voice or *the* sexuality, a warning against the commitment to any confessional mode as necessarily liberating, and a

challenge to the notion that simply speaking or writing frees us in any simple way from patriarchy or phallocentrism" (p. 15).

4. Roland Barthes, *Roland Barthes by Roland Barthes*, trans. Richard Howard (New York: Hill & Wang, 1977), p. 74.

5. I am thinking of Claudine Hermann who in her book, *Les voleuses de langue* (Paris: des femmes, 1976) catches out Barthes's subtle reinscription of cultural stereotypes of femininity; see pp. 16–18.

6. On the question of the relationship between feminist jouissance and Barthes, see Jane Gallop, "Beyond the *jouissance* principle," *Representations* (1984), 7: 110–115.

7. Stephen Heath, "Barthes on Love," *Sub-Stance* (1983), 37/38: 105. Not all readers of *A Lover's Discourse* share Heath's view that that discourse operates in a sexual limbo. Writing in *Christopher Street*, Richard Sennett assets: "I do not wish to leave you with the impression that *A Lover's Discourse* is a neutered book. It is clearly about love between men" (p. 27).

8. Jane Gallop, "Feminist Criticism and the Pleasure of the Text," *North Dakota Quarterly*, forthcoming.

9. John Sturrock, "Roland Barthes" in John Sturrock, ed., *Structuralism and Since: From Lévi-Strauss to Derrida* (Oxford: Oxford University Press, 1979), p. 73. See also p. 53 where Sturrock traces Barthes's life-long crusade against essentialism to the origins of his thought in Sartrean existentialism, which may indeed be the original modern French philosophical discourse of indifference.

10. Sarrasine's misprision relies on a triad of "enthymemes" or "imperfect syllogisms," what Barthes calls "the three proofs": narcissistic, psychological, aesthetic. Example: "all women are timid; La Zambinella is timid; therefore La Zambinella is a woman." Roland Barthes, *S/Z*, trans. Richard Miller (New York: Hill & Wang, 1974), p. 148.

11. Stephen Heath, *Vertige du déplacement* (Paris: Fayard, 1974), p. 20. All translations mine except where otherwise noted.

12. *S/Z*, p. 36. Cf. the almost identical analysis Barthes offers of the dramatis personae in *Sur Racine:* "The division of the Racinian world into strong and weak, into tyrants and captives, covers in a sense the division of the sexes: it is their situation in the relation of force that orchestrates [verse] some characters as virile and others as feminine, without concern for their biological sexes ... Here we find a first sketch of Racinian fatality: a simple relation, in origin purely circumstantial (captivity or tyranny), is converted into a biological datum; situation is converted into sex, chance into essence." From *On Racine* trans. Richard Howard, in *A Barthes Reader*, Susan Sontag, ed. (New York: Hill & Wang, 1982), p. 180. Here sexual difference is subordinated to positionality within a power structure; sexual difference is not primary, not a given, it is the consequence of the position a subject occupies in a configuration of power. Masculinity does not guarantee power, it is the possession of power that produces masculinity. Femininity, by the same token, is the sex of the powerless, irrespective of their biological sex.

13. Kaja Silverman, *The Subject of Semiotics* (New York: Oxford University Press, 1983), p. 272.

14. In her brilliant reading of Barthes's reading of Balzac's *Sarrasine,* Barbara Johnson has shown how by fetishizing castration, Barthes, unlike Balzac, reduces the tale to a mere "reversal" of the readerly/writerly paradigm, failing to account for Balzac's more radical deconstruction of the difference within the readerly: ". . . Balzac's text does not operate a simple *reversal* of the readerly hierarchy: Balzac does not proclaim castration as the truth behind the readerly's blindness in as unequivocal à way as Barthes' own unequivocality would lead us to believe," "The Critical Difference," *Diacritics* (June 1978), p. 8.

15. Roland Barthes, "Masculin, Féminin, Neutre," in *Echanges et Communications: Melanges offerts à Claude Lévi-Strauss à l'occasion de son 60ème anniversaire,* Jean Pouillon and Pierre Maranda, eds.; 2 vols. (The Hague: Mouton, 1970), 2: 899.

16. In his *De Rerum Naturae,* Lucretius writes: "While the first bodies are being carried downwards by their own weight in a straight line through the void, at times quite uncertain and uncertain places [sic], they swerve a little from their course, just so much as you might call a change of motion. For if they were not apt to incline, all would fall downwards like raindrops through the profound void, no collision would take place and no blow would be caused among the first-beginnings: thus nature would never have produced anything," tr. W.H.D. Rouse, Loeb Classical Library (Cambridge: Harvard University Press, 1975), p. 113, as quoted by Joan de Jean in her article, "*La Nouvelle Héloïse,* or the Case for Pedagogical Deviation," *Yale French Studies* (1982), 63: 98–116. Bloom's appropriation of the term in *The Anxiety of Influence* (New York: Oxford University Press, 1973) is typical of its recent usage: for him it is synonymous with "misprision," the felicitous misreading by a poet of his strong predecessor. Cf. Shoshana Felman, "De la nature des choses ou de l'écart à l'équilibre," *Critique* (January 1979), 380: 3–15.

17. Roland Barthes, *The Fashion System,* trans. Matthew Ward and Richard Howard (New York: Hill & Wang, 1983), p. ix.

18. Michel Foucault, *Power/Knowledge: Selected Interviews and Other Writings 1972–1977,* Colin Gordon, ed., Colin Gordon, et al., trs. (New York: Pantheon Books, 1980), pp. 219–220. Foucault goes on to contrast the desexualization of the women's movement with the fixation on sexuality in the gay rights movement.

19. Michel Foucault, *Herculine Barbin,* trans. Richard McDougall (New York: Pantheon Books, 1980), p. xiii.

20. But is this the only possible way to read Herculine's story? Herculine, Foucault notes, did not write her memoirs as a man because she never adjusted to her belated masculine identity. Rather like a wild child who cannot acquire human speech, Herculine-Abel could not learn to speak as a man, because, of course, masculinity is not just an anatomical fact, it is also the product of socialization. Nevertheless there are places in the memoirs where the narrator grapples with his dilemma by focusing on the signs of his difference from his fellow students and in so doing Herculine-Abel reinscribes one of the most stereotypical cultural differences between the sexes. He writes of his early school days:

    My progress was rapid, and more than once it aroused the astonishment of my excellent teachers.

It was not the same for handicrafts, for which I showed the deepest aversion and greatest incapacity.

The times my companions employed in making those little masterpieces intended to decorate a drawing room or dress up a younger brother, I myself spent reading. History, ancient and modern, was my favorite passion. (p. 8)

According to the dominant cultural code, women are naturally drawn to that lower order of the arts, handicrafts; patience, meticulous attention to details are some of woman's most time-honored virtues. The product of women's artistic endeavors are destined to brightening up the home and pleasing the family. To men belongs the world of public adventure and bold actions, even if only in the realm of phantasy. In short what I am suggesting is that despite her sexual indeterminacy Herculine Barbin was what we would call an essentialist.

21. Michel Foucault, *The Use of Pleasure,* trans. Robert Hurley (New York: Pantheon Books, 1985), pp. 5–6.

22. Michel Foucault, *Le souci de soi* (Paris: Gallimard, 1984), p. 175. Translations mine.

23. Myra Jehlen, "Against Human Wholeness: A Suggestion for a Feminist Epistemology," unpublished paper presented to the Columbia University Seminar on Women and Society.

24. The references here are to: Luce Irigaray, *Ce Sexe qui n'en est pas un* (Paris: Minuit, 1977), pp. 73–74; Annette Kolodny, "Dancing through the Minefields: Some Observations on the Theory, Practice, and Politics of a Feminist Literary Criticism," *Feminist Studies* (Spring 1980), 6: 1–25; Laura Mulvey, "Visual Pleasure and Narrative Cinema," *Screen* (Autumn 1975), 6: 6–18; Mary Ann Doane, "Film and Masquerade: Theorising the Female Spectator," *Screen* (September/October 1982), 23: 74–87; Teresa de Lauretis, *Alice Doesn't: Feminism, Semiotics, Cinema* (Bloomington: Indiana University Press, 1984), especially pp. 142–144; Sandra Gilbert and Susan Gubar, *The Madwoman in the Attic* (New Haven: Yale University Press, 1979), pp. 73 passim (interestingly palimpsest is indexed under duplicity); Sarah Kofman, *The Enigma of Woman: Woman in Freud's Writings,* trans. Catherine Porter (Ithaca: Cornell University Press, 1985); Elisabeth Berg, "The Third Woman," *Diacritics* (Summer 1982), 12: 11–20; Naomi Schor, "Female Fetishism: The Case of George Sand," *Poetics Today* (1985), 6: 301–310, and "Reading Double: Sand's Difference," *The Poetics of Gender,* Nancy K. Miller, ed. (New York: Columbia University Press, 1986); Jane Gallop, "Annie Leclerc Writing a Letter, with Vermeer," *October* (1985), 33: 103–118, rpt. in *The Poetics of Gender*; Biddy Martin, "Feminism, Criticism, and Foucault," *New German Critique* (Fall 1982), 27: 13.

25. Simone de Beauvoir, *The Second Sex,* trans. H. M. Parshley (New York: Knopf, 1971).

26. Hélène Cixous, "Sorties," trans. Ann Liddle in *New French Feminisms,* Elaine Marks and Isabelle de Courtivron, eds. (Amherst: The University of Massachusetts Press, 1980), p. 97.

Chapter 5   Is there a Lesbian in this Text? Derrida, Wittig, and the Politics of the Three Women

1. The texts I will be addressing will be, for the most part, the following: Elizabeth Berg, "The Third Woman," *Diacritics* 12 (1982); Jacques Derrida's "Choreographies,"

Diacritics 12 (1982); *Positions* (Chicago: University of Chicago Press, 1981) [in French, *Positions* (Paris: Les Editions de Minuit, 1972)]; *Spurs: Nietzsche's Styles / Eperons: Les styles de Nietzsche,* trans. Barbara Harlow (Chicago: University of Chicago Press, 1979); and Monique Wittig's *Le corps lesbien,* (Paris: Les Editions de Minuit, 1973) [in English, trans. David Le Vay (New York: William Morrow, 1975)]. Both page references for the French and English will be given in the case of *Spurs / Eperons.* I will cite other works as I refer to them in the course of the argument. Except in the case of Wittig, I use translations, providing the original texts in French (usually in endnotes) when it becomes necessary. As for *Le corps lesbien,* I will use the Minuit edition not only because the English translation has been heavily criticized, but because the format of the text changes so drastically from edition to edition. Where space allows, I have provided selections from Le Vay's translation. Wittig's introduction, however, appears only in the English editions. For an excellent review of Le Vay's translation of *Le corps lesbien,* see Namascar Shaktini's doctoral dissertation written at the University of California, Santa Cruz: "The Problem of Gender and Subjectivity Posed by the New Subject Pronoun j/e in the Writing of Monique Wittig," DIA (1983).

For her intellectual and emotional support (and proofreading to boot), I would like to thank Cathy Richardson; for their excellent editorial help, I am very grateful to Jonathan Goldberg, Adela Pinch, Jennifer Resnick, Ellen Rooney, Naomi Schor, and Mark Seltzer.

2. Berg's essay and McDonald's interviews appear together in a special issue of *Diacritics* dedicated to feminist theory and review articles of feminist work, and thus occupy a special position in the contemporary discourse of theory, feminism, and politics. Berg's essay is a review of Sarah Kofman's *L'énigme de la femme: la femme dans les textes de Freud* and Luce Irigaray's *Speculum: de l'autre femme* and *Amante marine: de Friedrich Nietzsche.* In the context of her critique of Kofman's and Irigaray's work, Berg culls the trope of the three women from the feminist essays she reads, traces the figures' intertextual relationships through writings by Freud, embellishes their distinctions, and relates them to Derrida's three women. An interesting question, although too lengthy and tangential for me to address here, would be the canonizing effect of Berg's and the other review articles contained in this volume; particularly because Berg's own text repeats the tripartite division she sees in the texts she reads. I will address this point later in this essay, but for now let me point out that Berg's essay is not only *about* the trope of the three women, but is *itself* a three-way interaction among the author, Kofman, and Irigaray. Significantly, Irigaray— the proponent of the second woman as far as Berg is concerned—shares the fate of the second woman in Berg's reading of Derrida; Berg finds her wanting in comparison to Kofman, and casts her out of the emerging canon of feminist-deconstructive writings.

3. Already I begin my admittedly "literal" and irreverent reading of the tortuous but fascinating relationship between Derrida's writings and feminist discourse. To assume that political deconstruction is possible is to ignore that deconstruction sees itself in the last instance as a *critique* of politics, and a disruption of the structures of "the political" in general. To be absolutely accurate, the only "deconstructive" text I address which is self-consciously political is Berg's—it is her project, after all, to cull a feminist political position from Derridean writings. But nevertheless my reading,

and all the texts that I read here, are characterized by the belief that deconstruction can have specific political effects in particular situations, even if deconstruction itself has no political agenda, or rather challenges all political agendas. I should also note that, like Berg, I emphasize the intertextuality of the three women to the extent that I am forced unavoidably to elide some crucial distinctions among the writings I address in this essay; I am aware that the differences among Berg's, Derrida's (which are really Nietzsche's), and Freud's three women are multiple and interesting. My only justification is that my project is to follow through with, and to criticize the often heterocentric assumptions made by these texts (particularly Berg's), and to that extent I am condemned to make—this time intentionally—the same mistakes.

4. Derrida, *Spurs,* pp. 38,39. Here I take liberties with the concept of bisexuality. For Berg, the term points to a particular type of subjectivity; the third woman embodies what Kofman sees as the deconstructive aspect of Freud's notion of femininity: her unconscious bisexuality. Yet in the other texts I read, the concept is much more slippery, and bisexual also refers to object choice. In the terms of modern sexual discourses, bisexuality is a—usually conscious—sexual preference. For Freud, the two problems are related: the subject's psychic constitution and her object choice reflect one another in various ways. In the limited context of this essay, I intend to outline the effects of "bisexual," "heterosexual," and "homosexual" as indices of object "choice," without closing off questions about the problems of, for example, homosexual subjectivity or lesbian "operations."

5. Derrida, *Spurs,* pp. 96–97. Harlow's translation renders the heterosexual closure of this sentence more dramatic than does the original. The French *"en elle-même et dans le homme"* (emphasis mine) underwrites the suspension between, and simultaneity of the masculine and feminine elements in Derrida's reading of the third woman's bisexuality. Berg adjusts the translation in "The Third Woman" to reflect this emphasis ("The Third Woman," p. 13).

6. This context, Derrida's critique of phallogoncentrism and self-presence, makes this passage difficult and in need of further explanation. For it is precisely the location of the feminine *within* phallogocentrism that makes her disruptive. For if feminine affirmation were "outside" the Law—and Derrida's work is committed to arguing that no such space exists—it would be devoid of deconstructive effects. Yet what is significant for my admittedly local reading is that in the attempt to disseminate sexuality into a multiplicity of sexualities—in other words "hetero"sexuality— Derrida comes up with a figure that, by more than an accident of the letter, cannot help but reinscribe *heterosexuality*.

7. Not only does the affirmative woman depend on masculinity for her textual and sexual gratification, she "dances" with men as well. If Nietzsche is the affirmative woman of *Spurs,* Emma "If I can't dance I don't want to be part of your revolution" Goldman embodies the theory in "Choreographies" because she is, in Derrida's words, "a sign of life, a sign of the dance" ("Choreographies," p. 67). Although Derrida imagines the sign of Goldman to be moving, slipping, and undetermined, it actually functions as a kind of bedrock for this example of Derrida's discourse, a discourse that returns to her name and the concept it represents over and over

as if Goldman were Derrida's dependable partner in his own theoretical dance. What Derrida's discourse represses is not only the independent dance of Goldman's "sign" but the "maverick" feminist's historical specificity: she was an early twentieth-century "free love" anarchist whose sexuality, no matter how liberated, was limited in the end to heterosexuality. When she danced, she danced with men. When she politicked, she was mostly critical of feminism and lesbianism in particular: historian Blanche W. Cook quotes Goldman as stating that the feminist movement is of "no interest except as an amusing and typical instance of feminine intellectual homosexuality." Cook writes further that "although [Goldman] was absolute about a person's right to sexual choice, she felt a profound ambivalence about lesbianism as a lifestyle." (See Blanche W. Cook, "Female Support Networks and Political Activism" in *A Heritage of her Own,* Nancy Cott and Elizabeth H. Pleck, eds. [New York: Simon and Schuster, 1979].) The sign "Emma Goldman" connates much more than Derrida's dance; in addition it refers to an affirmative, free love that liberates heterosexuality while expressing "profound ambivalence" about female homosexuality.

8. Sigmund Freud, "Female Sexuality" (1931), *The Standard Edition of the Complete Works of Sigmund Freud,* ed. James Strachey (London: Hogarth, 1974), vol. xxi, p. 230.

9. For the sake of brevity, I omit a lengthy discussion here of some rather fanciful footwork and some outright misreadings in Berg's text. The most interesting of these is the case of the second woman's narcissism. In Berg's reading of Kofman, the second woman is the narcissist: mute, and serving as an indifferent blank page on which men inscribe their truths. Yet here Berg affects a reversal on Kofman's text: in *l'énigme de le femme,* the narcissist is the affirmative woman—Berg's third woman. The very words Berg uses to describe the third, dionysian (and supposedly fetishistic) woman are those which Kofman uses in her subchapter "Narcissistic Woman" (Sarah Kofman, *The Enigma of Woman: Woman in Freud's Writings,* trans. Catherine Porter [Ithaca: Cornell University Press, 1985], pp. 50–64). " 'Affirmative,' a Nietzschean term," writes Kofman, "and 'narcissistic,' a Freudian term, are perhaps not irreconcilable" (p. 58). The fact that Berg sees them as totally irreconcilable is not a simple misreading; it is a symptom of the text's attempt to organize, define, personify, and then separate femininity into three different women. The problem is one of the difference: whereas Berg sees a difference between the narcissist and the fetishist, a more crucial difference *within* the figure causes her neat patterns to unravel. One also can read Berg's diversions as a symptom of her normalizing position as reader/referee in "The Third Woman"—a position that corresponds to the third element in a triangular formation with Kofman and Irigaray in the article. In a section titled "Cat Fights," the author tries to break up the hostilities between the two theorists she reads because, to Berg, the in-house quarrel repeats a "classic phallocentric move" (p. 15). Berg's position as the voice of order corresponds to her position as the third woman theorist in the discourse of "The Third Woman": a reading of Kofman and Irigaray by Elizabeth Berg. Whether or not Berg is her own affirmative woman, her position of authority is purchased here at the expense of the two women between whom she intervenes and sets things "straight."

10. This figuration of the second woman going about "distributing sexual identity cards"

interests me in particular because handing out sexual identity cards is precisely what the assertion of a homosexual identity does: the existence of an identified homosexual necessitates the redefinition of heterosexuality as *an* identity, not *the* identity. More exactly, heterosexuality becomes an identity as such, rather than a nameless status quo. Returning to Derrida's words, we see that, briefly, this is another moment when the deconstructive critique of self-presence (figured as a sexual identity card) slips into a critique of homosexuality (those women who look like men are handing them out).

11. Derrida, *Spurs*, pp. 96,97. The passage reads: "At the head of the prosecution this time is the masked artist who, because he himself still believes in castration, also does not escape the inversion of negation" ("*Mais celui-ci croit encore à la castration de la femme et en reste à l'inversion de l'instance réactive et négative*"). The term that psychologists, including Freud, used for homosexuality was, of course, "inversion" ("*Die Inversion*" in Freud's texts); I press on the intertextuality of this word, especially for my reading of the passage of *Positions* below.

12. Derrida, *Positions*, p. 42. The French text reads: "*Aussi faut-il, par cette écriture double, justement, stratifiée, décalée et décalante, marquer l'écart entre l'inversion qui met bas la hauteur, en déconstruit la généalogie sublimante ou idéalisante, et l'émergence irruptive d'un nouveau "concept," concept de ce qui ne se laisse plus, ne s'est jamais laissé comprendre dans le régime antérieur. Si tel écart, ce biface ou ce biphasage, ne peut plus être inscrit que dans une écriture bifide . . .*" (pp. 57–58).

13. Jacques Derrida, *Of Grammatology*, trans. Gayatri Chakravorty Spivak (Baltimore: Johns Hopkins University Press, 1976), p. lxvi.

14. *Spurs* itself was originally a lecture delivered to a group of theorists including Sarah Kofman (*Spurs*, p. 147, footnote 2).

15. Sigmund Freud, "Femininity" (1933), *The Standard Edition of the Complete Works of Sigmund Freud*, vol., XXII, pp. 116–117.

16. See Luce Irigaray's *Speculum of the Other Woman*, trans. Gillian C. Gill (Ithaca: Cornell University Press, 1985). For an alternative reading of Freud's comments, see Kofman's *The Enigma of Woman*, pp. 13–15.

17. An obvious example of such an intersection, and an obvious omission from my discussion of Derrida and homosexuality, being Derrida's own *Glas* (Paris: Les Editions de Galilée, 1974), a reading of Hegel and Jean Genet.

18. Monique Wittig, "The Straight Mind," *Feminist Issues 1* (Summer 1980), p. 110.

19. Monique Wittig and Sande Zeig, *Lesbian Peoples: Material for a Dictionary* (New York: Avon, 1976), p. 136.

20. The English text reads:
    "The novel effect of the movement of your cheeks and mouth and the difficulty the sounds have in making their way out of your mouth are so comical that I choke with laughter, I fall over backwards, m/y tears stream, I regard you still and silent, I am increasingly overcome by laughter, suddenly you too are affected, you burst out, your cheeks colour, you fall over backwards as the women's

clamour is heard outside their interpellations the long incomprehensible phrases pronounced by one of them and repeated interminable by many others." (p. 103).

21. Here is the poem in French (the English version can be found on pages 79–80 in the Morrow edition):

"Elles m//attirent jusqu'à tes morceaux dispersés, il y a un bras, il y a un pied, le cou et la tête vont ensemble, tes paupières sont fermées, tes oreilles détachées sont quelque part, tes globes oculaires ont roulé dans la boue, j/e les vois côte à côte, tes doigts sont coupés et jetés en un endroit, j//aperçois ton bassin, ton buste est ailleurs, il manque quelques fragments d'avant-bras, les cuisses et les tibias. A cette vision m/a vue se brouille, elles m/e soutiennent au-dessous des épaules, m/es genoux se fléchissent, m/es cris s'étouffent dans m/a poitrine, elles m/e demandent où te faire une sépulture dans quel ordre ramasser tes fragments ce qui fait que j/e m/e redresse hurlante, j/e prononce l'interdiction, d'enregistrer ta mort, que la traîtresse responsable de ton déchiquètement ne soit pas inquiétée, j/e prononce que tu es là vivante quoique tronçonnée, j/e cherche en toute hâte tes morceaux dans le boue, m/es ongles râclent les menues pierres et les cailloux, j/e trouve ton nez une partie de ta vulve tes nymphes ton clitoris, j/e trouve tes oreilles un tibia puis l'autre, j/e te rassemble bout à bout, j/e te reconstitue, j/e remets en place les yeux, j/e rapproche bords à bords les peaux séparéees, j/e produis avec empressement des larmes de la cyprine de la salive en quantité voulue, j/e t'en enduis à toutes tes déchirures, j/e mets m/on souffle dans ta bouche, j/e réchauffe tes oreilles tes mains tes seins, j//introduis tout m/on air dans tes poumons, j/e m/e redresse pour chanter, j//aperçois tout au loin la côte de l'île et le soleil briller sur la mer, j/écart les déesses de la mort assises sur leurs talon autour de toi, j/e commence autour de ton corps une danse violente, m/es talons s'enfoncent dans la terre, j/e dispose tes cheveux sur les mottes d'herbe, m/oi Isis la très puissante j/e décrète que comme par le passé tu vis Osiris m/a très chérie m/a très affaiblie j/e dis que comme par le passé nous pourrons faire ensemble les petites filles qui viendront après nous, toi alors m/on Osiris m/a très belle tu m/e souris défaite épuisée." (pp. 86–87).

Chapter 6 Commentary: Post-Utopian Difference

1. Sigmund Freud, *Three Essays on the Theory of Sexuality*, trans. James Strachey (New York: Basic Books, Inc.), p. 7.

2. Michel Foucault, *The History of Sexuality, Volume I: An Introduction*, trans. Robert Hurley (New York: Vintage Books, 1980); Stephen Heath, *The Sexual Fix* (London: The MacMillan Press Ltd., 1982).

3. Jean Laplanche, *Life and Death in Psycho-analysis*, trans. Jeffrey Mehlman (Baltimore and London: The Johns Hopkins University Press, 1976), p. 18.

4. Jean Laplanche and J.-B. Pontalis, *The Language of Psychoanalysis*, trans. Donald Nicholson-Smith (New York: W.W. Norton & Company, Inc., 1973), p. 420.

5. Roland Barthes, *Roland Barthes by Roland Barthes*, trans. Richard Howard (New York: Hill and Wang, 1977), p. 69.

6. Heather Findlay, "Strange Bedfellows: Feminine Sexuality and Feminist Theory," A.B. honors thesis, Brown University, 1986, p. 94.

7. Luce Irigaray, *Speculum of the Other Woman*, trans. Gillian C. Gill (Ithaca: Cornell University Press, 1985).

8. Luce Irigaray, *This Sex Which Is Not One,* trans. Catherine Porter (Ithaca: Cornell University Press, 1985), p. 72.

9. Irigaray, *This Sex Which Is Not One,* p. 68.

10. Heath, *The Sexual Fix,* p. 153.

11. Sigmund Freud, "Femininity," *The Standard Edition of the Complete Psychological Works,* vol. 22, trans. James Strachey (London: Hogarth Press, 1953), p. 135.

12. Stephen Heath, "Male Feminism," in Alice Jardine and Paul Smith, eds., *Men in Feminism* (New York and London: Methuen, 1987), p. 8.

13. Michèle Le Doeuff, "Women and philosophy," *Radical Philosophy,* no. 17 (Summer 1977), p. 3.

14. Jacqueline Rose and Juliet Mitchell, eds., *Feminine Sexuality: Jacques Lacan and the école freudienne* (New York: Pantheon Books, 1982), p. 40.

15. Heath, *The Sexual Fix,* pp. 153–54.

Chapter 7   Gender: A Useful Category of Historical Analysis

This essay was first prepared for delivery at the meetings of the American Historical Association in December, 1985. It was subsequently published in its current form in *The American Historical Review* Vol. 91, No. 5 (December 1986). The final version profited from comments by Ira Katznelson, Charles Tilly and Louise Tilly, Elisabetta Galeotti, Rayna Rapp, Christine Stansell, and Joan Vincent. I am grateful for the careful editing done at the AHR by Allyn Roberts and David Ransell. Discussions with Denise Riley, Janice Doane, Yasmine Ergas, Anne Norton, and Harriet Whitehead helped formulate my ideas on the various subjects touched in the course of this paper.

1. *Oxford English Dictionary* (Oxford: Oxford University Press, 1961), p. 4.

2. E. Littré, *Dictionnaire de la langue française* (Paris, 1876).

3. Raymond Williams, *Keywords* (New York: Oxford University Press, 1983), p. 285.

4. Natalie Zemon Davis, "Women's History in Transition: The European Case," *Feminist Studies* (1975–6) 3:90.

5. Ann D. Gordon, Mari Jo Buhle, and Nancy Shrom Dye, "The Problem of Women's History," in Berenice Carroll, ed., *Liberating Women's History* (Urbana, Ill.: University of Illinois Press), p. 89.

6. The best and most subtle example is from Joan Kelly, "The Doubled Vision of Feminist Theory," in her *Women, History and Theory* (Chicago: University of Chicago Press, 1984), pp. 51–64, especially p. 61.

7. For an argument against the use of gender to emphasize the social aspect of sexual difference, see Moira Gatens, "A Critique of the Sex/Gender Distinction," in J. Allen and P. Patton, eds., *Beyond Marxism?* (Leichhardt, N.S.W.: Intervention Publications, 1985), pp. 143–60.

8. For a different approach to feminist analysis, see Linda J. Nicholson, *Gender and*

History: The Limits of Social Theory in the Age of the Family (New York: Columbia University Press, 1986).

9. Mary O'Brien, *The Politics of Reproduction* (London: Routledge and Kegan Paul, 1981), pp. 8–15, 46.

10. Shulamith Firestone, *The Dialectic of Sex* (New York: Bantam Books, 1970). The phrase "bitter trap" is O'Brien's, *Politics of Reproduction,* p. 8.

11. Catherine MacKinnon, "Feminism, Marxism, Method, and the State: An Agenda for Theory," *Signs* (1982) 7:515, 541.

12. MacKinnon, "Feminism, Marxism, Method, and the State," pp. 541, 543.

13. For an interesting discussion of the strenghs and limits of the term "patriarchy," see the exchange between historians Sheila Rowbotham, Sally Alexander, and Barbara Taylor in Raphael Samuel, ed., *People's History and Socialist Theory* (London: Routledge and Kegan Paul, 1981), pp. 363–73.

14. Frederick Engels, *The Origins of the Family, Private Property, and the State* (1884; reprint ed., New York: International Publishers, 1972).

15. Heidi Hartmann, "Capitalism, Patriarchy, and Job Segregation by Sex," *Signs* (1976) 1:168. See also, "The Unhappy Marriage of Marxism and Feminism: Towards a More Progressive Union," *Capital and Class,* (1979) 8:1–33; "The Family as the Locus of Gender, Class, and Political Struggle: The Example of Housework," *Signs* (1981) 6:366–94.

16. Discussions of Marxist feminism include Zillah Eisenstein, *Capitalist Patriarchy and the Case for Socialist Feminism* (New York: Longmans, 1981); Annette Kuhn, "Structures of Patriarchy and Capital in the Family," in Annette Kuhn and Ann Marie Wolpe, eds., *Feminism and Materialism: Women and Modes of Production* (London: Routledge and Kegan Paul, 1978); Rosalind Coward, *Patriarchal Precedents* (London: Routledge and Kegan Paul, 1983); Hilda Scott, *Does Socialism Liberate Women? Experiences from Eastern Europe* (Boston: Beacon Press, 1974); Jane Humphries, "Working Class Family, Women's Liberation and Class Struggle: the Case of Nineteenth-Century British History," *Review of Radical Political Economics* (1977) 9:25–41; Jane Humphries, "Class Struggle and the Persistence of the Working Class Family," *Cambridge Journal of Economics* (1971) 1:241–58; and see the debate on Humphries's work in *Review of Radical Political Economics,* (1980) 12:76–94.

17. Kelly, "Doubled Vision of Feminist Theory," p. 61.

18. Ann Snitow, Christine Stansell, and Sharon Thompson, eds., *Powers of Desire: The Politics of Sexuality* (New York: Monthly Review Press, 1983).

19. Ellen Ross and Rayna Rapp, "Sex and Society: A Research Note from Social History and Anthropology," in *Powers of Desire,* p. 53.

20. "Introduction," *Powers of Desire,* p. 12; and Jessica Benjamin, "Master and Slave: The Fantasy of Erotic Domination," *Powers of Desire,* p. 297.

21. Johanna Brenner and Maria Ramas, "Rethinking Women's Oppression," *New Left Review,* (1984) 144:33–71; Michèle Barrett, "Rethinking Women's Oppression: A Reply to Brenner and Ramas," *New Left Review* (1984) 146:123–28; Angela Weir

and Elizabeth Wilson, "The British Women's Movement," *New Left Review* (1984) 148:74–103; Michèle Barrett, "A Response to Weir and Wilson," *New Left Review* (1985) 150:143–47; Jane Lewis, "The Debate on Sex and Class," *New Left Review* (1985) 149:108–20. See also Hugh Armstrong and Pat Armstrong, "Beyond Sexless Class and Classless Sex: Towards Feminist Marxism," *Studies in Political Economy* (1983) 10:7–44; Hugh Armstrong and Pat Armstrong, "Comments: More on Marxist Feminism," *Studies in Political Economy* (1984) 15:179–84; and Jane Jenson, "Gender and Reproduction: Or, Babies and the State," unpublished paper, June 1985, pp. 1–7.

22. For early theoretical formulations see *Papers on Patriarchy: Conference, London 76* (London: n.p., 1976). I am grateful to Jane Caplan for telling me of the existence of this publication and for her willingness to share with me her copy and her ideas about it. For the psychoanalytic position see Sally Alexander, "Women, Class and Sexual Difference," *History Workshop* (1984) 17:125–35. In seminars at Princeton University in early 1986, Juliet Mitchell seemed to be returning to an emphasis on the priority of materialist analyses of gender. For an attempt to get beyond the theoretical impasse of Marxist feminism, see Coward, *Patriarchal Precedents.* See also the brilliant American effort in this direction by anthropologist Gayle Rubin, "The Traffic in Women: Notes on the 'Political Economy' of Sex," in Rayna R. Reiter, ed., *Towards an Anthropology of Women* (New York: Monthly Review Press, 1975), pp. 167–68.

23. Nancy Chodorow, *The Reproduction of Mothering: Psychoanalysis and the Sociology of Gender* (Berkeley: University of California Press, 1978), p. 169.

24. "My account suggests that these gender-related issues may be influenced during the period of the oedipus complex, but they are not its only focus or outcome. The negotiation of these issues occurs in the context of broader object-relational and ego processes. These broader processes have equal influence on psychic structure formation, and psychic life and relational modes in men and women. They account for differing modes of identification and orientation to heterosexual objects, for the more asymmetrical oedipal issues psychoanalysts describe. These outcomes, like more traditional oedipal outcomes, arise from the asymmetrical organization of parenting, with the mother's role as primary parent and the father's typically greater remoteness and his investment in socialization especially in areas concerned with gender-typing." Nancy Chodorow, *The Reproduction of Mothering*, p. 166. It is important to note that there are differences in interpretation and approach between Chodorow and British object-relations theorists who follow the work of D.W. Winicott and Melanie Klein. Chodorow's approach is best characterized as a more sociological or sociologized theory, but it is the dominant lens through which object-relations theory has been viewed by American feminists. On the history of British object-relations theory in relation to social policy, see Denise Riley, *War in the Nursery* (London: Virago, 1984).

25. Juliet Mitchell and Jacqueline Rose, eds., *Jacques Lacan and the école freudienne* (London: Norton, 1983); Alexander, "Women, Class and Sexual Difference."

26. Teresa de Lauretis, *Alice Doesn't: Feminism, Semiotics, Cinema* (Bloomington, Ind.: University of Indiana Press, 1984), p. 159.

27. Alexander, "Women, Class and Sexual Difference," p. 135.

28. Denise Riley, "Summary of Preamble to Interwar Feminist History Work," unpublished paper, presented to the Pembroke Center Seminar, May 1985, p. 11. The argument is fully elaborated in Riley's book, *"Am I that Name?": Feminism and the Category of "Women" in History* (London: Macmillan, 1988, and Minneapolis: University of Minnesota Press, 1988).

29. Carol Gilligan, *In a Different Voice: Psychological Theory and Women's Development* (Cambridge, Mass.: Harvard University Press, 1982).

30. Useful critiques of Gilligan's book are: Judy Auerbach et al., "Commentary on Gilligan's *In a Different Voice*," *Feminist Studies* (1985) 11:149–62; and "Women and Morality," a special issue of *Social Research* (1983) 50. My comments on the tendency of historians to cite Gilligan come from reading unpublished manuscripts and grant proposals, and it seems unfair to cite those here. I have kept track of the references for over five years, and they are many and increasing.

31. *Feminist Studies* (1980) 6:26–64.

32. For a succinct and accessible discussion of Derrida, see Jonathan Culler, *On Deconstruction: Theory and Criticism after Structuralism* (Ithaca, N.Y.: Cornell University Press, 1982), especially pp. 156–79. See also Jacques Derrida, *Of Grammatology*, trans. Gayatri Chakravorty Spivak (Baltimore: Johns Hopkins University Press, 1976); Jacques Derrida, *Spurs* (Chicago: University of Chicago Press, 1979); and a transcription of Pembroke Center Seminar, 1983, in *Subjects/Objects* (Fall 1984).

33. Clifford Geertz, "Blurred Genres," *American Scholar* (1980) 49:165–79.

34. Michelle Zimbalist Rosaldo, "The Uses and Abuses of Anthropology: Reflections on Feminism and Cross-Cultural Understanding," *Signs* (1980) 5:400.

35. Michel Foucault, *The History of Sexuality*, 1, *An Introduction* (New York: Vintage Books, 1980); Michel Foucault, *Power/Knowledge: Selected Interviews and Other Writings, 1972–77* (New York: Pantheon, 1980).

36. For this argument, see Rubin, "The Traffic in Women," p. 199.

37. Rubin, "Traffic in Women," p. 189.

38. Biddie Martin, "Feminism, Criticism and Foucault," *New German Critique* (1982) 27:3–30; Kathryn Kish Sklar, *Catharine Beecher: A Study in American Domesticity* (New Haven: Yale University Press, 1973); Mary A. Hill, *Charlotte Perkins Gilman: The Making of a Radical Feminist, 1860–1896* (Philadelphia: Temple University Press, 1980).

39. Lou Ratté, "Gender Ambivalence in the Indian Nationalist Movement," unpublished paper, Pembroke Center Seminar, Spring, 1983; and Mrinalina Sinha, "Manliness: A Victorian Ideal and the British Imperial Elite in India," unpublished paper, Department of History, State University of New York, Stony Brook, 1984, and Sinha, "The Age of Consent Act: The Ideal of Masculinity and Colonial Ideology in Late 19th Century Bengal," *Proceedings of the Eighth International Symposium on Asian Studies*, 1986, pp. 1199–1214.

40. Pierre Bourdieu, *Le Sens Pratique* (Paris: Les Editions de Minuit, 1980), pp. 246–47; 333–461, especially p. 366.

41. Maurice Godelier, "The Origins of Male Domination," *New Left Review* (1981) 127:17.

42. Gayatri Chakravorty Spivak, "Three Women's Texts and a Critique of Imperialism," *Critical Inquiry* (1985) 12:243–46. See also Kate Millett, *Sexual Politics* (New York: Avon, 1969). An examination of how feminine references work in major texts of Western philosophy is carried out by Luce Irigaray in *Speculum of the Other Woman*, trans. Gillian C. Gill (Ithaca: Cornell University Press, 1985).

43. Natalie Zemon Davis, "Women on Top," in her *Society and Culture in Early Modern France* (Stanford: Stanford University Press, 1975), pp. 124–51.

44. Caroline Walker Bynum, *Jesus as Mother: Studies in the Spirituality of the High Middle Ages* (Berkeley: University of California Press, 1982); Caroline Walker Bynum, "Fast, Feast, and Flesh: The Religious Significance of Food to Medieval Women," *Representations* (1985) 11:1–25; Caroline Walker Bynum, "Introduction," *Religion and Gender: Essays on the Complexity of Symbols* (Boston: Beacon Press, 1987).

45. See, for example, T.J. Clarke, *The Painting of Modern Life* (New York: Knopf, 1985).

46. The difference between structuralist and post-structuralist theorists on this question rests on how open or closed they view the categories of difference. To the extent that post-structuralists do not fix a universal meaning for the categories or the relationship between them, their approach seems conducive to the kind of historical analysis I am advocating.

47. Rachel Weil, "The Crown has Fallen to the Distaff: Gender and Politics in the Age of Catherine de Medici," *Critical Matrix* (Princeton Working Papers in Women's Studies) (1985), 1. See also Louis Montrose, "Shaping Fantasies: Figurations of Gender and Power in Elizabethan Culture," *Representations* (1983) 1:61–94; and Lynn Hunt, "Hercules and the Radical Image in the French Revolution," *Representations* (1983) 1:95–117.

48. Edmund Burke, *Reflections on the French Revolution* (1892; reprint ed., New York, 1909), pp. 208–9; 214. See Jean Bodin, *Six Books of the Commonwealth* (1606; reprint ed., New York: Barnes and Noble, 1967); Robert Filmer, *Patriarchia and Other Political Works* (Oxford: Basil Blackwell, 1949); and John Locke, *Two Treatises of Government* (1690; reprint ed., Cambridge: Cambridge University Press, 1970). See also Elizabeth Fox-Genovese, "Property and Patriarchy in Classical Bourgeois Political Theory," *Radical History Review* (1977) 4:36–59; and Mary Lyndon Shanley, "Marriage Contract and Social Contract in Seventeenth Century English Political Thought," *Western Political Quarterly* (1979) 3:79–91.

49. I am grateful to Bernard Lewis for the reference to Islam. Michel Foucault, *Historie de la Sexualité*, 2, *L'Usage des plaisirs* (Paris: Gallimard, 1984). On women in classical Athens see Marilyn Arthur, "Liberated Woman: The Classical Era," in Renate Bridenthal and Claudia Koonz, eds., *Becoming Visible* (Boston: Houghton, Mifflin, 1976), pp. 75–78.

50. Cited in Roderick Phillips, "Women and Family Breakdown in Eighteenth Century France: Rouen 1780–1800," *Social History* (1976) 2:217.

51. On the French Revolution, see Darlene Gay Levy, Harriet Applewhite, and Mary Johnson, eds., *Women in Revolutionary Paris, 1789–1795* (Urbana, Ill.: University of

Illinois Press, 1979), pp. 209–20; on Soviet legislation, see the documents in Rudolph Schlesinger, *Changing Attitudes in Soviet Russia: Documents and Readings,* Vol. I, *The Family in the USSR* (London: Routledge and Kegan Paul, 1949), pp. 62–71, 251–54; on Nazi policy, see Tim Mason, "Women in Nazi Germany," *History Workshop* (1976) 1:74–113, and Tim Mason, "Women in Germany, 1925–40: Family, Welfare and Work," *History Workshop* (1976) 2:5–32.

52. Elizabeth Wilson, *Women and the Welfare State* (London: Tavistock, 1977); Jenson, "Gender and Reproduction"; Jane Lewis, *The Politics of Motherhood: Child and Maternal Welfare in England 1900–1939* (London: Croom Helm, 1980); Mary Lynn McDougall, "Protecting Infants: The French Campaign for Maternity Leaves, 1890–1913," *French Historical Studies* (1983) 13:79–105.

53. On English utopians, see Barbara Taylor, *Eve and the New Jerusalem* (New York: Pantheon, 1983).

54. Louis Devance, "Femme, famille, travail et morale sexuelle dans l'ideologie de 1848," in *Mythes et représentations de la femme au XIXe siècle* (Paris: Champion, 1977); Jacques Rancière and Pierre Vauday, "En allant à l'expo: l'ouvrier, sa femme et les machines," *Les Révoltes Logiques* (1975) 1:5–22.

55. Gayatri Chakravorty Spivak, " 'Draupadi' by Mahasveta Devi," *Critical Inquiry* (1981) 8:381–401, rpt. in Spivak, *In Other Worlds: Essays in Cultural Politics* (New York and London: Methuen, 1987); Homi Bhabha, "Of Mimicry and Man: The Ambivalence of Colonial Discourse," *October* (1984) 28:125–33; Karin Hausen, "The German Nation's Obligations to the Heroes' Widows of World War I," in Margaret R. Higonnet et al., eds., *Behind the Lines: Gender and the Two World Wars* (New Haven: Yale University Press, 1987), pp. 126–40. See also Ken Inglis, "The Representation of Gender on Australian War Memoria," *Daedalus* (1987) 116:35–59.

56. On the French Revolution see Levy *et al., Women in Revolutionary Paris.* On the American Revolution see Mary Beth Norton, *Liberty's Daughters: The Revolutionary Experience of American Women* (Boston: Little Brown, 1980); Linda Kerber, *Women of the Republic* (Chapel Hill, N.C.: University of North Carolina Press, 1980); Joan Hoff-Wilson, "The Illusion of Change: Women and the American Revolution," in Alfred Young, ed., *The American Revolution: Explorations in the History of American Radicalism* (DeKalb: Northern Illinois University Press, 1976), pp. 383–446. On the French Third Republic, see Steven Hause, *Women's Suffrage and Social Politics in the French Third Republic* (Princeton: Princeton University Press, 1984). An extremely interesting treatment of a recent case is Maxine Molyneux, "Mobilization without Emancipation? Women's interests, the State and Revolution in Nicaragua," *Feminist Studies* (1985) 11:227–54.

57. On Pro-natalism, see Riley, *War in the Nursery;* and Jenson, "Gender and Reproduction." On the 1920s, see the essays in *Stratégies des Femmes* (Paris: Editions Tierce, 1984).

58. For various interpretations of the impact of new work on women, see Louise Tilly and Joan Scott, *Women, Work and Family* (New York: Holt Rinehart and Winston, 1978; Methuen, 1987); Thomas Dublin, *Women at Work: The Transformation of Work and Community in Lowell, Massachusetts, 1826–1860* (New York: Columbia University

Press, 1979); and Edward Shorter, *The Making of the Modern Family* (New York: Basic Books, 1975).

59. See for example, Margaret Rossiter, *Women Scientists in America: Struggles and Strategies to 1914* (Baltimore: Johns Hopkins University Press, 1982).

60. Luce Irigaray, "Is the Subject of Science Sexed?," *Cultural Critique* (1985) 1:73–88.

61. Louis Crompton, *Byron and Greek Love: Homophobia in Nineteenth-Century England* (Berkeley: University of California Press, 1985). This question is touched on in Jeffrey Weeks, *Sex, Politics and Society: The Regulation of Sexuality Since 1800* (London: Leyman, 1981).

Chapter 8   The Body Politic

1. This paper was originally submitted for publication in this volume in the spring of 1985. Since then, I have published more detailed analyses of both the abortion debate and the sexologists' rhetoric in Carroll Smith-Rosenberg, *Disorderly Conduct: Visions of Gender in Victorian America* (New York: Alfred A. Knopf, Inc., 1985), pp. 217–297. Since then, as well, I have reconceived and reformulated many of the ideas found in the original 1985 essay. Of these I have been able to introduce some into this essay. As a consequence, "The Body Politic" offers a briefer but in some ways more recent analysis of the ways the physical body enters political discourse and the ways discourse reforms the body. So long and interrupted a gestation necessitates many acknowledgments. Most of all I would like to thank Alvia G. Golden who offered critical help at all the stages from conception to maturation. Lucienne Frappier-Mazur, Phyllis Rackin, and Gabrielle Spiegel also were generous of time and ideas. In many ways, the essay in its present form constitutes part of an ongoing discourse with my fellow members of the Gender Seminar, School of Social Science, Institute of Advanced Study, Princeton (1987–88). In researching and writing this essay, I was supported by fellowships from the Institute of Advanced Study, The American Council of Learned Societies, and the National Endowment for the Humanities.

2. It was Michel Foucault's *Archaeology of Knowledge* (New York: Pantheon Books, 1972), trans. A. M. Sheridan Smith, far more than any other book that drew historians' attention to these issues. In formulating the problems in the beginning of this essay I am indebted to the following critics and theorists: Catherine Belsey, *Critical Practice* (London and New York: Methuen, 1980), and *The Subject of Tragedy: Identity and Difference in Renaissance Drama* (London and New York: Methuen, 1985); M.M. Bakhtin, *The Dialogic Imagination*, ed. Michael Holquist, trans. Caryl Emerson and Michael Holquist (Austin: University of Texas Press, 1981); Mary Douglas, especially her *Natural Symbols: Explorations in Cosmology* (New York: Vintage Books, 1973).

3. For an excellent analysis of the social and medical history of abortion in America, see James Mohr, *Abortion in America: The Origins and Evolution of National Policy* (New York and Oxford: Oxford University Press, 1978). For the legal history of abortion, see Lawrence Lader, *Abortion* (New York: Bobbs-Merrill Co., 1966); David T. Smith, *Abortion and the Law* (Cleveland: Press of Case Western Reserve University, 1973).

For a clear statement of the history of the Roman Catholic Church's position, see Robert J. Huser, *The Crime of Abortion in Common Law* (Washington, D.C.: Catholic University of America Press, 1942); John Noonan, *Contraception: A History of Its Treatment by Catholic Theologians and Canonists* (Cambridge, Mass.: Belknap Press of Harvard University, 1965). The leader of this lobbying campaign was Harvard Medical School Professor Horatio R. Storer. The letters written and received by Storer during this campaign are in the Rare Book Room, Countway Medical Library, Harvard Medical School.

For forty-five years following independence, no state passed any law on abortion. By 1840 only eight states had passed any legislation regulating abortion in any way. Glenn Koopersmith, in "A Comparison of Early and Later Abortion Laws in 19th Century America," unpublished manuscript, University of Pennsylvania, has surveyed the statutes of Connecticut, New York, Iowa, Illinois, Arkansas, Missouri, Indiana, Oregon, California, New Jersey, Massachusetts, Vermont, New Hampshire, Maine, Wisconsin, Ohio, Michigan, Virginia, West Virginia, Mississippi, and Alabama. See also R. Sauer, "Attitudes Towards Abortion in America, 1800–1973," *Population Studies* XXVIII (March 1974): 53–67; Alfred S. Taylor, *Medical Jurisprudence,* 2nd American ed., from 3rd London ed., with notes and additions by R. Eglesfeld Griffith (Philadelphia: Lea and Blanchard, 1850); Alfred S. Taylor, *A Manual of Medical Jurisprudence,* 8th ed. (Philadelphia: J. B. Lippincott and Co., 1866); Alfred S. Taylor, *The Principles and Practice of Medical Jurisprudence,* 2nd ed. (Philadelphia: Henry C. Lea, 1973), vol. II.

4. For an excellent discussion of women reformers in post-Civil War America see Mari Jo Buhle, *Women and American Socialism, 1870–1920* (Urbana: University of Illinois Press, 1981), chap. 2.

5. Mohr, *Abortion in America,* p. 100. See also Wendell H. Bash, "Changing Birth Rates in Developing America: New York State, 1840–75," *Milbank Memorial Fund Quarterly* XLI (1963); Colin Forster and G.S.L. Tucker, *Economic Opportunity and White American Fertility Ratios, 1800–1860* (New Haven: Yale University Press, 1972); G. J. Barker-Benfield, "The Spermatic Economy: A Nineteenth-Century View of Sexuality," *Feminist Studies* I (1972): 45–74; and *The Horrors of the Half Known Life: Male Attitudes Toward Women and Sexuality in 19th Century America* (New York: Harper & Row, 1976). For somewhat less psychological interpretations, see Daniel Scott Smith, "Family Limitation, Sexual Control and Domestic Feminism in Victorian America," *Feminist Studies* I (1973): 40–57; Carroll Smith-Rosenberg and Charles Rosenberg, "The Female Animal: Medical and Biological Views of Woman and Her Role in Nineteenth-Century America," *Journal of American History* LX (1973): 332–56; Edward Shorter, "Female Emancipation, Birth Control and Fertility in European History," *American Historical Review* LXXVIII (1973): 605–40.

For two rather different studies of the history of newspapers see Raymond Ross, *Slavery and the New York City Newspapers, 1850–1860* (Ann Arbor, Mich.: University Microfilms, 1962); and Anthony Smith, *The Newspaper: An International History* (London: Thames and Hudson, 1979).

6. For examples of male medical rhetoric see: Simon M. Landis, *A Strictly Private Book . . . on the Secrets of Generation,* 20th ed. (Philadelphia: Landis Publishing Society,

1872); H. R. Storer, *Why Not? A Book for Every Woman, the Prize Essay* . . . (Boston: Lea and Shepard, 1866), p. 83; J. M. Toner, "Abortion in Its Medical and Moral Aspects," *Medical and Surgical Reporter* V (1861): 443; Walter Coles, "Abortion—Its Causes and Treatment," *St. Louis Medical and Surgical Journal* (1875): 252–53; M. M. Eaton, "Four and a Half Inches of Whalebone in the Uterus: Abortion," *Chicago Medical Examiner* IX (1868): 218; E. M. Buckingham, "Criminal Abortion," *Cincinnati Lancet and Obstetrician* n.s. X (1867): 139–43; Andrew Nebinger, *Criminal Abortion* (Philadelphia: Collins, printer, 1870), pp. 4–5, 7; rpt. New York: Arno Press, 1974. Mohr, *Abortion in America,* discusses the physicians' campaign in his chap. 6.

For a discussion of the Michigan findings see William D. Haggard, *Abortion: Accidental, Essential, Criminal, Address Before the Nashville Academy of Medicine, Aug. 4, 1898* (Nashville, Tenn., 1898), p. 10. See, as well, Ely Van De Warker, *The Detection of Criminal Abortion, and A Study of Foeticidal Drugs* (Boston, 1872); A. K. Gardner, *Conjugal Sins Against the Laws of Life and Health* (New York: Moulton, 1874), p. 131; Alexander C. Draper, *Observations on Abortion: With an Account of the Means both Medicinal and Mechanical, Employed to Produce that Effect* . . . (Philadelphia, 1839); Hugh Hodge, *On Criminal Abortion* (Philadelphia: T.K. and P.G. Collins, printers, 1854). Advocates of birth control routinely used the dangers and prevalence of abortion as one argument justifying their cause (H. R. Storer, *Report of the Suffolk District Medical Society on Criminal Abortion and Ordered Printed* . . . *May 9 [1857]* [Boston, 1857]; [N. F. Cook,] *Satan in Society: By a Physician* (Cincinnati: C. F. Vent, 1876); H. C. Ghent, "Criminal Abortion or Foeticide," *Transactions of the Texas State Medical Association at the Annual Session 1888–89* (1888–89). Certainly much of this literature was devoted to the task of convincing middle-class women not to use abortion as a form of family limitation (Mohr, *Abortion in America,* chaps. 3 and 4).

7. Walter Channing, "Effects of Criminal Abortion," *Boston Medical and Surgical Journal,* LX (1895): 134–35, 138–39.

8. E. Frank Howe, *Sermon on Ante-Natal Infanticide Delivered at the Congregational Church in Terre Haute, on Sunday Morning, March 28, 1869* (Terre Haute, Ind., 1869), pp. 2–3. Howe also quotes a typical editorial in *Harper's Magazine,* February 1859, which asserted that married women increasingly sought abortions because "women have become altogether immersed in pursuit of mere pleasure and fashion. Nothing must stand in the way of these objects" (p. 3). Storer, *Why Not?,* p. 85; Toner, "Medical and Moral Aspects," pp. 443–46; D. H., "On Producing Abortion: A Physician's Reply to the Solicitations of a Married Woman to Produce a Miscarriage for Her," *Nashville Journal of Medicine and Surgery* XVII (1876): 200–3.

9. Cover, *National Police Gazette* II (March 13, 1847): 209 (reprinted in Mohr, *Abortion in America,* p. 127). See also articles in the *National Police Gazette* for 1845 and 1846, passim. I am indebted to James Mohr's fine study for suggesting this source of popular male opinion on women and abortion.

10. Mary Douglas, *Natural Symbols* (New York: Vintage Books, 1973), p. 132.

11. Starr, Paul, *The Social Transformation of American Medicine* (New York: Basic Books, 1982), pp. 51–54, 96–102; Harris Coulter, *Divided Legacy: A History of Schism in Medical Thought* (Washington, D.C.: McGrath Publishing Co., 1973); Martin Kaufman, *Home-*

opathy in America: The Rise and Fall of a Medical Heresy (Baltimore: Johns Hopkins University Press, 1971); Kett, Joseph F., *The Formation of the American Medical Profession: The Role of Institutions, 1780–1860* (New Haven: Yale University Press, 1968), pp. 185–86; Alex Berman, "The Impact of the Nineteenth-Century Botanico-Medical Movement in American Pharmacy and Medicine," Ph.D. dissertation, University of Wisconsin, 1954; Richard Shryock, "Sylvester Graham and the Popular Health Movement, 1830–1870," in his *Medicine in America: Historical Essays* (Baltimore: Johns Hopkins Press, 1966).

12. For a classic analysis of Republican political discourse see J.G.A. Pocock, *The Machiavellian Moment: Florentine Political Thought and the Atlantic Republican Tradition* (Princeton: Princeton University Press, 1975). While Pocock does not draw explicit attention to the sexual nature of political rhetoric, the sexuality of its imagery is apparent throughout his presentation of it. See as well: Gordon Wood, *The Creation of the American Republic, 1776–1787* (Chapel Hill: University of North Carolina Press, 1969). I am particularly indebted to Istvan Hont of the Political Science Department, Columbia University for his suggestive comments about the sexualization of seventeenth- and eighteenth-century political and economic rhetoric. I look forward with great anticipation to his forthcoming book on the Scottish Enlightenment.

13. For a discussion of the role gender played in the sexualization of the political subject see Carroll Smith-Rosenberg, "Domesticating Virtue," in Elaine Scarry, ed., *Literature and the Body* (Baltimore: Johns Hopkins University Press, 1988).

14. For an analysis of this early social purity rhetoric see Carroll Smith-Rosenberg, "A Richer and a Gentler Sex," *Social Research*, LIII (Summer, 1986): 283–309.

15. See, for example, the following women authors: Mrs. E. B. Duffey, *The Relations of the Sexes* (New York: Wood & Holbrook, 1876); Elizabeth Blackwell, *Essays in Medical Sociology* (London: Ernest Bell, 1902); Alice Stockham, *Karezza: Ethics of Marriage* (Chicago: Alice B. Stockham & Co., 1896); Lucinda B. Chandler, *The Divineness of Marriage* (New York: Great American Printing Company, 1872); Victoria Woodhull, *Scare-Crow of Sexual Slavery* (New York: Woodhull & Claflin, 1874).

16. For an analysis of nineteenth-century women's reform movements see, for example: Eleanor Flexner, *Century of Struggle* (Cambridge, Mass.: Harvard University Press, 1959), chaps. 3, 4, 6, 8; Blanche Glassman Hersch, *The Slavery of Sex: Feminist Abolitionists in America* (Urbana: University of Illinois Press, 1978), chap. 2; Barbara Berg, *The Remembered Gate: Origin of American Feminism* (New York: Oxford University Press, 1978); Buhle, *Women and American Socialism*, chap. 2.

17. For a fuller discussion see Smith-Rosenberg, "The New Woman as Androgyne," in *Disorderly Conduct*, pp. 245–296.

18. For studies of the beginnings of women's higher education in the post-Civil War years in America, see Mabel Newcomer, *A Century of Higher Education for American Women* (New York: Harper and Row, 1959); Thomas Woody's encyclopedic *A History of Women's Education in the United States* (New York: Science Press, 1929), 2 vols.; Keith Melder, "Mask of Oppression: The Female Seminary Movement in the United States," *New York History* LV (1974): 261–79; Dorothy McGuigan, *The Dangerous Experiment: 100 Years of Women at the University of Michigan* (Ann Arbor: Center for the

Continuing Education of Women, 1970); Charlotte Williams Conable, *Women at Cornell: The Myth of Equal Education* (Ithaca, N.Y.: Cornell University Press, 1977); Edward Potts Cheyney, *History of the University of Pennsylvania, 1740–1940* (Philadelphia: University of Pennsylvania Press, 1940); Dorothy A. Plumb and George B. Dowell, *The Magnificent Enterprise: A Chronicle of Vassar College* (Poughkeepsie, N.Y.: 1961); Arthur Charles Cole, *A Hundred Years of Mount Holyoke College: The Evolution of an Educational Ideal* (New Haven: Yale University Press, 1940); Cornelia Lynde Meigs, *What Makes a College? A History of Bryn Mawr* (New York: Macmillan and Co., 1956).

For some New Women's discussions of what college education meant to them, see Vida Scudder, who commented in her autobiography, *On Journey* (New York: E. P. Dutton and Co., 1937), that she had harbored "a private fairy tale wherein, disguised as a boy, she crept into Harvard" (p. 58). Education was as critical to Florence Kelley: see Josephine Goldmark's biography, *Impatient Crusader* (Urbana: University of Illinois Press, 1953), chap. 2. "Entering College," Kelley told Goldmark, "was for me almost a sacramental experience." Commenting specifically on her years at Cornell, she wrote: "Little did we care that there was no music, no theater . . . that the stairs to the lecture halls were wooden and the classrooms heated with coal stoves. No one, so far as I know, read a daily paper, or subscribed for a monthly or a quarterly. Our current gossip was Froude's life of Carlyle. We read only bound volumes." Florence Kelley, *Survey Graphic* (February 1, 1927), p. 559, reprinted in Goldmark, *Impatient Crusader*, pp. 11–12. Mary Kingsbury Simkhovitch reported similar feelings in her autobiography, *Neighborhood: My Story of Greenwich House* (New York: W. W. Norton and Co., 1938), to Alice and Edith Hamilton—see Madeleine P. Grant, *Alice Hamilton: Pioneer Doctor in Industrial Medicine* (New York: Abelard-Schuman, 1967), pp. 35–55. See women's bitter response to Edward Clarke's *Sex in Education; or, A Fair Chance for the Girls* (Boston: J. R. Osgood & Co., 1873) in Julia Ward Howe, *Sex and Education: A Reply to Dr. E. H. Clarke's "Sex in Education"* (New York: Arno Press, 1972; reprint of 1874 ed.). M. Carey Thomas, in Marjorie Housepian Dobkin, *The Making of a Feminist: Early Journals and Letters of M. Carey Thomas* (Kent, Ohio: Kent State University Press, 1979), pp. 48–49, 57–58. See also Conable, *Women at Cornell*, chap. 3; Thomas, in Dobkin, *Making of a Feminist*, pp. 66–67, 103–6, 109.

In the 1930s, Vida Scudder maintained the enthusiastic, reforming vision of women's education that she had taken with her to Smith College as an entering freshman in 1880:

> I must regard the success of colleges for women as one of the few triumphs of idealism, in an age when the shipwreck of former standards and the disintegration of older cultures have precipitated society into a chaos before which men are helpless. I do not know for what reason this throng of educated women has been released into the larger life, just in the period when an old order of civilization is passing away, and the new order emerges in confusion. . . . But I recognize that in general they mean for civilization the introduction of a new element; and for women, a change not only of social opportunity but of psychological make-up, resulting from a transformation of status, actual and prospective, which is no less than epoch-making. (*On Journey*, pp. 63–64)

19. Grant, *Alice Hamilton;* Goldmark, *Impatient Crusader;* Buhle, *Women and American Socialism, 1870–1920,* chaps. 2 and 3; Allen F. Davis, *Spearheads of Reform: Social Settlements and the Progressive Movement, 1890–1914* (New York: Oxford University Press, 1967), passim; Ellen Lagemann, *A Generation of Women* (Cambridge, Mass.: Harvard University Press, 1979).

20. Anna Mary Wells, *Miss Marks and Miss Woolley* (Boston: Houghton Mifflin Company, 1978). Vida Scudder dedicates her autobiography (as she did her first book) to Florence Converse, "Comrade and Companion." See also Nan Bauer Magler's fine article concerning Vida Scudder and Florence Converse, "Vida to Florence, Comrade and Companion," *Frontiers* IV (1979): 13–20. For Scudder's more general comments on friendships between women, see *On Journey,* pp. 104–15. Blanche Wiesen Cook presents a detailed study of this pattern in her excellent *Women and Support Networks* (New York: Out & Out Books, 1978); Liela Rupp traces this phenomenon to women politically active in the suffrage movement and later, in the 1920s, 1930s, and 1940s, in Alice Paul's Women's Party. See her sophisticated analysis, " 'Imagine My Surprise': Women's Relationships in Historical Perspective," *Frontiers* V (1981): 61–70 (I am indebted to Sarah Begus for first drawing my attention to this article). See also Grant, *Alice Hamilton,* chap. 4, especially pp. 66–68; Scudder, *On Journey,* chap. 3; Allen Davis, *The American Heroine: The Life and Legend of Jane Addams* (New York: Oxford University Press, 1973), pp. 85–91.

21. Lillian Faderman, *Surpassing the Love of Men* (New York: William Morrow and Co., 1981); Nancy Ann Sahli, "Changing Patterns"; Smith-Rosenberg, "The Female World of Love and Ritual," in *Disorderly Conduct;* George Chauncey, Jr., "From Sexual Inversion to Homosexuality: Medicine and the Changing Conceptualization of Female Deviance," *Salmagundi* LVIII–LIX (Fall 1982/Winter 1983): 114–46. Samuel Gregory, *Facts and Important Information for Young Women on the Subject of Masturbation* (Boston: George Gregory, 1857); Gross and Co., *Hygieana: A Non-Medical Analysis of the Complaints Incidental to Females* (London: G. Booth, 1829), see especially pp. 64 and 66. See also Thomas, in Dobkin, *Making of a Feminist,* pp. 90–93, 69; O. S. Fowler, *Amativeness or Evils and Remedies of Excessive and Perverted Sexuality* (New York: Fowlers and Wells, 1856), pp. 28–29.

22. For its most famous male explication, see Clarke, *Sex in Education.* See, as well, Victorian women's response to Clarke in Howe's *Sex and Education.*

23. Thomas Addis Emmett, *The Principles and Practice of Gynecology* (Philadelphia: H. C. Lea, 1879), p. 21; Thomas Smith Clouston, *Female Education from a Medical Point of View* (Edinburgh: Macniven & Wallace, 1882), p. 20.

24. Consider Clarke's statement: "The results [of higher education for women] are monstrous brains and puny bodies; abnormally active cerebration, and abnormally weak digestion; flowing thought and constipated bowels; lofty aspirations and neuralgic sensations" (p. 41). The body (female/lower)—mind (male/higher) polarity that was central to Victorian medical thought is clear in this quote: women torn between male intellectual achievement and female reproductive achievement literally tore their bodies in half. For other pleas against education for women, see Lawrence Irwell, "The Competition of the Sexes and Its Results," *American Medico-Surgical*

Bulletin X (September 19, 1896): 319–20. All the doyens of American gynecology in the late nineteenth century—Emmett, J. Marion Sims, T. Gaillard Thomas, Charles D. Meigs, William Goodell, and S. Weir Mitchell—shared the conviction that higher education and excessive development of the nervous system might interfere with woman's proper performance of her maternal functions. Mitchell was especially pointed in his attacks on women's colleges, and specifically his criticisms of Vassar (Mitchell, *Fat and Blood* [Philadelphia: J. B. Lippincott Co., 1885], and *Doctor and Patient* [Philadelphia: J. B. Lippincott Co., 1888], passim).

25. Clarke, *Sex in Education,* passim. For specific references to hermaphroditism, see pp. 44, 93, 115.

26. For an elaborate feminist refutation of Clarke by a variety of bourgeois women born during the first third of the nineteenth century, all educated before the Civil War, all schoolteachers or writers, see Howe, *Sex and Education.* The women include Julia Ward Howe herself; Mrs. Horace Mann (Mary Tyler Peabody, sister of Elizabeth Peabody and of Sophia Peabody Hawthorne, a teacher until she married Mann at the age of thirty-seven); Reverend Olympia Brown (feminist and minister, graduate of Antioch, 1860); Elizabeth Stuart Phelps (best-selling novelist); Caroline H. Dall (feminist, abolitionist, and writer, born 1822); Mercy B. Jackson; Maria A. Elmore; Ada Shepart Badger. Howe also includes official endorsements of women's higher education from Vassar, Antioch, and Oberlin colleges and from the University of Michigan. See also Sarah H. Stevenson, *The Physiology of Woman, Embracing Girlhood, Maternity and Mature Age,* 2nd ed. (Chicago: Cushing, Thomas & Company, 1881), pp. 68, 77; Alice Stockham, *Tokology: A Book for Every Woman,* rev. ed. (Chicago: Sanitary Publishing Co., 1887), p. 257. Stevenson noted acidly that "the unerring instincts of woman have been an eloquent theme for those who do not know what they are talking about" (p. 79). Health reformers, frequently critical as well of the medical establishment whose arguments I have been describing, were often sympathetic to women's claims that not too much, but too little, mental stimulation was the cause of their ills, especially psychological ones. See Martin Luther Holbrook, *Hygiene of the Brain and Nerves and the Cure of Nervousness* (New York: U.S. Book Co., 1878); James C. Jackson, *American Womanhood: Its Peculiarities and Necessities* (Dansville, N.Y.: Austin, Jackson & Co., 1870).

27. Richard von Krafft-Ebing, *Psychopathia Sexualis with Especial Reference to the Antipathetic Sexual Instinct,* trans. F. J. Rebman (Brooklyn: Physicians and Surgeons Book Co., 1908), pp. 333–36. This book was originally published in Stuttgart in 1886.

28. *Ibid.,* pp. 334–35, 351, 355.

29. *Ibid.,* p. 355.

30. For three excellent analyses of the sexologists' attitudes toward homosexuality, see Chauncey, "From Sexual Inversion to Homosexuality"; Jane Caplan, "Sexuality and Homosexuality," in *Women in Society,* ed. Cambridge Women's Studies Group (London: Virago, 1980), pp. 149–67; Sheila Rowbotham and Jeffrey Weeks, *Socialism and the New Life: The Personal and Sexual Politics of Edward Carpenter and Havelock Ellis* (London: Pluto Press Limited, 1977). See also Richard von Krafft-Ebing, *Psychopathia Sexualis with Especial Reference to the Antipathic Sexual Instinct,* trans. F.J. Rebman (Brooklyn:

Physicians and Surgeons Book Co., 1908), p. 333. This book was originally published in Stuttgart in 1886. Pp. 342, 345–46, 351, 353, and 355 provide examples of Krafft-Ebing's concern with hereditary patterns. See, as well, J. C. Kiernan, "Sexual Perversion in the White Chapel Murders," *Medical Standard* (Chicago) IV (1888): 170–72.

31. For a classic anthropological discussion of this symbolic trope see David Kunzle, "World Upside Down: The Iconography of a European Broadsheet Type," in Barbara A. Babcock, ed., *The Reversible World: Symbolic Inversion in Art and Society* (Ithaca: Cornell University Press, 1978), pp. 39–94.

32. For a provocative and highly influential analysis of "The Woman-on-Top" rituals and iconography of the Middle Ages and early modern period, see Natalie Zemon Davis, "Woman on Top," in *Society and Culture in Early Modern France* (Stanford, Calif.: Stanford University Press, 1975), pp. 124–51.

33. Sigmund Freud, "Contribution I. The Sexual Aberrations," in *Three Contributions to the Theory of Sex* (New York: E.P. Dutton, 1962 [1905]), pp. 1,6. See also Caplan, "Sexuality and Homosexuality," pp. 153, 155–57; Weeks, "Havelock Ellis and the Politics of Sex Reform," in Rowbotham and Weeks, *Socialism and the New Life*, p. 151–55, 160, 163, 172, 178; David Kennedy, *Birth Control in America: The Career of Margaret Sanger* (New Haven: Yale University Press, 1970), pp. 29–35. Jonathan Katz cites Emma Goldman's letter to German sexologist Magnus Hirschfeld praising Ellis's work on behalf of male homosexuals. Ellis also wrote an introduction to Radclyffe Hall's *Well of Loneliness*. See Katz, *Gay American History: Lesbians and Gay Men in the U.S.A., A Documentary* (New York: Thomas Crowell, 1976), pp. 379, 403.

34. Ellis, "Sexual Inversion in Women," *Alienist and Neurologist*, XVI (1895): 147–48, states that women who are attracted to true inverts, and who, in turn, attract them are "the pick of the women whom the average man would pass by." See as well, Ellis, pp. 145–46.

35. *Ibid.*, pp. 146–48, 152–53, 155–57. For Ellis's distinction between "homosexuality" and "inversion," see his "Sexual Inversion with an Analysis of Thirty-three New Cases," *Medico-Legal Journal*, XIII (1895–96): 262–64. To compare Ellis's attitudes towards male homosexuals and lesbians, see his *Sexual Inversion* (Philadelphia: F. A. Davis, 1901), p. 283. For an early article attacking European sodomy laws, see Ellis, "Sexual Inversion in Relation to Society and the Law," *Medico-Legal Journal*, XIV (1896–97): 279–88. Caplan offers an insightful analysis of Ellis's thought on male homosexuality in "Sexuality and Homosexuality," pp. 156–67. See also Weeks' analysis of Ellis and male homosexuality, "Havelock Ellis," in Rowbotham and Weeks, *Socialism and the New Life*, pp. 153–55, 160–61. Weeks presents a forceful case for Ellis's essentially conservative attitude toward women, pp. 169–80. For Ellis on the biological and social differences between women and men, see his *Men and Women* (London: Walter Scott, 1894).

36. Havelock Ellis, "Sexual Inversion in Women," *Alienist and Neurologist* XVI (1895): 155–56.

37. R.W. Shufeldt, "Dr. Havelock Ellis on Sexual Inversion," *Pacific Medical Journal* XLV (1902): 199–207.

38. William Lee Howard, "Effeminate Men and Masculine Women," *New York Medical Journal* LXXI (1900): 687.

39. Thomas, in Dobkin, *Making of a Feminist*, pp. 86–87. Lorine Pruette makes a similar observation, commenting that the sexual reformers had now made impossible the easy flow back and forth between homosexual and heterosexual relations that had previously characterized female adolescence (Pruette, "The Flapper," ed. Victor F. Calverton and Samuel D. Schmalhausen, *The New Generation: The Intimate Problems of Modern Parents and Children* [New York: Macaulay, 1930], pp. 574–77). Christina Simmons opens her pathbreaking article on the companionate-marriage movement with this point (Simmons, "Companionate Marriage and the Lesbian Threat," *Frontiers* IV [1979]: 54–59). See, as well: Wein, "Women's Colleges and Domesticity, 1875–1918," pp. 38–39, 44; and Ellen Ross and Rayna Rapp, "Sex and Society: A Research Note from Social History and Anthropology," *Comparative Studies in Society and History* XXIII (1981): 51–72.

40. For a discussion of Alice Stone Blackwell and of Wellesley College's changing politics, see Nancy Ann Sahli, "Smashing." See, as well, Margaret Otis, "A Perversion Not Commonly Noted," *Journal of Abnormal Psychology* (1913). Kate Richards O'Hare's article, "Prison Lesbianism" (1919–20), and Charles A. Ford's article, "Homosexual Practices of Psychology" (1929), are both cited and abstracted in Jonathan Katz's invaluable *Gay American History: Lesbians and Gay Men in the U.S.A.* (New York: Crowell, 1976). pp. 65–74, where there is also an abstract of the Otis article. See, as well, William S. Barker, "Two Cases of Sexual Contrariety," *St. Louis Courier of Medicine* XXVIII (1903): 269–71.

41. The list of companionate-marriage advocates and sex reformers is vast, but see Christine Simmos' path-breaking article, "Companionate Marriage and the Lesbian Threat," *Frontiers* IV (1979): 54–59. For specific attacks on women who were hostile or indifferent to heterosexual relations, see Floyd Dell, "Sex in Adolescents," in *Sex Education: Facts and Attitudes* (New York: Child Study Association of America, 1934), p. 49; Dorothy Dunbar Bromley and Florence Haxton Britten, *Youth and Sex: A Study of 1300 College Students* (New York: Harper and Row, 1938), p. 129; John F. W. Meagher, "Homosexuality: Its Psychopathological Significance," *The Urologic and Cutaneous Review* XXXIII (1929): 508, 512; Edward Podolsky, " 'Homosexual Love' in Women," *Popular Medicine* I (February, 1935): 375; Ralph Hay, "Mannish Women or Old Maids?" *Know Thyself* I (July, 1938) and Floyd Dell, *Love in the Machine Age: A Psychological Study of the Transition from Patriarchal Society* (New York: Farrar, 1930).

42. Buhle, *Women and American Socialism,* chap. 4; Elaine Showalter, "Introduction," *These Modern Women* (Old Westbury, N.Y.: Feminist Press, 1978), pp. 3–29; Judith Schwarz, *Radical Feminists of Heterodoxy: Greenwich Village, 1912–1940* (Lebanon, N.H.: Victoria Publishers, Inc., 1982). See Gertrude Stein's attacks on M. Carey Thomas for being a single-minded feminist and sexually forbidding: *Fernhurst*, in *Fernhurst, QED and Other Early Writings* (New York: Liveright, 1971; originally written 1904?). See, as well, Edna St. Vincent Millay, "First Fig," in *The Norton Anthology of Modern Poetry*, ed. Richard Ellmann and Robert O'Claire (New York: W. W. Norton & Company, 1973), p. 492; and her "Love Is Not All: It Is Not Meat Nor Drink"—Love is not

all: it is not meat nor drink / nor slumber nor a roof against the rain / . . . It well may be that in a difficult hour, / Pinned down by pain and moaning for release, / Or nagged by want past resolution's power, / I might be driven to sell your love for peace, / Or trade the memory of this night for food. / It well may be. I do not think I would (p. 494)—for this generation's view of the centrality of sexuality and love to their life aims.

43. Sandra M. Gilbert, "Costumes of the Mind: Transvestism as Metaphor in Modern Literature," *Critical Inquiry* (Winter 1980): 391–417.

44. Virginia Woolf, *Orlando: A Biography* (New York: Harcourt Brace Jovanovich, 1956 [1928]); Djuna Barnes, *Nightwood* (New York: New Directions, 1961 [1937]); Radclyffe Hall, *The Well of Loneliness* (New York: Coucici-Friede, 1934 [1928]). For suggestive analyses of these novels, see Catherine Stimpson, "Zero Degree Deviance: The Lesbian Novel in English," *Critical Inquiry* (Winter, 1981): 363–79 and Kenneth Burke, "Version, Con-, Per-, In- (Thoughts on Djuna Barnes's Novel *Nightwood*)," in *Language as Symbolic Action* (Berkeley: University of California Press, 1966), pp. 240–53.

45. Gilbert, "Costumes," pp. 404–07, proposes this vision of Orlando. I am indebted to Lucineene Frappier-Mazur for bringing the European male literary tradition of the novel of initiation to my attention. Frappier-Mazur has explored George Sand's *The Countess of Rudolstadt* as a feminist inversion of this form. See her article in the special issue on psycho-poetics in *Poetics* (Spring/Summer, 1984), "Desire, Writing and Identity in the Romantic Mystical Novel: Notes for a Definition of the Feminine."

46. See Newton's interpretation of *The Well of Loneliness*: "The Mythic Mannish Lesbian," *Signs IX* (Fall, 1984): 557–75; Barnes, *Nightwood*, pp. 1–7.

47. For a superb analysis of the Trickster, see Barbara Babcock-Abrahams, " 'A Tolerated Margin of Mess': The Trickster and His Tales Reconsidered," *Journal of Folklore Institute* XI (1975): 147–86.

48. For Djuna Barnes's presentation of Frau Mann and her fellow circus characters, see *Nightwood* (New York: New Directions, 1949), pp. 11–13, 113.

Chapter 9   The Problem of Race in Women's History

1. Elizabeth Hyde Botume, *First Days amongst the Contraband* (Boston: Lee and Shepard Publishers, 1893), 53 quoted in Eugene D. Genovese, *Roll Jordon Roll: The World the Slaves Made* (New York: Random House, 1974), 494.

2. John Hope Franklin, "The Place of Carter G. Woodson in American Historiography," *Negro History Bulletin* (May 1950): 174–176; also see Jacqueline Goggin, "Carter G. Woodson and the Movement to Promote Black History" (Ph.D. diss., University of Rochester, 1984).

3. Robert Harris, "Coming of Age: The Transformation of Afro-American Historiography," *Journal of Negro History* 47 (Summer 1982): 107–121; Melville Herskovits, *The Myth of the Negro Past* (Boston: Beacon Press, 1958).

4. Katherine Kish Sklar, "American Female Historians in Context, 1770–1930," *Feminist*

Studies (Fall 1975): 171–184; Gerda Lerner, *The Majority Finds its Past* (New York: Oxford University Press, 1979); Elizabeth Fox-Genovese, "Placing Women's History in History," *New Left Review* (May–June 1982): 5–29; Joan W. Scott, "Women in History: The Modern Period," *Past & Present* (November 1983): 141–157.

5. See articles by Ellen DuBois, Mari Jo Buhle, Temma Kaplan, Gerda Lerner, and Carroll Smith-Rosenberg in "Politics and Culture in Women's History: A Symposium," *Feminist Studies* 6 (Spring 1980): 26–64; also see Elizabeth Fox-Genovese on "cultural separatism" in Fox-Genovese, "Women's Studies in the 1980s: Now More than Ever," *Women's Studies Quarterly* 12 (Fall 1984): 25–28.

6. Rosalyn Terborg-Penn, "Discrimination against Afro-American Women in the Woman's Movement, 1830–1920," in Rosalyn Terborg-Penn and Sharon Harley, eds., *The Afro-American Woman: Struggles and Images* (Port Washington, N.Y.: Kennikat Press, 1978), 17–27; Angela Davis, *Women, Race and Class* (New York: Random House, 1981); Bettina Aptheker, *Woman's Legacy: Essays on Race, Sex, and Class in American History* (Amherst: The University of Massachusetts Press, 1982); Gerda Lerner, "The Community Work of Black Clubwomen" and also "Black Women in the U.S.: A Problem in Historiography," in Lerner, *The Majority Finds its Past;* Paula Giddings, *When and Where I Enter: The Impact of Black Women on Race and Sex in America* (New York: William Morrow, 1984).

7. See for example: Eleanor Flexner, *Century of Struggle: The Woman's Rights Movement in the United States* (Cambridge, Mass.: Belknap Press of Harvard University Press, 1959; paperback edition, New York: Atheneum, 1973); Aileen S. Kraditor, *The Ideas of the Woman Suffrage Movement, 1890–1920* (New York: Columbia University Press, 1965); Ellen DuBois, *Feminism and Suffrage: The Emergence of an Independent Women's Movement in America, 1848–1869* (Ithaca: Cornell University Press, 1978).

8. Rosalyn Terborg-Penn, "Discontented Black Feminists: Prelude and Postscript to the Passage of the Nineteenth Amendment," Lois Sharf and Joan M. Jensen, eds., *Decades of Discontent: The Women's Movement, 1920–1940* (Westport, Conn.: Greenwood Press, 1983); and the introduction by Philip S. Foner in Philip S. Foner, ed., *Frederick Douglass on Women's Rights* (Westport, Conn.: Greenwood Press, 1976).

9. See for example: Bogart R. Leashore, "Black Female Workers: Live-in Domestics in Detroit, Michigan, 1860–1880," *Phylon* 45 (June 1984): 111–120; Claudia Goldin, "Female Labor Force Participation—The Origin of Black and White Differences, 1870 and 1880," *Journal of Economic History* 37 (March 1977): 87–108; Barbara Klaczynska, "Why Women Work: A Comparison of Various Groups—Philadelphia, 1910–1930," *Labor History* 17 (Winter 1976): 73–87; Lawrence B. deGraf, "Race, Sex, and Region: Black Women in the American West, 1850–1920," *Pacific Historical Review* 49 (May 1980): 285–313; Walter R. Allen, "Family Roles, Occupational Statuses, and Achievement Orientations among Black Women in the United States," *Signs* 4 (1979): 670–686; James Oliver Horton and Lois E. Horton, *Black Bostonians* (New York: Holmes and Meier, Inc., 1979), ch. 2.

10. Suzanne Lebscok, *The Free Women of Petersburg: Status and Culture in a Southern Town, 1784–1860* (New York: W.W. Norton & Company, 1984), ch. 4.

11. Lebscok, *The Free Women of Petersburg,* 111.

12. See, for example, the introduction by Filomina Steady for the "Pan-Africanist" perspective toward black women's culture in Filomina C. Steady, ed., *The Black Woman Cross-Culturally* (Cambridge, Mass.: Schenkman Publishing Company, Inc., 1981), 2–32.

13. See: John W. Blassingame, *The Slave Community: Plantation Life in the Antebellum South* (New York: Oxford University Press, 1972); Genovese, *Roll Jordon Roll*; Herbert G. Gutman, *The Black Family in Slavery and Freedom, 1750–1925* (New York: Random House, 1976).

14. Deborah G. White, "Female Slaves: Sex Roles and Status in the Antebellum Plantation South," *Journal of Family History* 8 (Fall 1983): 248–251, 256.

15. Deborah G. White, *Ar'n't I A Woman?* (New York: Norton, 1985), ch. 3; also see Steady on the same theme in Steady, *Black Woman Cross-Culturally*, 29–30.

16. White, "Female Slaves," 256–259.

17. White, "The Lives of Slave Women," *Southern Exposure* (November/December 1984): 32–37.

18. Jacqueline Jones, *Labor of Love, Labor of Sorrow: Black Women, Work, and the Family from Slavery to the Present* (New York: Basic Books, Inc., 1985), introduction.

19. Sociologist Charles Valentine developed the term "biculturation" to denote the dual socialization of blacks into mainstream and Afro-American culture. See Charles Valentine, "Deficit, Difference and Bicultural Models of Afro-American Behavior," *Harvard Educational Review* 44 (May 1971); also see Bonnie Thornton Dill, "The Dialectics of Black Womanhood," *Signs* 4 (Spring 1979): 543–555.

20. Dorothy Sterling, ed., *We Are Your Sisters* (New York: W.W. Norton & Company, 1984), xiii.

21. Lawrence Levine, *Black Culture and Black Consciousness* (New York: Oxford University Press, 1977), 138–143; E. Franklin Frazier, *Black Bourgeoisie* (New York: Macmillan Publishing Company, 1957), 56.

22. W.E. Burghardt Du Bois, *The Souls of Black Folks* (New York: Washington Square Press, 1970), 3.

23. Evelyn Brooks, "The Women's Movement in the Black Baptist Church, 1880–1920," (Ph.D. diss., University of Rochester, 1984); also Elizabeth H. Pleck, "A Mother's Wages," in Elizabeth H. Pleck and Nancy F. Cott, eds., *A Heritage of Her Own* (New York: Simon & Schuster, 1979), 378–379.

24. John P. McDowell, *The Social Gospel in the South* (Baton Rouge: Louisiana State University Press, 1982).

25. Brooks, "The Women's Movement in the Black Baptist Church"; also see William Breen, "Black Women and the Great War: Mobilization and Social Reform in the South," *Journal of Southern History* 44 (August 1978): 421–440.

26. Genovese, *Roll Jordan Roll*, 490; Gutman, *Black Family*, 168; Pleck, "Mother's Wages," 384–385; E. Franklin Frazier, *The Negro Church* (New York: Shocken Books, 1974), 39; Jacqueline Jones, *Soldiers of Light and Love* (Chapel Hill: University of North

Carolina Press, 1980); Brooks, "The Women's Movement in the Black Baptist Church."

27. Valentine, "Deficit, Difference, and Bicultural Models," 144.

28. See for example: William Muraskin, *Middle-Class Blacks in White Society* (Berkeley: University of California Press, 1979), 4–25; Jesse Bernard, *Marriage and Family among Negroes* (Englewood Cliffs, N.J.: Prentice-Hall, 1966), 28–33.

29. Brooks, "The Women's Movement in the Black Baptist Church."

30. Sojourner Truth expressed her displeasure at women not receiving the vote in the Fifteenth Amendment: "There is a great stir about colored men getting their rights, but not a word about the colored women; and if colored men get their rights, and not colored women theirs, you see the colored men will be masters over the women, and it will be just as bad as it was before." See Bert James Lowenberg and Ruth Bogin, eds., *Black Women in Nineteenth-Century American Life* (University Park: The Pennsylvania State University Press, 1976), 258.

31. Sharon Harley, "Black Women in a Southern City: Washington D.C., 1890–1920," in Joanne V. Hawks and Sheila L. Skemp, eds., *Sex, Race, and the Role of Women in the South* (Jackson: University of Mississippi, 1983), 59–74.

32. Fox-Genovese, "Placing Women's History in History," 14; also see Elizabeth Fox-Genovese, "Gender, Class and Power: Some Theoretical Considerations," *The History Teacher* 15 (February 1982): 255–276.

33. Delores Janiewski, "Sisters under Their Skins: Southern Working Women, 1880–1950," in Hawks and Skemp, eds., *Sex, Race, and the Role of Women,* 13–35; also Janiewski, *Sisterhood Denied* (Philadelphia: Temple University Press, 1986). In the North domestic service did not carry the connotation of being strictly black women's work during the nineteenth century; see David Katzman, *Seven Days a Week* (New York: Oxford University Press, 1978).

34. Jacquelyn Dowd Hall, *Revolt against Chivalry: Jessie Daniel Ames and the Women's Campaign against Lynching* (New York: Columbia University Press, 1979), 129–157, 220; also see Ida Wells Barnett, *On Lynchings* (1892; reprinted, New York: Arno Press, 1969).

Chapter 10 Commentary: Feminism and the Consolidations of "Women" in History

1. I.A. Richards, *The Philosophy of Rhetoric* (1936; New York: Oxford University Press, 1965).

2. Franz Fanon, *Black Skin, White Masks,* trans. Charlesham Markmann (London: Macgitbom and Kee, 1968).

3. Christina Crosby, *The Ends of History: Victorians and "The Woman Question"* (forthcoming Routledge).

4. Jeffrey Minson, *Genealogies of Morals* (London: MacMillan, 1985).

Chapter 11 Feminism and Cross-Cultural Inquiry: The Terms of the Discourse in Islam

1. See my *A Common Past: Women in Middle Eastern History* (forthcoming).

2. Sufism as a tradition of mystical/religious belief (as distinct from a religious and socio-political movement) continued to thrive throughout Islamic history, and indeed is an active tradition down to our own day.

3. Nabia Abbott's *Two Queens of Bagdad* (Chicago: University of Chicago Press, 1946) gathers together considerable material on male-female relations among royalty from this period.

4. Jalal al-Din al-Siyuti, *Tarikh al-Khulafa'*, ed. Ibrahim Abu al-Fadl (Cairo: Dar Nahdat Misr, 1975), p. 557.

5. Margaret Smith, *Rabi'a The Mystic and her Fellow-Saints in Islam* (Cambridge: Cambridge University Press, 1928), p. 9.

6. Smith, *Rabi'a*, p. 14.

7. Smith, *Rabi'a*, p. 9.

8. Smith, *Rabi'a*, pp. 16, 36.

9. A.J. Arberry, *Muslim Saints and Mystics* (London: Routledge and Kegan Paul, 1979), p. 51.

10. Cited in Bernard Lewis, *The Arabs in History* (London: Arrow Books, 1958), p. 109. See also, Nasser Khusrau, "Kittab Safar Nama," in Suhail Zakkar, *Akhbar al-Qarammita* (Damascus: Dar Hassan, 1982, 2nd ed.).

11. See, for a discussion of this, M.J. De Goeje, "Carmatians," *Encyclopedia of Religion and Ethics* (New York: Scribner and Sons, 1961) and *Mémoire sur les Carmates du Bahrein et les Fatimides* (Leyden: E.J. Brill, 1886).

Chapter 12 "It's you, and not me": Domination and "Othering" in Theorizing the "Third World"

1. Lu Xun, "The New Year's Sacrifice," *The Complete Stories of Lu Xun*, trans. Yang Xianyi and Gladys Yang (Bloomington: Indiana University Press and Beijing: Foreign Languages Press, 1981), pp. 157–171.

2. An analysis of Asian concepts of power in these terms can be found in Lucian W. Pye (with Mary W. Pye), *Asian Power and Politics* (Cambridge, Mass. and London: The Belknap Press of Harvard University Press, 1985). Unfortunately, the potential import of the book is annulled by what particularly from an Asian perspective is its racist methodology.

3. My formulation of the relation between subjectivity and culture here is much influenced by a theoretical environment informed by the writings of Jacques Lacan and Louis Althusser. In the case of Lacan, I am indebted to Kaja Silverman's analyses in *The Subject of Semiotics* (New York: Oxford University Press, 1983).

4. Marston Anderson, "The Morality of Form: Lu Xun and the Modern Chinese Short

Story," in *Lu Xun and His Legacy*, ed. Leo Ou-fan Lee (Berkeley, Los Angeles, and London: University of California Press, 1985), pp. 32–53.

5. See Anderson's succinct argument on p. 44 of "The Morality of Form."

6. Jacques Derrida, "Racism's Last Word" and "But, beyond . . . (Open Letter to Anne McClintock and Rob Nixon)," trans. Peggy Kamuf; McClintock and Nixon, "No Names Apart: The Separation of Word and History in Derrida's 'Le Dernier Mot du Racisme,' " This exchange was first published in *Critical Inquiry*, vol. 12, no. 1 and vol. 13, no. 1 (Autumn 1985 and Autumn 1986) and then in *"Race," Writing, and Difference*, ed. Henry Louis Gates, Jr. (Chicago and London: The University of Chicago Press, 1986), pp. 329–369. Hereafter page references of the exchange are made in parentheses in the text.

7. Elizabeth Weed, in editorial correspondence regarding this essay.

8. See Georg W.F. Hegel, *The Philosophy of History*, trans. J. Sibree (New York: Dover Publications, 1956), especially the Introduction and the section on China; see also *Introduction to the Lectures on the History of Philosophy*, trans. T.M. Knox and A.V. Miller (Oxford: Clarendon Press, 1985).

9. Jean-Jacques Rousseau and Johann Gottfried Herder, *On the Origin of Language*, trans. John H. Moran and Alexander Gode (New York: Frederick Ungar Publishing Co., 1966), pp. 86–166.

10. Hegel, *Philosophy of History*, p. 99.

11. Hegel, *Introduction*, p. 171.

12. Raymond Williams, *Politics and Letters: Interviews with "New Left Review"* (London: Verso, 1979), p. 252; quoted in Edward W. Said, "An Ideology of Difference," *"Race," Writing, and Difference*, p. 46.

13. Homi K. Bhabha, "Signs Taken for Wonders: Questions of Ambivalence and Authority under a Tree Outside Delhi, May 1817," *"Race," Writing, and Difference*, p. 173.

14. Bhabha, "Signs Taken for Wonders," p. 177.

Chapter 13 Commentary: "All that is inside is not center": Responses to the Discourses of Domination

1. Rosaura Sánchez, "Ethnicity, Ideology and Academia," *The Americas Review* 15 (1987), p. 82.

2. Leila Ahmed, "Western Ethnocentrism and Perceptions of the Harem," *Feminist Studies* 8,3 (1982), p. 525.

3. Domitila Barrios de Chungara, *Let Me Speak*, with Moema Viezzer, trans. Victoria Ortiz (New York: Monthly Review Press, 1979) and *Aquí tambien*, Domitila, ed. David Acebey (Mexico: Siglo Veintiuno, 1985).

4. Nawal el-Saadawi, *Memoirs from the Women's Prison* (Cairo: Dar al-Mustaqbal al-Arabi, 1984), p. 214. In Arabic.

5. Angela Weir and Elizabeth Wilson, "The British Women's Movement," *New Left Review* 148 (1984).

6. Jenny Bourne, "Homelands of the Mind: Jewish Identity and Feminist Politics," *Race and Class* 29,1 (1987), p. 2.

7. Gayatri Chakravorty Spivak, "Can the Subaltern Speak?" in *Marxism and the Interpretation of Culture,* ed. Cary Nelson and Lawrence Grossberg (Urbana, IL: University of Illinois Press, 1988), p. 295.

8. Marjorie Agosin, "Metaphors of Female Political Ideology: The Cases of Chile and Argentina," *Women's Studies International Forum* 10,6 (1987), p. 572.

9. Cornel West, "Religion and the Left: An Introduction," *Monthly Review* (July–August 1984), p. 9.

10. Kumari Jayawardena, *Feminism and Nationalism in the Third World* (London: Zed Books, 1986), p. 2.

11. Faysal Draj, "National Culture and Dependent Culture: Preliminary Observations," *Ai-Muwajana* 5 (1985). In Arabic.

12. Rey Chow, "Rereading Mandarin Ducks and Butterflies: A Response to the 'Postmodern' Condition," *Cultural Critique* 5 (1986–87), p. 71.

13. Irene Eber, "The Reception of Lu Xun in Europe and America: The Politics of Popularization and Scholarship" in *Lu Xun and His Legacy,* ed. Leo Ou-fan Lee (Berkeley, Los Angeles, and London: University of California Press, 1985), p. 242. I want to thank Yvonne Chang for her discussion with me of Chinese "modernism" and Comparative Literature.

14. Armand Mattelart, "Introduction" to A. Mattelart, X. Delcourt, and M. Mattelart, *La culture contre la démocratie· l'audiovisuel à l'heure transnationale* (Paris: La découverte, 1984), p. 10. In French.

15. Manlio Argueta, *Cuzcatlán Where the Southern Sea Beats,* trans. Bill Brow (New York: Random House, 1987), p. 5.

16. Roberto Fernandez Retamar, *Caliban: Apuntes sobre la cultura en nuestra América* (Mexico: Editorial Diogenes S.A., 1974), p. 40.

17. Laila al-Hamdani, "A Palestinian Woman in Prison" in Khamsin, *Women in the Middle East* (London: Zed Books, 1987), p. 40.

18. Nancy Taylor Day, *Represa* (Austin, TX: Plain View Press, 1987).

Chapter 14   A Manifesto for Cyborgs: Science, Technology, and Socialist Feminism in the 1980s

Research was funded by an Academic Senate Faculty Research Grant from the University of California, Santa Cruz. An earlier version of the paper on genetic engineering appeared as "Lieber Kyborg als Gottin: Für eine sozialistisch-feministische Unterwanderung der Gentechnologie," in Bernd-Peter Lange and Anna Marie Stuby, eds., (Berlin: Argument-Sonderband 105, 1984), pp. 66–84. The cyborg manifesto grew from my "New Machines, New Bodies, New Communities: Political Dilemmas of a Cyborg Feminist," "The Scholar and the Feminist X: The Question of Technology," Conference, Barnard College, April 1983.

The people associated with the History of Consciousness Board of UCSC have had an enormous influence on this paper, so that it feels collectively authored more than most, although those I cite may not recognize their ideas. In particular, members of graduate and undergraduate feminist theory, science, and politics, and theory and methods courses have contributed to the cyborg manifesto. Particular debts here are due Hilary Klein ("Marxism, Psychoanalysis, and Mother Nature"); Paul Edwards ("Border Wars: The Science and Politics of Artificial Intelligence," *Radical America*, vol. 19, no. 6 [1985]: 39–52); Lisa Lowe ("Julia Kristeva's *Des Chinoises*: Representing Cultural and Sexual Others"); James Clifford ("On Ethnographic Allegory," in James Clifford and George E. Marcus, eds., *Writing Culture, the Poetics and Politics of Ethnography* [Berkeley: University of California Press, 1985], pp. 98–121).

Parts of the paper were my contribution to a collectively developed session, "Poetic Tools and Political Bodies: Feminist Approaches to High Technology Culture," 1984 California American Studies Association, with History of Consciousness graduate students Zoe Sofoulis, "Jupiter Space"; Katie King, "The Pleasures of Repetition and the Limits of Identification in Feminist Science Fiction: Reimaginations of the Body after the Cyborg"; and Chela Sandoval, "The Construction of Subjectivity and Oppositional Consciousness in Feminist Film and Video." Sandoval's theory of oppositional consciousness was published as "Women Respond to Racism: A Report on the National Women's Studies Association Conference," Center for Third World Organizing, Oakland, California, n.d. For Sofoulis's semiotic-psychoanalytic readings of nuclear culture, see Zoe Sofia, "Exterminating Fetuses: Abortion, Disarmament and the Sexo-Semiotics of Extraterrestrialism," Nuclear Criticism issue, *Diacritics*, vol. 14, no. 2 (1984), pp. 47–59. King's manuscripts ("Questioning Tradition: Canon Formation and the Veiling of Power"; "Gender and Genre: Reading the Science Fiction of Joanna Russ"; "Varley's *Titan* and *Wizard*: Feminist Parodies of Nature, Culture, and Hardware") deeply inform the cyborg manifesto.

Barbara Epstein, Jeff Escoffier, Rusten Hogness, and Jaye Miler gave extensive discussion and editorial help. Members of the Silicon Valley Research Project of UCSC and participants in SVRP conferences and workshops have been very important, especially Rick Gordon, Linda Kimball, Nancy Snyder, Langdon Winner, Judith Stacey, Linda Lim, Patricia Fernandez-Kelly, and Judith Gregory. Finally, I want to thank Nancy Hartsock for years of friendship and discussion on feminist theory and feminist science fiction. I also thank Elizabeth Bird for my favorite political button: "Cyborgs for Earthly Survival."

1. Useful references to left and/or feminist radical science movements and theory and to biological/biotechnological issues include: Ruth Bleier, *Science and Gender: A Critique of Biology and Its Themes on Women* (New York: Pergamon, 1984); Ruth Bleier, ed., *Feminist Approaches to Science* (New York: Pergamon, 1986); Sandra Harding, *The Science Question in Feminism* (Ithaca: Cornell University Press, 1986); Anne Fausto-Sterling, *Myths of Gender* (New York: Basic Books, 1985); Stephen J. Gould, *Mismeasure of Man* (New York: Norton, 1981); Ruth Hubbard, Mary Sue Henifin, and Barbara Fried, eds., *Biological Woman, the Convenient Myth* (Cambridge, Mass.: Schenkman, 1982); Evelyn Fox Keller, *Reflections on Gender and Science* (New Haven: Yale University

Press, 1985); R. C. Lewontin, Steve Rose, and Leon Kamin, *Not in Our Genes* (New York: Pantheon, 1984); *Radical Science Journal* (from 1987, *Science as Culture*), 26 Freegrove Road, London N7 9RQ; *Science for the People,* 897 Main St., Cambridge, Mass. 0213°.

2. Starting points for left and/or feminist approaches to technology and politics include: Ruth Schwartz Cowan, *More Work for Mother: The Ironies of Household Technology from the Open Hearth to the Microwave* (New York: Basic Books, 1983); Joan Rothschild, *Machina ex Dea: Feminist Perspectives on Technology* (New York: Pergamon, 1983); Sharon Traweek, "Uptime, Downtime, Spacetime, and Power: An Ethnography of U.S. and Japanese Particle Physics," Ph.D. dissertation, UC Santa Cruz, History of Consciousness, 1982; R. M. Young and Les Levidov, eds., *Science, Technology, and the Labour Process,* vols. 1–3 (London: CSE Books, 1981); Joseph Weizenbaum, *Computer Power and Human Reason* (San Francisco: Freeman, 1976); Langdon Winner, *Autonomous Technology: Technics Out of Control as a Theme in Political Thought* (Cambridge, Mass.: MIT Press, 1977); Langdon Winner, *The Whale and the Reactor* (Chicago: Chicago University Press, 1986); Jan Zimmerman, ed., *The Technological Woman: Interfacing with Tomorrow* (New York: Praeger, 1983); Tom Athanasiou, "High-tech Politics: The Case of Artificial Intelligence," *Socialist Review,* no. 92 (1987): 7–35; Carol Cohn, "Nuclear Language and How We Learned to Pat the Bomb," *Bulletin of Atomic Scientists* (June 1987): 17–24; Terry Winograd and Fernando Flores, *Understanding Computers and Cognition: A New Foundation for Design* (New Jersey: Ablex, 1986); Paul Edwards, "Border Wars: The Politics of Artificial Intelligence," *Radical America,* vol. 19, no. 6 (1985): 39–52; *Global Electronics Newsletter,* 867 West Dana St., #204, Mountain View, Cal. 94041; *Processed World,* 55 Sutter St., San Francisco, Cal. 94104; *ISIS, Women's International Information and Communication Service,* P.O. Box 50 (Cornavin), 1211 Geneva 2, Switzerland, and Via Santa Maria dell'Anima 30, 00186 Rome, Italy. Fundamental approaches to modern social studies of science that do not continue the liberal mystification that it all started with Thomas Kuhn, include: Karin D. Knorr, *The Manufacture of Knowledge* (Oxford: Pergamon, 1981); Karin Knorr-Cetina and Michael Mulkay, eds., *Science Observed: Perspectives on the Social Study of Science* (Beverly Hills, Cal.: Sage, 1983); Bruno Latour and Steve Woolgar, *Laboratory Life: The Social Construction of Scientific Facts* (Beverly Hills, Cal.: Sage, 1979); Robert M. Young, "Interpreting the Production of Science," *New Scientist,* vol. 29 (March 1979): 1026–1028. More is claimed than is known about room for contesting productions of science in the mythic/material space of "the laboratory"; the 1984 *Directory of the Network for the Ethnographic Study of Science, Technology, and Organizations* lists a wide range of people and projects crucial to better radical analysis; available from NESSTO, P.O. Box 11442, Stanford, Cal. 94305.

3. Fredric Jameson, "Post-modernism, or the Cultural Logic of Late Capitalism," *New Left Review,* vol. 146 (July/August 1984); 53–94. See Marjorie Perloff, " 'Dirty' Language and Scramble Systems," *Sulfur,* II (1984): 178–183; Kathleen Fraser, *Something (Even Human Voices) in the Foreground, a Lake* (Berkeley, Cal.: Kelsey St. Press, 1984). For feminist modernist/post-modernist "cyborg" writing, see *How(ever),* 871 Corbett Ave., San Francisco, Cal. 94131.

4. Frans de Waal, *Chimpanzee Politics: Power and Sex among the Apes* (New York: Harper & Row, 1982); Langdon Winner, "Do artifacts have politics?," *Daedalus* vol. 109, no. 6 (Winter 1980): 121–36.

5. Jean Baudrillard, *Simulations,* trans. P. Foss, P. Patton, and P. Beitchman (New York: Semiotext(e), 1983). Jameson ("Postmodernism," p. 66) points out that Plato's definition of the simulacrum is the copy for which there is no original; i.e., the world of advanced capitalism; of pure exchange. See *Discourse,* 9 (Spring/Summer 1987), for a special issue "On Technology (Cybernetics, Ecology, and the Postmodern Imagination)."

6. Herbert Marcuse, *One-Dimensional Man* (Boston: Beacon, 1964); Carolyn Merchant, *The Death of Nature* (San Francisco: Harper & Row, 1980).

7. Zoe Sofia, "Exterminating Fetuses," *Diacritics,* vol. 14, no. 2 (Summer 1984): 47–59; and "Jupiter Space," California American Studies Association, Pomona, 1984.

8. For ethnographic accounts and political evaluations, see Barbara Epstein, "The Politics of Prefigurative Community: The Non-Violent Direction Action Movement," *The Year Left,* forthcoming; and Noel Sturgeon, Qualifying Essay on feminism, anarchism, and non-violent direct action politics, UCSC, 1986. Without explicit irony, adopting the spaceship earth/whole earth logo of the planet photographed from space, set off by the slogan "Love Your Mother," the May 1987, Mothers and Others Day action at the nuclear weapons testing facility in Nevada nonetheless took account of the tragic contradictions of views of the earth. Demonstrators applied for official permits to be on the land from officers of the Western Shoshone tribe, whose territory was invaded by the U.S. government when it built the nuclear weapons test ground in the 1950s. Arrested for trespassing, the demonstrators argued that the police and weapons facility personnel, without authorization from the proper officials, were the trespassers. One ˙affinity group at the women's action called themselves the Surrogate Others, and in solidarity with the creatures forced to tunnel in the same ground with the bomb, they enacted a cyborgian emergence from the constructed body of a large, non-heterosexual desert worm.

9. Powerful developments of coalition politics emerge from Third World speakers, speaking from nowhere, the displaced center of the universe, earth: "We live on the third planet from the sun"—"Sun Poem by Jamaican writer Edward Kamau Braithwaite," review by Nathaniel Mackey, *Sulfur,* II (1984): 200–205. *Home Girls,* ed. Barbara Smith (New York: Kitchen Table, Women of Color Press, 1983), ironically subverts naturalized identities precisely while constructing a place from which to speak called home. See esp. Bernice Reagan, "Coalition Politics, Turning the Century," pp. 356–368. Trinh T. Minh-ha, ed., "She, the Inappropriate/d Other," *Discourse,* 8 (Fall/Winter 1986–87).

10. Chela Sandoval, "Dis-Illusionment and the Poetry of the Future: The Making of Oppositional Consciousness," Ph.D. qualifying essay, UCSC, 1984.

11. Bell Hooks, *Ain't I a Woman?* (Boston: South End Press, 1981); Bell Hooks, *Feminist Theory: From Margin to Center* (Boston: South End Press, 1984); Gloria Hull, Patricia Bell Scott, and Barbara Smith, eds., *All the Women Are White, All the Men Are Black, But Some of Us Are Brave: Black Women's Studies* (Old Westbury, Conn.: Feminist Press,

1982). Toni Cade Bambara, in *The Salt Eaters* (New York: Vintage/Random House, 1981), writes an extraordinary post-modernist novel, in which the women of color theater group, The Seven Sisters, explores a form of unity. See Elliott Butler-Evans, "Race, Gender and Desire: Narrative Strategies and the Production of Ideology" in "The Fiction of Toni Cade Bambara, Toni Morrison and Alice Walker," Ph.D. dissertation, UCSC, 1987.

12.　On orientalism in feminist works and elsewhere, see Lisa Lowe, "Orientation: Representations of Cultural and Sexual 'Others,' " Ph.D. thesis, UCSC, 1986; Edward Said, *Orientalism* (New York: Pantheon, 1978); Chandra Talpade Mohanty, "Under Western Eyes: Feminist Scholarship and Colonial Discourse," *boundary,* 2 (no. 12), and 3 (no. 13) (1984): 333–357, and "Many Voices, One Chant: Black Feminist Perspectives," *Feminist Review,* 17 (Autumn, 1984).

13.　Katie King has developed a theoretically sensitive treatment of the workings of feminist taxonomies as genealogies of power in feminist ideology and polemic: Katie King, "Canons without Innocence," Ph.D. dissertation, UCSC, 1987, and "The Situation of Lesbianism as Feminism's Magical Sign: Contests for Meaning in the U.S. Women's Movement, 1968–72," *Communication,* vol. 9, no. 1 (1985): 65–91. King examines an intelligent, problematic example of taxonomizing feminisms to make a little machine producing the desired final position. See also Alison Jaggar, *Feminist Politics and Human Nature* (Totowa, N.J.: Rowman & Allanheld, 1983). My caricature here of socialist and radical feminism is also an example.

14.　The feminist standpoint argument is being developed by: Jane Flax, "Political Philosophy and the Patriarchal Unconsciousness," in Sandra Harding and Merill Hintikka, eds., *Discovering Reality* (Dordrecht: Reidel, 1983); Sandra Harding, "The Contradictions and Ambivalence of a Feminist Science," ms.; Nancy Hartsock, *Money, Sex, and Power* (New York: Longman, 1983) and "The Feminist Standpoint: Developing the Ground for a Specifically Feminist Historical Materialism," in Harding and Hintikka, *Discovering Reality*; Mary O'Brien, *The Politics of Reproduction* (New York: Routledge & Kegan Paul, 1981); Hilary Rose, "Hand, Brain, and Heart: A Feminist Epistemology for the Natural Sciences," *Signs,* vol. 9, no. 1 (1983): 73–90; Dorothy Smith, "Women's Perspective as a Radical Critique of Sociology," *Sociological Inquiry,* 44 (1974) and "A Sociology of Women," in J. Sherman and E. T. Beck, eds., *The Prism of Sex* (Madison: University of Wisconsin Press, 1979). For rethinking theories of feminist materialism and feminist standpoint in response to criticism, see chapter 7 in Harding, *The Science Question in Feminism*; Nancy Hartsock, "Rethinking Modernism: Minority and Majority Theories," paper presented at the 1987 meeting of the Western Political Science association and forthcoming in *Cultural Studies*; Hilary Rose, "Women's Work: Women's Knowledge," in Juliet Mitchell and Ann Oakley, eds., *What Is Feminism? A Re-examination* (New York: Pantheon, 1986), pp. 161–83.

15.　Catherine MacKinnon, "Feminism, Marxism, Method, and the State: An Agenda for Theory," *Signs,* vol. 7, no. 3 (Spring 1982): 515–544. See also MacKinnon, *Feminism Unmodified* (Cambridge, Mass.: Harvard University Press, 1987). I make a category error in "modifying" MacKinnon's positions with the qualifier "radical," thereby generating my own reductive critique of extremely heterogeneous writing, which does explicitly use that label, by my taxonomically interested argument about writing which does not use the modifier and which brooks no limits and thereby adds to the various dreams of a common, in the sense of univocal, language for feminism. My category error was occasioned by an assignment to write from a particular taxonomic position which itself has a heterogeneous history, socialist feminism, for *Socialist Review*. A critique indebted to MacKinnon, but without the reductionism and with an elegant feminist account of Foucault's paradoxical conservatism on sexual violence (rape), is Teresa de Lauretis, "The Violence of Rhetoric: Considerations on Representation and Gender," *Semiotica,* 54 (1985): 11–31, and de Lauretis, ed., *Feminist Studies/Critical Studies* (Bloomington: Indiana University Press, 1986). A theoretically elegant feminist social-historical examination of family violence, that insists on women's/men's/children's complex agency without losing sight of the material structures of male domination, race, and class, is Linda Gordon, *Cruelty, Love, and Dependence: Family Violence and Social control, Boston 1880–1960,* forthcoming with Pantheon.

16. My previous efforts to understand biology as a cybernetic command-control discourse and organisms as "natural-technical objects of knowledge" are: "The High Cost of Information in Post-World War II Evolutionary Biology," *Philosophical Forum,* vol. 13, nos. 2–3 (1979): 206–237; "Signs of Dominance: From a Physiology to a Cybernetics of Primate Society," *Studies in History of Biology,* 6 (1983): 129–219; "Class, Race, Sex, Scientific Objects of Knowledge: A Socialist-Feminist Perspective on the Social Construction of Productive Knowledge and Some Political Consequences," in Violet Haas and Carolyn Perucci, eds., *Women in Scientific and Engineering Professions* (Ann Arbor: University of Michigan Press, 1984), pp. 212–229.

17. E. Rusten Hogness, "Why Stress? A Look at the Making of Stress, 1936–1956," available from the author, 4437 Mill Creek Rd., Healdsburg, Cal. 95448.

18. A left entry to the biotechnology debate: *GeneWatch, a Bulletin of the Committee for Responsible Genetics,* 5 Doane St., 4th floor, Boston, Mass. 02109; Susan Wright, "Recombinant DNA Technology and Its Social Transformation, 1972–82," *Osiris,* 2nd series, 2(1986):303–60, and "Recombinant DNA: The Status of Hazards and Controls," *Environment* (July/August 1982); Edward Yoxen, *The Gene Business* (New York: Harper & Row, 1983).

19. Paula Treichler, "AIDS, Homophobia, and Biomedical Discourse: An Epidemic of Signification," *Cultural Studies,* vol. 1, no. 3 (Oct. 1987): 263–305.

20. Starting references for "women in the integrated circuit": Pamela D'Onofrio-Flores and Sheila M. Pfafflin, eds., *Scientific-Technological Change and the Role of Women in Development* (Boulder, Col.: Westview Press, 1982); Maria Patricia Fernandez-Kelly, *For We Are Sold, I and My People* (Albany, N.Y.: SUNY Press, 1983); Annette Fuentes and Barbara Ehrenreich, *Women in the Global Factory* (Boston: South End Press, 1983) with an especially useful list of resources and organizations; Rachael Grossman, "Women's Place in the Integrated Circuit," *Radical America,* vol. 14, no. I (1980): 29–50; June Nash and Maria Patricia Fernandez-Kelly, eds., *Women and Men and the International Division of Labor* (Albany, N.Y.: SUNY Press, 1983); Aihwa Ong, "Japanese Factories, Malay Workers: Industrialization and the Cultural Construction of Gender

in West Malaysia," in Shelley Errington and Jane Atkinson, eds., *Power and Difference* (Palo Alto: Stanford University Press, forthcoming); Aihwa Ong, *Spirits of Resistance and Capitalist Discipline: Factory Workers in Malaysia* (Albany, N.Y.: SUNY Press, 1987); Science Policy Research Unity, *Microelectronics and Women's Employment in Britain* (Sussex, Eng.: University of Sussex, 1982).

21. The best example is Bruno Latour, *Les Microbes: buerre et paix, suivi de irreductions* (Paris: Metailie, 1984).

22. For the homework economy and some related arguments: Richard Gordon, "The Computerization of Daily Life, the Sexual Division of Labor, and the Homework Economy," paper delivered at the Silicon Valley Workshop Group conference, 1983; Richard Gordon and Linda Kimball, "High-Technology, Employment and the Challenges of Education," *SVRG Working Paper*, no. 1 (July 1985); Judith Stacey, "Post-industrial Conditions and Postfeminist Consciousness in the Silicon Valley," *Socialist Review*, vol. 96 (November–December, 1987); Barbara F. Reskin and Heidi Hartmann, eds., *Women's Work, Men's Work* (Washington, D.C.: National Academy of Sciences Press, 1986); *Signs*, 10, no. 2 (1984), special issue on women and poverty; Stephen Rose, *The American Profile Poster: Who Owns What, Who Makes How Much, Who Works Where, and Who Lives with Whom?* (New York: Pantheon, 1986); Patricia Hill Collins, "Third World Women in America," and Sara G. Burr, "Women and Work," in Barbara K. Haber, ed., *The Women's Annual, 1981* (Boston: G. K. Hall, 1982); Judith Gregory and Karen Nussbaum, "Race against Time: Automation of the Office," *Office: Technology and People*, 1 (1982): 197–236; Frances Fox Piven and Richard Cloward, *The New Class War: Reagan's Attack on the Welfare State and Its Consequences* (New York: Pantheon, 1982); Microelectronics Group, *Microelectronics: Capitalist Technology and the Working Class* (London: CSE, 1980); Karin Stallard, Barbara Ehrenreich, and Holly Sklar, *Poverty in the American Dream* (Boston: South End Press, 1983) including a useful organization and resource list.

23. Rae Lessor Blumberg, "A General Theory of Sex Stratification and Its Application to the Position of Women in Today's World Economy," paper delivered to Sociology Board, UCSC, February 1983. Also Blumberg, *Stratification: Socioeconomic and Sexual Inequality* (Boston: Little, Brown, 1981). See also Sally Hacker, "Doing It the Hard Way: Ethnographic Studies in the Agribusiness and Engineering Classroom," California American Studies Association, Pomona, 1984, forthcoming in *Humanity and Society;* Sally Hacker and Lisa Bovit, "Agriculture to Agribusiness: Technical Imperatives and Changing Roles," Proceedings of the Society for the History of Technology, Milwaukee, 1981; Lawrence Busch and William Lacy, *Science, Agriculture, and the Politics of Research* (Boulder, Col.: Westview Press, 1983); Denis Wilfred, "Capital and Agriculture, a Review of Marxian Problematics," *Studies in Political Economy*, no. 7 (1982): 127–154; Carolyn Sachs, *The Invisible Farmers: Women in Agricultural Production* (Totowa, N.J.: Rowman & Allanheld, 1983). International Fund for Agricultural Development, *IFAD Experience Relating to Rural Women, 1977–84* (Rome: IFAD, 1985). Thanks to Elizabeth Bird, "Green Revolution Imperialism," I & II, ms. UCSC, 1984.

24. Cynthia Enloe, "Women Textile Workers in the Militarization of Southeast Asia," in Nash and Fernandez-Kelly, *Women and Men*; Rosalind Petchesky, "Abortion, Anti-

Feminism, and the Rise of the New Right," *Feminist Studies,* vol. 7, no. 2 (1981). Cynthia Enloe, *Does Khaki Become You? The Militarization of Women's Lives* (Boston: South End Press, 1983).

25. For a feminist version of this logic, see Sarah Blaffer Hrdy, *The Woman That Never Evolved* (Cambridge, Mass.: Harvard University Press, 1981). For an analysis of scientific women's story-telling practices, especially in relation to sociobiology, in evolutionary debates around child abuse and infanticide, see Donna Haraway, "The Contest for Primate Nature: Daughters of Man the Hunter in the Field, 1960–80," in Mark Kann, ed., *The Future of American Democracy* (Philadelphia: Temple University Press, 1983), pp. 175–208.

26. For the moment of transition of hunting with guns to hunting with cameras in the construction of popular meanings of nature for an American urban immigrant public, see Donna Haraway, "Teddy Bear Patriarchy," *Social Text,* no. 11 (Winter 1984–85):20–64; Roderick Nash, "The Exporting and Importing of Nature: Nature-Appreciation as a Commodity, 1850–1980," *Perspectives in American History,* vol. 3 (1979): 517–560; Susan Sontag, *On Photography* (New York: Dell, 1977); and Douglas Preston, "Shooting in Paradise," *Natural History,* vol. 93, no. 12 (December 1984): 14–19.

27. For crucial guidance for thinking about the political/cultural implications of the history of women doing science in the United States, see: Violet Haas and Carolyn Perucci, eds., *Women in Scientific and Engineering Professions* (Ann Arbor: University of Michigan Press, 1984); Sally Hacker, "The Culture of Engineering: Women, Workplace, and Machine," *Women's Studies International Quarterly,* vol. 4, no. 3 (1981): 341–353; Evelyn Fox Keller, *A Feeling for the Organism* (San Francisco: Freeman, 1983); National Science Foundation, *Women and Minorities in Science and Engineering* (Washington, D.C.: NSF, 1982); Margaret Rossiter, *Women Scientists in America* (Baltimore: Johns Hopkins University Press, 1982); Londa Schiebinger, "The History and Philosophy of Women in Science: A Review Essay," *Signs* 12, no. 2 (1987): 305–332.

28. John Markoff and Lenny Siegel, "Military Micros," UCSC Silicon Valley Research Project conference, 1983, forthcoming in *Microelectronics and Industrial Transformation.* High Technology Professionals for Peace and Computer Professionals for Social Responsibility are promising organizations.

29. Katie King, "The Pleasure of Repetition and the Limits of Identification in Feminist Science Fiction: Reimaginations of the Body after the Cyborg," California American Studies Association, Pomona, 1984. An abbreviated list of feminist science fiction underlying themes of this essay: Octavia Butler, *Wild Seed, Mind of My Mind, Kindred, Survivor,* and *Dawn;* Suzy McKee Charnas, *Motherliness;* Samuel Delany, *Tales of Neveryon;* Anne McCaffrey, *The Ship Who Sang,* and *Dinosaur Planet;* Vonda McIntyre, *Superluminal* and *Dreamsnake;* Joanna Russ, *Adventures of Alyx, The Female Man;* James Tiptree, Jr., *Star Songs of an Old Primate,* and *Up the Walls of the World;* John Varley, *Titan, Wizard,* and *Demon.*

30. Mary Douglas, *Purity and Danger* (London: Routledge & Kegan Paul, 1966) and *Natural Symbols* (London: Cresset Press, 1970).

31. French feminisms contribute to cyborg heteroglossia. Carolyn Burke, "Irigaray through

the Looking Glass," *Feminist Studies,* vol. 7, no. 2 (Summer 1981): 288–306; Luce Irigaray, *Ce sexe qui n'en est pas un* (Paris: Minuit, 1977); Luce Irigaray, *Et l'une ne bouge pas sans l'autre* (Paris: Minuit, 1979); Elaine Marks and Isabelle de Courtivron, eds., *New French Feminisms* (Amherst: University of Massachusetts Press, 1981); *Signs,* vol. 7, no. I (Autumn, 1981), special issue on French feminism; Monique Wittig, *The Lesbian Body,* trans. David Le Vay (New York: Avon, 1975; *Le corps lesbien,* 1973). See especially *Feminist Issues: A Journal of Feminist Social and Political Theory* (1980 ff); and Claire Duchen, *Feminism in France: From May '68 to Mitterand* (London: Routledge & Kegan Paul, 1986).

32. But all these poets are very complex, not least in treatment of themes of lying and erotic, decentered collective and personal identities. Susan Griffin, *Women and Nature: The Roaring Inside Her* (New York: Harper & Row, 1978); Audre Lorde, *Sister Outsider* (New York: Crossing Press, 1984); Adrienne Rich, *The Dream of a Common Language* (New York: Norton, 1978).

33. Audre Lorde, *Zami, a New Spelling of my Name* (New York: Crossing Press, 1982); Katie King, "Audre Lorde: Layering History/Constructing Poetry," in "Canons without Innocence," Ph.D. dissertation, UCSC, 1987.

34. Jacques Derrida, *Of Grammatology,* trans. and Introd. Gayatri Chakravorty Spivak (Baltimore: Johns Hopkins University Press, 1976), esp. part II, "Nature, Culture, Writing"; Claude Lévi-Strauss, *Tristes Tropiques,* trans. John Russell (New York, Atheneum, 1961), esp. "The Writing Lesson"; Henry Louis Gates, Jr., "Writing 'Race' and the Difference It Makes," in " 'Race,' Writing and Difference," special issue of *Critical Inquiry,* ed. Gates, vol. 12, no. 1 (Autumn 1985): 1–20; Douglas Kahn and Diane Neumaier, eds., *Cultures in Contention* (Seattle: Real Comet Press, 1985), Walter Ong, *Orality and Literacy: The Technologizing of the Word* (New York: Methuen, 1982); Cheris Kramarae and Paula Treichler, *A Feminist Dictionary* (Boston: Pandora, 1985).

35. Cherríe Moraga, *Loving in the War Years* (Boston: South End Press, 1983). The sharp relation of women of color to writing as theme and politics can be approached through: "The Black Woman and the Diaspora: Hidden Connections and Extended Acknowledgements," An International Literacy Conference, Michigan State University, October 1985; Mari Evans, ed., *Black Women Writers: A Critical Evaluation* (Garden City, N.Y.: Doubleday/Anchor, 1984); Barbara Christian, *Black Feminist Criticism* (New York: Pergamon, 1985); Dexter Fisher, ed., *The Third Woman: Minority Women Writers of the United States* (Boston: Houghton Mifflin, 1980); several issues of *Frontiers,* esp. vol. 5 (1980), "Chicanas en el Ambiente Nacional" and vol. 7 (1983), "Feminisms in the Non-Western World"; Maxine Hong Kingston, *China Men* (New York: Knopf, 1977); Gerda Lerner, ed., *Black Women in White America: A Documentary History* (New York: Vintage, 1973); Paula Giddings, *When and Where I Enter: The Impact of Black Women on Race and Sex in America* (Toronto: Bantam, 1985); Cherríe Moraga and Gloria Anzaldua, eds., *This Bridge Called My Back: Writings by Radical Women of Color* (Watertown, Mass.: Persephone, 1981); Robin Morgan, ed., *Sisterhood Is Global* (Garden City, N.Y.: Anchor/Doubleday, 1984). The writing of white women has had similar meanings: Sandra M. Gilbert and Susan Gubar, *The Madwoman in the*

Attic (New Haven: Yale University Press, 1979); Joanna Russ, *How to Suppress Women's Writing* (Austin: University of Texas Press, 1983).

36. James Clifford argues persuasively for recognition of continuous cultural reinvention, the stubborn non-disappearance of those "marked" by Western imperializing practices. See Clifford's "On Ethnographic Allegory" in Clifford and Marcus, *Writing Culture,* and his "On Ethnographic Authority," *Representations,* vol. I, no. 2 (1983): 118–146.

37. The convention of ideologically taming militarized high technology by publicizing its applications to speech and motion problems of the disabled-differently abled takes on a special irony in monotheistic, patriarchal, and frequently anti-semitic culture when computer-generated speech allows a boy with no voice to chant the haftorah at his bar mitzvah. See Vic Sussman, "Personal Tech: Technology Lends a Hand," *The Washington Post Magazine* (November 9, 1986):45–46. Making the always context-relative social definitions of "abledness" particularly clear, military high-tech has a way of making human beings disabled by definition, a perverse aspect of much automated battlefield and Star Wars R&D. See John Noble Welford, "Pilot's Helmet Helps Interpret High Speed World," *The New York Times* (July 1, 1986):21, 24.

38. Page DuBois, *Centaurs and Amazons* (Ann Arbor: University of Michigan Press, 1982); Lorraine Daston and Katharine Park, "Hermaphrodites in Renaissance France," ms., n.d.; Katharine Park and Lorraine Daston, "Unnatural Conceptions: The Study of Monsters in 16th and 17th Century France and England," *Past and Present,* no. 92 (August 1981): 20–54. The word *monster* shares its root with the verb to *demonstrate.*

Chapter 16   Commentary: Cyborgs, Origins, and Subjectivity

1. Claude Lévi-Strauss, *Structual Anthropology* (New York: Basic Books, 1963), p. 224.

Chapter 18   The Political Economy of Women as Seen by a Literary Critic

1. Heleieth I.B. Saffioti, "Pathways of Feminism in an Underdeveloped Socio-Economic Context," p. 1, a paper delivered at the Pembroke Center conference on "Feminism/Theory/Politics," March, 1985.

2. *New Left Review* 148 (November–December 1984).

3. Lydia Sargent, *Women and Revolution: A Discussion of the Unhappy Marriage of Marxism and Feminism* (Boston: South End Press, 1981).

4. Jonathan Rée, *Proletarian Philosophers: Problems in Socialist Culture in Britain* (Oxford: Oxford University Press, 1984).

5. Karl Marx, *Grundrisse,* tr. Martin Nicolaus (New York: Vintage Edition, 1973), p. 548. I have cited this passage in Spivak, "Speculations on Reading Marx—After Reading Derrida," in Derek Attridge et al. eds., *Post-Structuralism and the Question of History* (Cambridge: Cambridge University Press, 1987), p. 55, and developed a similar line of argument.

6. Theodore Levitt, "The Globalization of Markets," *Harvard Business Review* 61, iii (May-

June 1983), 95. I have quoted this and the passage in note 7 in Spivak, "Scattered Speculations on the Question of Value," *In Other Worlds: Essays in Cultural Politics* (New York: Methuen, 1987), p. 168f and developed a similar line of argument.

7.   "The Wiring of Wall Street," *The New York Times,* Sunday, Oct. 23, 1983, p. 47.

8.   June Nash and Maria Patricia Fernandez-Kelly, eds., *Women, Men, and the International Division of Labor* (Albany: SUNY Press, 1983).

9.   *Subaltern Studies II* (Delhi: Oxford University Press, 1983).

10.   Paul de Man, *Allegories of Reading* (New Haven: Yale University Press, 1979), p. 240.

11.   Ashis Nandy, "Sati: A Nineteenth-Century Tale of Women, Violence and Protest" in *At the Edge of Psychology: Essays in Politics and Culture* (Oxford: Oxford University Press, 1980), pp. 1–31.

12.   Nicholas and Maria Torok, "A Poetics of Psychoanalysis: "The Lost Object—'Me'," *SubStance* 42 (1984), 5.

Chapter 19   Commentary: What Is To Be Done

1.   Jenny Bourne, "Homelands of the Mind: Jewish feminism and Identity Politics," *Race and Class* 29:1 (Summer 1987): 1–24.

2.   Gayatri Chakravorty Spivak, "Subaltern Studies: Deconstructing Historiography," *In Other Worlds: Essays in Cultural Politics* (London and New York: Methuen, 1987), p. 201, my emphasis.

3.   Louis Althusser, "Ideology and Ideological State Apparatuses," *Lenin and Philosophy and Other Essays* (New York and London: Monthly Review Press, 1971), pp. 182. Althusser suggests that interpellation "can be imagined along the lines of the most commonplace everyday police (or other) hailing: 'Hey you there' " (174)! The ease with which this formulation can be rewritten to describe a woman who is heckled in the street and thus inscribed in one of the discourses of femininity suggests the aptness of Althusser's model for addressing the construction of sexual difference. Further references to this essay (A) will be given in the parentheses in the text.

4.   The phrase is Nancy K. Miller's; see her essay in this volume. Certain popular narratives of the Progress of feminism imagine a scenario in which North American activists of all kinds appear as the naive though energetic Before to French post-feminisms' knowingly philosophical After; what French theory is said to know is that the subject has no essence. See Toril Moi, *Sexual/Textual Politics: Feminist Literary Theory* (London: Methuen, 1985), for a text that draws this distinction very sharply. Moi excludes discussion of black or lesbian feminist criticism in the United States on the grounds that "so far, lesbian and/or black feminist critics have presented exactly the same *theoretical* problems as do 'straight' feminist critics" (86). On the contrary, efforts by women of color, lesbians, and working-class women to articulate their "double jeopardy" inevitably undermine the essentialism that blocks a radical analysis of subjectivity. For an early instance of this "dream of dissymmetry," as Naomi Schor calls it, see Frances M. Beal, "Double Jeopardy: To Be Black and Female," *Sisterhood is Powerful,* ed. Robin Morgan (New York: Vintage, 1970), pp.

340–59. Admittedly, many U.S. feminisms have looked primarily to one side of the "ambiguity" of subjectivity, assailing the status of woman as "a subjected being, who submits to a higher authority, and is therefore stripped of all freedom" in the name of an unexamined notion of "a free subjectivity, a centre of initiatives, author of and responsible for its actions" (A, 182). But as Foucault suggests, resistance, "the antagonism of strategies," is a privileged starting place for an analysis of subjectivity. In "The Subject and Power," (*Critical Inquiry* 8:4 [1982]), he urges particular attention to "struggles which question the status of the individual: on the one hand, they assert the right to be different, and they underline everything which makes individuals truly individual. On the other hand, they attack everything which separates the individual, breaks his links with others, splits up community life, forces the individual back on himself, and ties him to his own identity in a constraining way. These struggles are not exactly for or against the 'individual' but rather they are struggles against the 'government of individualization' " (781).

5. Bell Hooks, *Feminist Theory: From Center to Margin* (Boston: South End Press, 1984), pp. 43–44. Hooks emphasizes that the problem of who "we" are emerged early for feminism, but was consistently brushed aside by women who dominated organizations. She cites Florynce Kennedy criticizing "the sisterhood mystique" that insisted " 'we are sisters, Don't criticize a 'sister' publicly,' etc." in 1970. Kennedy had judges in mind: "When a female judge asks my client where her bruises are when she complains about being assaulted by her husband (as did Family Court Judge Sylvia Jaffin Liese), and makes smart remarks about her being overweight, and when another female judge is so hostile that she disqualifies herself but refuses to order a combative husband out of the house (even though he owns property elsewhere with suitable living quarters)—these judges are not my sisters . . . Such females, in my opinion, are agents of an oppressive System." "Institutionalized Oppression vs. The Female," *Sisterhood is Powerful,* p. 445.

6. The Crash of October 1987 provides an ironic comment on this point. Money moving at the speed of light accelerated the fall of prices as the computerized crash swept around the globe, from Tokyo to London, London to New York. Only the anachronism of closing markets at twilight and the fact that the sun does set on specific outposts of electronic capital put any brake whatsoever on the panic selling.

7. See Helen I. Safa, "Runaway Shops and Female Employment: The Search for Cheap Labor," *Signs* 7:2 (Winter 1981): 418–33. June Nash points out that for these "footloose" concerns, movement can literally be a weekend's work. In one example, she cites electronic assembly companies attracted to New England mill towns by tax rebates and CETA funds that don't last forever: "with no laws restricting the movement of such operations, workers in one of these plants recalled showing up for work on Monday to find a sign stating 'Gone to Jamaica' on the door of the factory." "The Impact of the Changing International Division of Labor on Different Sectors of the Labor Force," *Women, Men and the International Division of Labor,* eds. June Nash and Maria Patricia Fernandez-Kelly (Albany: State University of New York Press, 1983), p. 6. Jamaican workers, of course, receive the same treatment and much worse. See A. Lynn Bolles, "Kitchens Hit by Priorities: Employed Working-

Class Jamaican Women Confront the IMF," *Women, Men and the International Division of Labor,* pp. 138–60.

8. Spivak suggests that "the history of the institutional study of literature is one of great permissiveness." On the contrary, I would argue that, until very recently, the only permissiveness that characterized literary studies in the United States was a willingness to indulge fantasies of individuality, no matter how impressionistic. A certain apparent *methodological* permissiveness in fact masked a rigorous *ideological* program that deflected critique by remaining consistently and aggressively under-theorized. At best the history of literary studies has been one of resistance to theory as a defense of its ideological interests; this strategy has only recently been disrupted as a result of intense political struggle.

9. See Gayatri Chakravorty Spivak, "Explanation and Culture: Marginalia," *In Other Worlds,* pp. 103–117.

10. The very term Women's Studies raises the problem of the subject of study. See Jane Gallop's suggestion that "one of the goals of what we so ambiguously call women's studies [might] be to call into question the oppressive effects of an epistemology based on the principle of a clear and nonambiguous distinction between subject and object of knowledge." *Reading Lacan* (Ithaca: Cornell University Press, 1986), pp. 15–16. For an extremely interesting analysis of the politics of feeling at home, see Biddy Martin and Chandra Talpade Mohanty, "Feminist Politics: What's Home Got to Do with It?" *Feminist Studies/Critical Studies,* ed. Teresa de Lauretis (Bloomington: Indiana University Press, 1986), pp. 191–212.

11. Barbara Harlow, *Resisting Literature* (New York: Methuen, 1987), pp. 13–14.

12. See Donna Haraway, "A Manifesto for Cyborgs: Science, Technology, and Socialist Feminism in the 1980s," this volume. Haraway's analysis is fundamentally at odds with Spivak's interpretation. Haraway emphasizes the opportunity presented by the unprecedented "networks of connection" that encircle the globe. She sees these networks as escape routes, leading away from the organic oppositions of nineteenth-century concepts of identity and toward the "fractured identities" of the cyborg; Haraway projects the figure of the fracture inward and leaps over the problems of constituency. Spivak sees the networks themselves as creating a crisis that can only be managed by the super-exploitation of a subproletarian class of women, necessarily enlarging the distances between women.

13. See Elizabeth Berg, "Iconoclastic Moments: Reading the *Sonnets for Helene,* Writing the *Portuguese Letters,*" for a discussion of partiality as both incompleteness and partisanship. *The Poetics of Gender,* ed. Nancy K. Miller, (New York: Columbia University Press, 1986), pp. 208–21; Martin and Mohanty make the same point in "Feminist Politics."

14. For an extended treatment, see Gayatri Chakravorty Spivak, "Scattered Speculations on the Question of Value," *Diacritics* 15:4 (Winter 1985):73–93, reprinted in *In Other Worlds* (New York and London: Methuen, 1987).

Contributors

Leila Ahmed is Associate Professor of Women's Studies at the University of Massachusetts, Amherst. She is the author of numerous articles on women in the Middle East and of a forthcoming book, *A Common Past: Women in Middle Eastern History*.

Evelyn Brooks-Higginbotham is Assistant Professor of History at the University of Pennsylvania. She has written on Afro-American women's history and is at work on a book on black women's organizations in Washington D.C. at the turn of the century.

Rey Chow is Assistant Professor of Comparative Literature, and an affiliated member of the departments of East Asian Studies and Women's Studies at the University of Minnesota, Minneapolis. Her book, *Stories of Chinese Modernism*, is forthcoming from the University of Minnesota Press.

Christina Crosby, Associate Professor of English at Wesleyan University, has a book, *The Ends of History: Victorians and "The Woman Question,"* forthcoming from Routledge. Her current project is on Angela Carter.

Mary Ann Doane is Associate Professor of Modern Culture and Media at Brown University. She is the author of *The Desire to Desire: The Woman's Film of the 1940's* and co-editor of *Revision: Essays in Feminist Film Criticism*.

Margaret W. Ferguson, Professor of English and Comparative Literature at Columbia University, is the author of *Trials of Desire: Renaissance Defenses of Poetry*. She has co-edited *Rewriting the Renaissance: the Discourses of Sexual Differences in Early Modern Europe* and *Re-membering Milton: The Texts and the Traditions*. She is currently working on a book on female literacy and literary production in Renaissance France and England.

Heather Findlay is a graduate student in English at Cornell University. She is at work on a dissertation on witchcraft, sexuality, and politics in Renaissance drama.

Barbara Harlow is Associate Professor of English at the University of Texas, Austin. She is author of *Resistance Literature* and articles on Third World literature and theory. She is currently working on a study of women, writing, and political detention for Cornell University Press.

Donna Haraway is Professor in the History of Consciousness Board at the University of California, Santa Cruz. She is the author of *Primate Visions: Gender, Race, and Nature in the World of Modern Science*, forthcoming from Routledge, and *Simians, Cyborgs, and Women: The Reinvention of Nature*, forthcoming from Free Association Books (London). She is currently writing on feminist theory, science fiction, and fictions of science and on the material and semiotic productions of the immune system in late capitalism.

Nancy K. Miller, Distinguished Professor of English at Lehman College and the Graduate Center, CUNY, is author of *The Heroine's Text: Readings in the French and English Novel, 1722–1782* and *Subject to Change: Reading Feminist Writing;* she is editor of *The Poetics of Gender.*

Ellen Rooney is Assistant Professor of English at Brown University. She is author of *Seductive Reasoning: Pluralism and the Problematic of Contemporary Literary Theory*, forthcoming from Cornell University Press, and is at present writing on "Criticism and the Subject of Sexual Violence."

Jacqueline Rose is on the faculty of the University of Sussex. She is co-editor and translator of *Feminine Sexuality: Jacques Lacan and the école freudienne* and author of *The Case of Peter Pan or the Impossibility of Children's Fiction* and *Sexuality in the Field of Vision*. She is currently writing on Sylvia Plath.

Naomi Schor is Nancy Duke Lewis Professor and Professor of French Studies at Brown University. She is author of *Zola's Crowds, Breaking the Chain: Women, Theory, and French Realist Fiction*, and *Reading in Detail: Aesthetics and the Feminine;* she is co-editor of *Flaubert and Postmodernism*. At present she is completing a book on Georges Sand and is co-editor of *differences, A Journal of Feminist Cultural Studies.*

Joan W. Scott, Professor of Social Science at the Institute for Advanced Study (Princeton, NJ), is author of *The Glassworkers of Carmaux* and *Gender and the Politics of History*, and co-author of *Women, Work, and Family*. She is at work on a book on "French Feminism and the Rights of Man."

Carroll Smith-Rosenberg is Professor of History at the University of Pennsylvania. She is the author of *Religion and the Rise of the American City* and *Disorderly Conduct: Visions of Gender in Victorian America.*

Gayatri Chakravorty Spivak is Andrew W. Mellon Professor of English at the University of Pittsburgh. Her writings include the introduction to and translation of Jacques Derrida's *Of Grammatology* and her *In Other Worlds: Essays in Cultural Politics.*

Denise Riley lives in London. She is the author of *War in the Nursery: Theories of the Child and Mother* and of several collections of poetry, including *Dry Air*. Her most recent book is *"Am I That Name?" Feminism and the Category of "Women" in History*.

Elizabeth Weed is Associate Director of the Pembroke Center at Brown University and is co-editor of *differences, A Journal of Feminist Cultural Studies*.